# BACKPACK LOOPS AND LONG DAY TRAIL HIKES IN SOUTHERN OHIO

*A descriptive trail guide to major hiking areas of interest to the serious hiker in Southern Ohio.*

### By Robert H. Ruchhoft
Associate Professor Emeritus of History
The University College, University of Cincinnati

Copyright© 1984 by Robert H. Ruchhoft
**SIXTH PRINTING**

All photographs by the Author except where otherwise noted

𝕿𝖍𝖊 𝕻𝖚𝖈𝖊𝖑𝖑𝖊 𝕻𝖗𝖊𝖘𝖘

P.O. Box 19161
Cincinnati, Ohio 45219

# ACKNOWLEDGEMENTS

In producing this volume there were so many physical and mental trail turns that had to be transformed into a standardized context and outline with easily read word descriptions that I fear, without the help of others this author would have found himself hoplessly lost in the literary equivalent of the labyrinth at Strabo. In turning my original tape recorded trail description to the final printed page I know the manuscript's organization, information and readability has been improved by the special knowledge and talents provided by the following individuals: To my University College colleagues Franchot Ballinger, Bill Bocklage, Marvin Garrett, Ed Richardson and Jack Stevens for reading the original manuscript and giving me their experienced judgement on content and style; to Mike and Linda Sears who carefully proofread the original and corrected galley proofs as well as the final paste up pages finding many a previously unnoticed mistake or misspelled word, and often sucessfully challenging my word structure; to Shirley Thorpe who cleaned up some of my sloppy lettering and trail markings on many of the included maps; to many of my hiking friends who are members of the Miami Group of the Ohio Chapter of the Sierra Club who accompanied me on some of the many hikes made for this book; and to the many employees of both the forestry and parks divisions of the O.D.N.R., employees of the Ironton district of the U.S. Forest Service in the Wayne National Forest and Boy Scout leaders whose names are mentioned in the text who answered my many questions and gave generous help and suggestions when I researched the hiking areas they oversaw. If the book is successful in its purpose all of the persons mentioned above added substantially to that success. On the other hand, any error, shortcoming, omission or over all failure of this book's purpose must rest soley on the shoulders of its author.

## TABLE OF CONTENTS

I.     INTRODUCTION .................................................. 1

        Basic objective/4. What is not in the book/6. Rating the trails - Difficulty and time/7. Maps/8. Why all the signs?/8. Something about the snakes/10. Rules, regulations and backcountry etiquette/10. To the trailhead/14.

II.     TAR HOLLOW .................................................. 17

        Introduction and area development/17. How to get there, Where to stay/22. Hiking the Logan Trail and its variations/23. Backpack and dayhike possibilities/23. Finding the trailheads/25. North Loop/27. South Loop/35.

III.     HOCKING HILLS .................................................. 44

        Introduction/45. How to get there/46. Where to stay/46. Special events/47. Geology of the area/49. General trail classifications/51. Scenic locations and suggested hikes/51. Unit One - Granny Gatewood Trail (Upper, Lower and Cedar Falls, Old Man's Cave, Ash Cave)/56. Indian Run Loop Trail/67. East Rim Loop Trail/69. Gulf Trail/71. Rose Lake Trail/72. Unit Two - Location of the three areas/73. Conkle's Hollow/73. Rock House/76. Cantwell Cliffs/79.

IV.     VESUVIUS RECREATION AREA ............................... 83

        Introduction and area development/83. How to get there/89. Where to stay/89. The Vesuvious loop trails and their variations/90. Backpack loop/93. Bluegrass trail/102. Lakeshore trail/108.

V.     ZALESKI .................................................. 112

        Introduction and area development/112. How to get there/113. Where to stay/113. Zaleski loop variations/119. South loop/122. Central loop/127. North loop/129. Olds Hollow trail/141.

VI.     BURR OAK AND WILDCAT LOOPS .......................... 143

        Introduction and area development/143. How to get there/143. Where to stay/144. Burr Oak - Wildcat trails and variations/148. Burr Oak loop/153. Wildcat loop/168.

VII.     SHAWNEE .................................................. 174

        Introduction and area development/174. How to get there/175. Where to stay/175. Shawnee Backpack loops and variations/175. North loop/192. South loop/200. Wilderness Side trail/215. Silver Arrow trail/220.

VIII.     EAST FORK .................................................. 225

        Introduction and area development/225. How to get there and finding the trailheads/230. Places to stay/230. Hiking the Backcountry and Backpack trails and their variations/230. Backcountry Trail/231. Backpack Trail/252.

## MAPS

### GENERAL LOCATION MAP .................................260

### TAR HOLLOW
Logan Trail North Loop ...................................... 18
Logan Trail South Loop....................................... 20

### HOCKING HILLS
Area location map/44. Unit #1 area map/52. Old Man's Cave map/54. Cedar Falls map/63. Ash Cave map/66. Conkle's Hollow map/74. Rock House map/77. Cantwell Cliffs map/81.

### VESUVIUS
Backpack and Lakeside Trail ............................... 84
Backpack and Bluegrass Trail .............................. 86

### ZALESKI
South Loop map ............................................ 114
Central and North Loop map................................ 116

### BURR OAK-WILDCAT
Burr Oak map .............................................. 144
Wildcat map ............................................... 146

### SHAWNEE
West segment of North Loop ............................... 176
East segment of North Loop ............................... 178
East segment of South Loop................................ 180
West segment of South Loop ............................... 182
Wilderness side trail ....................................... 184

### EAST FORK
West segment.............................................. 226
East segment .............................................. 228

IV.

# INTRODUCTION

"What? Real backpacking in Ohio! aw come-on, you can't be serious," said the young man in total disbelief. He is a native Ohioian and an experienced backpacker who, like so many fellow Buckeyes, erroneously believes the state is basically a megalopolis patchworked by corn fields bordered by a polluted lake to the north and a polluted river in the south. In recent years marvelous progress has been made in the improvement of the water quality of the lake to the north, and the rolling Appalachian foothills in the southeastern part of Ohio offer thousands of acres of high forested hills. Much of this land is protected within the boundaries of our state and national forests, with no really large metropolitan area nearby.

But of course, there are limitations. Even though there is an Indiana county named Switzerland, whose borders touch the southwestern part of Ohio, don't expect to round a corner on any of these trails and see a Matterhorn or Jungfrau suddenly rising triumphantly thousands of feet above the mist. If you do you have problems that should be looked into by professionals in other areas. There is a man-made minature Matterhorn at an Ohio ski resort, but only a climber the size of an inchworm would find the ascent of that twenty foot plastic mountain exhilerating. O.K., we don't have a Gannet Peak or a Mt. Whitney but we have many a mile of fine trail to use. Yes I'd rather backpack in Colorado, Wyoming or Alaska and I try to get one trip a year up to the rarified air of the high mountains. But the rest of the year, I can have several shorter backpacking trips at a fraction of the cost in time and money right in my Ohio backyard. This also offers me the feeling of getting away from it all with the added bonus that if I do make a western trip I'll be in better shape and know that my gear is functioning well.

"Why", you may reasonably ask, "does one need a book like this at all since various governmental agencies issue trail maps and the trails themselves are usually well marked?" Why not just go out and hike them, which is successfully done by hundreds of hikers each year? As you hike down a trail that is perfectly obvious, you might wonder why I went to all the bother of spending the spare time of several years of my life to write this guide. There are a number of valid reasons, which began occurring to me after the publication of my first guide to the Red River Gorge - Natural Bridge area called KENTUCKY'S LAND OF THE ARCHES. With the moderate success of that book, I learned several things. Although that book was written as a general guide that was just as valid for automobile sightseers as hikers, by far the greatest number of people using that book were hiker - backpackers. I also learned that the fifty odd miles of beautiful trail in that area are now being loved to death.

I also learned from my many friends who work in backpack related stores in the Cincinnati area the question that they hear frequently is "Where can we go backpacking in Ohio?" I decided to find out and found no less than seven major areas where serious backpacking can be done on marked trails, usually in loops that are often short enough to do on a weekend. The list is not comprehensive but does offer about 250 miles of trail for the interested hiker. "But," you say, "All that one needs is a list of the names of the available places then go to them." However, if you want to get rid of some of the frustrations and just enjoy the hiking, here's how this book can help.

If you think you can do all the trails without getting lost a few times, Lotsa luck. You'll never be so far afield that you'll start looking for brandy carrying St. Bernards, but sometimes trails seem to disappear or to branch out in three directions, signs are missing or purposely turned around by pranksters and road crossings seem to be eaten up by the asphalt strip. Unofficial trails suddenly appear with no real indication about which way is the official path. Erosion and man - made changes sometimes make a once easily followed trail do a disappearing act. I once spent almost an hour trying to find a trail on the other side of a road crossing which shouldn't have taken ten seconds. The sign indicating the turn off was missing and rapid summer growth of underbrush had obliterated all signs of the usual, obvious turn. On another occasion I traveled 200 miles by auto to a loop trail only to find that so much of the trail was under water that hiking it was impossible even though my arrival at the trailhead was three full days after the last rain. I once talked to a backpacking couple who were forced to walk about three extra miles from their campsite after a long, tiring hiking day to obtain water because the water supply for that camp had been moved from its original location. The new site was only about 200 yards from their tent, but its location was hidden from view, buried in high weeds.

Even trailheads are sometimes hard to find and nearby government offices, where hiking information and sometimes maps are cheerfully given during the week, are often closed when the weekend backpacker arrives. If you are totally new to an area, you may spend a great deal of time learning the general orientation of it, finding the right road to the trail head and the location of parking areas, water drops and campgrounds.

Most of us, with our busy urban existence forcing us to hike a trail within a very restricted time frame, would rather escape these frustrations and delays and concentrate on enjoying the hike.

To eliminate or reduce these frustrating time wasters - plus letting the potential hiker know that these hikes exist - are the major raison d' etre for this book and I won't deny there is a modicum of ego satisfaction in seeing it in print.

So this book offers a variety of trails for almost all endurance levels of healthy people. If hikers know about the location of the available trails and the ability level necessary to comfortably hike them, it may also have the desired effect of spreading out the hiking population, cutting out the concentration of vibram footprints in the more popular areas.

I have a few close friends (and others of casual and momentary acquaintance) who usually scoff at the idea of following trails at all, preferring to roam the many thousands of trailless public areas with topo maps and compass in hand, bushwacking their way, rarely following an occasional trail. But it takes a special breed to climb over all those dead falls, mush through swamps, heavy underbrush and briar patches, having only a general idea of where they are and only a rougher one of how long it will take to hike to their objective. Covering a single mile may take hours instead of minutes and, if injury is sustained, help is often many trailless miles away.

Several times during the research walks for this book, when I was safely following the lifeline of a trail, I wondered and marveled at those pioneers who penetrated these areas before any trails or roads and managed to find their way about. Many must have felt like that great pathfinder Daniel Boone when someone asked him if he ever got lost and he replied "No but sometimes I was mighty confused for two or three days." Bushwacking is a marvelous experience for those trained and conditioned enough to do it and mentally able to cope with the uncertainties, but most of us are a little too far removed from the frontiersman pathfinder. The trail is a sort of umbilical cord to civilization which we would rather not break. Our retreat to the wilderness is desired only partly. Prepared trails and guide books provide a certain cushion of comfort and safety.

Since most of us are necessarily geared to the recreational week-end clock, we appreciate trails that lead us into the semi-wilderness environment. We like to have some idea of the hours necessary to make these hikes and work out a pre-arranged time frame that permits us to unhurriedly switch hats back to our Monday morning world.

I am somewhat amused (and also a bit worried) at the general public's attitude toward long day hikers and backpackers. It is as if we belonged to some kind of conspiracy against the common weal, that there is something basically sinful about people who knowingly would go out and torture their bodies by walking excessive miles carrying several pounds of equipment through sunshine, snow and rain, cooking packaged gruel over midget stoves, fitting our sweat drenched bodies into miniscule tents and lying uncomfortably on the ground, when instead we could be snugly ensconced in a lodge or motel room, shower handy with the T.V. to help us through the lonely hours before sleep. I can answer simply by saying that for many of us it is fun and it is not in any way masochistic.

I remember hearing Arthur Miller say during a T.V. interview that after he moved out of the city a concerned friend asked him, "But when you go for a walk in the country where do you go?" I'm afraid that those types, especially when they become tourists, will always look at us with our hiking clothes and packs as if we were mentally deranged morons who are quite dangerous and should be caged for safe viewing in some side show alongside the wild man from Borneo. I particularly remember returning from a strenuous day hike one hot August afternoon when I took a short cut to my car through the well populated outdoor swimming pool area of one of our state park lodges. I had been treking through some marshy and over grown weedy country so my appropriate hiking clothes were mud spattered and briar covered. My sudden appearance brought a look of amazement and disapproval from most of the bathers whose only previous concern prior to my arrival was soaking up the poolside sun. Those with young children immediately began to urge the toddlers toward them for protection as if I had been the local distributor of venereal disease.

How many times have you heard "But what if you get hurt or sick out there?" It is something that could happen, but the seasoned sensible hiker rarely finds himself a victim. In the few cases where serious impairment has happened, it is usually the unprepared - particularly the macho type - that are found dead from hypothermia or a serious fall. A seasoned hiker would not knowingly start on any overnighter if he felt a chronic illness coming any more than a star tennis player would participate against top competition with a body temperature of 104° F. Sure there are dangers but the greatest of them is the possibility of getting creamed by a eighteen wheeler or a drunk driver when you travel by car to or from the trailhead.

**The dangers of getting yourself seriously hurt are not much different than someone driving to Florida for a Disneyland visit.**

Those of us that have this urge to break away into the natural world, even for a single night, may be affected by a subliminal attachment to that two million year evolutionary period of human development from the simplest hunter - gatherer societies to the first small urban communities. After all, civilization is just a few thousand years old, and we lived as hunter - gatherers for millions. Anthropoligists studying modern hunter - gatherer societies have determined that the women in these primitive groups walk about 3000 miles a year.

When someone learned to plant crops the long walk gradually disappeared and, as urban civilization grew from simple village living to our present day complexities, we now see people circling parking lots in their cars trying to find a parking place that will save them from walking thirty or forty extra feet. For many the long walk has shrunk to the point that our pedal extremities may be in evolutionary danger.

Some us may have a subconscious desire to, at least partially, return to the long walk of our hunter - gather ancestors, but few would wish to entirely turn back the clock to live in such an economy. Anyway, it would be impossible in Ohio to return to

*Winter Backpackers near the end of the Lakeshore Trail - Vesuvius Recreation Area*

a Grizzly Adams existance except in fantasy, for it takes about a square mile of territory to support one person in a hunter - gather economy. In Ohio there are about 235 people for each square mile, so there would be a tremendous amount of head bashing to get rid of the excess of 234 extra bodies. And, if such a blood bath were possible, most of us would find it excessively painful to live in that primitive way for very long. But it's fun for a week-end, with no head - bashing necessary and it tends to make us more appreciative of some of our civilized amenities. The boring daily shower we find becomes an absolute savored luxury after a few sweaty days on the trail. If an abrupt change in weather finds you slogging through buckets of rain and Lake Erie sized puddles you may find both your "waterproof" boots and rain jacket have become sieve-like receptacles of water and the snug, bone dry tent has suddenly developed a seam leak transforming its interior into a misty shower, you become painfully aware of how nice it is to have a roof at home that doesn't leak.

Such walks remove us just far enough from our nest that we have less chance to fall victim to temptation. If you are nicely ensconced in a back country campground and suddenly get a fat attack at 11:30 p.m., there are no handy delis or pizza parlors to run your calorie counter crazy. I often think of how nice it is to wake up on a backpack morning knowing that no one during the early hours delivered to the front of my tent that chronicle of human stupidity and daily horrors known as the morning newspaper.

## BASIC OBJECTIVE

It is sometimes fascinating for me to daydream about how I am going to carry out the main idea of a proposed book which, at first, can only be loosely structured. I learned, while writting my book, KENTUCKY'S LAND OF THE ARCHES, that trying to figure out an exact format and organizational pattern at the beginning only led to monstrous frustration.

But as the research and writing went along logical patterns began to emerge that could not have been forseen earlier. I am well aware that writing an ideal guide book for a wide spectrum of hikers is a bit like seeking the Holy Grail. Nonetheless I started with the basic idea that there are many Ohio hikers looking either for week-end backpack loop trips or day hikes with some real bite to them that are not too far from home where they could hike on hilly forested land mostly removed from civilization. The Buckeye Trail, as wonderful as it is, does not lend itself well to this type of format for covering its thousand mile loop would require months, not days.

Knowing that there are hundreds of miles of many types of trail in southern Ohio and that writing something about all of them would have produced a work slightly longer than "War and Peace," I set up some criteria for what areas would have to be included in this trail guide.

FIRST.
An area should have at least one good backpack loop of a single night or more where primitive camping is legal.

SECOND.
The trails must be official trails on public land that are marked and maintained.

THIRD.
The trails must be at least eight miles in length.

FOURTH.
A high percentage of the trail miles must be away from public highways. They should traverse rugged hilly terrain of mostly forested land that, by-and-large, is removed from developed civilized area.

The above criteria, although generally followed in this book, are not rigid and were liberalized a few times to best fit the overall purpose of producing a good and usable guide. When I began my hiking research I knew of two major areas that would fit this type of format. Before I was finished, I had found six more suitable areas containing close to 300 miles of trail and all but one of these areas are included in this book.

Interestingly enough, all but one of these areas were organized around locations that were set aside as a result of congressional action for a quite different purpose. The year after the worst Ohio River flood in recorded history Congress passed the Flood Control Act of 1938 authorizing a series of dams to be built for controlling water run off during periods of heavy rain. The impounded waters would serve as recreation centers as well as resevoirs to keep streams from going near or completely dry when long periods of little or no rain ensued. Dams were built at Tar Hollow and Vesuvius before World War II. Others followed after the war and the last one was completed in 1978. All but one of the eight areas have long trails that circle the lake but only three of them stay relatively close to the impounded water. There has been a great deal of controversy about the feasibility of these dams, some suggesting that they destroy more than they protect. Since I belong to organizations that have questioned their desirability, I know the ecological arguments against them. But I am also old enough to have witnessed the disastrous 1937 flood of the Ohio River that crested at Cincinnati just a sliver short of eighty feet. Recent engineering studies suggest that if the existing dams had been built before 1937 the crest of the river would have been at least ten feet lower. So there are strong arguments on both sides. But from the pragmatic point of view the dams and the lakes they created are a fact of life. The

*Two backpackers crossing the large open area in the East Fork spillway*

areas are generally attractive and often downright beautiful. With the multiple use concept of land both the state and federal governments have utilized these lands for recreational purposes with many miles of delightful trail on or near the lakes. So why not use them and enjoy?

## WHAT IS NOT IN THE BOOK

The present title for this book might lead one to believe most or all of the Buckeye Trail has been included. To encompass that large loop of over 1000 miles in detail in this volume would have resulted in something reminiscent of the size of the Encyclopedia Britannica. Descriptions of that trail, broken down into sections, have already been done by the Buckeye Trail Association. If you are interested in a free brochure, or in joining our membership and following the blue blazes write to the

BUCKEYE TRAIL ASSOCIATION
P.O. BOX 254
WORTHINGTON, OHIO 43058

Originally I intended to write a general, brief geological and human history of the overall areas as I had done in the opening pages of my Red River Gorge Guide. I especially wanted to have an extensive section about Ohio's pre-historic Indian cultures but several factors make these ideas unrealistic. In my Kentucky book I was dealing with one centralized area. This book deals with seven. To have written about all of them in any detail would have taken up so much research time that with my procrastinating slowness the completion of this volume would have probably occured when I was tripping over my long and ancient beard bending over a tome that had increased in size until it was as fat as an unabridged Websters. I have briefly introduced each area, and there is a bit of geology in the Hocking Hills chapter. There are already excellent books on the Indian cultures which can be purchased at The Mound City group National Monument near Chillcothe, Cincinnati Nature Center and the Cincinnati Museum of Natural History. Also, the diaramas of these early Indian cultures found in that museum give a beautiful display of how these people probably lived.

I had also intended to follow the idea of describing all trails in both directions as I had done in my Kentucky book, but as new miles of trail were discovered, I realized that such a plan would have stretched the size of this book way past the point of where it could be called a portable volume.

I have left out one hiking area that seems ideal for the general format of this book. Caesar Creek State park with a hiking loop of over thirty miles seems just right and would have been included except for one major problem. The trail is less than half finished at this writing and this book is already a year behind its proposed publishing date.

For those interested in the proposed Caesar Creek loop, I am beginning a book about the hiking and canoeing areas on and near the Little Miami River and intend to include a description of the Caesar Creek trail in the book.

## RATING THE TRAILS - DIFFICULTY AND TIME.

Finding the perfect system for rating the time and difficulty of trails for people of diverse ages, levels of fitness and determination is a little bit like trying to write an income tax law that everyone agrees is equally fair for all payees. Although I consider myself a seasoned hiker-backpacker I am not a fast one, for I have had hikers pass me as if they were snarling Corvettes charging onwards and upwards leaving me in the dust as if I were a geared-down loaded cement truck with flat tires on my drive wheels. On the other hand, I've seen groups much younger than myself, who were the **most enthusiastic healthy looking hikers at the trailhead, experience a drastic mood change after a two mile stretch of hills. They had been transformed to forlorn** pessimists on the threshold of serious muscular pain and exhaustion. Such trail ratings will always be somewhat arbitrary; I have noticed that trails I hiked late in the day always tended to seem harder and longer. But these ratings, at least, give you some sort of framework from which to plan hikes and, after a hike or two, you'll know if your level conforms to mine or if your pace is a level or two faster or slower. It will also help you to determine which hikes best suit your capacity and mood.

I have devised six levels of trail difficulty: VERY EASY, EASY, MODERATE, MODERATE TO STRENUOUS, STRENUOUS, VERY STRENUOUS. These ratings take into account elevation gain, steepness of grade, trail surfaces and distance. Trails marked VERY EASY would be about the same as walking two level city blocks and its use in this book is rare. EASY is a little more demanding than a pancake flat city-type stroll with some gentle grades and a mite more distance. I believe most conditioned hikers will find that the MODERATE level is their idea of pleasant hiking conditions where being in shape will pay off and present no great physical challenge, while many new and out-of-shape walkers will find this level fairly difficult. STRENUOUS means that the average hiker in relatively good condition is going to get a workout and VERY STRENUOUS requires a concentrated effort of body and soul with possibly more than just a little suffering. However, sinewy youths who are used to carrying heavy packs over hilly terrain for some miles over ten, and those of the older generation who have the inherited ability of a Granny Gatewood will find that even 'VERY STRENUOUS' is a bit of a lark.

Walking times are even more difficult to determine since such times tend to vary greatly between the beginning and the end of the walking day. Even the speed of experienced and conditioned hikers varies from slothful plodders to marathon runners. I have tended to favor walkers with a moderately slow pace who are not out to test their endurance limits but to savor the out-of-doors, examining the natural surroundings in an unhurried way. Almost all conditioned hikers will find they can cover the trails in considerably less time than indicated if they wish, for the walking times suggested for each trail were not designed to test cross country runners. Beware of the numbers game especially if you are a beginner. You can easily get caught up in this trap when braggarts sound off about the number of miles they covered in a given time and you feel like some sort of an unfit weakling unless you too can boastfully tell about hiking into the double figures in a single day. Unless you have done a lot of distance hiking you will find that miles are longer than you think, and any type of **incline or uneven trail surfaces squares the difficulty. If your one aim is to see how many miles you can squeeze into a day, hike alongside roads for you can move much** faster and inclines are almost never steep. But hiking along a paved public highway with the constant buzz of traffic excites me about as much as waiting for the mating season of giant sloths.

If you are interested only in the speed you can make from point to point you might take up hiking along a limited access Interstate. Quite illegal of course, but the singing eighteen wheels of a semi passing you at sixty plus may give you the feeling of speed you are after. The spirit of adventure is there too as you wonder if some passing drunks might pelt you with beer cans or maybe swerve off the road to see if you are fleet enough to dive into the nearest ditch. Or, you may enjoy seeing if you can out-wit the state police who will take umbrage at your hike alongside the fast lane.

Walking times given here are an average for the time you are moving because they do not take into account time taken for comfort stops, lunch, gorp or photographic breaks.

## MAPS

All maps with exception of the individual small area maps at Hocking Hills were made from the appropriate U.S.G.S. 7.5 minute series topographic maps. Although I was often aided by existing area maps issued by the state and federal governments the trail markings in this book were made by me. I feel they are adequate for giving the hiker, regardless of his/her map reading ability, a good general idea of where the trails go. I found many small errors in the existing trail maps and made appropriate corrections. Some minor mistakes may turn up in mine and with time, new trail routings caused by man and nature will call for occasional revisions. Even though I make no claims to be any professional type of cartographer I think I am reasonably safe in stating that, at this writing, my trail maps, if not as artistically done, are more accurate than any other trail maps of these areas in existance. For those fond of reading topo maps who wish to do some bushwacking I have included the names of the quadrangles for each area. Since most of the trails discussed in this book are not shown on the U.S.G.S. maps, trail hikers will find the maps herein more useful and a good deal less expensive, for the hiking areas of this book are on twenty two different quadrangles which, at the current price of $2.00 apiece, will cost considerably more than this book.

## WHY ALL THE SIGNS?

Many readers may wonder why I have included most trail signs and their locations at trail heads, important junctions and other specific points. I did not mean to be redundant (which will often be the case) but hikers can often notice that as they leave

***The largest recess Cave in Ohio on Hocking Hill's Granny Gatewood Trail***

the trailhead walking away from the road there seems to be an inverse ratio between two factors,:

As the number of beer cans, pop can tops, discarded fried chicken boxes and other offal discarded along the trail decreases the amount of wildflowers, box turtles, and general undisturbed wildlife increases. The same ratio generally holds true for trail signs. With a few unfortunate exceptions the destruction and defacement of trail signs is the worst on or near roads but this vandalism usually decrease as one moves further into the backcountry. When witnessing this unnecessary destruction I am reminded of a saying that is applied to certain parts of Asia. "If something shows movement shoot it. If it is standing still hack it down." Not only has wholesale destruction of signs reached runaway proportions but I have also witnessed examples in the back country where signs have been deliberately turned around or changed to face in a misleading direction often causing hikers to make a wrong turn at a junction which could take them miles out of their way. By describing the exact **location of signs in this text, I hope that attempts to deliberately mislead the hiker by hooligans will be largely frustrated by preventing the hiker from making a wrong** turn. When I see the mutilated signs, the erosion producing short cuts on trails, paint spray can messages on natural rock surfaces, wholesale picking of wildflowers, the hacking down of live trees, garbage and unnecessary fire rings in the backcountry, I am reminded of a remark I once heard by an acquaintance when she said, "Man was the worst mistake that God could afford to make."

I belong to the group of people who believe that to destroy a wildflower is to disturb a star to which we are all connected and interelated with things in the universe both big and small, and the less we fool around with this natural system, especially in these sanctuaries removed from civilization, the better for us the living and those to follow. In the backcountry, extreme ego and arrogance seem more out of place than anywhere else. John Muir summoned it up nicely by saying "When we try to pick out anything by itself, we find it hitched to everything else in the universe."

## SOMETHING ABOUT THE SNAKES

Along with a variety of non-poisonous snakes, there are two venomous varieties, the copperhead and the timber rattler, that are native to Ohio which might be encountered on almost any trail described in this book. However the likelihood of that happening is extremely remote. As far as I know, no one has ever been bitten by a poisonous snake on any of these trails and during my hundreds of miles of walking I have yet to see my first one in Ohio. That doesn't mean that they are not there but they do tend to shy away from areas that are heavily traveled by humans and the ones that do generally get killed or captured before they grow to the larger sizes. Even on back trails your chances of seeing one of these species are so slim that it shouldn't be a major concern. But precautions are suggested especially when hiking in the less frequented areas during the warmer seasons of the year. Don't hike barefoot or in shorts for many reasons including better snake protection. Wear shoes that cover your ankles since about 90% of all snake strikes are in that region. By wearing long pants you add a little more protection, because a snake bites when he contacts a surface and he may penetrate no more than the air between pants and leg. Don't put your hands under rocks or logs until you have given them a good visual examination. Watch sunny areas on cool days and shady spots on the warmer ones especially during the afternoon and early evening. Fortunately neither the timber rattler nor the cooperhead is aggressive and both will generally leave your alone if they don't feel threatened. Remember that the evolutionary reason for the poison is for hunting, not for attacking people. There has never been a human death by a copperhead bite in the state of Ohio, and the few that happened anywhere occured when those unlucky persons fell into a snake pit and suffered multiple bites from many snakes. The timber rattlers do get big, but, again, statistics are on your side for, on the average, there are about 14 deaths a year from poisonous snake bites in the entire United States. This means that Ohio should have one snake fatality about once in every three and a half years and it probably isn't that many. A far higher percentage of people are killed annually from insects stings, and the most dangerous viper of them all is the one tanked up on booze or drugs that is zinging down the highway at unreasonable speeds.

The jury is still out on the worth and practicability of a snake bite kit, for in the hands of the inexperienced user, it sometimes causes more damage than the snake. I carry one, almost more for psychological security than for any practical reason. If you really have an abnormal dread of snakes to the point where just thinking about them ruins the pleasure of any hike but otherwise love to hit the trail, wait until the first hard frost in the fall. That is when the snakes usually hibernate for the winter giving you almost six months of worry-free hiking along the snakeless trails.

## RULES, REGULATIONS AND BACKCOUNTRY ETIQUETTE

Since all trails in this book are either on state or federal property the rules concerning their use in some cases vary slightly but in others are exactly the same. To acquaint you with special rules of each area I have written an individualized introduction for each one. The following are general rules and trail tips for all areas of which you should be aware.

Backcountry camping on state land must be done in designated primitive backcountry camps and not wherever you'd like to pitch your tent. There are no campgrounds along the trails in the Wayne National Forest, and except for the area immediately surrounding the lower part of Lake Vesuvious one may camp anywhere it is prudent to do so. Several of the state trails require registration for overnight stays in backcountry campgrounds. This policy varies from area to area, but in every case, where it is necessary, registration is done by self registration at the trailhead as you begin your hike. At this writing there is no registration required for hiking and camping in the backcountry of the Wayne National Forest. Drinking water is available in most but not all of the backcountry overnight areas on the state trails but not on federal lands. All water taken from streams, lakes and springs should be considered contaminated; therefore it should be purified before drinking. Out-house type laterines are found at the state backcountry camps, but there are none on the backcountry trails in the Wayne National Forest. Those wishing to have hot food should not rely on campfire cooking. Although it is legal in some but not all areas to burn dead fallen timber in designated fire rings, territory immediately adjacent to the campgrounds is usually picked clean and the supplies in the other areas are rarely plentiful and often too wet to burn. Carry a backpack stove and leave your axe at home. Although I fully support the major purposes of the Boy Scouts of America, I feel that competent scout leaders should stand at the trailhead and collect all the hatchets of the younger scouts. Too often I have seen some poor overweight father who was neither physically in shape nor experienced in leading such overnighters drafted into leading a hike for his son's troop. The father might have experienced the following scenario. After walking many more miles than he had in years, while lying exhausted in front of his tent in the dim evening light, the dozing scout leader felt like he might be dying and half wished his demise would occur before the hike would commence on the following morning. Meanwhile the unsupervised young scouts, bleary-eyed and soot covered from campfires which seem more to smoke than burn, after consuming a supper of sorts where the only things that seemed to get hot were their fingers from attempts at fire building and cooking, take off into the surrounding forest, hatchets in hand --- for revenge. The main targets seem to be small live trees and sign posts. Don't interpret this as an anti-Boy Scout generality. Two trails in this book are maintained and kept in beautiful hiking condition by Scout Councils and troops. They are competently led by experienced leaders and are a credit to their organization. My only advice to those unprepared fathers is if someone calls you to lead an overnighter because no one else is available --- don't do it. Go with experienced leaders until you have a feel for it. The same holds true for women too. I once saw a group of young Girl Scouts all dressed in shorts and tennis shoes beginning their first backcountry overnighter. Their two women leaders were mothers who had never camped out in their lives and were leading these quite small girls into a backcountry area in Kentucky that has the highest concentration of copperheads in that state. They were beginning this hiking adventure during a season when the snakes are most active. I asked one of the women what she would do if she saw a snake. Her incredible reply was, "But there aren't any snakes here." Since the odds were with them on the snakes, I felt that enlightening the lady would only terrify her and thought that this was a classic example of the old adage, "Where ignorance is bliss, tis folly to be wise."

Hikers should stay on designated trails avoiding short cuts particularly at switchbacks which cause serious erosion problems. This does not mean that you may never leave the trail to bushwack to a vantage point for exploration but to keep erosion to a minimum, when following the main trails, stay on them. All refuse should be packed out. It is also a nice idea to take an extra plastic bag along to help pick up the carriable debris left behind by thoughtless litterers. Remember, there are no garbage cans along the trail.

*Author checking notes and maps in Iron Ridge Campground after a day hike. Vesuvious Recreation Area.*

Since many miles of these trails are in a close proximity to lakes one should be aware that swimming, except in designated areas, is forbidden. Only one of these swimming locations is reasonably close to a trail, so swimming at any point where the trail is near the water's edge is *verboten*.

Groups using the state's primitive backcountry campgrounds are limited to no more than ten persons. Camp etiquette includes leaving the campsites as clean or cleaner than you found them. No person should disturb the peace and tranquility of other campers after 11:00 p.m. and before 8:00 a.m. This generous rule, I feel, should be interpreted to include the following. Within reasonable limits no person should disturb others at any time on or off the trail. Always maintain the solitude most of us seek during our walking adventures. Be careful with anything that burns. If you are addicted to nicotine, don't smoke while hiking but wait for a rest stop, lunch or the evening camp before lighting up.

If you hike during the hunting seasons wear bright clothes and be cautious. I've found most hunters, especially natives of the vicinity, to be courteous, experienced, and careful but the woods may have a few over anxious beginners who might shoot before they're sure.

It is highly unlikely that you would lose all evidence of trails on any of these hikes and find yourself lost. But if this should happen the best procedure will usually be to follow the course of a stream downhill until it reaches a road. This will usually occur in a mile or less. The only area in this book where following such a proceedure could be highly dangerous is Hocking Hills, where streams frequently drop off suddenly a hundred feet or more over cliffs. But Hocking Hills has such easy, official trails to follow that your chances of getting lost there are about as likely as losing your way in the middle of a supermarket.

If you do become lost and feel you must use this downstream procedure, don't try to find your way out in darkness, for one unseen deadfall, large rock, or small cliff face could result in a broken leg. I know of one incident where this happened. The lady involved not only spent a pain-filled night with her broken ankle but had to wait until late the next afternoon before she was rescued.

Most hiking books suggest that you should not hike alone for you can be quite helpless if a fall results in a serious injury, or if the flu germs you picked up in the city blossom forth on the second day of the hike. I had such an experience and I was mighty happy that I had someone along when I tumbled and broke an ankle on an exceptionally easy stretch of trail on the Burr Oak loop. My companion suddenly transformed himself into a modern Saint Christopher. Still, hiking alone has its own fascination and rewards. Many do it, and even after my accident I have still occasionally gone by myself. Better than 80% of the hiking that I did for this book was done on solo walks. Not always because I wanted it that way, but often I found no available hiking companions when I had the time to go. Although inherently more dangerous, hiking alone isn't as risky as it might seem. Solo hiking tends to make one more cautious, and great numbers do it every year without mishap. There are two suggestions for this activity that I strongly recommend you follow. First, don't hike alone until you are an experienced overnighter who is healthy and has hiked a few times in very nasty weather. In addition, always tell someone, who is reliable and cares, where you are going and when you expect to be back.

Generally my personal opinions are addressed equally to men and women but when hiking alone women face a serious problem not often encountered by men. Not only do they have the previous hazards to contend with, but women also are in far greater danger of personal attack, not from other backpackers but from road hoodlums who can go far afield when the spirit moves. This brings up one of the problems with the rules for a possible deterrent. Dogs, except those used as seeing eye dogs for the blind, are prohibited in the state parks and forest backcountry campgrounds. It is legal to have your pet along for day hikes and you may camp out with them in the Wayne National Forest. I have mixed feelings about dogs in the back country. It is marvelous to have Fido along if the dog is well behaved, obeys you and does not menace other hikers. Human nature being what it is makes certain breeds of dogs very useful and helps insure the safety of women hiking alone, lessening their chances of being molested. But with that option goes a certain responsibility not always followed. On two occasions during trail hikes while I was minding my own business, I was threatened and came very close to being attacked by two breeds of dogs that are often trained as attack animals. Their lone female owners seemed little concerned if I got chewed up or not and did nothing to restrain their bad tempered animals. After a few very scary moments the women offered no apology for my fright **as if their attitude seemed to be "if my dog scares the hell out of everybody coming down the trail, innocent or not, that assures me that I won't be bothered."** Far from wanting to deny women this protection I am all for increasing its effectiveness while at the same time not violating the rights of others on the trail. This can be achieved if the dog is trained to quickly obey the command to "Sit!" as the stranger approaches. If the dog instantly obeys keeping his eye on the approaching stranger, any hiker noticing this conduct will automatically assume that the dog will as quickly obey a command to attack savagely if the lady hiker feels it necessary. This will act as a stronger deterrent for any would be molester while allowing an innocent hiker to **proceed without being physically harassed. Single women are hardly the only ones who hike with menacing dogs that are unrestrained.** Often I have encountered small groups appearing to be an affluent, married couple or two with an unleashed expensive pedigreed dog rather huge in size known for his devotion to a single master or mistress and viciousness towards all others. These hounds approached me as if they were right out of the Baskerville tale, suspicious and ill tempered. The owners, if they noticed me at all, would say, "Oh don't worry about Thunderspreck. He's just showing he likes you." But their canine companion seemed to be imparting a totally different response. The dog's drooling jaws baring glittering teeth, without any tailwagging relief, made me assume that the drooling which was accompanied by a deep-throat growl, was meant to tell me that the dog expected to get a chunk of my bodily meat. It's a little like being inside a cage with a tiger whose trainer standing outside the bars assures you that the big beast is just an overgrown friendly pussy cat. These irresponsible dog owners, who are horrified at tree and sign defacement and would never litter, seem to feel they have a right to let their nasty - tempered beasts freely roam the trails unrestrained just as others feel their rights include cutting down trees and throwing away beverage cans. Although it has never happened to me, I know of at least one case where a hiker was attacked by a group of roaming dogs. One deterrent that gives me a certain peace of mind is my stout hiking stick which also functions as a monopod for my camera. It is stiff enough that it could act as a powerful deterrent to fend off an unwarranted attack.

## TO THE TRAILHEAD

It is most irritating to read and possibly have spent a great deal of money buying guide books where it soon becomes painfully obvious that the author has only a superficial knowledge of the areas being described. I've never kept exact track of the distances I hiked in preparing this book, but I'm fairly confident that the miles I covered on foot would come close to a thousand. With this in mind, even if you disagree with my descriptions I hope you don't feel that my writings came from a perfunctory knowledge of the trails. One of the nicest compliments. I ever received for my guide to Kentucky's Red River Gorge came second-handed when a friend of mine asked another person who was using the guide what she thought of it. Her reply was "He sure has been there."

This is very much a personal guide - my opinions, my judgements and some of my experiences - as I hiked these trails. Sometimes writing trail descriptions is about as exciting as picking gnats out of the oatmeal or pancake mix and they can be equally dull for the reader. I can't guarantee that these descriptions, dull or otherwise, will always prevent you from making a wrong turn or losing the trail but it can greatly reduce the chances of that happening. It happened to me dozens of times so I tried to write clear descriptions in trouble spots to keep you from making the same time-consuming mistakes. I don't consider myself as any great Guru of Ohio hiking for I have friends (and I'm sure there are others I know not of) whose total hiking mileage in Ohio far exceeds mine. There are hundreds of Ohio trail miles that lie ahead of me. Yet I have covered almost every trail segment in this book at least twice, many in both directions. Where my notes seemed vague I went back again. In some cases I've hiked some stretches as many as four times.

Changes will soon occur on these trails and undoubtedly already have because during the six plus year time lapse from the beginning of this project to the end both man and nature have been at their erosive processes. I am astounded to think that about seven years of calendar pages will have found their way to the floor from the first attempts of serious notetaking for this book until it appears in print, and that my little grade school daughter who accompainied me on some of my first walks for this book is fast approaching college age. Although repeated hikes have taken me to each area in different years and seasons, I'm sure there are changes of which I am not aware. For that reason I intend to rehike one or two areas each year and make corrections and additions where necessary in future editions. Since I can't cover all the trails each year this is where you, the hiker, can help me. If you should find substantial differences between actuality and the printed page that you think I should know about, please write to me using the address on the first page of this book.

Even though I am obviously fond of hiking, my thousand mile adventure had many unpleasant moments. Since the times that I was able to hit the trails were restricted by my teaching position and family responsibilities, I was often forced to hike in weather not to my liking. Anytime of year can have great weather for hiking, but the times I could grab often resulted in a sweat-soaked body climbing ridges in 90° July and August heat. The humidity often was so heavy that it felt as if it could be cut with a knife. Sometimes I found myself plodding through mucky marshlands in a freezing December rain with the temperature remaining just high enough to keep the precipitation from turning to delightful snow. The temperature highs and lows for my research walks were 95° on top and 20° on the bottom. For me the high end walks are miserable, but the hikes made when it got below freezing were exhilarating delights, especially if it were snowing. For most of us the ideal hiking temperatures fall in the 40 to 60° range. Passing through the sun warmed crop of spring flowers or the scarlet and yellow shades of our colorful dying season makes walking for us addicts a great elixir of life. Such days I cherish, but if I had waited for those occasions to gather my trail notes for this book, it would have taken so long to finish that it most likely would have had a celestial conclusion. But I have also found that hiking in nasty weather **and coming home healthy has a sort of exhilaration too. I'm not masochistic enough to favor torrential rains over sunshine but if one is prepared for hiking in such weather it often beats spending too many consecutive weekends in our "televised" brick cocoons.**

If you are strictly a fair weather hiker who expects constant sunshine, well manicured trails and no more obstacles than one would meet walking on a sidewalk, you will find most of the hikes in this book unpleasant. If going around or fighting your way over trees that have fallen across the trail makes you unhappy, you are not going to enjoy these loops for, in spite of excellent trail maintenence, nature is always at work with windfalls and deadfalls, an inevitable part of the system. I remember walking an easy and attractive stretch of trail one beautiful crisp fall morning with nary a dead fall to slow up the brisk pace. Covering the same stretch the following spring, I encountered no less than five groups of dead and wind falls across the trail, some with multiple downed trees containing great snarls of branches in less than a quarter mile. They turned this usually easy seven to eight minute stroll into a slow and exasperating fight, bending, crawling, and climbing over, under and through a **jungle of twisted branches that often snagged the top of my backpack frame. So be prepared for the unexpected, like downpours that seem to come from nowhere on a** predicted sunny day and finding usually dry stretches of trails that you cover during a near drought that have mysteriously turned into quagmires sucking your boots into the slime. But the real hiker - backpacker will accept these inconveniences as part of it all. Like myself, you will probably find the things that are most uncomfortable and hardest to get used to are not the natural inconveniences but the human indignities committed on and near the trails. Observing malicious destruction of signs and trees, picking of wildflowers by the armload, parents who let young children run wild in areas that are dangerous or approvingly watch as their young fry scratch, or carve initials into stone surfaces or trees; polaroid snap shooters who drop the negative part of their instant pictures on the trail, fishermen who leave on the bank empty bait containers, pop or beer cans, and bottles that are usually broken, maliciously set fires and other offensive acts - these are the things that are hard to get used to. But on a happier note I've walked entire loops described in this book and found nothing more offensive or out of place than a single gum wrapper. On one occassion the only piece of paper I found was a dollar bill lying, unattended, on the trail.

*Ruins of Pioneer Farmhouse on Wildcat Trail*

So, in conclusion to this rather lengthy introduction, if your own personal discovery and appreciation of these lovely southern Ohio hiking areas are enhanced by the reading of this book and if it leads you to paths you otherwise might have missed, I will have succeeded in my major purpose for writing it. As you follow me down the trail in all kinds of weather and a variety of personal moods, I hope you find this guide a friendly and helpful companion to have along.

# TAR HOLLOW STATE PARK AND FOREST

## INTRODUCTION AND AREA DEVELOPMENT

Although Tar Hollow is a somewhat secluded and quietly beautiful area of high forested hills located close to Chillicothe, and easily accesible from the Columbus, Cincinnati and Dayton areas, it is overlooked by many campers and hikers. They are drawn away by the more scenic but many times more populated Hocking Hills about twenty miles to the northeast, leaving Tar Hollow in a state of splendid islolation. Tar Hollow's lake is not quite big enough to attract the serious boaters. The pit type toilets, and lack of showers and electricity discourage those campers with sensitive noses who look at a camping experience as an appendage of their living rooms complete with stereos and color T.V. Consequently, the Tar Hollow Campgrounds are almost never crowded. On at least two of the occasions that I stayed there during the camping season, I was the campground's sole occupant.

Tar Hollow State Park's 540 acres are surrounded by a 1600 acre state forest with the same name, making it the third largest state forest in Ohio. Like the other hiking areas described in this book, it has loop trails over public land that are located close to a man-made lake. But Tar Hollow has a couple of unique differences too. Like the Vesuvius Recreation Area, it's beginnings as a public park date back to the depression days of the 1930's starting entirely as a federal project.

The lowlands of Ross County are particularly fertile areas for farming, but the surrounding hills are mostly restricted to timber as a successful economic crop. Even before the coming of the white man the modern tribes of the Shawnee and Mingos used the area only as a hunting preserve, considering the area as bad for settling; therefore, the hill country was little known before the beginning of the nineteenth century.

Despite the restrictions of low economic gain, the name of the park and the forest comes from an important by-product of its many evergreen trees, pine tar. Derived from the native pitch pine, it was widely used in nineteenth century Ohio households for soft ointments and mechanical lubricants necessary for the limited pioneer technology. As the demands for their products decreased, economic necessity, semi-wilderness isolation, inaccesability, and abundance of a high yield but poor paying corn crop resulted in profitable but illegal moonshining operations. The residents of the hollow were often considered by many of the outside population to be a group of troublemaking squatters who would best be removed from the area. Under the federal government's Bankhead - Jones Farm Tenant Act of the 1930's the Ross-Hocking Land Untilization project was begun and the squatters of Ross and Tar Hollow were relocated by U. S. Revenue Agents into agricultural areas of better economic opportunity. On one of my stays in the Hollow, I camped next to a man who was a member of a family removed under this act. He told a far different story, claiming that the Federal Government literally drove out several well-established families from land they had legally owned for generations and had no desire to leave. After the removal of the former residents, the land was envisioned as a recreation area and then was so converted by the famous C.C.C. Camping areas and roads were built by these young men and a dam was constructed that created the present fifteen acre lake.

Unlike the Vesuvious Recreation Area which had its beginnings in quite similar circumstances, Tar Hollow did not remain under the jurisdiction of the federal government, but was leased to the state in 1939. The entire area was administered by

17

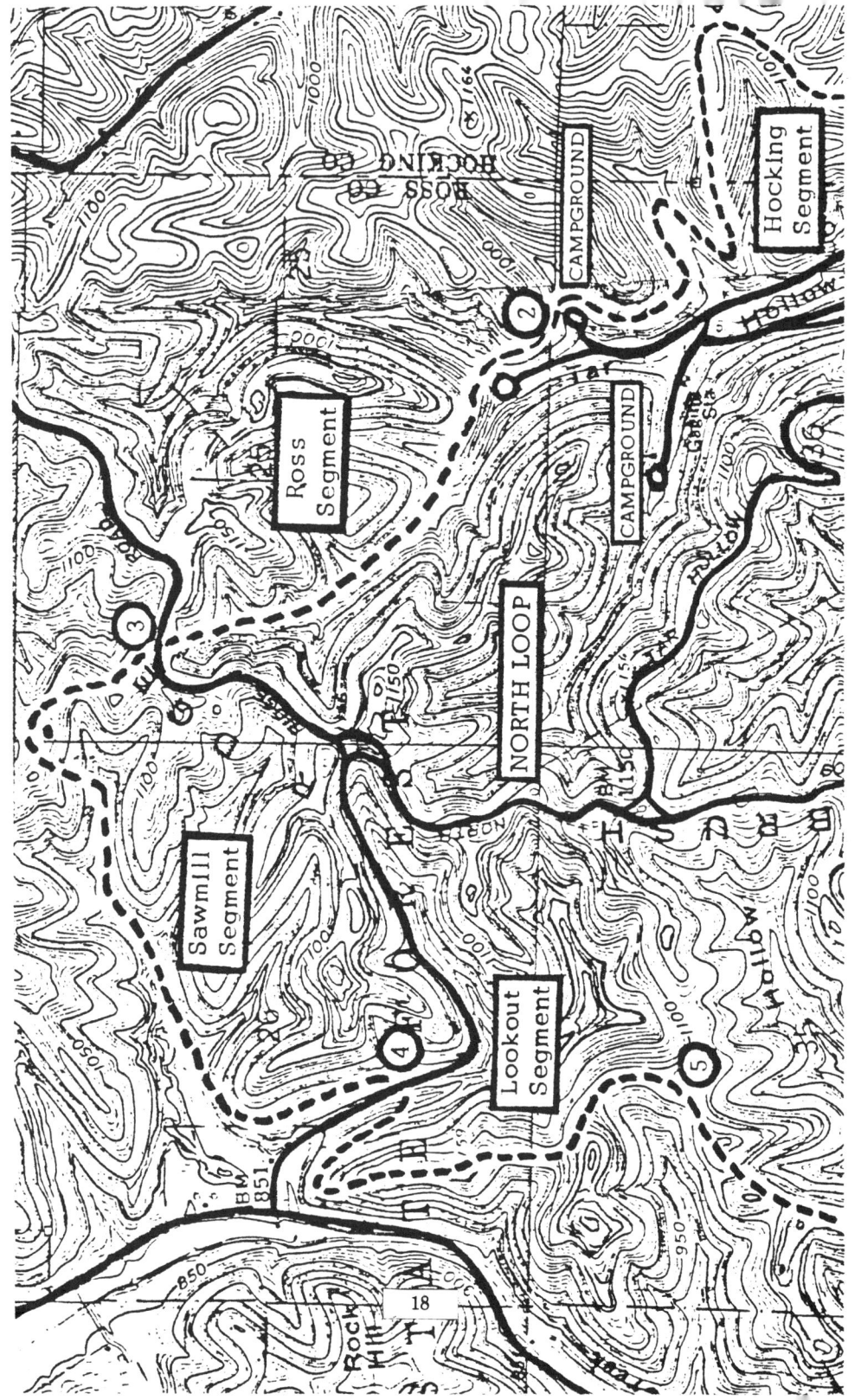

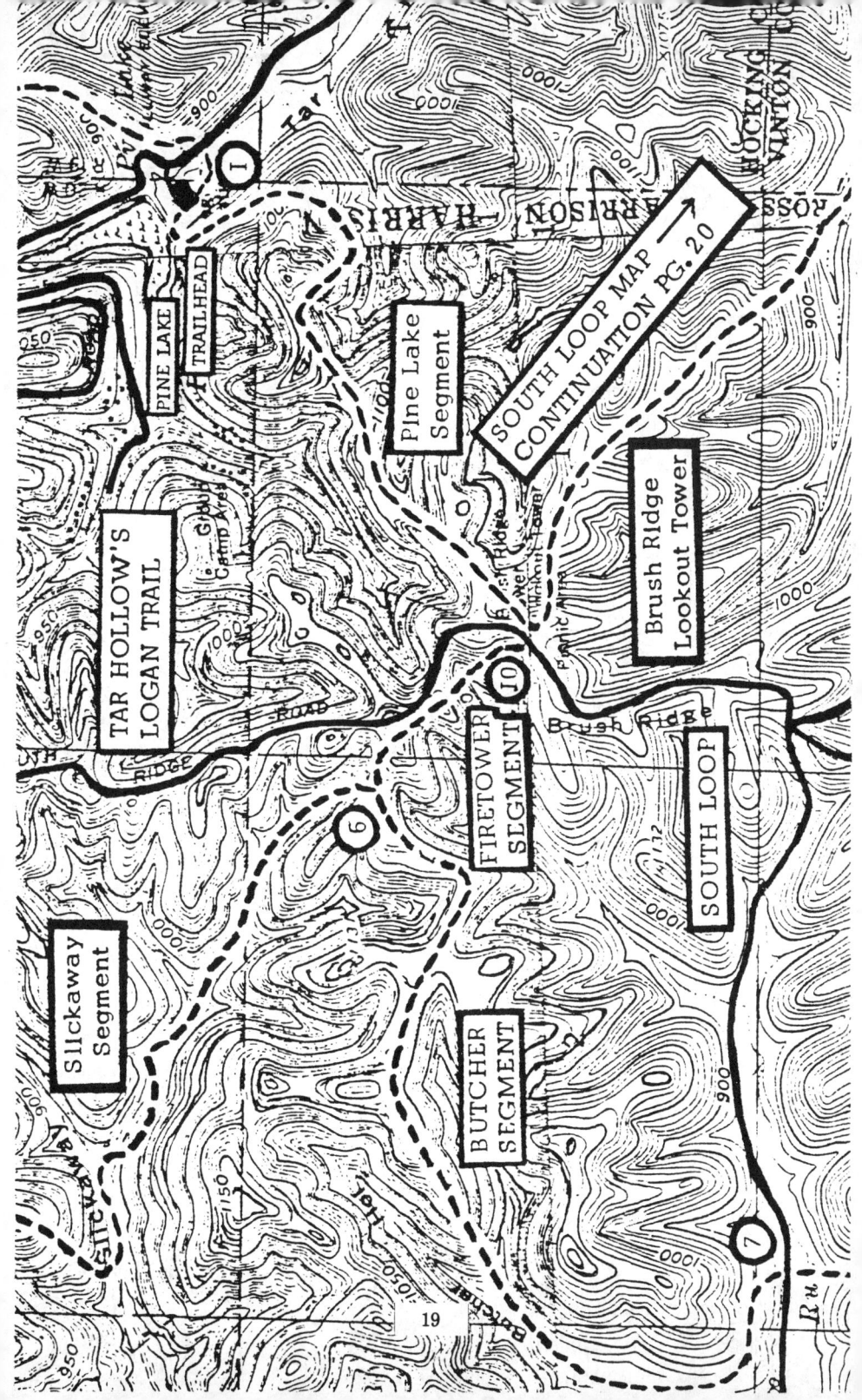

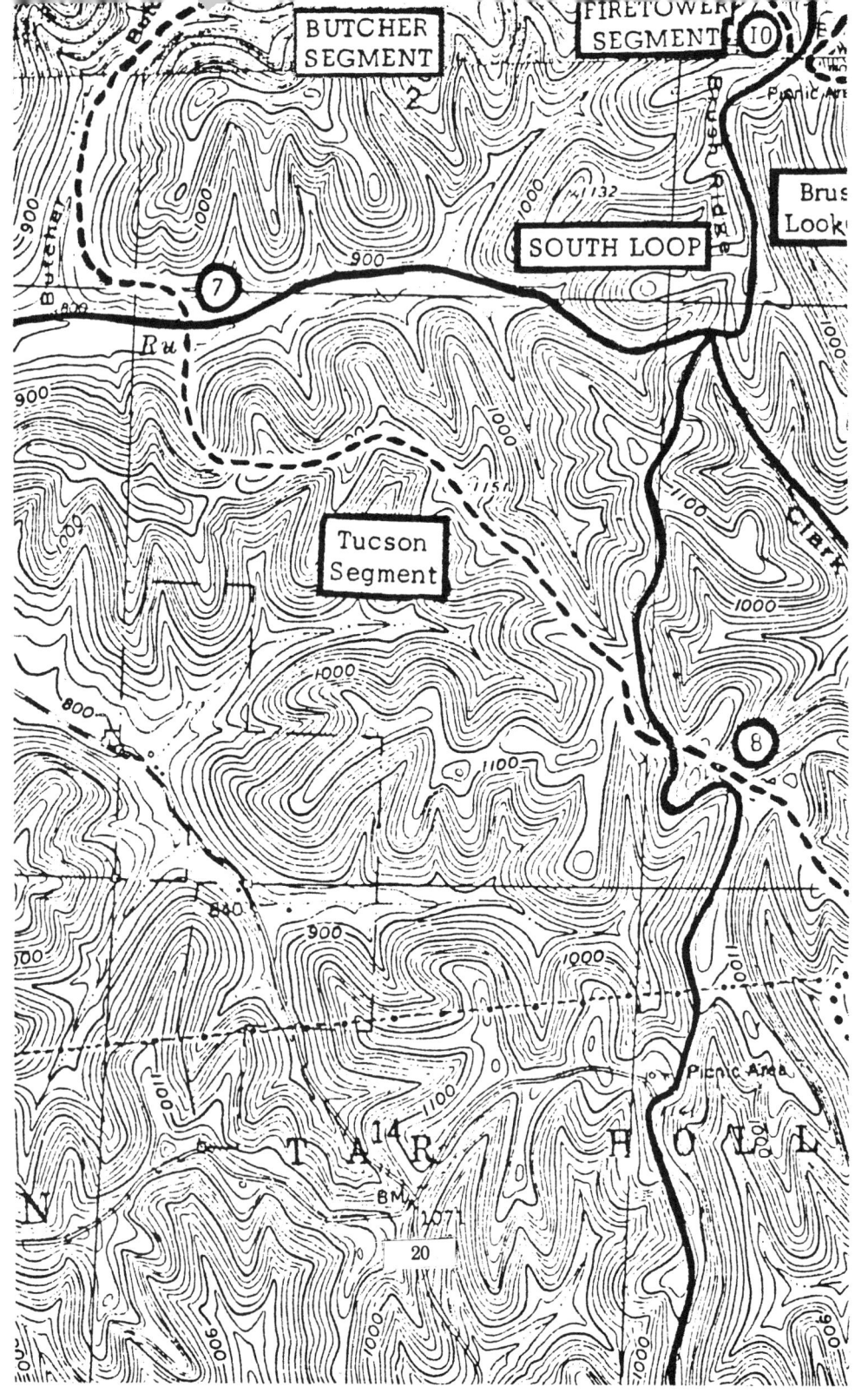

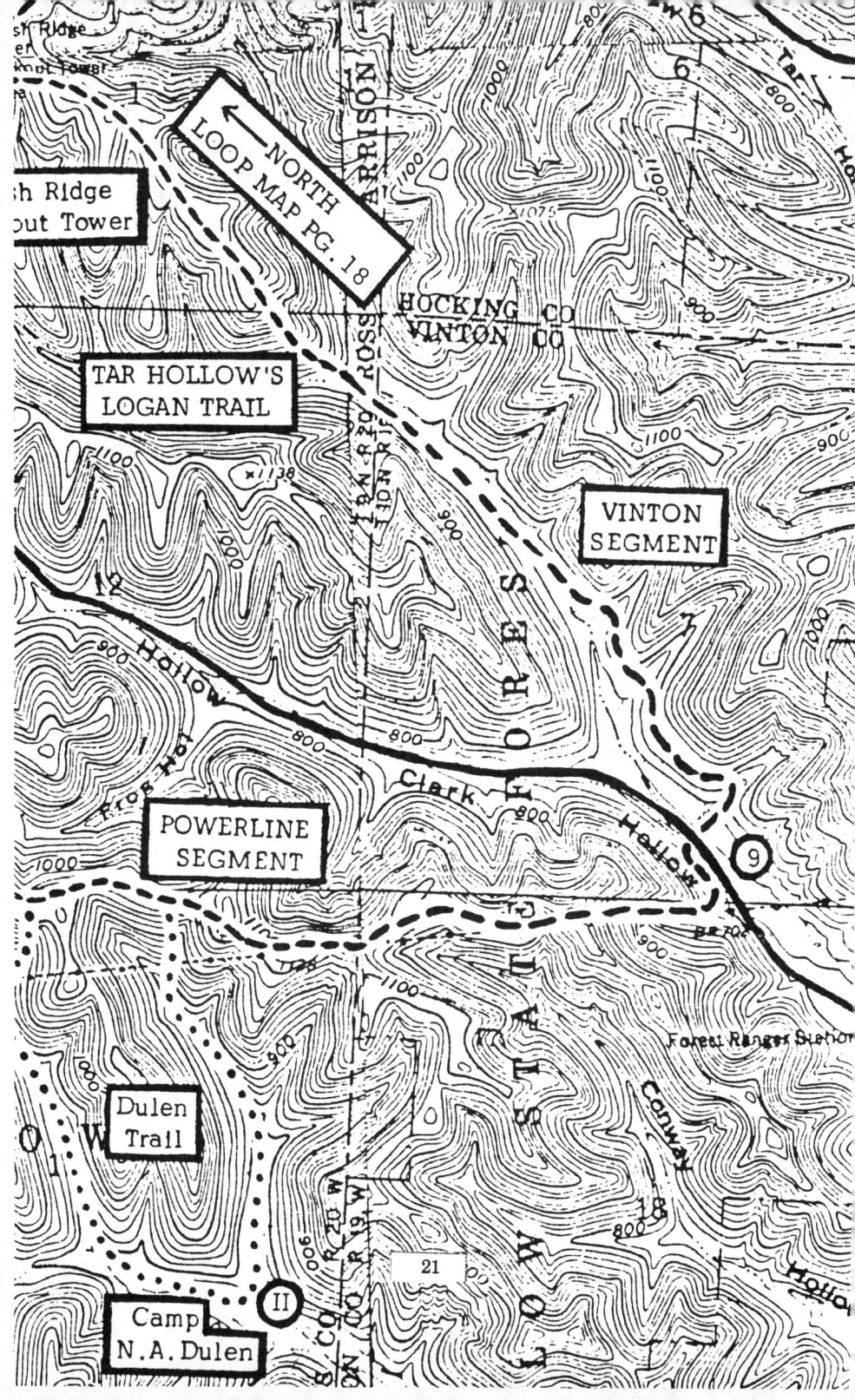

the state's Division of Forestry until the Division of Parks was created in 1949. The prime recreation areas, consisting of 540 acres, became Tar Hollow State Park while the rest remained under the control of the forestry division.

Another unique difference from the other state park trails described in this book, is that this path was envisioned and created by a group of enlightened scout leaders from Troop 195 in Columbus, Ohio and the trail is still maintained by that troop. **Named after the famous Indian Chief Logan of the Mingo tribe, the original trail openend in 1958, utilizing many park and forest roads.** This first routing of the trail proved unpopular because of the high percentage of road walking. It soon fell into disuse and was finally closed. Realizing that the major drawback of the original trail was its reliance on roads, a trail committe of Troop 195 completely rerouted the trail which eliminated walking along public roads and reopened the new trail in 1965. Even **the crossing of public roads has been reduced and it does so only five times in its entire 23 mile length.** Scouts who make the North loop in one hike are eligible for a Logan Patch Award. Those scouts who complete both loops in one continuous hike are eligible for a special Logan Trail patch. Such qualifying hikes, however, are only done under group supervision. Scouting groups wishing to participate should obtain a touring permit from their local council. No permit is required for others wishing to walk the trail.

I had some original apprehension that scouting leaders might be unhappy about others walking a trail maintained by the scouts and might want to discourage its use by others. Such original fears disappeared immediately when one of my hikes there coincided with a work party of the troop led by Roy Case, the present Logan Trail Chairman. By sheer coincidence I met him on the south loop where he was checking a short section of rerouted trail. That evening I spent some enjoyable hours around his campfire where he told me much about the activities relating to the trail and assured me the scouts never intended it to be an exclusive hiking area. The trail committee was pleased that other lovers of the outdoors could enjoy the trail too.

This is one of two trail areas discussed in this book that is maintained by scouts. The other is the Silver Arrow loop in the Shawnee State Forest.

## HOW TO GET THERE

Tar Hollow is conveniently located for people that live in or near the Columbus, Cincinnati Dayton area. It is almost due south of Columbus and about 140 miles northeast of Cincinnati. For those coming from Columbus, take U.S. Route 23 south to Circleville; then go southeast on State Route 56 to Adelphi; then take State Route 327 south to the park entrance on the right. Residents who live in or near Cincinnati have a choice of taking the southerly U.S. Route 50 to Chillicothe or the longer but faster I-71 north to exit 65. Those who prefer to take the Interstate should turn right at **the exit and follow U.S. 35 east which eventually goes around the north side of Chillicothe. People from the Dayton area should take Route 35 to the same location** north of Chillicothe. Both groups should follow Route 35 around Chillicothe until it links up with U.S. Route 50 east of the city. Continue on Route 50 east and follow it to Londonderry; then turn left on State Route 327 and follow it to the state park entrance.

## WHERE TO STAY

Although Tar Hollow has no lodge or cabins that can be rented individually it has the Ross Hollow and Logan Hollow Class B campgrounds with 96 sites located just north of Pine Lake. They can be reached from Tar Hollow Road the main park thorofare and begins at the park entrance of Route 327. There is also a primitive camping area with 16 sites beyond the first two campgrounds farther up the ridge on Tar Hollow Road as it climbs up to Brush Ridge. A larger group primitive area is located just beyond the Logan Hollow campground but reservations are necessary for this group camp made at least 14 days in advance. There is also the large Four Hills Resident Camp which is designed for groups for 175 or more open from May 1 until November 1. Reservations are necessary and are made up to a year in advance. For reservations or information for either group camp write to:

> Tar Hollow State Park
> 16396 Tar Hollow Road
> Laurelville, Ohio 43135
> Telephone (614) 887-4818

The closest motel accomodations are found in Chillicothe.

## HIKING THE LOGAN TRAIL AND ITS VARIATIONS

**TOPOGRAPHIC MAPS:** Ratcliff, Laurelville and Londonderry quadrangles.

**TRAIL BLAZES:** Red.

|  | **Page** |
|---|---|
| Backpack and day hike possibilities | 23 |
| Finding the Trailheads, Fire Tower and water drops | 25 |
| North Loop | 27 |
| South Loop | 35 |
| Dulen Loop | 42 |
| **MAPS** | |
| North Loop | 18 |
| South Loop | 20 |

## BACKPACK AND DAY HIKE POSSIBILITIES

This delightful and well marked trail has many different alternatives in loop hikes for both the day hiker and the backpacker. Although steep in places, the trail is one of the easiest to follow, for trail blazes painted red are plentiful and losing the trail is almost never a problem since the red blaze marks are well maintained by Troop 195. Since there are some confusing trail forks and sudden turnoffs you can assume that if you walk more than 100 feet without seeing a red blaze, you've probably taken the wrong fork or turn off. But though the trail is relatively easy to follow, walking it isn't easy for it offers little for the out-of-shape stroller except agony. Any of the following loop suggestions are demanding enough that they should be considered only by the serious walker in good physical condition.

The Logan Trail is divided into a North and a South loop and each can be begun at the Pine Lake Picnic Area parking lot. Both loops are divided into named segments and are described separately. The North loop consists of seven segments and is a stiff walk of just under twelve miles. This is a bit much for all but the sturdiest of hikers to complete in a single day. The Boy Scout pamphlet suggests a walking time of four hours which concur with the fastest times I have suggested, but for most of us, my more conservative slow time is about seven hours. So a realistic walking time for this loop considering the average hikers abilities would be between five and six hours.

The South loop makes an even more demanding day hike with its six segments covering about fifteen miles from the Pine Lake parking lot. That still is a bit ambitious for many walkers in a single day and walking time should be somewhere between six and eight and a half hours.

There are a couple of nice alternatives for both loops if some want to shorten the distance and still have a rather full day. Beginning at map point 2 bordering the Logan Hollow Camp area and having someone to pick you up at the Pine Lake Picnic area would shorten the day hike of the north loop to about 9½ miles and cut out a very stiff climb on the first segment of this trail. If you can arrange for someone to pick you up at the fire tower, you can shorten the walk to about eight miles. A shorter version of the south loop also begins and ends at the fire tower, making the distance a trifle over ten miles.

The two loops tie in together so they both may be combined into a single trip for a combined length of just under twenty-three miles. This is a good distance for a two night backpack trip, with two short days at either end and a full one in the middle. But there's a fly in the ointment, for there is a nice overnight back country stop at Camp Dulen situated ideally for a second night's stop but no camp at all on the north loop. Since overnight camping outside of organized campgrounds is forbidden, a one night backpack trip would require a rugged 16 mile hike on the first day to reach Camp Dulen, leaving a shorter second day of about six and a half miles back to the trailhead. This might not seem to be much, but the stretch has one of the steepest climbs of the trail up to the Brush Ridge Fire Tower. With the mini-marathon tuckering you out on the first day, this second day climb may make you feel as if the **position of Hades has been reversed and, at best, you are marching up to purgatory. To add to your general misery, there is no safe water supply on the loops and Dulen is a dry camp so your upward climb might also be a parched one.**

If you want a not too strenuous overnighter, Camp Dullen is nicely situated on the south loop for that purpose. By taking the Brush Ridge Trail from the Pine Lake parking area with an overnight stop at Dulen, you can cover over half of the 15 mile loop on the first day's hike leaving a managable walk of under 7 miles for the second day. The scout pamphlet suggests that the twenty-one mile double loop (minus the Dulen side trail) can be done in an incredible eight hours. Impossible, I thought, and when I questioned Roy Case about this he told me there are a few of the older and well seasoned scouts that do make it in about that time. He even introduced me to two young men that had accomplished it. I felt like asking them to repeat the "Scout Oath" when they confirmed their time for completing both loops but they were a couple of wiry sixteen year olds, on whose body fat was an unknown substance; so I believed them. Of course, for most of us, such speed over this distance and terrain is a physical impossibility and even those who are young and conditioned enough to attempt it by doing so would only transform a pleasant hiking experience into a marathon of misery, leaving no time to enjoy the scenery.

## BEWARE OF THE THREE BEARS

For those of you that have hiked in the Smokies, Yellowstone and other areas where bears are a problem and sometimes a threat to hikers the above title has nothing to do with those marvelous culprits of the wild. Although once prevalent in this state, they have long since been exterminated by man. The name came to me as I was struggling up one of the worst climbs on these twin loop trails. When I was about half way up this particularly taxing ridge, sweating profusely and gasping for air, I said out loud to myself, "This climb is a real bear." On later recollection I realized that this and two other climbs have more bite in their ascent than all the rest. Climbing over 300 feet in **a relatively short distance, the name for this trio of ascents suddenly occured to me. One is on the north loop and two on the south and are identified in the trail description. They are not really terrible but are far more exhausting than other**

*Author bicycling back to the Tar Hollow Campground after a day of hiking and note taking along the Logan Trail*

climbs at Tar Hollow and the average backpacker will suffer a little more on these rises as I have.

### FINDING THE TRAILHEADS, FIRE TOWER AND WATER DROPS

You may begin either loop at Pine Lake or for a shorter trip on the south loop you may want to start at the fire tower. Both the Pine Lake parking lot and the Brush Ridge Fire Tower are patrolled by Park Rangers, but I feel your vehicle is probably safer for overnight stays by utilizing the Pine Lake lot. To find it turn off State Route 327 into the park. You will pass the park office on the right in about .8 mile (Public telephone here). In just a little over a mile from the Park entrance you will see a sign on the left side of the road that says:

### PINE LAKE
### PICNIC AREA

You turn left down a short drive that enters a large parking area at the foot of the dam that forms Pine Lake.

To find the NORTH LOOP trailhead after you are in the parking lot, turn left away from the dam where there is a narrow gravel road that leads away from the parking lot. A sign on the left side of the gravel road facing you says:

### THE LOGAN TRAIL BEGINS
### AT THIS POINT

Just as the road goes into the trees, there is a red arrow painted point up on the trunk of a tree next to the left side of the road. That is the trail head for the North loop. For trail description see page 27.

To find the SOUTH LOOP trailhead continue across this same parking lot paralleling the dam which is on the right. At the other end of the parking lot, there is a wooden fence. When you reach that end, look right and you will see a cement spillway for the dam runoff to the right. There is a foot bridge with metal railings that crosses the spillway. The trailhead for this Pine Lake section of the trail which takes you to the Brush Ridge Fire Tower is on the other side of that bridge. For trail description see page 35.

## FINDING THE BRUSH RIDGE FIRE TOWER

Follow the park road from State Route 327 past the park office and past Pine Lake. Continue on past a campground road fork, staying to the left. Almost immediately beyond it, a little over two miles from the park entrance, there is a second fork with the right fork again going into another section of the campground. There are many signs there. Some of them read:

⟵ GROUP CAMPGROUND
⟵ FIRE TOWER PICNIC AREA
⟵ PRIMITIVE CAMPING

Take the left fork; the road begins to climb the ridge. You will now pass the group campground entrance on your left as you begin climbing the ridge. Use caution here, for the road is narrow with sharp curves. In not quite a mile you will pass the primitive campground on your right. In less than a half mile, you hit another fork in the road. Take the left fork, and almost immediately it T's into South Ridge Road. Turn left and in about a mile and a half, Brush Ridge Fire Tower will be on your left.

## FINDING THE WATER DROPS ON THE NORTH AND SOUTH LOOPS

For those who are making longer trail hikes and would like to cache water by car previous to the hike, there is a convenient place where this may be done on both loops.

### NORTH LOOP WATER DROP

Follow the directions to the fire tower until you get to the fork in the road that is about a half mile beyond the primitive campground. Instead of taking the left fork, take the right fork and it will soon curve to the right, into North North Ridge Road. Continue north and, in less than a half mile, the road comes to another fork. Take the left fork which puts you on Swamp Hill Road. Follow the road downhill, and shortly after it takes a decided curve to the right about 7/10 mile from the fork, look for the trail at map point 4.

### SOUTH LOOP WATER DROP:

Follow the directions to the fire tower but continue on past it. In about a half mile there is a road intersection. Pass the intersection and follow the road that stays on the ridgetop. In a little less than a mile from the intersection, the road makes a sweeping curve to the left, then almost immediately makes another to the right. Just as you reach the right curve, there is an unused dirt road. Beside it there is a sign which says

*Brush Ridge Fire Tower*

**MOTOR
VEHICLES
PROHIBITED**

This is point 8 on the map and the closest road point to Camp Dulen.

# NORTH LOOP

The north loop is divided into seven sections covering map points 1 through 6, then 6 to 10 and back to 1 for the complete loop. For available options on this loop see page 24.

### HOCKING SEGMENT

From Pine Lake Parking lot (Point #1) to Logan Hollow Class B Campground (Point #2)
Distance: 2.4 miles
Hike: First ½ mile very strenuous. The rest of this section is moderate.
Walking Time: 1 hour to 1 hour and 30 minutes.

GENERAL REMARKS: The trailhead starts almost at the line between Ross and Hocking Counties. To find trailhead see page 25. This is the only segment found in Hocking County and it stays in that county for about ¾th of its distance, giving this section its name. This trail gives you little chance to warm up, for it immediately starts up the first of the Three Bears. In about ½ mile, your elevation gain is close to 400 feet.

TRAIL DESCRIPTION: Beginning your hike from the trailhead on the narrow gravel road that leads away from the Pine Lake Parking Lot, you will find that in a very short time the road comes to a creek crossing. Just before reaching the creek there is a sign to the right of and facing the trail which says:

⟶ **1** **LOGAN TRAIL**

You do not cross the creek, but take a left turn there where another red arrow attached to a tree assures you that you are on the right trail. The trail quickly climbs above the creek and skirts along the edge of a steep embankment then turns and heads towards the main park road and crosses it close to a vehicle sign that indicates a series of auto curves. Climbing rapidly above the road the trail levels off in a beautiful man-planted grove of pine trees. Here the forest floor is a thick blanket of brown pine needles completely obliterating the trail but the red blazes on the trees keep you from straying from the righteous path. Leaving the pine plantation behind, you enter a deciduous forest where the trail descends, crosses a small wash, immediately turns right following alongside the wash for a short distance, then angles away from it starting up the ridge. Here the climbing starts in earnest up the moderately steep slope with a few very steep stretches that would be troublesome for someone carrying a heavy pack or on a wet slippery day.

Once the top of the ridge is reached, the hardest climb of the first of the Three Bears is behind you as you follow the up and down elevation changes of the ridge top.

After about a ten minute walk on the ridge top, the trail makes a decided left turn and begins a very gradual decline on another finger of the ridge. After a few minutes **of this downhill walking, the descent gets noticeably steeper and you have the feeling that the trail will follow the backbone of the ridge down to the end.** It almost does, but watch for a painted red arrow on the right side of the trail which indicates an abrupt right turn off the ridge top. From here it drops rather quickly down to the bottom of a hollow where it T's into another trail. Turn right here, for a left turn takes you back toward the main park road. A few feet after the right turn, the trail turns left and crosses a small wash, turns left again and starts angling up and around the end of the ridge on the other side of this side hollow. The trail climbs about a third of the way up this ridge, then levels off and parallels the park road which is below on the left. There is a very definite fork in the trail and I once took the wrong left fork which gradually descends down into the park. I quickly realized I was wrong, for even though I was on a well established trail, the red blazer marks had disappeared. These blazes are very handy, particularly in areas near campgrounds where all kinds of unofficial trails abound. When I retraced my steps, I discovered at the junction that a red arrow was pointing to the right fork, but its view was partially blocked by foliage and I had breezed right by. Remember that on any part of the Logan Trail when you have not seen a blaze mark within a trail distance of approximately a hundred feet, you are probably off the official trail.

Very soon you will see picnic tables below you on the left which are part of the Class B Campground. You can see another trail that leads off to the left going down to a **turnaround in the campground, but the official trail continues to the right dropping down to another hollow bottom where it again T's into another trail coming from the Campground. Again the trail turns right and very shortly turns left to cross another small wash. This is point 2 and you can see it painted on a large tree just before** crossing the wash.

By looking left at the trail junction you can see campsites 95 and 96 of the Logan section of the Campground.

## ROSS SEGMENT

From Class B Logan Hollow Campground (Point #2) to North Ridge Road (Point #3)
Distance: 1.8 miles
Hike: Moderate to strenuous
Walking time: 45 minutes to 1 hour

GENERAL REMARKS: During the downhill section of the Hocking segment, the trail crossed back into Ross County. Although all but one of the remaining sections of the Logan Trail are in Ross County, this section is the first completely within it and was so named. Its close proximity to campsites 95 and 96 in the Logan Hollow section of the Tar Hollow Campground make some other hiking options possible. Even if you wanted to hike the whole loop you might hide your packs or cache water in the woods nearby and walk the Hocking segment several pounds lighter and probably happier. This section goes up Tar Hollow proper, at first skirting along its edge. But once you've passed the Campgrounds, it is right in the bottom of the hollow following it straight out to the end. When I first looked at this section on a topo map I felt I was in for another uphill struggle, for the trail climbs about 300 feet but on my first walk it didn't seem to be all that difficult. I was suspicious of that feeling but having walked it a couple more times I found my first impression was a valid one. I hope it is for you too.

TRAIL DESCRIPTION: From the map point #2 the trail crosses the little wash at the hollow bottom and rises moderately steep above the campground before leveling off and angling around the end of the ridge. There are several trails in this vicinity that intersect the Logan Trail going left steeply down to the Campground made by campers climbing up to the Logan Trail and often on up to the top of the ridge. The Logan Trail hangs on the side of the ridge and goes neither up nor down until it descends moderately steep down into a flat bottomed major part of Tar Hollow. When it reaches the wash in the bottom of the hollow, it seems that the trail turns right at that point on a well defined trail and follows up the wash. It doesn't however, for it immediately crosses the wash and goes into a weed patch on the other side.

Sometimes during the growing season these weeds are so high it may be difficult to see the trail. If that is the case, keep the wash at your back and walk directly away from it towards the hill. As soon as you hit the tree line you should be able to pick up a blaze marker to locate the trail which goes a bit left and up the hill. Again there is another trail coming from the left that proceeds up the hollow to your right. This trail comes from a group primitive camp area that is often used by Boy Scout Troop 195 when they are doing trail maintenance. The trail neither turns left into the camp nor right up the hollow. Instead it proceeds rather steeply up the hill. It soon levels off again, hanging on the side of the ridge keeping about the same altitude. You will soon notice that the Campground on the left below the trail finally ends and is replaced by forest.

The trail then curves gently right before dropping very steeply into a small side hollow, and immediately crosses the wash at its bottom. In about 50 yards, the trail crosses a second wash which is the main stream at the bottom of this section of Tar Hollow.

Again the trail T's into another trail that is coming from the direction of the primitive campground and is following the bottom of the hollow.

Here the Logan Trail turns right at this T and proceeds up the hollow. At first this section is fairly level, following along the wash and crossing it twice. There is one short, steep, six foot drop down to a side wash, then it goes up again. For awhile the trail is actually in the bed of the main wash, but, as the hollow rises, the wash becomes fragmented into a group of tributary runoffs as the trail continues up the narrowing valley floor. The greatest rise in elevation comes near the head of the hollow gaining about 200 feet of elevation as it starts up the ridge with a wash below on each side. Despite the togetherness of the grid lines on the topo map, the climb is never much more than moderate and rather quickly hits the paved North Ridge Road. The trail crosses the road and leaves it a few feet to the left which is indicated by a red arrow affixed to the tree pointing up and away from the road.

Proceeding directly away from the road you arrive at point #3 after just a few feet. The sign to the left of the trail reads:

## 3 ⟶
## LOGAN TRAIL

### SAWMILL SEGMENT

From North Ridge Road (Point #3) to Swamp Hill Road (Point #4).
Hike: Easy to moderate
Distance: 2.0 miles
Walking time: 40 minutes to 1 hour

GENERAL REMARKS: Near the end of this segment there is a large pile of lumber scraps, once the site of a sawmill, which gives this segment its name. The first part of this section follows the ridgetops briefly before beginning an easy descent into a hollow which eventually drains into Walnut Creek. But the trail doesn't quite follow this hollow to its end, for it rises slightly, curving to the left around the edge of the ridge. It then follows another tributary hollow of Walnut Creek before dropping down to Swamp Hill Road to point #4.

TRAIL DESCRIPTION: In just a very short distance from point #4 the trail hits an easily seen trace road and turns left on it. The trail stays on the road until it comes to a small rise where the road skirts around the right side of the rise, but the trail leaves the road and goes around the left side. Then the trail skirts around the right side of a small pond and goes into the forest. Just beyond the pond, the trail again briefly joins another trace road, following it to the left. But an arrow painted on a tree to the left indicates the trail and the road soon part company, with the trail turning left. It is at this point that the trail begins a moderate drop off the ridge into the head of a hollow. The trail twice crosses a small wash that develops on the right, then crosses another wash also developing in the head of the hollow just before the two washes join together. Here the hollow widens and has a rather flat bottom. Proceeding down the hollow, the trail crosses the usually dry stream bed several times before entering an open weedy section. It is here that the trail momentarily joins an old road which leads to an old dump that is visible on the right. But the trail does not follow the road to the dump but abruptly turns left off the road, crosses a small wash and begins climbing somewhat steeply in places a ridge finger to the left of the hollow. As the trail goes up the first rise of this ridge, you can look left and see the large pile of decaying scrap wood about eight feet high and twenty feet long that indicates the location of the old sawmill. The sawmill ceased operations some years ago, for the pile of rotting wood now has plants growing from its top. After climbing just a short distance up the ridge the trail levels off briefly. Then there is another short steep uphill section before it levels off a second time and swings left around the end of the ridge. This takes you into the hollow that has Swamp Hill Road at its bottom. The trail hangs evenly about half way up the ridge and it is not long before you can see the paved surface of Swamp Hill Road beneath you on your right. Just as the trail hits another smaller side hollow, it cuts right and drops steeply down to Swamp Hill Road and crosses it. The Point 4 marker is just on the other side of the road.

## LOOKOUT SECTION

From Swamp Hill Road (Point #4) to the ridge top above Slickaway Hollow (Point #5)
Hike: Moderate
Distance: 1.5 miles
Walking time: 20 to 40 minutes

GENERAL REMARKS: Although most of the trail covered in this section is on a ridgetop, it is also enclosed in a heavy forest with nary a single overlook area that would give a clue to its name. The trail angles up the other side of the ridge above Swamp Hill Road, then follows the end of the finger of that ridge to its top for an altitude climb of about 250 feet. The trail is engineered in such a way that most of it is gruntingly quite bearable with only a couple of short sections to make the sweat glands flood. But, in total, the climb is far less taxing than the Three Bears. This is followed by some easy ridge top forest walking which should soon cool down the heat producing elements of your human engine and allow thoughts of walking enjoyment to replace the unpleasant stressful thoughts that one might have entertained on the way up. Its end at point 5 is the only one on either loop that does not begin or end near a modern road.

TRAIL DESCRIPTION: Leaving sign post 4 from Swamp Hollow Road, the trail quickly crosses a major tributary of Walnut Creek. Once across the creek, the trail turns right going steeply up for a short distance reaching a ledge of this ridge. The level walking here was nicely arranged by nature to give you comparative rest and solace before the climb. It starts easily enough, gently angling up the slope until there is no more room to angle. Out of necessity the trail turns left and charges up a finger of the ridgetop with a vengeance and there are a couple of places that will make you feel its wrath. But once you gain elevation, the ridgetop is gentle and you can enjoy yourself for the next mile.

The trail follows the ridgetop in heavy secondary forest where it eventually hits and turns left on an old trace road. In less than ten minutes of walking, there is a junction with a sign to the right of the road which says:

```
           5 ⟶
           L
           O
           G
           A
           N
```

The trail turns right at the junction leaving the trace road at Point 5.

## SLICKAWAY SEGMENT

From the ridge top (Point #5) to the Brush Ridge Fire Tower — Butcher Junction (Point #6)
Hike: Strenuous
Distance: 2.3 miles

Walking Time: 1 hour to 1 hour 30 minutes

GENERAL REMARKS:   After about a half mile of ridge top walking, the trail drops, sometimes abruptly and steeply over ground of unsure footage for an elevation drop of about 300 feet, into the attractive Slickaway Hollow after which this segment is named. The walk up the hollow, which is mostly flat, pleasant, and easy, finally gives way to more serious climbing up the ridge side. But the uphill part is of a moderate sort and it is the more tricky downhill section that earns this segment its rating of strenuous.

TRAIL DESCRIPTION:   From Point 5 the trail leaves the trace road but continues on the top of the ridge for about a half mile before it begins to drop down in earnest to Slickaway Hollow. Most of the descent is in a straight line with no switchback aids to make the elevation decrease more gentle. This straight line approach has also added to the erosion problem, for the destruction of plant life in the path is slowly turning the downward trail into a rock laden runoff gulley. Most of the decline is moderately steep with an underfooting of loose stone making it a hazardous descent. There are a couple of places that are very steep which can be quite tricky, especially for those who are carrying a backpack and for those who are in too much of a hurry to get to the bottom. Once down you will find yourself in a delightful flat wooded hollow. If another primitive campground were ever added for backpackers who wanted to do both loops in a two-night, three-day trip or an easy overnighter on the north loop, this hollow would offer a prime location for its establishment. Once on the bottom, the trail goes straight across the hollow until it is almost to the wash that drains it. There, a left turn is made and the trail follows alongside the usually dry creek bed. After crossing the creek twice, the trail blends into an old trace road running along the left side of the streambed. When the trace road reaches and begins crossing the wash, it appears that the trail does too; but, just before the crossing, the trail cuts left and goes about twenty feet upstream just above a point where two tributaries come together to form the bigger stream. Here the trail turns right and crosses both tributaries. Once across the two streams the trail again joins the old trace road which becomes quite indefinite at times. The trail and road cross the right fork twice more, and, when this wash also splits, there is another left turn over the right branch which has an attractive little rock ledge on its upstream side.

From here, the trail follows the left fork into a narrowing and very attractive ravine, crossing back and forth over its stream bed and tributaries several times. At one point, the trail goes right up the floor of the wash which is, fortunately usually dry.

Eventually leaving the wash, the trail begins angling out of this ravine, up the ridge on the right with a moderately steep section. About half way up the ridge, it levels off briefly, then once again turns and angles moderately for a short distance to the top of the ridge that brings you to Point 6, where this trail T's into another. As you approach the junction, there is a sign mounted high on a large tree facing you which says:

```
              LOGAN TRAIL
                   6
              SOUTH LOOP
              CAMP DULEN———►
              NORTH LOOP
         ◄——— FIRE TOWER
```

If you are doing both loops on the same hike, you turn right here and begin the Butcher segment (see page 37). To complete the north loop you turn left here.

## FIRE TOWER SEGMENT

From north-south loop junction (Point #6) to the Brush Ridge Fire Tower (Point #10)
Distance: ½ mile
Hike: easy
Walking Time: 10 to 20 minutes

GENERAL REMARKS: This short segment functions as a connection for those who wish to do either the north or south loop as complete but separate round trips. If you are doing the combined loops as a long single hike you will miss this segment entirely. The only unusual feature is the fire tower itself and, since a later segment on the south loop takes you to the tower you will miss nothing of scenic importance by avoiding this segment.

TRAIL DESCRIPTION: From this junction at point #6, the trail climbs slightly then abruptly turns right into a well-defined logging road. Turn left on the road and in about ten feet you will see that the trail turns to the right, away from the road. A sign post on the right side of the trail says:

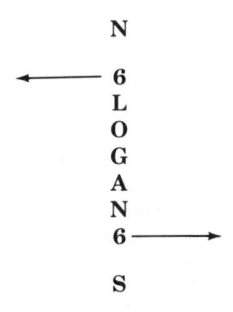

```
            N
    ←―― 6
            L
            O
            G
            A
            N
            6 ――→
            S
```

If you have a good reason for getting to the fire tower more quickly, you may skip this section of trail by not leaving the road at the trail cutoff but proceeding straight ahead and in a short distance you will hit a paved road. This is South Ridge Road. Make a right turn into the road and in 1/3 mile you will be at the fire tower.

If you opt for staying on this official trail, you will find that, after leaving the dirt road, the trail goes easily down and around the head of a ravine. Then it climbs gently over a little knob. Beyond the knob, there is a gradual descent to a wash, followed by a very steep twenty-foot section climbing out of the wash. Beyond this, there is an easy uphill section that soon arrives at the Brush Ridge Fire Tower.

If you wish to complete the north loop back to the Pine Lake parking lot, cross the paved road and walk past the left side of the Fire Tower until you hit the gravel driveway that circles the tower. On the other side of this driveway, there is a brown sign with yellow letters that says: **LOGAN TRAIL** with four yellow footprints on the bottom of the sign. The Pine Lake trailhead leaves the gravel driveway about twenty feet to the left of that sign.

## PINE LAKE SEGMENT or BRUSH RIDGE TRAIL

From the Brush Ridge Fire Tower (Point #10) to the Pine Lake Parking Lot (Point #1).
Hike: Very easy.
Distance: 1.3 miles
Walking time: 40 minutes to 1 hour.

GENERAL REMARKS: In its length of just under 1½ miles, this trail follows a long finger of Brush Ridge almost to its end before beginning a long but gentle descent of over 300 feet down to the Pine Lake parking lot. From its width and its well defined outlines, you can correctly assume that it is the most frequently walked section of the entire Logan Trail. Many use it as an easy day hike up from Pine Lake to the Fire Tower and back. Many others make an easier hike out of it by having someone drive them to the fire tower. This way the auto has made the elevation gain and the hiker walks only the downhill part from the fire tower to the lake. For those of you who wish to make this short and pleasant hike and are driving up from the State Park see road directions on page 26.

TRAIL DESCRIPTION: The trail begins by rounding the head of a ravine on the right, and, in less than ¼ mile, there is a fork in the trail. A sign, facing you, located between the forks says:

### BRUSH RIDGE TRAIL ⟶
### ⟵ TO GROUP CAMP

The trail to the left is maintained and does go into the large group facility located on Pine Lake.

The right fork is the correct one for walking to the Pine Lake parking lot. Beyond the sign, there is a gentle climb which takes you over the 1100 feet mark. From there the trail begins its easy descent skirting around a couple of more ravines on the right. Beyond the ravines, the trail becomes just slightly steeper, gradually swinging left around the end of a ridge finger. In wet weather, there is one short mucky section where ground water surfaces just above the trail. Shortly beyond this point, the trail crosses an open swath that has been cleared for electric lines. This trail then makes a sharp left turn. At the turn, on your right, there is a sign that says:

### BRUSH RIDGE TRAIL ⟶

The arrow is pointed in the direction you have just come, for the people going up to the fire tower.

In just a few feet beyond the left turn there is a sign to the right of the trail which says:

### LOGAN TRAIL ENDS
### THE FIRST SEGMENT BEGINS
### ON THE FAR SIDE OF THE PARKING LOT

Looking down beyond the sign, you can see there is a trail of sorts that goes very steeply down to a creek. On my first and second walks there, I assumed that the official trail went down that embankment trail, crossed the creek, and climbed out of the creek bed to the parking lot on the other side. I found that going down to the creek could be very treacherous, especially with a loaded backpack, and I couldn't figure out why, after descending quite easily on a well maintained trail, it abruptly ended on a dangerously angled slope with very unsure footing. One of my hiking companions who did a bit of exploring discovered what I had not reasoned out. The official trail does not end at the sign and it offers a much easier and safer way to get to the parking lot. Do not go down to the creek here but keep the sign on your right and proceed straight ahead. In less than 50 yards you will pass signs on the left which indicate trail names and distances. There, a cement foot bridge takes you over the dam spillway. Once across, it's an easy drop down to the parking lot.

# SOUTH LOOP

The South Loop is divided into six sections plus one optional side section to Camp Dulen. If you wish to make the shorter version of this loop at the fire tower, start on page 36. The longer section begins at the Pine Lake Parking Lot (see below.)

### PINE LAKE SEGMENT or BRUSH RIDGE TRAIL

From Pine Lake (Point #1) to Brush Ridge Fire Tower (Point #10)
Distance: 1.3 mile
Hike: Moderate to strenuous
Walking time: 40 minutes to one hour.

**GENERAL REMARKS:** If you are going to make the complete south loop this stretch is the only segment that you will walk in both directions. Although the trail rises almost 400 feet from Pine Lake to Brush Ridge, the elevation rise is fairly gradual and should not prove difficult for any walker that is not badly out of shape. For those carrying a loaded backpack intending to stay overnight at Camp Dulen, the climb is a bit testier. It is the most used section of the Logan Trail, since many day hikers go up and return from the Fire Tower this way. The trail is wide, well-maintained, and easy to follow.

**TRAIL DESCRIPTION:** (To find the trailhead see page 25). The trail begins at the cement footbridge that crosses the dam spillway above the west end of the Pine Lake parking lot. Once across the bridge, turn left and, immediately on the right side of the trail are several signs. The first one reads:

⟵ **BRUSH RIDGE TRAIL**
**FIRE TOWER 1.5 MILES**

The next sign says:

⟵ **TO BUCKEYE TRAIL**
**1.6 MILES**

There is a third sign that says horses and vehicles are prohibited. In a little over a hundred feet there is a sign on the left side facing the trail which says:

**LOGAN TRAIL ENDS**
**THE FIRST SEGMENT BEGINS**
**ON THE FAR SIDE OF THE PARKING LOT**

If you look down to the creek below, you can see that going over the spillway bridge is a much easier way to get to this point than scrambling up that embankment. Continuing ahead just beyond that sign, there is another sign, facing you, which says:

**BRUSH RIDGE TRAIL** ⟶

This sign indicates a sharp right turn. From this point, the trail starts angling up the hill and soon crosses an area cleared of trees for electric wires. Just beyond it, you might encounter a short mucky stretch of trail if there has been some rainy weather, for a water runoff surfaces just above the trail. As the trail gradually climbs, it slowly swings to the right around the edge of a ridge. It then skirts around the head of two ravines on the left before reaching the ridge to  The trail approaches a sign on the right which faces the opposite direction. When you walk past it, you can see that it says:

**BRUSH RIDGE TRAIL ⟶**
**⟵ TO GROUP CAMP**

You can look to the right and see a trail that leads down to the group camp. This a nice short loop walk from Pine Lake parking lot if you are with an organization that has rented the camp and is staying there. But for the fire tower, you continue straight ahead. The trail again rounds the head of a ravine on the left, then immediately comes into the cleared opening at the fire tower.

**FIRE TOWER SEGMENT**

From Brush Ridge Fire Tower (Point #10) to the North-South Loop junction (Point #6).
Distance: ½ mile.
Hike: Easy
Walking time: 10 to 20 minutes.

GENERAL REMARKS: To find the Brush Ridge Fire Tower by road, see page 26. The Brush Ridge Fire Tower gives a beautiful view of many ridges to the west with Mount Logan, the high hill that appears on the State Seal of Ohio, visible from the upper steps of the tower. The tower is maintained by the State of Ohio and it is legal to go up the tower which will take you just below the viewing cabin. For most people, it is well worth the climb, unless one has a touch of acrophobia, which would make it a spooky trip indeed. Only those who are masochists or fools will carry their packs to the top.

This easy section takes you to the connecting point of the North and South Loop. It is used in this direction primarily for those doing only the South Loop. It is also used by some day hikers walking up from Pine Lake who might want to add another mile to their hike.

TRAIL DESCRIPTION: To find the trailhead, walk under the fire tower toward the paved Brush Ridge Road. When you reach the road, cross it, turn left, and walk along the road. In a few feet, you should see a large red arrow, nailed to a tree and pointing up away from the road and into the forest. This is the trailhead. If the arrow has disappeared because of vandalism, look for the path leaving the paved road almost directly across and slightly left of the fire tower.

From the trailhead, the walk starts off fairly level and gentle, but soon drops quite steeply for about twenty feet over a wash. On the other side of the wash. the trail splits. Take either one, for they soon join up again. You have a steady moderate climb to the ridge top, where you soon run into a logging road. A post to the left of the trail just as it comes out of the trees at the road says:

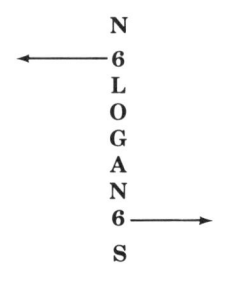

N
⟵ 6
L
O
G
A
N
6 ⟶
S

Turn left on the road and in about ten feet the trail turns right, off the road. If you wish, it is not necessary to make this turn, for after the junction at Point 6, the Butcher Segment of the trail returns to this road and follows it. After your left turn on the logging road, continue on until you see red blaze markers on the tree which will tell you that you are on the trail again.

If you want to stay on the official trail, soon after it leaves the road, it turns left and parallels the road. It turns away from the road for a short distance before another trail T's into it from the right at Point 6. There is a sign on a large tree to the left, facing the trail, which says:

**LOGAN TRAIL**
**6**
**SOUTH LOOP ⟶**
**CAMP DULEN**
**⟵ NORTH LOOP**
**FIRE TOWER**

For the Butcher Segment, don't turn right but continue straight ahead in the direction of Camp Dulen.

**BUTCHER SEGMENT**

From the North-South Loop junction (Map 6) to Piney Run Road (Map 7).
Distance: 2.4 miles
Hike: Moderate
Walking Time: 1 to 1½ hours

GENERAL REMARKS: This segment gets its name from Butcher Hollow into which it eventually drops and follows almost to its end. There is easy ridge top walking for almost a mile before it begins a 300 foot drop with only one very steep section down to the hollow bottom. It eventually leaves the hollow, swinging left around another ridge before dropping again down to North Piney Road.

TRAIL DESCRIPTION: Shortly after leaving Point 6, the trail bends slightly left until it runs into and turns right onto a logging road. As you walk along the ridge top section, you will occasionally see smaller side roads going down hill on the left where recent logging operations have been carried out.

There is a fork in the ridge top road, but a red arrow on a large oak tree between the fork indicates that the trail follows the left fork. There is another fork, but it is easy to see the left fork is again correct, for the right one now is full of high weeds.

Beyond this point the road becomes far less distinct and finally drops off the ridge top to the left, but the trail continues straight ahead on the ridge top, following it to the end where the gradual descent into Butcher Hollow begins. It goes straight down the ridge with water runoff casuing erosion problems which makes a trough of parts of the trail. It ends in one steep difficult stretch going down a small gulley with many loose rocks. At the end of this steep section, the trail takes an abrupt left turn, and, in a few feet, hits the logging road again, turning right onto it. The trail and road curve gently left, crossing a small wash in a semi-open area. After crossing the wash, the trail swings right into another small open area with a pile of old logs left over from past timbering operations on the right. Just beyond the scrap logs, the road and trail cross a larger wash. This is the main runoff stream at the bottom of Butcher Hollow. The trail stays on this level dirt road for about a quarter of a mile, then turns left leaving the road and immediately crossing the creek. It's easy to walk past the turn;

watch for a red arrow nailed to a maple tree on the right side of the road which indicates the turnoff point to the left. Once over the stream bed, the trail leaves the bottom of the hollow and begins angling up the ridge side of the road which indicates the turnoff point to the left. Once over the stream bed, the trail leaves the bottom of the hollow and begins angling up the ridge at an easy rate, crossing several small branches on the way up. The first time I walked this section, the trail was almost non-existant and only the red blaze markers kept me going in the right direction. On subsequent walks, I found the trail far more distinct and guessed rightly that it was a new routing and had been traversed by few hikers before my first walk.

The trail swings gradually around the end of the ridge and moves into the valley of Piney Run. Then, climbing further up the ridge, it levels off far below the ridge crest and goes easily down into an area where the trees have been thinnned. Many small pine trees killed during severe winters of 77-78 and 78-79 have been cut down. As you approach the paved Piney Run Road, there are two ways to get to Point 7. Cross the road and the Point 7 marker is just to the left of the trail.

## TUCSON SEGMENT

From North Piney Road (Point #7) to South Ridge Road (Point 8).
Distance: 2.1 miles
Hike: Very strenuous to ridge top, then easy
Hiking time: 40 minutes to 1 hour 10 minutes

GENERAL REMARKS: North Piney Road, in its westerly direction, reaches the small hamlet of Tucson in about 2½ miles, giving this segment its name. You have one of the stiffer climbs of this entire trail almost immediately ahead of you. The altitude gain is about 300 feet which, in itself, is not particularly bad, since several climbs on the Logan Trail go up as much or more than this and are not overly difficult. What delivers the mean bite in this one is that the altitude gain is accomplished in about a quarter of a mile. It's a lung buster without a pack, and, with one, this short climb can take on the feeling of an Everest ascent with foilage. This is the second of the Three Bears, but, if my description tends to depress you, there is a brighter side too. Once up the ridge, you've got easy ridge top walking for well over two miles, and, if you are not going to Camp Dulen, your next serious uphill section is almost fives miles away.

**TRAIL DESCRIPTION:** After leaving Point 7, the trail crosses Piney Run, one of the main tributaries of Walnut Creek. Although Piney Run usually has water in it, a dry crossing is easy except after periods of heavy rain. Once across the stream, the climb starts out deceptively easy as the trail moves directly away from the creek, gradually climbing up a beautiful side hollow. But, very quickly, the trail gradient shows its ugly side and stretches before you like a great green wall. I was almost reduced to tears on my first trip up the slope, for a well defined trail goes more or less directly right to the top. Once there the friendly red blaze markers had disappeared like the setting sun and I knew that I had missed a turn. Going reluctantly down again, I found the overlooked turnoff about a third of the way to the bottom. As you struggle upwards, keep your eyes peeled for a red arrow attached to a tree on the left side of the trail, showing a left turn off the more pronounced straight up path. Once you have made the turn, the trail goes up at an angling grade making it slightly easier than the straight up version. However, if perspiration clogs your eyes and you miss the turn, after you arrive damp and hot at the top, don't go back down. Instead turn left on the ridge top trace road, and, in a short distance, you will pick up the red blaze marks telling you that you're back on the official trail again.

If you made the turn successfully, there is a gradual climb until you reach the trace road on top of Locust Ridge. Turn left on the road. Both the trail and the road follow the up and down sections of this ridge top for about a mile before the trail turns off to the right. Because of the easy walking along the old road, it is easy to walk right by the turnoff. There is a red arrow on a pine tree indicating a right trail turn off the road. If you miss it, the trace road soon ends at a paved road. Backtrack about a hundred yards and keep your eye peeled for the trail turnoff now on your left.

Once you have made the turn, you will see that in just a few feet the trail forks. A red arrow on a tree tells you that the left fork is the correct one. The trail ambles along in a meandering nature until it crosses directly over the paved South Ridge Road. Across the road, a tree to the right of the trail has a red arrow pointing upwards with a rectangular blue patch below the arrow and a red blaze below the blue patch.

Blue patches are markings used by the Buckeye Trail Association and this is one of two places along this trail that the Logan and Buckeye Trail share the same path. Here again the trails are on some kind of old trace road, and, except for one brief separation of about thirty feet, the trails stay together along the ridge top to Point 8.

In less than ¼ mile, the trails again come out of the trees along South Ridge Road. The trails part company here, for the Buckeye Trail proceeds south on the paved road while the Logan Trail skirts around the outside curve of the road but does not cross it. In just a few feet along a trace road that goes left away from South Ridge Road, there is a sign that says:

### MOTOR VEHICLES PROHIBITED

As you approach the sign you will find just to the left of it but to the right of the trace road, a post facing you which indicates you have completed the Tucson Section. It has an arrow pointing upward with the number 8 below the arrow. This is the point suggested earlier in the book where water might be cached by auto prior to the hike since it is the closest road point on the trail to Camp Dulen.

### POWER LINE SEGMENT

From South Ridge Road (Point #8) to Clark Hollow Road (Point #9).
Distance: 2.3 miles
Hike: Moderate
Walking time: 1 hour to 1 hour 30 minutes.

**GENERAL REMARKS:** About half the length of this segment continues along the ridge top. This occurs before the clearing made for the power lines that give this section its name. From there it follows or skirts this clearing with a spectacular 400 foot drop down to Clark Hollow at its end. If you are planning an overnight stay at Camp Dulen and have added to your weight by previously storing water here, you will be glad to know there are no real uphill sections between Point 8 and the camp, with the distance to Dulen about 1¼ miles.

**TRAIL DESCRIPTION:** As the trail moves away from South Brush Ridge Road, the trace road becomes more defined and easy to follow except for a few spots that seem to stay mucky in all but the driest periods. In about a ten minute walk along the road, you will see high up on a tree facing you to the right of the trail a sign that reads:

LOGAN TRAIL
CAMP DULEN
⟶

*Powerline clearing showing drop down to Clark Hollow*

If you are going to Camp Dulen, see trail description beginning on page 42. If you are not and wish to stay on the main trail, do not turn right here but proceed straight ahead. On the same tree that holds the Dulen turnoff sign, there is another sign facing the main trail that you pass that says:

← POST 9 FIRE TOWER

In about ¼ miles of easy walking, you will see a well used trail coming up the ridge from the right that T's into the main trail. This is where the return section of the Camp Dulen Trail again joins the South Loop.

After a short walk from this junction, you hit the the power line clearing and turn left. During the growing months the weeds are quite high in the clearing and although usually not difficult to follow, the high weeds keep much breeze from getting through, but you are exposed to the full rays of the sun. This, it would seem, might be a section of trail that would be uncomfortably hot and, for hay fever sufferers, a very watery and sneezy one as well. But the trail soon returns to the cover of the forest to the left of the power lines and parallels them.

There is a second brief return to the cleared area which gives you a marvelous view of the uphill-downhill terrain usually hidden by the forest. Once more the trail returns to the woods, but it is not long before it returns to the clearing for the third and last time. The trail is right on the crest of the ridge, giving you a marvelous view of Clark Hollow and the road at its bottom, almost 400 feet below where you will soon arrive. The total trip is covered in about ¼ mile, so the walk down is moderately steep. If this bothers you, think of what it would be like if you were doing the trail in reverse.

The trail starts down the slope in the middle of the cleared area, but gradually swings left back into the woods and stays there all the way to the creek at the bottom of the hollow. There is a very steep 20 foot descent to the creek, and when you cross it, you are at the lowest elevation on either loop. When you climb out, turn left on the paved Clark Hollow Road and in about 100 yards there are two ancient maple trees facing the right side of the road. There is a red blaze on one tree and a blue blaze on the other, which means the trail turns right between the two trees with the Logan and Buckeye Trails again running together. Just beyond the tree with the red blaze on the left side of the trail, there is a sign post which reads:

9 ⟶
L
O
G
A
N

## VINTON SEGMENT

From Clark Hollow Road (Point #9) to Brush Ridge Fire Tower (Point #10)
Distance: 2.9 miles
Hike: Strenuous
Walking time: 1 hour 15 minutes to 1 hour 45 minutes.

**GENERAL REMARKS:** While walking along the Power Line Segment you crossed over from Ross County to Vinton County, making the two loops in at least part of three counties. Slightly over half of the Vinton segment is in that county before returning to Ross County. All of the walking of this segment in Vinton County is easy and gives you a chance to ease off before you approach the last of the Three Bears. This segment has the greatest elevation gain on the entire trail, rising well over 400 feet but at least 100 feet of that gain is spread over a mile of trail, so it is almost not noticeable. When you cross the county line back into Ross County, you run into the more difficult elevation gain of about 300 feet in slightly more than ¼ of a mile climbing the heights of Brush Ridge. Beyond that, there is an easy to moderate half mile to cover before arriving at the fire tower. In actual climbing versus distance, this is the easiest of the Three Bears. But, for most hikers, it will not seem so, for much of the elasticity of the legs has been stretched a good deal by the miles of walking covered to get to this point. Since it comes so close to the end of the hike, the tired walker usually finds it trying; but a happy bolstering thought is that if you began your trek at the fire tower you are on the last lap of the loop. For those who still have the stretch to Pine Lake to do from the fire tower, from there it is downhill almost all the way.

**TRAIL DESCRIPTION:** Walking directly away from Clark Hollow Road in an easterly direction, you cross an open field where the high weeds during the summer months can make the trail a little difficult to follow. But, as the trail gets closer to the ridge, it soon comes to the tree line where it becomes easy to follow. Once into the trees, the trail comes up to a small wash, turns left, crosses it, and begins an easy uphill section that goes partially up the ridge before leveling off along the ridge side. Twice more, the trail descends to cross side ravines and their washes before angling left into the open brush area of the main hollow. It crosses the flat area of the hollow to the other side where it joins and turns right into an old logging road which skirts the side of the valley. This bottom area was clear cut timbered in 1979 and you can see how quickly nature has refilled the area with brush and small trees. As you proceed up the hollow road with the brush area to your right and a creek on your left, you have about a half mile of easy walking, giving you plenty of time to rest up for the last of the Three Bears.

Eventually the road forks, the right fork staying in the valley bottom while the left one drops down into the forest and crosses the creek. The trail leaves the road following the left fork across the creek just above a point where another tributary joins the main stream and proceeds upstream between the two small creeks.

Just a short distance beyond, the blue markers of the Buckeye Trail turn left away from the Logan Trail. Although both trails go to Brush Ridge fire tower, they do so separately. This may change for the policy of the Buckeye Trail Association is to eliminate such divisions and use other maintained trails whenever possible. But, at this writing, each trail goes its separate way. From here your climb begins in earnest on the last of the Three Bears. When I told Mr. Case of my names for the three stiffer climbs, he told me the scouts have their own name for this one, "Heartbreak Hill".

Actually the climb is never more than moderately steep but is a steady pull which is usually behind you in 15 to 20 minutes.

Once at the top there is less than ¾ mile to cover before reaching the fire tower. Except for one short steep down and up section over a ravine and a moderate uphill section just prior to the tower, the walking on this last stretch is easy. On the left side of the trail, there is a sign which says:

10 ⟶

L
O
G
A
N

Immediately beyond the sign, the trail breaks into the clearing surrounding the Brush Ridge fire tower. If you have walked the entire two loops in one hike this will be your first and only time at the fire tower. If you are not too tired and it is a moderately clear day, the view from the tower is worth the climb.

If you wish to return to Pine Lake by trail, turn right on the gravel driveway in front of the tower. Walk by a sign that says LOGAN TRAIL with yellow footprints beneath the letters. Just a few feet beyond this sign, the trail leaves the gravel driveway on the right. The trail description begins on page 33.

## DULEN TRAIL

From the Powerline Segment near Point #8 to Camp Dulen (Point #11) and return to the Powerline Segment of the South Loop.
Distance: Powerline to Camp Dulen 1.1 miles. Camp Dulen back to Powerline .8 miles.
Hike: To Camp Dulen from Powerline - easy. The Powerline from Camp Dulen -moderate to strenuous.
Walking time: From Powerline to Dulen - 25 to 30 minutes. From Dulen to Powerline - 25 to 35 minutes.

**GENERAL REMARKS:** This very pleasant camp was once the homesite of N. A. Dulen. He apparently lived there for many years until his death in 1932, and he is buried nearby. The camp itself is in a pleasant, flat, grassy area surrounded by woods bordered by one side by a logging road and an often dry creek. There are pit toilets and fire rings at the camp, but no drinking water. Since the camp is in a hollow, it is well protected from high winds and is a nice location for an overnight stay.

**TRAIL DESCRIPTION:** After the turnoff from the Powerline Segment of the

*Trail sign maintained by Columbus Boy Scout Troop 195*

south loop, the trail goes down somewhat steeply until you can see a wash developing both to the left and right of you. As the two washes join, the trail comes into an open weedy segment cut for the power lines and passes under them. From this point on, the trail is no longer steep and is fairly easy walking to the camp. Once back in the forest, the trail goes down a pretty but narrow ravine, sometimes being in the wash at its bottom. As this little ravine curves to the left, it joins a bigger one coming from the right and crosses it several times. As you walk down the hollow, you can see areas to the left up the ridge where selective timbering has taken place. There are remnants of old timber trails coming from these areas, meeting the trail on the left. But rapid vegetation growth is making them less distinguishable. As you are walking down this ravine, you become aware that the trail is gradually becoming an old trace or lumber road. This faint outline of a road then joins a far more prominent one. It is at a junction point where two smaller hollows join. The trail turns left into the more distinct road. Follow this road until you see a pleasant, cleared area to the left with two brown privies in easy view. You've arrived at Camp Dulen.

**RETURN TRAIL FROM CAMP DULEN:** Unlike the first part of the Dulen loop, the return section is never on a trace road and is slightly shorter in length. To find the return trailhead, keep the logging road that brought you to the camp at your back, walk away from it, passing close to the privies and keeping them on your left side. By walking in that direction, you will find the return trail on the other side of the campground. The trail is in the bottom of a side hollow and stays in it until you pass under the power lines. The uphill grade is quite gentle and hardly noticeable up to this cleared area. The trail crosses the wash at the bottom of the hollow several times, going up this very pretty hollow. Once you have crossed under the electric wire and the cleared area, you are very close to the trail junction. Yet there is a stiff 200 foot climb ahead of you to get there. It is a moderately steep climb to get up the ridge which should take you five to ten minutes. Once the trail gains the ridge top, it T's into the Powerline Segment of the South Loop. There are two definite forks on the trail, one just before a creek crossing and another almost on top of the ridge. In both cases, take the right fork. To find notes for Powerline Section see page 40.

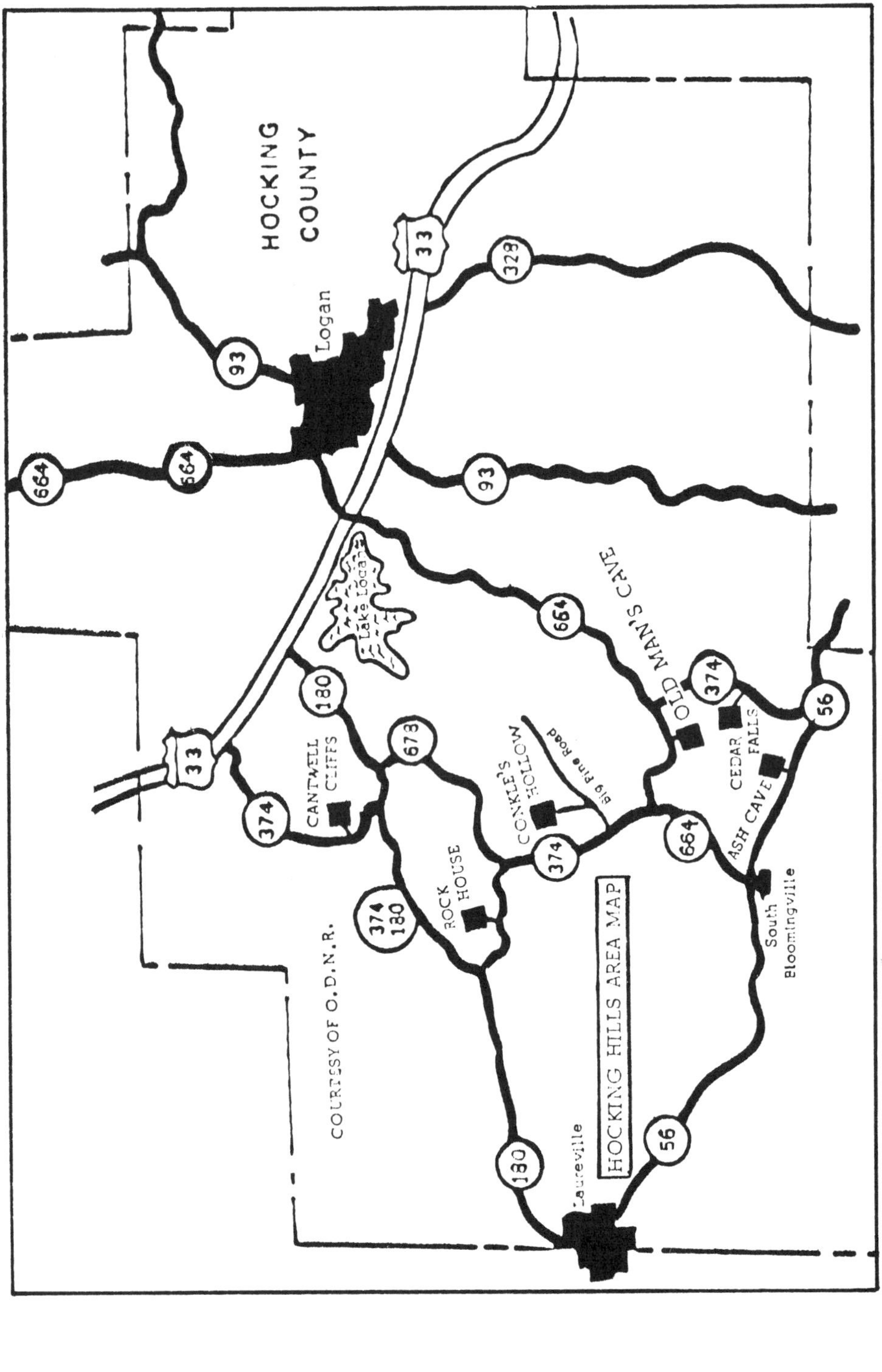
HOCKING HILLS AREA MAP
HOCKING COUNTY
Logan
Lake Logan
OLD MAN'S CAVE
CEDAR FALLS
ASH CAVE
South Bloomingville
CANTWELL CLIFFS
CONKLE'S HOLLOW
Big Pine Road
ROCK HOUSE
Laurelville
COURTESY OF O. D. N. R.
33
93
664
328
180
673
374
56
130

# HOCKING HILLS

## INTRODUCTION AND AREA DEVELOPMENT

If the trails in the Shawnee State Forest are the longest and provide the greatest physical difficulties, by contrast Hocking Hills crams in the most spectacular natural scenery found in Ohio on short easy walks that are a breeze for any seasoned hiker. Since the book's primary purpose is to acquaint hikers with some good backpack loops and long hikes for the day walker, I debated whether to include Hocking Hills for it has no backpack loops and camping is prohibited in all but the authorized campgrounds. All of its six major attractions are quite close to paved public roads and are reached by trails less than a half mile in length that are yearly tramped by 1½ million people. Such heavy use negates the long solitary walks sought out by the hiker wishing to trade his urban existance for the refreshing long walk in the semi wilderness. But despite the drawbacks, I felt Hocking Hills should be included for the following reasons. The outstanding features here are geologic and are better viewed during the winter season. The forest of large hemlocks growing in the narrow gorges, sometimes to a height of over 100 feet, means there is an abundance of greenery year around, and, if one can plan a visit after a prolonged spell of freezing weather, the formation of giant icicles turn much of the area into an iced fairyland. Only during the famous "Winter" walk held on the third Saturday of January will you ever find crowds of people during the so called off season. Even if you are unable to come during the colder months or you're a basically warm weather hiker, the in-season walks may still be enjoyed. The hiker should plan walking the more popular areas in the morning, for the modern version of Attila and his littering hordes seldom appear much before 11:00 a.m. From some of the gigantic breakfasts I've seen them put away in the campground, I'm surprised they can venture out at all. The largest crowds are mostly found on pleasant weather weekends from the spring through the fall with long holiday weekends like Labor Day often attracting over 40,000 visitors. In contrast, I once walked the area for five consecutive weekdays in December and encountered only two people.

Another of my own rules that I broke here is that a trail should be at least six, and, more properly, 8 miles in length to be included. On my first visit to the area, only the trail from Old Man's Cave Gorge to Ash Cave, now known as the Granny Gatewood Trail just barely qualified. But in the last few years the addition of the 12 mile Indian Run Trail, made several pleasant day loop hikes possible.

But even without these qualifications, the grandeur of the many high sandstone cliffs with their accompanying recess caves and lovely waterfalls within these narrow gorges make the scenic beauty of Hocking Hills unique and, in the eyes of many, including this writer, unequaled elsewhere in the state.

Still another reason for its inclusion is that many of the walks in the bottom of the gorges are excellent places to break in very young children of hiking parents by having them walk easy distances to attractive scenery. I once made the mistake of over extending the mental but not physical limits of my own young children on a walk to see one of the Smoky Mountain's magnificent waterfalls. They were so cranky that by the time we got there the cascading water appealed to them about as much as a smelly garbage dump. Extreme caution should be taken, however, particularly with the small fry when doing rim walks, because the cliffs are high and people do fall off and get killed. If you have unruly children who will not obey you do not take them on the upper trails. However, cliff walks are not dangerous if one stays on the trails. In times past the park area averaged about three falling deaths a year. Most, but not all, occurred at Conkle's Hollow and with only a rare exception all victims were young men between the ages of 15 and 21. In 1977 several large warning signs were posted in dangerous areas and have resulted in a decided drop in fatalities. Futhermore, arrests are made and citations given for those venturing off the trails on cliff tops.

And a last reason for including Hocking Hills (I'm sure I could think of others) is the marvelous job the park personnel do in keeping the most frequented areas litter free and the surroundings so natural giving little or no clue of the thousands that walk these gorges each year. Litter laws, too, are strictly enforced and those in violation are cited, taken to a local court and fined a heavy monetary penalty. One upset violator exclaimed to the judge, "All I did was to drop one Polaroid negative". The judge replied "and after you've paid this fine you probably never will do it again".

If you are the victim of some physical impairment that makes longer hikes impossible but still wish to surround yourself in outstanding natural settings where the work-a-day world seems remote, you can utilize the very short walks to one of the six major sightseeing areas in the morning or any time of day during less popular seasons and enjoy.

## HOW TO GET THERE

From the Cincinnati-Dayton area there are a number of ways but I find that the easiest and fastest, if not the shortest, is to go south east on Route 35 (Cincinnatians will turn right off of Interstate 71) and follow it almost to Chillicothe. Turn left on Route 159. Follow it to Route 180 which comes in only on the right. Follow 180 to and through Aldelphi where it runs into Route 56. Turn right on Route 56 following it through Laurelville to South Bloomingdale. Here you have the option of following 664 left to the Old Man's Cave area and Lodge or continuing on 56 to Ash Cave.

There are two main routes from Columbus. One is to follow Route 23 south east to South Bloomingdale. There you can stay on 56 to Ash Cave or go north east on 664 to the Old Man's Cave area.

The other Columbus Route is to follow Route 33 south with two options. You can turn left on Route 374 and visit Cantwell Cliffs and Rock House on your way down to Old Man's Cave. But if you want to go directly to Old Man's Cave and the lodge area, continue on Route 33 to Route 664. Turn right on 664 and follow it south to the Old Man's Cave area.

## WHERE TO STAY

Because backpack camping in the Hocking Hills State Park areas is not allowed and the hikes are often short, one must find overnight accommodations in the area if one wants to stay long enough to see the major scenic attractions. There are two state campgrounds in the park and both are open year around. For those with back pack equipment who want to rough it, the primitive campgrounds would best fill your needs. It is on state Route 374 between Old Man's Cave and Cedar Falls. From its parking lot campers walk in to their campsites making it unhandy for those with large tents and impossible for those with vans, campers, motorhomes and trailers. Before picking a campsite you must register at the Class B Campground office. The entrance to the Class B campgrounds is just east of the Old Man's Cave parking lot and fords the stream just a few yards above the Upper Falls. Although rated as a Class B Campground, 26 sites of the 170 in the park have electricity.

Unlike other Class B sites it does have one location with hot showers, flush toilets and even a swimming pool. This is one of the most popular campgrounds in the state and during the seasonable months it is often full. Both campgrounds are open all year but the shower and flush toilet facilities are closed during the winter months so one must rely on the pit toilets. Water is available and the electricity on those sites so equipped is also left on year round. Because of heavy demand during the season, especially for the electric sites, it is possible to reserve a campsite by payment in advance. This policy could change. If you want information concerning reservations and fees, write to:

Hocking Hills State Park
20160 State Route 664
Logan, Ohio 43138
Camp Phone (in season) (614) 385-6165

No need to worry about campground reservations during the winter season. I once spent five days in the Class B campground in December and for three of those five days I had the entire campground to myself. There is a private campground on Chapel Ridge Road that is open during the spring through fall. To find it, turn west on Chapel Ridge Road from 374 between Ash Cave and Cedar Falls and you will soon see the campground on the left.

There is a very attractive lodge in the park with dining facilities, gift shop, game room and outdoor swimming pool but there are no overnight accommodations. At this writing the dining lodge is open daily except for the months of January, February and March. Headquarters for the park is also in this building and it is open the year round.

For those not having camping equipment the park has modern housekeeping cabins that sleep up to six people. The demand for these deluxe facilities is so high that they can be rented only by the week from Saturday to Saturday from Memorial Day through Labor Day. Early reservations for the period should be be made many months ahead of time for they are booked solid long before the season begins. This is not so during the winter months when single night bookings are accepted and week end bookings are usually available. To encourage people to use these facilities during the winter months, there are often specials when you can rent a cabin for two nights for the price of one. Since the so called off season is a particularly rewarding time to hike the trails at Hocking Hills, it seems a wonderful and not expensive way to break the winter doldrums of the city.

## SPECIAL EVENTS

Each year two special events are held at Hocking Hills which may interest hikers. The first, which has been held for many years, is the annual "Winter Hike", which covers the Granny Gatewood Trail from the Old Man's Cave parking lot to Ash Cave -a distance of just under 6 miles. Transportation is furnished from the Ash Cave parking lot back to Old Man's Cave, and at the half way point the Logan Kiwanis Club serves a delicious bean soup at a very reasonable price. Conducted groups leave from 9 to 11 o'clock in the morning. There is a patch that you can buy that says Hocking Hills Winter Walk. Another smaller one can be purchased that gives the year you made the walk. Some people come each year, and below the large patch they may have several year patches sewn on below. My introduction to this area occurred on the Winter Walk, and I had suspected that there would be 200 to 300 hikers participating. How wrong I was, for unless the weather is absolutely awful, the usual number of winter walkers is above 3,000. The Winter Walk is always held the third Saturday in January.

The other big special event is the Indian Run, a 20 KM (12.43 miles) or the shorter 10

*Participant finishing Indian Run Loop*

KM (6.215 miles) loop foot race which is held on the third weekend of September. The course is a combination of road and cross country running which passes through forests, crosses streams and climbs hills. The run, originally the idea of Shell Johnson of Logan, who still functions as race chairman, was first run in 1979. It was then called the Indian Marathon and attracted only about 100 runners because of unseasonably heavy showers. But since then the race has become more widely known and has attracted better than 400 runners about equally divided in numbers between the Saturday and Sunday race days and numbers up to a thousand are predicted for future runs. The race offers runners the unique experience of completing the loop on Saturday then again on Sunday to see if they can better their time on the first day run. The trail is well marked and easy to follow and can be utilized by hikers on all but race days. A far different experience awaits the runner who is used to the usual marathons on roads for there are far steeper hill climbs, forest floors to cross full of exposed roots where a runner can easily be tripped up and small bridgeless creeks to cross. There is no mass start because most of the course is narrow enough to restrict to solo runners, although there is always enough room for the speedy rabbit-like competitors to pass the plodding turtles. Small groups are started at intervals between 10 a.m. and 1:30 p.m. on each day with the runners competing against the clock. Due to the general topography and trail surfaces this race should be considered only by experienced runners in excellent physical condition. Seasoned marathon racers should consider that their times will be about 10 to 15 minutes slower than their usual run on hard surfaces. Even so, the record for the 20 KM event stands now at one hour and 9 minutes flat. That's just a hair over 5½ minutes a mile. Classifications include:
Male - Under 16, 16-20, 21-30, 31-40, 41-50, 51-60, over 60.
Female - Under 16, 16-20, 21-30, 31-40, 41-50, over 50.

Awards are given to the 1st, 2nd and 3rd place winners in each category for each sex. In addition there is a best overall time award.

Of course the major goal for all but a few superb athletes is not to win but to finish and do so in a respectable time for the individual's capacity. There is a small entrance fee and the race is sanctioned by the Ohio Amateur Athletic Union. For those wishing entry blanks or additional information write to:

>Hocking Hills Indian Run
>P. O. Box 838
>Logan, Ohio 43138

Because of its centralized location I have been able to use parts of it in conjunction with other existing trails for interesting shorter loop hikes. For the trail description **see page 65.**

## GEOLOGY OF THE AREA

Although geologic history has generally been omitted in this book to keep it from reaching Tolstoyan size, the geologic features at Hocking Hills are so striking that a short description of their formations may enhance the viewer's appreciation. Most of these features are found in a massive bed of sandstone which varies in thickness in Hocking Hills from 100 to over 200 feet. It is known as the Black Hand sandstone because a high cliff of this strata above Ohio's Licking River east of the present town of Newark had a large black hand inscribed on its surface by Indians. It is believed the hand was placed there to direct the ancient red men to one of the best outcroppings of flint in Ohio at Flint Ridge just south of the Licking.

This Black Hand sandstone is divided into three fairly distinct layers or zones with the top and bottom quite hard and resistant to erosion because of heavy natural cementing. In contrast the much softer middle zone gives way far more easily to the cutting agents of water, ice and wind. As constant stream erosion cuts through the tougher zones creating narrow gorges such as the ones that contain Old Man's Cave and Conkle's Hollow, the middle zone is cut back by sapping action leaving the harder capstone of the upper zone in place with an overlap creating the recess caves or rock shelters such as Old Man's Cave and Ash Cave. These are not caves at all in the usual sense of the word since the entire side length toward the cliff is open. The only formation here that resembles the usual concept of a cave is found at Rock House. **Even it has several openings fairly close together that makes it different from the large limestone caves in southern Indiana and Kentucky such as Mammoth Cave.**

Another interesting geologic feature commonly seen in this and other cliff areas in Ohio is the creation of slump blocks created by vertical joint fractures. Because of cross bedding or some other cause erosion works vertically down a soft crack near a cliff face eventually causing the rock with the enlarged crack to separate from the rest of the cliff. This is a vertical joint fracture. Fat Woman's Squeeze at Cantwell Cliffs is a text book example. With time, these large separate blocks slowly slide downhill away from the original cliff. These are called slump blocks. Some of recent geologic times are still close to the cliff. Others have slid a great distance over a longer period of time.

## HUMAN ACTIVITIES IN THE AREA

Because of the protective advantages of the various recess caves, it is known that prehistoric Indians used these locations both as permanent and temporary areas of shelter before the birth of Christ. Archeological evidence suggests human occupation as early as 7000 years ago, and future discoveries and archeological techniques may push that date far earlier in time. It is certain that humans inhabited these shelters before the building of the great Egyptian pyramids at Giza. Several prehistoric groups now at least partially known by outstanding anthropologic studies have been identified and dates for the rise and demise of these various cultures have been established. The well-known Adena Culture inhabited the area from sometime around the birth of Christ to about the time of death of Charlemagne (Circa 1 to 800 A.D.) . Other well known groups inhabited the area, but for reasons not entirely known, these well established ancient cultures gave way to the more nomadic modern Indian who apparently used these recess caves only temporarily during hunting forages into the region. We know that one of the important Indian highways from the south east to their town of Chillicothe (in a different location from the modern one) passed along the banks of Queer Creek. In those rather bloody years spanning most of the latter half of the 18th Century when the Indians fought bitterly against the encroachemnts of their white competitors, the inhabitants of the area on both sides were subject to many horrible brutalities. White prisoners were marched along this Indian road and from this we have one of the first local historical remnants of those blood thirsty days. A large beech tree that once stood close to the village of Bloomingville bore a carving on its smooth bark which read "This is the road to Hell. 1782." It has been assumed that the carver had been an Indian captive tortured in one of the nearby rock shelters who escaped just long enough to carve his pathetic message on the tree.

But the tide against the Indians had already turned, for the outcome of Lord Dunmore's War in 1774 doomed Indian supremacy and by the end of the 18th century white homesteaders had little to fear from Indian attack. With these permanent settlements the rapid demise of the region as a prime hunting area began. In 1799 the last wood bison was reportedly killed near the banks of Queer Creek. There soon followed the elimination of the black bear, wild turkey, passenger pigeon and almost the entire deer population. Today the white tailed deer have made a healthy comeback. During one December visit I saw ten of them in three days and five at one sighting. Wild turkey have been restocked and are again thriving in the area. I accidentally startled a pair of them near Chapel Ridge Road, and, as stupid as ever, one of them flew directly into a barbed wire fence. Fortunately the only damage to the bird was the loss of a few feathers.

By 1835 a grist mill was operating just above Cedar Falls, a plant at Gibsonville was briskly making gun powder from salt-peter readily available in the surrounding rock shelters and a tourist hotel was operating at Rock House, indicating that the scenic interest in the area began well over 150 years ago. By the time of the Civil War all of the parks six major areas were popular for picnics and sightseeing.

It is not surprising that Hocking Hills became the first area in the state where lands were purchased by the state government for scenic recreation. A far sighted state forester, whose name was Edmund Secrest, guided a state forest law through the Ohio Legislature which enabled the state government to buy or receive as gifts, lands that were highly desirable to preserve as scenic areas for the general public. In 1924 the first land purchase was made and included 146 acres at Old Man's Cave Gorge. The following year three more major land purchases were made and included 50 acres at Rock House, 100 acres at Conkle's Hollow and 50 acres at Ash Cave. In 1925 the last two of the scenic areas were purchased: 50 acres at Cedar Falls and another 50 acres at Cantwell Cliffs. During the late 1930's a large C.C.C. Camp was established at the present site of the Hocking Hills State Forest Office. The young men did extensive development in the areas making trails, carving steps and tunnels in the rock, and constructing numerous stone footbridges, many of which are still in use today. Land acquisitions continued until the park complex included over 19,000 acres with much of this park land surrounded by the Hocking Hills State Forest.

The 17 acre Rose Lake was added and named after the hollow it occupies which is very close to the state park campground.

## GENERAL TRAIL CLASSIFICATIONS

Because there are so many different hiking and sightseeing possibilities on walks that are not physically demanding I have dispensed with the usual trail difficulfy and walking times given for all other trails. Except for the brief but somewhat strenuous sections from a gorge bottom to a rim, steep up and down trail sections are almost non-existent. Every trail discussed in this chapter would be classified between very easy to moderate. On the other hand, moderate ratings may extend into strenuous for some of the longer loop trails because of their distance of several miles. The only real difficulty one might find on the very short loops such as the Old Man's Cave Gorge, Cedar Falls, Ash Cave, Rock House and Cantwell Cliffs are their many steps. Anyone who can manage going up 100 steps at one time without being overly tired will find no difficulty in any of the aforementioned places for, although you may have slightly more than 100 in some locations, they are never in one continuous series.

## SCENIC LOCATIONS AND
## SUGGESTED HIKES

**TOPOGRAPHIC MAP:** Bloomingville quadrangle.

There are six major sightseeing areas in the Hocking Hills complex which include the Old Man's Cave Gorge, Cedar Falls, Ash Cave, Conkle's Hollow, Rock House and Cantwell Cliffs. All are well worth seeing and all near modern public main roads with parking lots. These six areas conveniently divide into two distinct units for planning excursions. The first unit contains the Old Man's Cave Gorge, Cedar Falls and Ash Cave, the three most visited areas which are linked together by the short 6 mile **Granny Gatewood Trail or are a short drive from the Old Man's Cave parking lot.** Other walks centered around this area, such as the East Rim walk, the Indian Run Loop and the Gulf Trail are all included in unit one.

Conkles Hollow, Rock House and Cantwell Cliffs comprise the second unit and are best reached separately by auto. The parking lots for all six areas are either on or **close to State Route 374. See the road map on page 44. All six areas have short loop walks which can be negotiated by healthy walkers who don't mind walking up and down a great number of steps.** If you are going to do only short hikes, follow the map for that area because trail descriptions are necessarily brief. The helpful maps in each case show not only the possible routes but also the locations on those routes where one will encounter steps both up and down. These are slightly modified versions of the maps included in an excellent 18 page illustrated publication put out by the Division of Parks and Recreation and can be purchased at this writing at the park headquarters for 25 cents. The state park publication even included the number of steps along the trail but time and much people erosion has changed the number. Also, in a few cases the trails have been modified somewhat. The steps that I have used on the detailed maps are only to be used as an approximation, for erosion and repairs keep changing the numbers. I have deviated from the originals only where the passage of time has made such changes necessary.

52

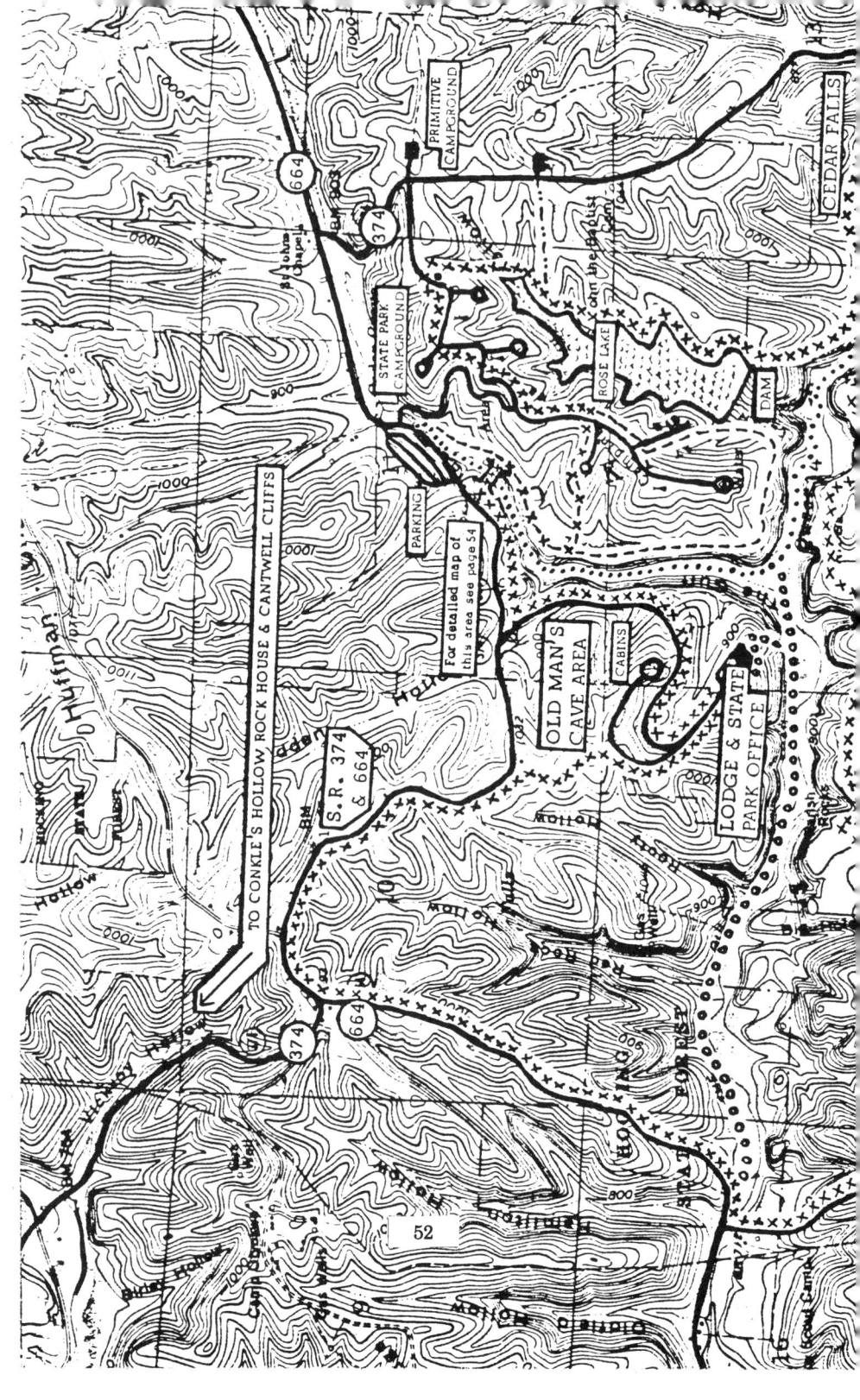

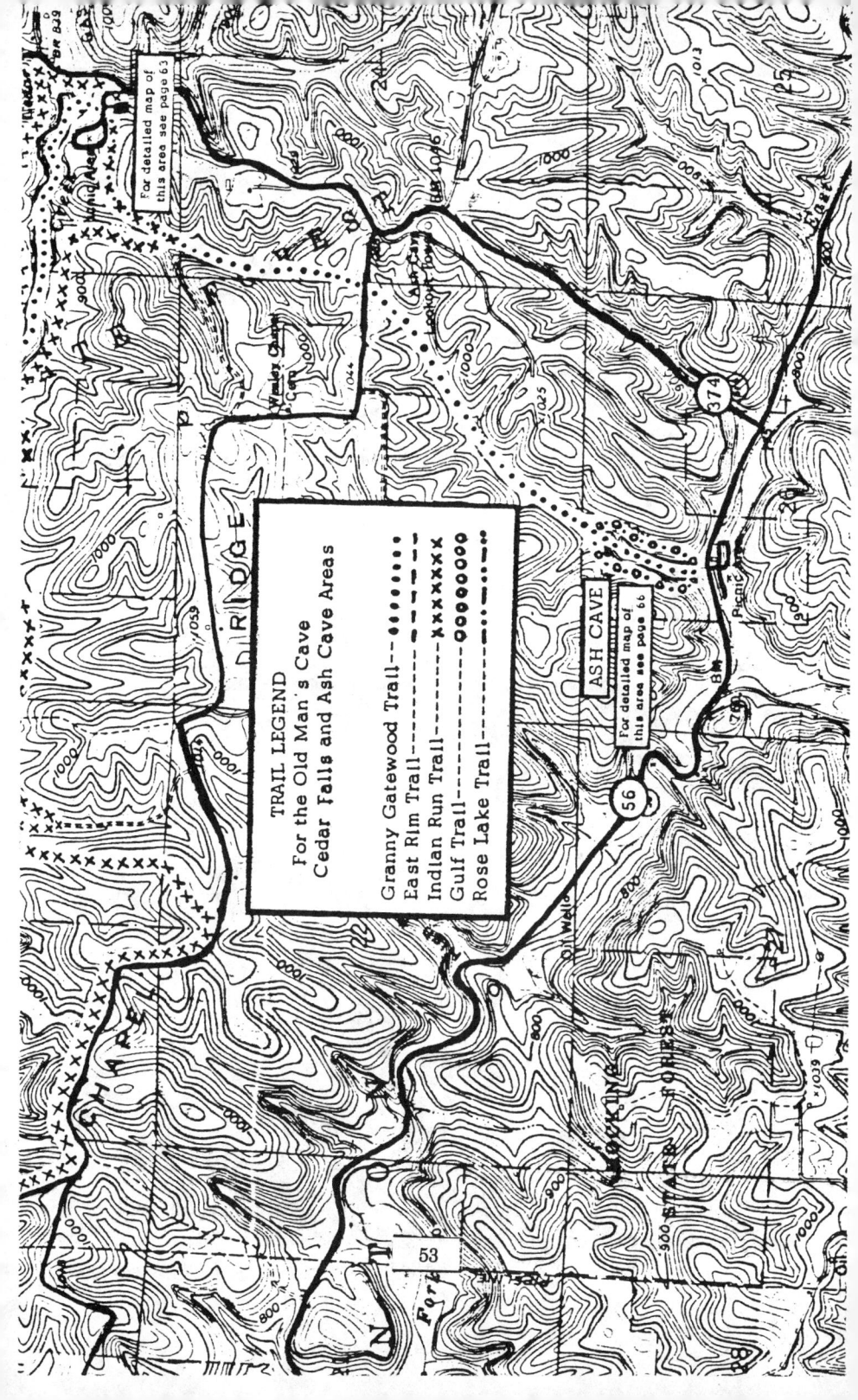

TRAIL LEGEND
For the Old Man's Cave
Cedar Falls and Ash Cave Areas

Granny Gatewood Trail — ••••••••
East Rim Trail — ————————
Indian Run Trail — ××××××
Gulf Trail — ○○○○○○○
Rose Lake Trail — ——————

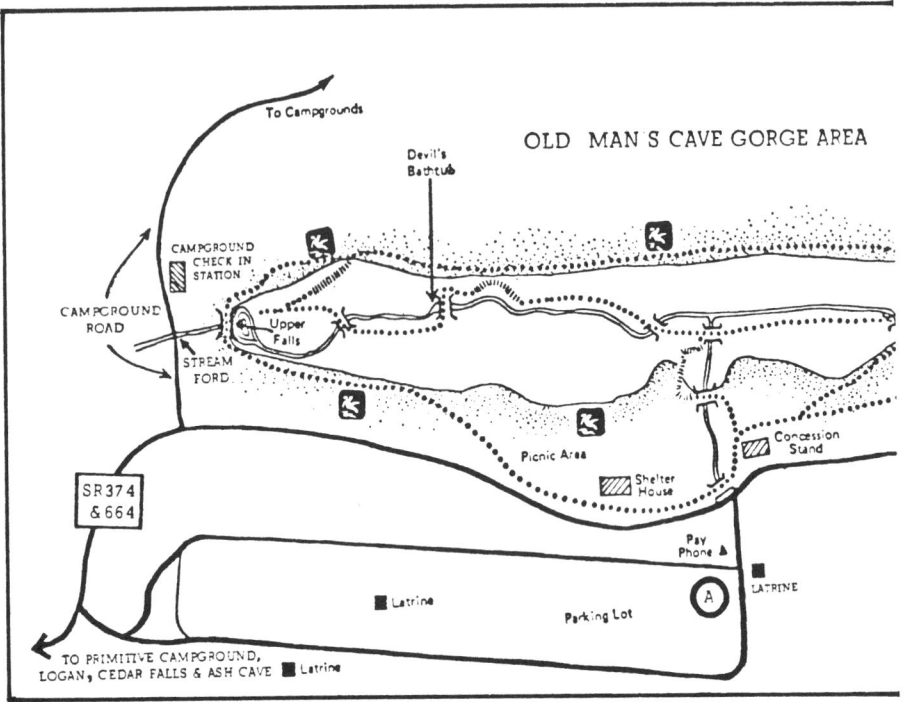

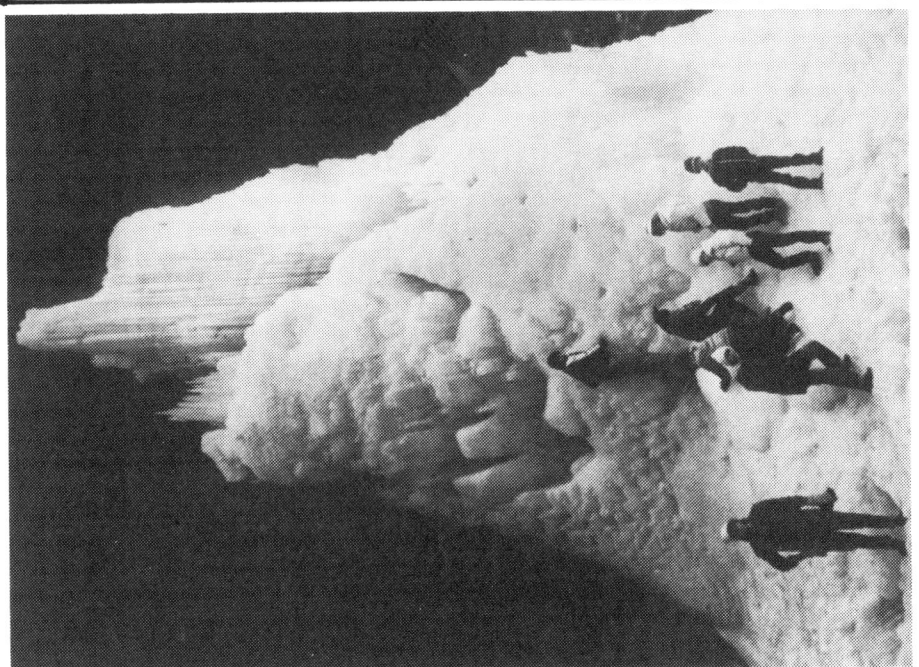

*Ice formation below Ash Cave Falls in Winter. Photo - Rich Fischer*

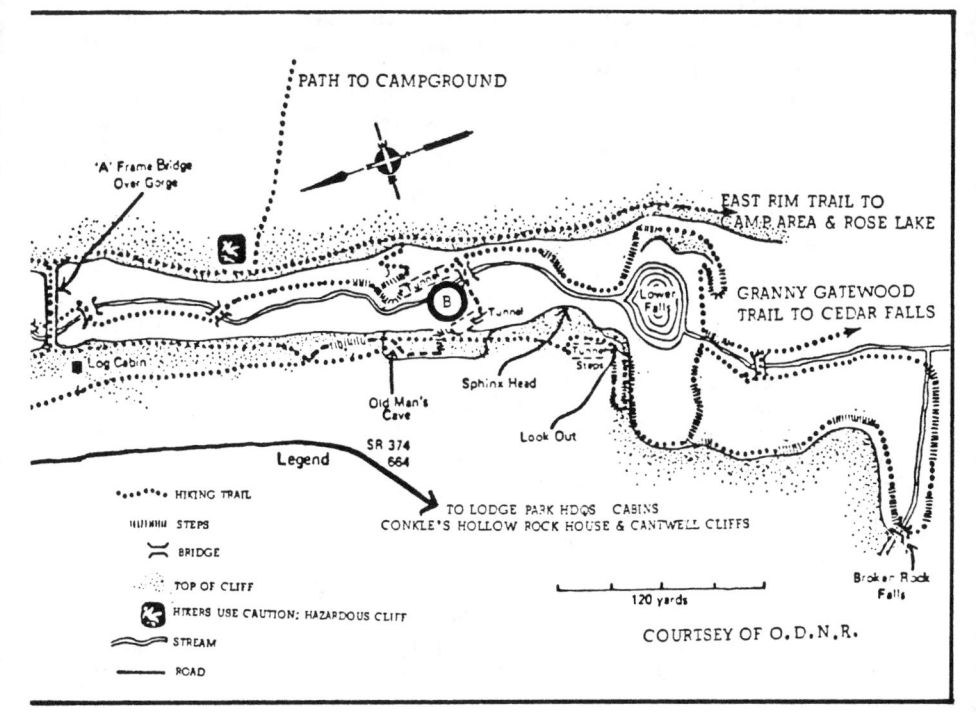

*Members of The Logan Chamber of Commerce making bean soup for the annual Winter Hike*

55

If you have someone in your party whose walking abilities are severely limited, the walks along the gorge floor from the parking lots to both Ash Cave and the head of Conkle's Hollow are two of the rare walks suggested in this book for which the trails are classified as very easy. If a person is capable of walking a mile on fairly even level ground, these walks should be within their capacity, but the rim walks of these two areas require much more physical effort.

## SUGGESTED HIKES FOR UNIT ONE

The three most popular areas for sightseers, Old Man's Cave Gorge which includes the Upper and Lower Falls, Cedar Falls and Ash Cave are linked together by the Granny Gatewood Trail of just under 6 easy miles. This is the most popular longer walk in the area and is the trail used for the famous "Winter Walk". Its moderate length and non strenuous climbs makes for a nice and fairly easy single day hike which includes all of the sightseeing highlights of Unit One. Its one drawback is that unless you have someone to pick you up at the Ash Cave parking lot you have to trek the six miles back again. But there are options for this. With those having only one car, the walks can be broken into two fairly easy one-day loop trips by using part of the Indian Run Trail. The first Old Man's Cave-Cedar Falls Loop is about 8 miles in length and the page number for the return is given in the text at Cedar Falls. The other loop, using the Granny Gatewood Trail is the Cedar Falls-Ash Cave Loop of 9 miles. Following the Granny Gatewood Trail from Cedar Falls to Ash Cave, you have to backtrack the first mile of that trail from Ash Cave to Chapel Ridge Road. The return loop turns left on that paved road following it for a delightful 1.9 mile walk along the open ridge top passing Wesley Chapel and continuing until it joins the Indian Run Trail. At that point they both turn off the road. This turnoff is easy to find for there is a well kept green mobile home on the left side across the road from the junction turnoff. The return loop turns right off Chapel Ridge Road and follows the Indian Run Trail into the forest and returns to the Cedar Falls parking lot. Follow the directions of the Indian Run Trail starting on page 68.

There are at least three different versions of short loop trips around the Old Man's Cave Gorge along the Granny Gatewood Trail for those who do not wish to hike on to Cedar Falls. (See detailed map on page 54.) Other hikes that center in the Unit One area are the 12 mile Indian Run Loop (see page 67), the 1½ mile Gulf Trail and the trail down to it from the dining lodge (page 71) and a short half mile trail connecting Rose Lake with State Route 374 (see map on page 54). There is a Chief Leatherlips Trail shown on the map included in the official state park brochure but because so much of its routing was alongside busy public highways, it has fallen into disuse and is no longer maintained.

## SUGGESTED HIKES FOR UNIT TWO

Since all three of these areas are of intense geologic interest, quite scenic, and easily seen with a minimum of difficult walking, turn to page 72 for an easy description of how to get to them followed by maps and other suggestions.

## UNIT ONE

| | Page |
|---|---|
| Overall map of all the trails in Unit One | 52 |
| Old Man's Cave Gorge map | 54 |
| Cedar Fall's map | 63 |
| Ash Cave map | 66 |
| Granny Gatewood Trail | 57 |
| From Old Man's Cave Parking Lot to Cedar Falls | 61 |

From Cedar Falls to Ash Cave ............................................... 64
Indian Run Loop Trail ...................................................... 67
East Rim Loop Trail ........................................................ 69
Lodge Trail to Gulf Trail ................................................... 70
Gulf Trail .................................................................. 71
Rose Lake Trail ............................................................ 72

## THE GRANNY GATEWOOD TRAIL

From the Upper Falls of the Old Man's Cave Gorge to Ash Cave.
Distance: Just under 6 miles.

GENERAL REMARKS: Many of us long trail hikers felt a great deal of satisfaction when this most popular six mile stretch of the Buckeye Trail was named after and dedicated to the memory of Ohio's most famous trekker. Mrs. Emma Gatewood, an Ohio farm lady, one of fifteen children, raised eleven of her own before she began the adventures that made her a legend in her lifetime. In her middle sixties, she read a magazine article about the Appalachian Trail which described it as a lovely, somewhat easy trail rather than the treacherously difficult path that it is. The article changed her life, for despite having no previous long trail hiking experience and being closer to seventy than sixty, she decided she wanted to walk all 2000 miles of it. Her first attempt at feeling out a small section of the trail in Maine almost turned out to be her last, for she made a wrong turn in that state's rugged backcountry and was lost for two days. According to Grandma she wasn't lost but just, "misplaced." After this disheartening experience she momentarily gave up the idea of doing the trail, but an inner urge kept growing until May of 1955 when she arrived at Mt. Oglethrope, Georgia which was then the southern end of the trail to begin the long hike to Maine. 145 days later she arrived at Baxter Peak on Mt. Katahdin, the northern terminus of the trail just a month short of her sixty eighth birthday. She became the first woman to walk the entire trail as well as the first female to do the trail in one continual journey.

She averaged between fourteen and sixteen miles per day with one Bunyonesque day of twenty seven miles. She had dropped in weight from 155 to 120 pounds and her foot width had increased one full size. Her equipment and clothing for this long walk would hardly delight the manufacturers of backpacking equipment. She never carried a stove saying that cold food was good enough. Her scanty cupboard consisted of chipped beef, bullion cubes, raisins, powdered milk, peanuts, and salt. She augmented these meager rations by food abandoned by other hikers and occasional meals offered by admirers who met her along the way. She spurned the use of a canteen and used instead two plastic eight ounce baby bottles for water. Although any through hiker faces many days of wind driven rain and temperatures below freezing neither tent, rain coat nor sleeping bag was part of her equipment. She carried one light wool blanket and a plastic sheet for covering. Equally spartan were the clothes she carried: a blouse, light jacket, a sweater, scarf and pants. To this scanty list she added only a **rain hat plus a cape for inclement weather that she cut from an old piece of plastic sheeting. The rest of her equipment consisted of a household flashlight, a teaspoon** and the only piece of gear she carried regularly found in all outfitting stores --- a Swiss Army knife. She later added a tin cup she found abandoned near a spring. She transported these items in a cloth bag with one shoulder strap that she had fashioned from a piece of denim. All in all Granny's pack usually weighed less than twenty pounds and was sometimes as light as fourteen. Her hiking shoes were sneakers and she wore out five pairs of them on the trek. She tried leather hiking boots briefly and got the only foot blisters she ever had in her life. In contrast I am an overweighted multi-equipped sissy, for an eleven day wilderness trip I made, my backpack weighed over 50 pounds and my gun boat sized boots weighed over five pounds apiece. But unlike Granny, my full grained leather boots have never given me a blister in thousands of miles of hiking.

Just seventeen months after completing the entire Appalachian hike she was off on the same trail again.

On the second trip she wore out six pairs of sneakers and cut three days off her total time for an incredible average of 14½ miles a day. She became the first hiker, male or female, to hike the trail in one continual stint twice. She completed this second trip a few days short of her seventieth birthday. When asked why she decided to do the whole trail a second time, she simply answered that she wanted to see some of the things she had missed the first time.

She managed to hike the trail a third time in segments during her seventies. When she was 72 she hiked the Oregon Trail and later did other long trail walks in Vermont, Pennsylvania and Maryland. At eighty five Granny Gatewood lay down for her last bivouac and began her eternal walk in the Big Sky. As mentioned before the Granny Gatewood Trail can be done in one hike or broken up into loop walks. All of these loop walk possibilities will again be mentioned in this description. The most popular walking area is the short walk through Old Man's Cave Gorge from the Upper Falls to the Lower Falls. Unless a person is physically unable to make this bottom gorge walk of less than half a mile but with many steps, or has had totally no interest in its high scenic rewards, it should not be missed. There are a number of short loop options mentioned in the text for those not wishing to walk on to Cedar Falls. If you are making the walk during the popular seasons try to do so in the morning before the trail becomes a sort of crowded people interstate highway. If you make this walk on a pleasant winter weekday, you and the spirit of the old man may silently chat alone on equal terms on why you both appreciate it being there. This will take you past two of the most beautiful waterfalls in the state as well as the old man's residence and the bath tub for the ruler of the nether world. Beyond this gorge the trail leads to Cedar Falls and Ash Cave, each of them far different than those things seen before.

TRAIL DESCRIPTION: To find the trailhead after crossing the road from the parking lot at Point A, turn left walking in front of the picnic shelter and follow the path to the stone bridge just above the Upper Falls. Just before you reach it, there is a sign to the left which should be taken seriously. It says:

**WARNING
CLIMBING ON ROCKS PROHIBITED
STAY ON CONSTRUCTED TRAILS
WATCH FOR FALLEN OBJECTS
CLOSELY CONTROL CHILDREN**

Once down in the gorge there is no worry about high cliff areas until you climb out of this gorge or reach Ash Cave almost 6 miles away. Just past the sign, the trail curves right and crosses the stone bridge across Old Man's Cave Creek. As you cross it look right over the top of the Upper Falls and the plunge pool below.

Following the rim top around the head of the gorge to the right, you come to a sign facing the trail on the left at the head of a group of steps which says:

⟵ PARKING LOT
EAST RIM TRAIL ⟶

You turn right here and go down the steps, which are mostly in cement, to the view of the Upper Falls and its plunge pool. The rim of the Upper Falls is the top of the very hard upper zone Black Hand sandstone.

After viewing the falls, turn around and begin your walk through the narrow and attractive upper gorge. The resistant quality of the capstone has kept this gorge narrow with near vertical cliffs enclosing you and allowing little sunlight to hit the gorge floor. Just before you cross the second bridge, which is the first one in stone on the gorge floor, look just in front of it to see the Devil's Bathtub. This is actually a large pot hole caused by the eroding away of a pocket of weaker conglomerate made by the swirling action of water driven sand.

After you have crossed the fourth bridge, look up to see the A frame bridge that crosses the gorge rim connecting the east and west rim and is used both by people walking from the campground and by those on the yearly Indian Run. After passing under the A frame and crossing two more wooden bridges you can look right and see the upper part of the cascade that drops below Old Man's Cave. Do not leave the trail for you get a better look at it from the cave itself.

As you come down 10 stone steps, there is a sign to the left of the trail facing it which says:

## OLD MAN'S CAVE ⟶

You will notice there are steps right next to the sign that go straight ahead and up but take you to the East Rim Trail. Turn right at the sign and come down about 10 more steps which brings you to the mouth of a man made tunnel. After passing through its approximate 35 foot length you are at point B on the detail map. On the left facing the trail there is a sign which says:

## ⟵ UPPER FALLS
## LOWER FALLS ⟶

Look straight ahead at this point and see the Sphinx Head on the lower part of the right cliff walk. The protruding chin of this profile rock was caused by the stream undercutting the rock. Other features of the face are the result of uneven erosion in this middle zone of the Black Hand sandstone with some layers being more resistant to weathering than others.

On your right you can see Old Man's Cave above you, a large recess cave that was also cut into the softer middle zone of the Black Hand sandstone by sapping action undercutting the hard capstone of the upper zone above it. Its floor is about 75 feet above the creek. The opening of the cave is just under 200 feet long but only 50 feet high and its sloping ceiling receeds more than 50 feet. It is not nearly as large or awesome as Ash Cave but is more frequently visited because of the old man who once called it home and the beautiful gorge in which he lived.

There is no documented evidence of who the old man was but many legends abound about him. His name was Richard Rowe or Roe. He was probably a hunter and trapper, and most accounts have him occupying this shelter after the Civil War although one account has him living there considerably before that time. Some stories related that he was a fugitive from West Virginia; others say that he migrated with his family from Tennessee. The time of his death is unknown but almost all accounts have him buried in the cave. One story tells how one very cold winter morning he went down to the creek for water and tried to break the ice with the butt of his musket. The jar caused the gun to discharge, the shot hitting him under the chin and killing him.

Visiting the cave gives one a beautiful view of the cascading creek below and some idea why this old hermit choose this cave to live in. The floor is high enough and the strata are such that the cave is dry in most areas. The shelter faces in a direction that allows natural daylight to fall into its interior for the greater part of the day. It has a reliable water supply below and the relatively low ceiling at the back of the shelter would make it easier to wall up a section for heating during the colder seasons. To get there turn right crossing the stone bridge across the creek; then pass through another man made tunnel and up about 50 steps to the cave.

It is at this point you have your first option of available loop trips. If you intend to continue on the Granny Gatewood Trail to Cedar Falls or include the Lower Falls and Broken Rock Falls in a shorter loop recross Old Man's Creek and head down the gorge. For persons who will not endanger their health by going up or down many steps the Lower Falls should not be missed. But if you have someone who is unwell or, for some reason, finds the stress a little too much, there is an easy access from the cave back to the rim top with less than 50 steps to climb. Walk through the rock shelter in the upstream direction and you will see the path and steps up to the rim.

For those continuing on, once back across the stone bridge there is a climb of just under 50 steps before a long descent of about 70 steps leading to the plunge pool at the bottom of Lower Falls. When there is ample water going over the 40 foot drop, this is one of the most beautiful scenes in Ohio and one might think he is in western Colorado rather than in the middle of the Buckeye state. Before 1978 there was a large rock shelter just to the right of the falls. A sign there tells what happened to it. Since it has been mutilated once and repaired I add it here in case the vandals get at it again.

**The creation or the cutting of the Old Man's Cave Gorge into the Black Hand sandstone took ten thousand years. Rarely in one's lifetime does a change take place to form a new landscape. But sometime during the morning of January 7, 1978, such a change took place. Here a main part of this cliff gave way resulting in the formation of a totally new picture. Will more fall? No one knows, but in this area we urge extreme caution. Massive changes may be an instant or a thousand years in the future.**

Behind the sign you can notice a large pile of rock debris that now forms a small hill and was once the overhang of the shelter.

You can also see that the gorge widens considerably below the falls for erosion has cut completely through the Black Hand sandstone and the gorge floor is now in softer rock strata. While viewing the falls by the plunge pool look to the left across the stream and you can see a very tall tree. It is a giant hemlock which is 120 feet high; still not a record however, for there is one hemlock somewhere in the valley of Queer Creek reported to reach up 146 feet.

To continue either the short loop or on to Cedar Falls, walk downstream from the plunge pool retracing your walk back up about 13 steps across a flat space and when you go down about 6 steps you come to the trail division. The path to the left is the continuation of the Granny Gatewood Trail to Cedar Falls while the right one over the stone bridge is to Broken Rock Falls and a demanding climb to the rim. People who only wish to do this short loop and are afraid of heights would best retrace their steps and gain the rim through Old Man's Cave, for the return below the falls is spooky and has a climb where small children should be watched carefully.

As you cross the stone bridge you will see a sign facing you which says:

**BROKEN ROCK**
⬅ — — — **FALLS**

a right turn will almost immediately take you to the climb to the rim but by turning left you can take the slightly longer loop that includes the falls. In just a few yards you

*View of Lower Falls from Granny Gatewood Trail*

will cross the wash of that falls and come to the steps that lead up to it. Just under 90 steps takes you to its base, but you can get an excellent view of it about halfway up. If there has been recent rain, this tributary falls is so different in character from the two already seen that it is well worth the little extra effort to get there. Cut into the Black **Hand Sandstone cliff, it cascades better than 70 feet cutting a diagonal gash in the cliff. The trail loops through the rock shelter at its base and returns along the cliff** base to a set of wooden steps that begins the climb up the cliff. At this writing the bridge immediately below the falls has been washed out, so it does make for some scrambling. The bridge is scheduled to be replaced, but if it hasn't been yet and the short climb is a bit much for someone in your party you can go back the way you came passing by, but not crossing, the stone bridge across Old Man's Cave Creek which soon leads you to the steps beginning the climb out. If you do make the Broken Falls loop over the repaired bridge you will soon junction with the direct trail from the Lower Falls at the top of a flight of 60 stone steps. In front of you there are a series of 30 wooden steps that take you up the side of a near vertical cliff. If you have young children in the party, have an adult go up first, for the steps lead to a cliff ledge very close to a drop off. More stone steps lead you to another tunnel in which you ascend 68 more steps to the rim. Once up, there is a fenced overlook to the right, which gives you a somewhat restricted view of the gorge below

### GRANNY GRATEWOOD TRAIL CONTINUED TO CEDAR FALLS

As you walk downstream alongside the creek, you see the gorge has widened even more. Soon you will see a sign facing you which says:

GULF TRAIL ⟶
HOCKING LODGE ⟶

This very attractive trail follows along Queer Creek reaching Route 664 in 1½ miles or to the Lodge in ¾ miles. For trail description see page 71. **A sign to your left facing the trail says:**

*Ash Cave on the Granny Gatewood Trail*

CEDAR FALLS 1.5 MI ⟶<br>
OLD MANS CAVE 1.5 MI ⟵

which indicates that you have reached the halfway point between the Upper Falls and Cedar Falls. In case the signs are missing the trail to the right is the Gulf Trail while the Granny Gatewood Trail continues straight ahead. The vandalism of the signs is extreme here so if the signs were down there is a sure way to tell which trail you are on. If you continue on very briefly to a stream crossing and once across the stream you find a stream on your left and you are following it in the downstream **direction you are on the Gulf Trail. If you find a stream on your right going upstream you're on the trail to Cedar Falls, for both these trails are now following Queer Creek in opposite directions.**

After covering another easy half mile you will pass a sign on the right facing the trail which says:

⟵ CEDAR FALLS 1 MI<br>
OLD MANS CAVE 2 MI ⟶

Not far beyond this sign there is a fork in the trail. The right fork takes you down to the creek and the left one up some well worn steps. Go up the steps which leads you through some narrow passages between slump blocks. Shortly beyond this point the trail winds under a high but shallow rock shelter with just the barest trickle of a waterfall from the rim. Skirting behind this spray, the hiker is aided across the swampy bottom of the shelter by a boardwalk. The cliff indicates that the gorge is narrowing and is back in the Black Hand Sandstone zones. The whole nature of the area becomes like the first part of this walk with less sunlight reaching the bottom and with a marvelous forest grove of large hemlocks. Passing more rock shelters on the left, the trail curves around on a narrow ledge about two feet wide on the side of a

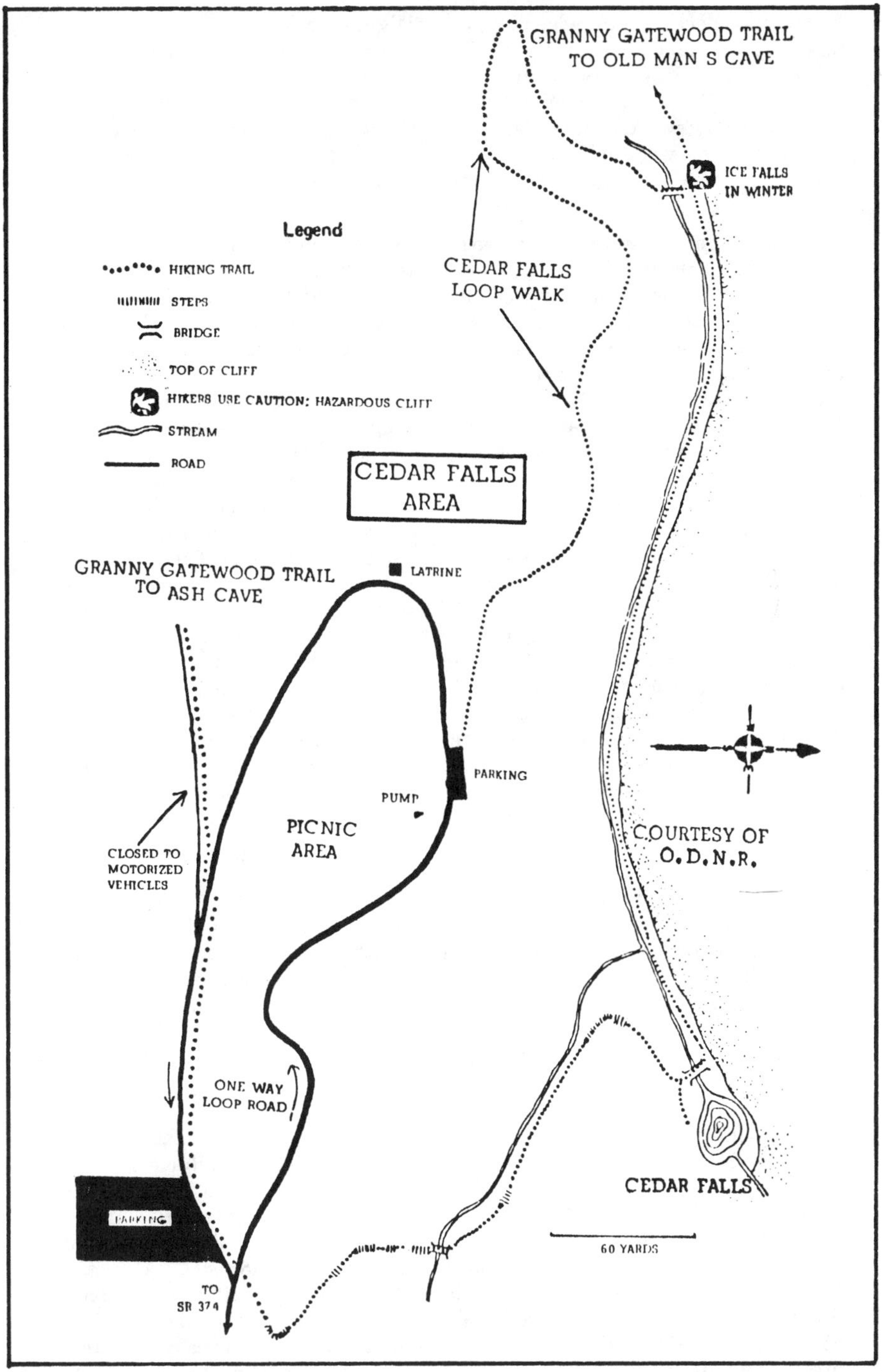
GRANNY GATEWOOD TRAIL
TO OLD MAN S CAVE
ICE FALLS
IN WINTER
Legend
HIKING TRAIL
STEPS
BRIDGE
TOP OF CLIFF
HIKERS USE CAUTION: HAZARDOUS CLIFF
STREAM
ROAD
CEDAR FALLS
LOOP WALK
CEDAR FALLS
AREA
GRANNY GATEWOOD TRAIL
TO ASH CAVE
LATRINE
PARKING
PUMP
PICNIC
AREA
CLOSED TO
MOTORIZED
VEHICLES
COURTESY OF
O.D.N.R.
ONE WAY
LOOP ROAD
CEDAR FALLS
PARKING
60 YARDS
TO
SR 374

huge slump block with the edge dropping straight to the creek. Some hand holding might be advisable here for the small fry. Just beyond the ledge you will pass an attractive rock shelter which brings you into view of a sturdy wooden foot bridge across Queer Creek. The bridge is used as part of the short Cedar Falls loop walk, but the Granny Gatewood trail does not cross it but proceeds straight ahead until you come to a second wooden bridge where you cross Queer Creek. Once across it Cedar Falls is immediately on your left and the stairway to the parking lot is to the right.

## CEDAR FALLS

Because the early settlers in the area mistook the abundant giant hemlocks as the cedars of biblical fame, the falls was so named. You can easily see the caprock which is the upper zone of the Black Hard Sandstone just above the falls. It is about 15 feet thick and two vertical joint fractures are easily seen on its surface. The falls are more like a large cascade which falls about 50 feet down a semi-circular cliff. At the head of the gorge the water carrying sand as an abrasive agent has carved two separate grooved water passages which can be seen during times of normal run off. In the 1830's a grist mill was built above the falls and operated for many years. Although it is long gone, some of its millstones are on display in the Nature Center near Old Man's Cave.

When you walk back towards the bridge take the stone stairs to the left to get up to the parking lot. There you will pass alongside a very attractive tributary stream on the right and will soon cross that stream on a small wooden bridge. Then it is an easy, short climb to the parking lot road. Once at the road you have two hiking alternatives. If you are making a day loop hike, turn left on the road and follow the sign posts for **the Indian Run trail (see page 68). If you are going on to Ash Cave, you walk across the two sections of this one-lane loop road and turn right following the road. As the road curves to the right you will see a F.W.D. service gravel road straight ahead that is the beginning of the Ash Cave section of the Granny Gatewood trail. Cedar Falls is the half way point between the Lower Falls and Ash Cave, and it is in this parking lot** that the Logan Kiwans Club serves the bean soup during the January Winter Walk. I remember one warm September day passing this point and suddenly developing a craving for that soup that I remembered being served steaming hot on a cold January Saturday.

## GRANNY GATEWOOD TRAIL
## FROM CEDAR FALLS TO ASH CAVE

Once on the one lane dirt service road you will soon see that another service road goes off to the right in a large horse shoe curve. Although you proceed straight ahead at this point, the road on the right is used as part of the Indian Run trail and, if you are doing the Cedar Falls Ash Cave loop, you will return to this point. Although the trail proceeds straight ahead on the orginal road, it does not do it for very long, for just about 50 yards beyond this junction the road begins going uphill. There the trail turns left off the road and a sign to the left says:

## ←——— ASH CAVE

After leaving the road the trail crosses a wash three times using narrow wooden bridges and then climbs at an easy gradient up to the top of Chapel Ridge. This is the highest elevation of the walk at 1,068 feet a rise of a little over 300 feet above the lowest point on Queer Creek. A short distance after reaching the crest, the trail crosses the paved Chapel Ridge Road which is the half way point between Cedar Falls and Ash Cave. From here on it is downhill all the way to Ash Cave.

If you are going to make the Cedar Falls, Ash Cave loop you will turn west here on **this road when you return from Ash Cave. You might also want to make a side trip here to the Ash Cave Lookout Tower if you are finding the hike easy and are not pressed for time. If you climb its 8 platforms and just under a hundred steps you will** be rewarded with an impressive panoramic view of the rolling countryside. To get there turn left on Chapel Ridge Road and in 1/10 mile it dead ends into State Route 374. Look right and between the two paved roads you will see a small gravel road. Follow it taking the left fork when it divides, and in about a three minutes walk from the first road junction you will arrive at the tower. See page 68 for loop return.

Continuing on the Granny Gatewood Trail, shortly after passing Chapel Ridge Road, the trail crosses a clearing for telephone poles and soon crosses a series of small washes, some with bridges. During the summer months there is a lovely corridor of about 100 feet lined on each side by Joe Pye weed seven to eight foot tall. You will reach a sign on the right side of and facing the trail which reads:

◄──── ASH CAVE
CEDAR FALLS ────►

The first time I walked this trail the word ASH in the sign had been vandalized to read HASH CAVE, but a new sign has again eliminated the unwanted first letter. This sign is also an indication that you are close to this enormous rock shelter and you will soon see a sign on the left side and facing the trail which reads:

DANGER
CLIFF AREA
WATCH YOUR CHILDREN

If you generally ignore signs make this an exception for the drop off is close, sudden and severe. Rambunctious children should be taken by the hand. When you come to a low wooden foot bridge across the stream you are practically at the edge of the top of the cave, and it is now underneath you. The trails going left and right from this bridge are the rim walk of the cave and, in just a few feet beyond it, the stream goes over the top with a straight plunge of 90 feet. To get down to the cave turn left going over the small bridge and follow the rim walk a few feet until you come to the wooden steps. There are three tiers of them containing almost 50 steps. Once down you can look to the right and follow the path into this huge rock shelter.

## ASH CAVE

This is the largest recess shelter, rock shelter or recess cave in all of Ohio. The distance of its curving open side is over 700 feet. The outside rim is 90 feet. The outside rim is 90 feet above the floor and the ceiling recesses back over 100 feet. The geologic formation of this famous shelter was caused by the upper zone capstone of the Black Hand Sandstone being far more resistant to erosion than the middle zone. This capstone became the roof of the cave as the softer middle layers were and still are being sapped away by water and wind erosion. Ash Cave has amazing acoustic qualities for in certain areas along the back wall a person may whisper against the rock surface and be easily heard by others along the back wall some distance from the speaker.

Its name came from the huge piles of ash that were discovered here by the early white inhabitants. One such pile was over 100 feet long, 30 feet in width and 3 feet deep. Such accumulations were formed over the centuries, for pre-historic tribes would cover ash beds with sand and begin a new one on top until such beds sometimes reached a thickness of 10 feet. One excavation of this cave in 1877 turned up pottery bits, arrow heads, flint working tools and many animal bones including elk, deer, skunk, wildcat, wild turkey, bear and the now extinct passenger pigeon.

Due to its size it was an important ceremonial site and meeting place for large groups of Indians both modern and prehistoric. What a story could have been pieced together of the human history taking place here by today's archeologists with modern techniques if they had been able to do careful scholarly excavation of its floor

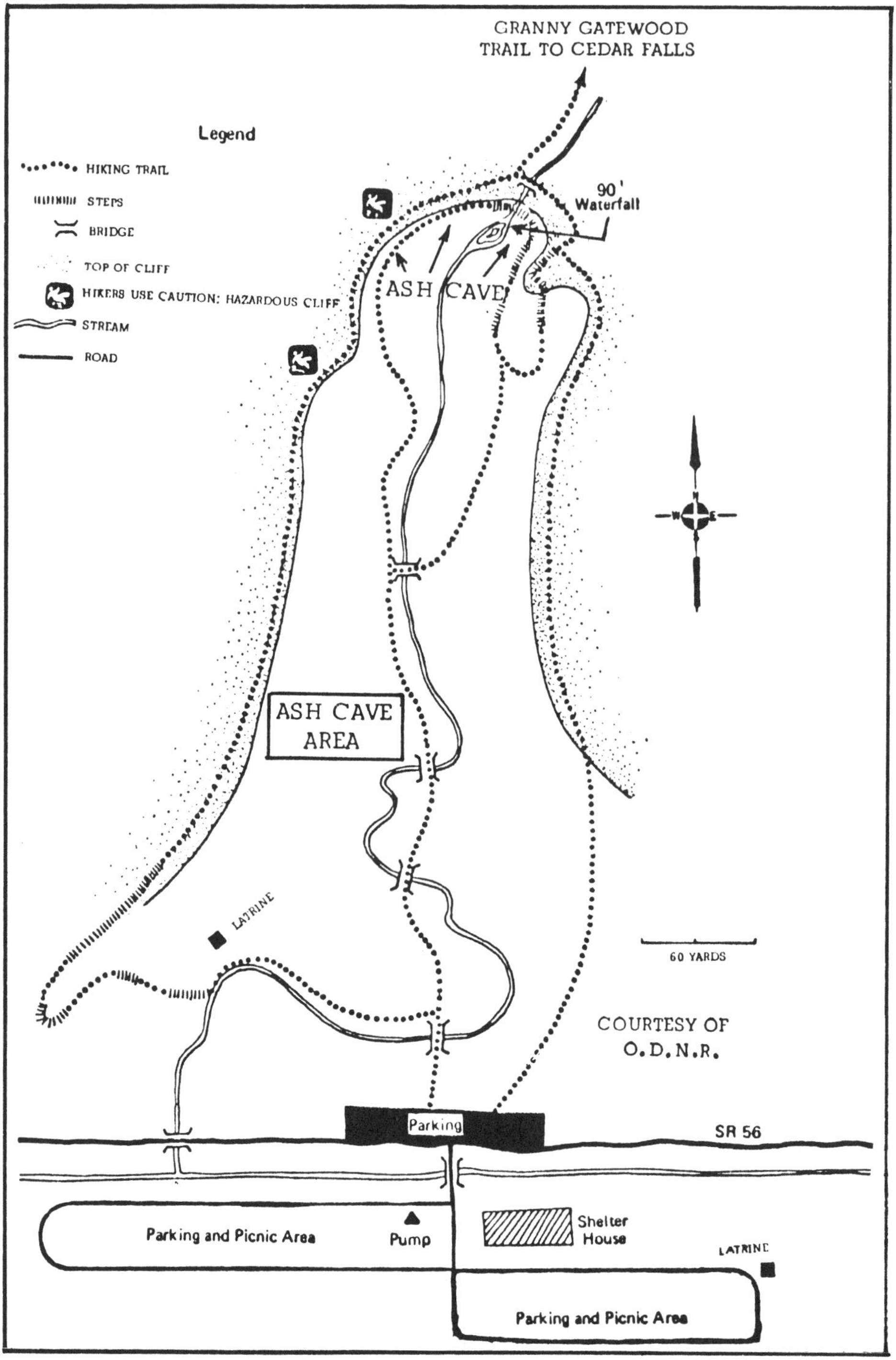
GRANNY GATEWOOD
TRAIL TO CEDAR FALLS
Legend
HIKING TRAIL
STEPS
BRIDGE
TOP OF CLIFF
HIKERS USE CAUTION: HAZARDOUS CLIFF
STREAM
ROAD
90'
Waterfall
ASH CAVE
ASH CAVE
AREA
LATRINE
60 YARDS
COURTESY OF
O.D.N.R.
Parking
SR 56
Parking and Picnic Area
Pump
Shelter
House
LATRINE
Parking and Picnic Area

before it was disturbed. But because of its marvelous acoustics and the ability to shelter many people it was used widely as a gathering place for white settlers for over 100 years. It was a favorite place for camp meetings and revivals.

You can see a huge slump block which is centrally located and not quite under the rim which was used by Divines to deliver their fire and brimstone sermons. It is also quite likely that at important Indian powwows the great chiefs would make their deliverances from this same boulder hence its name, "Pulpit Rock."

Those making a winter visit, when there have been long periods of freezing weather, may see a sizable chunk of ice at the bottom of the falls in the middle of the plunge pool. In the severe winter of 1978 the falls froze all the way to the top forming a giant 90 foot icicle. There is an excellent color photograph of this amazing freeze hanging inside the dining lodge just in front of the park offices.

## INDIAN RUN LOOP TRAIL

Distance 12 1/3 miles.

GENERAL REMARKS: Although laid out for the yearly Indian Run in September all but one weekend of the year the trail is there for hikers to use. For information on the race itself see page 47. Hikers can do the entire loop in a day and the only really difficult part is the distance. Unfortunately the first part of the trail follows along very busy roads but after milepost #3 the Indian Run Trail makes a very pleasant walk and includes a couple of beautiful stretches that are on no other trail. Except on the race days much of the trail covers areas that are seldom used so you will encounter few people. It avoids all the heavily congested areas except around the A frame bridge over Old Man's Cave Gorge.

Parts of this trail fit in nicely for loop trails at Cedar Falls and Ash Cave. This is a very well marked trail with square brown wooden posts used as mile and kilometer markers and to indicate turns on the trail. The last time I field checked this trail all posts but two were on the left side of the trail and all were in good shape. The posts furnished by the Logan Chamber of Commerce were wisely hewn thick enough to resist all but the most dedicated axe wielders.

TRAIL DESCRIPTION: Beginning at the covered driveway at the entrance of the Dining Lodge, the trail runs through the parking lot to the lodge road but almost immediately turns left on the driveway to the cabin area. Just after passing cabin number 11 the trail turns left off the road and passes through the middle of a playground and a break in the trees, then turns left. In about 50 yards the trail turns right on a dirt road and runs to State Route 374 and 664. The trail does not cross the road but turns left and stays on the left hand side. The first wooden post after you turn alongside the highway is the one mile marker and you have about two miles of running along Route 664. The second mile marker comes just after State Route 374 turns to the right off 664. The trail follows 664 downhill until you see a large sign on the left side of the road facing you which says:

### LEAVING HOCKING STATE FOREST
### DEPARTMENT OF NATURAL RESOURCES
### DIVISION OF FORESTRY

Just beyond the sign you pass mile marker 3 and turn left onto a narrow gravel road and begin a climb that is so steep it makes Boston Marathon's Heartbreak Hill seem like its going downhill. For in about a half mile the trail climbs better than 300 feet. Although other climbs are still ahead this lung buster is the worst. The gravel road dead ends into the paved Chapel Ridge Road where the trail turns left following alongside the road. After about a half mile on Chapel Ridge Road you will pass mile marker 4. As the forest gives way to open fields on the right side of the road you will soon see a green mobile home on the right. The trail turns left there going on a F.W.D. type forest service road and into a beautiful pine forest. **It is at this point that the Ash Cave loop joins the Indian Run Trail.** Soon the conifers give way to the hardwoods and a half mile into the forest mile marker 5 is on the left. Just beyond this marker the trail makes a U turn to the right. Then it turns left again and crosses the stoney bottom of a wash and T's into and turns left on another forest road. The trail is now running close to the south rim of the Queer Creek Gorge and there are a few places where you can see cliff areas to your left. As you pass the six mile marker on the left you will notice a vehicle turn around for this is where the vans deliver the runners that are starting the 10 kilometer run. The 10 km post where they start is just a bit beyond this point and you will soon pass it on the left. The road soon U turns into another forest road turning left on it. This short stretch to the Cedar Falls Parking lot is shared by both the Granny Gatewood and the Buckeye Trail. About a hundred yards from this junction you pass mile marker 7. When the forest road runs into the paved Cedar Falls drive the Indian Run Trail turns right alongside this road past a parking lot on the right.**This is where the Old Man's Cave-Cedar Falls hiking loop joins the Indian Run Trail.** You must cross this paved road to the left side before it reaches State Route 374. Turn left alongside State Route 374 and follow the paved road and cross two stone bridges. About 15 yards after crossing the second bridge the trail turns left on a very narrow forest road and is now running along the north side of the Queer Creek Gorge where mile post 8 is soon on the left. Shortly after the trail goes over a wash with a solid stone floor, the trail curves to the right up the side of Rose Hollow. This is another very steep uphill section climbing 100 feet in less than a quarter mile up to the Rose Lake Dam where there is a sign which says:

## DANGER
## NO SWIMMING
## WATER 55 FEET DEEP

The trail begins following the right side of the lake around an inlet then leaves the lakeshore temporarily going uphill into the woods. It then declines passing out of the woods and an easy descent down to the lake where it follows around another inlet. Then again it leaves the lakeshore going up very steeply but fortunately not long. Just after the trail passes the hillcrest, it passes mile marker 9. The trail then goes down toward a third inlet where the bottom can be mucky. It again leaves the lakeshore and goes easily uphill and then eventually goes down to the lakeshore passing a sign which says:

## SWIMMING PROHIBITED

As you get close to the headwaters of the lake, there are cat tails alongside the trail and the trail jumps a small wash. The trail turns left around the head of the lake and crosses a two plank wooden bridge over the wash at the head of the lake. It then turns right on an F.W.D. service road that has a gentle but long uphill climb until you see a gray house on the left where the road curves to the left and hits a gravel road. The trail turns left on the road and U turns around the house. At this writing there was talk of demolishing the house; therefore in some future year it may not be there. Once around the house the trail and gravel road goes a short distance to the paved main campground road turning right on it and following its left side passing mile marker 10 next to campsite #97. You continue until you see a stop sign on the right side of the road and a sign facing you which says: THIS WAY OUT. The trail turns left here and crosses over the paved campground road and runs along its right side. Just after passing campsite # 20, you turn right on a short paved campground spur which has a sign marked - NATURAL RESOURCES 7. Going down to the turning circle at its end just beyond campsite # 27, there are two signs facing the road saying: PARK CLOSES AT DARK and to the left of it DANGER KEEP ON TRAIL. To the left of the latter sign the trail leaves the road with a sign on its left facing the trail which says RIM TRAIL. As the trail heads into the woods, it goes easily downhill hitting another narrow F.W.D. road and turns right. The trail follows it until a post indicates a left turn at which point you are in sight of the A frame bridge that goes over the Old Man's Cave Gorge. You cross the bridge and continue straight ahead briefly until the trail turns left in front of a log cabin which has a sign on it identifying it as the **"NATURALISTS CABIN". In about 50 yards beyond this left turn the trail goes off diagonally to the right leaving the main path and follows what once was a narrow** wooded road. You will come to the 11 mile marker, which indicates a right turn just before the trail comes to a small ravine. The trail crosses the ravine's wash, then turns right and climbs a small ridge. As the trail comes out of the forest, it turns left, goes downhill, crosses another wash on a 2 plank bridge, runs around the right side of a tan cinder block building, and goes up 30 cement steps to the lodge road. The trail turns left and follows alongside the paved road, which has a gradual climb back up to the lodge. You will pass mile marker 12 as you go uphill, which means you have about 3/10 mile to go before finishing in front of the lodge's 'main' entrance.

### EAST RIM LOOP TRAIL

Distance: 2.6 miles

GENERAL REMARKS: This loop trail gives you pleasant views of the upper part of the Old Man's Cave Gorge and you can see the gorge gradually widening before the trail swings away from it into Rose Hollow and up to Rose Lake. Better than half of the walk is on or near dangerous cliff areas so extreme caution should be used especially with young children. It also offers some shorter versions if you do not wish to do the entire loop. A very short loop walk can be done by following the rim to the A frame bridge, then cross the bridge back to the parking lot. There are two safe places quite close together where you can descend to the gorge bottom. One is directly across from Old Man's Cave, the other close to the Lower Falls, so it is possible to do a loop trip by returning by the less interesting West Rim that can be reached both at Old Man's Cave and the Lower Falls. There are even alternative ways to follow from the Rose Lake dam. Pick the one that suits you best

TRAIL DESCRIPTION: The trail head is the same as the Granny Gatewood Trail going across the stone bridge just above the Upper Falls. As the trail swings right around the head of the gorge, there is a sign to the left of the trail facing it which says:

◄———— PARKING LOT<br>
EAST RIM TRAIL ————►

You continue straight ahead at this point passing the steps on the right. This first part of the gorge walk is one of the prettiest, for as you walk along the rim which is sometimes uncomfortably close to the edge, there are some excellant views down into the narrow gorge.

It is only about a five minute walk to the A frame bridge. The rim trail continues straight ahead at the bridge, and there is a sign just beyond it facing the trail which says:

## ←——— EAST RIM TRAIL ———→

When you get to the area of Old Man's Cave it is a bit confusing to follow the trail you want, for you have the option of going down to the gorge in front of Old Man's Cave, going on to the Lower Falls or continuing on the rim trail with no signs to aid you. When you can see Old Man's Cave across the gorge from you, you will see three stone steps curving down to the right. Take them and head diagonally for a few feet until you see some badly deteriorated steps going up to the left. Take these steps for continuation of the rim trail or to the Lower Falls. If you wish to go down to Old Man's Cave for a shorter loop, don't take these worn steps but curve around to the right and you will see the path that takes you down.

To continue on to the Lower Falls or the rim trail after going up the badly worn steps, you proceed just a little ways before coming to a small stone bridge. To get to the Lower Falls Trail, cross the stone bridge and proceed straight ahead, and you will soon join the Granny Gatewood Trail. If you wish to continue on the rim trail, walk to but don't cross the little bridge. Look left and you will see about 22 stone steps going up. Take them and turn right at the top where the trail again becomes easy to follow. You will now see that the gorge has considerably widened, but the view is not as interesting, for it is mostly blocked by high trees and shrubbery.

The trail finally joins a narrow dirt service road and turns right on it. This trail road eventually makes a sharp curve to the left and starts uphill. This is the turn for Rose Hollow and a sign to the right at the curve facing the trails says:

## OLD MAN'S CAVE ———→

You don't climb very far before there is a fork in the trail with the left fork most predominant. A sign there says:

## ←——— CAMPING AREA

indicating that the left fork leads to the campground. The fork to the right which goes into the forest is the one you should take if you wish to complete the loop and take in Rose Lake. The trail starts angling down but soon curves to the left and comes out of the forest in front of the Rose Lake dam and hits a cement drain that runs diagonally down the side of the earthen dam. Follow the drain up to the top of the dam. To the left there is a trail going up to 19 wooden steps around the cinder block pump house up to the road that takes you by the group campground and the swimming pool. Once by the bath house, turn right on the campground road and almost immediately turn left on a campground road spur and follow the Indian Run signs back to the Old Man's Cave picnic area.

## LODGE TRAIL TO GULF TRAIL

Distance ¼ mile.

GENERAL REMARKS: Those wishing to walk into the Old Man's Cave area from the cabins or the lodge parking lot may do so by using this short trail to the Gulf Trail, turning left on the Gulf Trail and turning again on the Granny Gatewood Trail, or it can be used as a way to reach the lovely walk of the Gulf Trail itself. It is less than a 10 minute walk to the Granny Gatewood junction.

TRAIL DESCRIPTION: To find the trail head when facing the lodge there is a set of cement steps on the right side of the parking lot. Take them down and turn left following a wall on the left around to the back of the lodge. There you will hit a blacktop walk heading away from the lodge. On the right side of the trail there is a sign facing it, which says:

| **CEDAR FALLS 2.2 MI.**
| **OLD MAN'S CAVE 2.2 MI.**

Beyond this, the trail goes down about 100 wooden steps. There is a lookout platform to the left, but the trail turns right on a wide level path. Another sign here indicates the right turn. The level path then narrows considerably as it starts down. Almost immediately there is a very steep downhill stretch that takes you through a gap in the cliff wall and then past a rock shelter on your right. From here the trail easily descends to the junction of the Gulf Trail. There is a sign to the right of the trail facing it, which says:

| **GULF TRAIL**
| **HOCKING LODGE** ⟶

As the trail T's into the Gulf Trail there is another sign facing you which says:

⟵ **CEDAR FALLS**
**OLD MAN'S CAVE**

If you turn left, you are going up the valley of Queer Creek, which you will see on your right. You will soon cross a stream, which is Old Man's Cave Creek just before it empties into Queer Creek. About 50 yards beyond this crossing, you join the Granny Gatwood Trail.

If you turn right you will be on the Gulf Trail which ends at State Route 664 in 1.2 miles. See Trail description below.

### GULF TRAIL

From Granny Gatewood Trail to State Route 664
Distance: 1½ miles

GENERAL REMARKS: This very pretty walk in the valley of Queer Creek is off the beaten path and offers the hiker an easy short hike with only one or two testy places without the annoyance of the hiking hordes in the more popular locations. If it has no large geologic wonders it makes up for it with the quiet isolation it affords in the deep woods.

TRAIL DESCRIPTION: When you reach the halfway point of the Granny Gatewood Trail between the Upper Falls and Cedar Falls, you turn right on this trail that follows the valley of Queer Creek. In about 50 yards you cross a stream which is Old Man's Creek just a few yards away from the point where it joins Queer Creek. You will soon see Queer Creek on your left and you will stay on this side of the creek for the rest of the walk. In a short distance the trail floor turns to sand which is an indication you are close to the junction with the lodge trail. Shortly thereafter you will see a sign facing you which says:

| **GULF TRAIL**
| **HOCKING LODGE** ⟶

and a sign to the left of the trail facing it which says:

← CEDAR FALLS
← OLD MAN'S CAVE

pointing in the direction you have just come. If you wish to return to the lodge, turn right here. The distance is only about a quarter mile, but there is one somewhat difficult section to go up just after passing a rock shelter on your left as the trail turns left and goes steeply up a gap in the cliff wall. Beyond this, the walking is easy and after climbing up about 100 wooden steps follow the trail left around the back of the lodge to get to the parking lot.

If you continue on the Gulf Trail, you will see that the trail narrows at this point. Few hikers go past the junction with the lodge trail, although here is where it becomes its loveliest. It will take less than an hour to complete it. Shortly you will pass an attractive but wild looking side gorge where the trail has a short steep climb partly up the ridge side. There are a few up and down sections but only one of them that requires a brief stretch of some steep climbing. At one point slump blocks along the bank of Queer Creek force a detour away from the bank. You must climb steeply about 20 feet where you will see a gap between two of these slump blocks. After passing through the opening, you drop rather steeply down near the stream bank again. As you continue, you will find the side hollows are becoming larger. After crossing one wash in a rather deep ditch you climb up the other side and turn right following that wash away from Queer Creek. It soon hits a narrow dirt F.W.D. road. Turn left and follow it. You will pass through a grove of very large pine trees and just beyond the trail ends at Route 664.

## ROSE LAKE TRAIL

The easiest way to Rose Lake for those not staying in the campground, is to take a short half mile trail from Route 374. Take 374 from the Old Man's Cave parking lot east in the direction of Cedar Falls. Just about 7/10 mile after 374 turns right away from route 664, you will see a sign on the left which says: **FISHERMANS PARKING.** A sign on the right says: **ROSE LAKE .5 MILE.** This easy half-mile walk starts out in a beautiful grove of man planted pines. The trail is mostly level until you get to the lake where the going gets rather steep down to the bank.

## UNIT TWO

### VISITING CONKLE'S HOLLOW, ROCK HOUSE AND CANTWELL CLIFFS

**GENERAL DISCUSSION:** See Below.

| | Page |
|---|---|
| Location of the three areas. See below. | |
| Conkle's Hollow description | 73 |
| Rock House description | 76 |
| Cantwell Cliffs description | 79 |

GENERAL DESCRIPTION: Since there are no maintained woodland trails connecting the Old Man's Cave area to these three prime scenic locations, it is best to drive to their respective parking lots. Conkle's Hollow is the closest, being only 3 road miles from the Old Man's Cave Parking Lot with Cantwell Cliffs at 15 miles the furthest. Rock House at 7 miles is in between. All three areas have short loop hikes; the longest is just over 2 miles in length, so all three can be comfortably seen and hiked in a rather full single day. Since all three locations have picnic areas, you might want to pack along a lunch. If none of the walks are long, all but the short and lovely walk on the gorge bottom of Conkle's Hollow have many steps, which can make for a tiring day. Some may wish to spread them out over a two-day period. Parts of all three loop walks have high cliff areas, so caution is advised. None of these areas are dangerous if you stay on the official trails and the previously mentioned walk up the floor of Conkle;s Hollow is safe for everyone.

## LOCATION OF THE THREE AREAS

Along with the location road map on page 44 the following description should make them all easy to find since all are on or near State Route 374. From the Old Man's Cave parking lot, go west on 374, and in less than 2 miles 374 turns right away from 664 and goes downhill. If you wish to go to Conkle's Hollow first when you reach the bottom of the hill turn right on Big Pine Road. You will see the United Methodist Church on the corner. After you make the turn, just 1/10 mile will take you to the Conkle's Hollow Drive on the left and the parking lot. If you wish to go to Rock House don't turn right but stay on 374 until Route 678 comes in on the right and 374 curves to the left. After this left turn it is 1.7 miles to Rock House Drive on the right. From Rock House Drive to Cantwell Cliffs, continue north on 374 and in just over a mile it T's into Route 180. Follow both routes to the right for about 4.7 miles where 374 turns left away from 180. After this left turn, the Cantwell Cliffs Drive is just over 1½ miles on the right.

## CONKLE'S HOLLOW

Conkle's Hollow is a very deep narrow gorge about a half mile long enclosed by sandstone cliffs that rise vertically for over 200 feet, making them possibly the highest cliffs in the state. The top of the cliffs are the case hardened upper zone of the Black Hand Sandstone and at the head of the gorge the cliffs on each side are a mere 300 feet apart. There are a profusion of ferns and huge hemlocks that thrive on the restricted amount of sunlight that reaches the floor of the gorge. This hollow has been designated as a nature preserve to protect its unique growing habitat and walkers are required to stay on the official trails to protect the delicate growth of the surrounding area.

Its name comes from a carving found on a rock surface which is the first existing proof that white men had penetrated this hollow as early as the late Eighteenth Century. Chiseled on this surface and surrounded by a rectangular frame of stars are the names:

### W. J. CONKLE 1794
### A. O. COW 1898

Until recently I knew of no information of who W. J. Conkle was until one day, seeking information for the book I paid one of many visits to the State Park Office and was introduced to the assistant manager whose name happened to be Robert Conkle. He told me that he was a direct decendant of the person whose name was engraved in the stone and told the story of the family tradition that placed him here.

W. J. Conkle was one of three sons brought over from Germany by his father. The father sent the sons to three different areas to look over land interests they held. One son went to Pennsylvania, one to the Hocking Hills area where many of his descendants still live but it is unknown where the third son was sent.

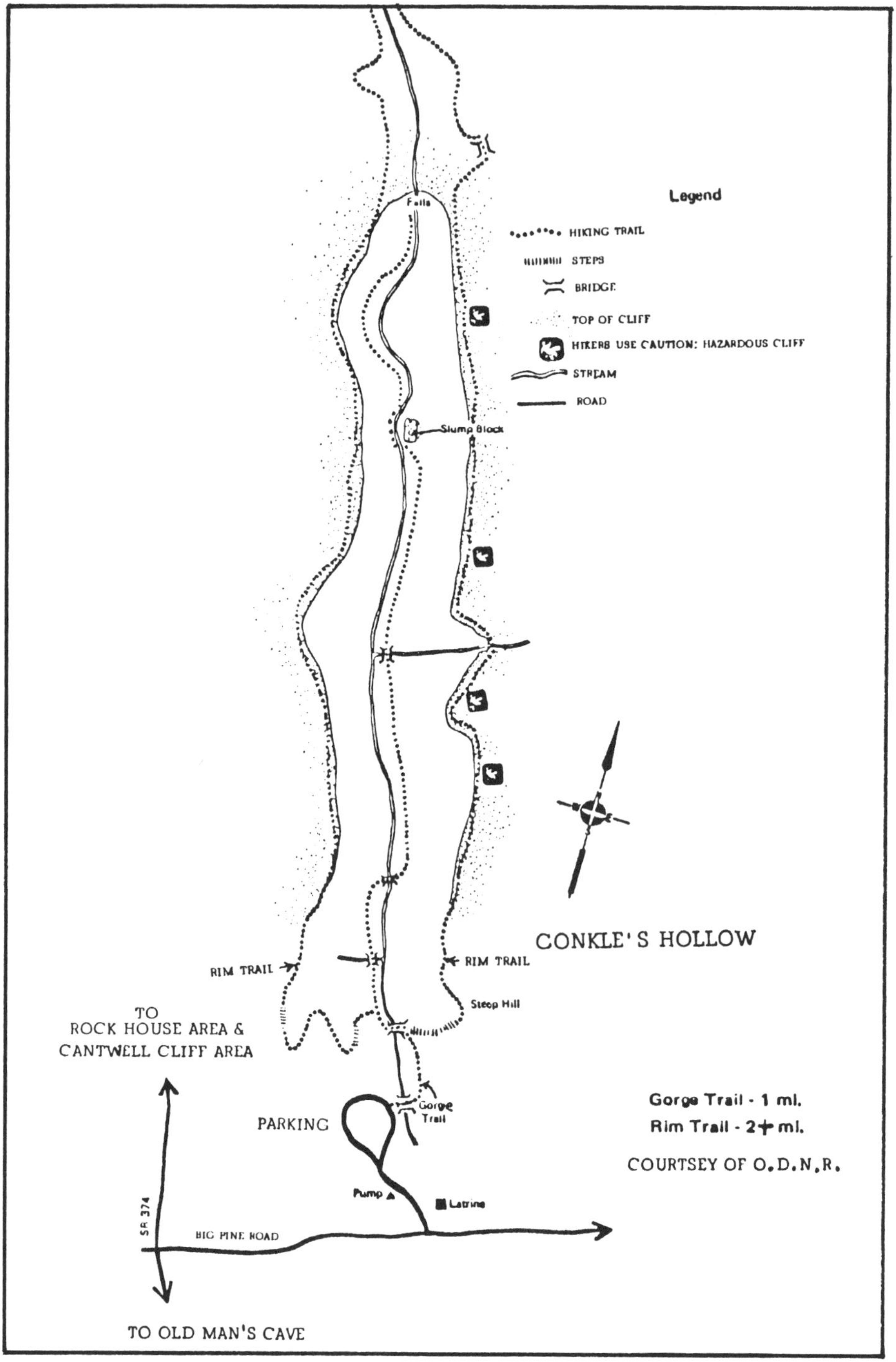

Legend
HIKING TRAIL
STEPS
BRIDGE
TOP OF CLIFF
HIKERS USE CAUTION: HAZARDOUS CLIFF
STREAM
ROAD
Falls
Slump Block
CONKLE'S HOLLOW
RIM TRAIL
RIM TRAIL
Steep Hill
TO
ROCK HOUSE AREA &
CANTWELL CLIFF AREA
PARKING
Gorge Trail
Gorge Trail - 1 mi.
Rim Trail - 2+ mi.
COURTSEY OF O.D.N.R.
Pump
Latrine
SR 374
BIG PINE ROAD
TO OLD MAN'S CAVE

*Rim view of Conkle's Hollow*

    The two walks to consider here are the easy gorge bottom walk of one half mile ending at the head of the gorge where an attractive cascade comes shooting through a rock chute before falling about 40 feet into the plunge pool. This complete trip is a very easy one mile walk where there is no fear for little ones wandering over an edge.
    The rim walk which is slightly over 2 miles in length is more demanding but far from being difficult. It is quite hazardous for the foolhardy and unsupervised young children.

TRAIL DESCRIPTIONS: By using the Conkle's Hollow map a trail description seems a bit redundant but I might offer some suggestions. The walk along the hollow bottom should not be missed. There are some excellent views of the hollow from the rim and most of them occur during the first part of the trip if you go up the East Rim side which I feel is the easiest, for you have just under 50 steps that carry you up a little less than half of the altitude gain you make. When you come to a sign on the right side of the trail facing you which says:

### DANGER KEEP ON TRAIL

you are on the top. After a couple of small bridge crossings you will come to a large sign facing the left side of the trail which should be taken very seriously. It says:

### DANGER
### PLEASE STAY ON TRAIL
### THIS WATERFALL PLUNGES 95 FEET TO THE HOLLOW FLOOR. HAZARDOUS FOOTING AND SLIPPERY ROCKS HAVE RESULTED IN SERIOUS INJURY AND DEATHS HERE. DON'T BECOME A STATISTIC

Shortly after this sign you will come to a small wooden bridge crossing that takes you over the creek that drops down into the hollow. A sign just across the bridge and facing the trail says:

◄─────── WEST RIM TRAIL
EAST RIM TRAIL ───────►

The West Rim Trail is not as open as the East Rim Trail, and the overlooks are fewer, but there are a couple of very nice ones shortly before the trail begins the descent to the hollow bottom.

Although the trails are usually well marked by signs, in case they are vandalized, here is a brief description of the trail locations.

After you cross the sturdy bridge which is to the right of the parking lot and the trail is heading into the hollow, the first trail to the right with visible steps is the East Rim Trail. By staying on the hollow floor you cross the first bridge, and the first turn off to the left is the West Rim Trail. Whatever trail you take from this point a compass is hardly necessary.

## ROCK HOUSE

GENERAL REMARKS: In this region of marvelous and contrasting scenery, Rock House is unique. You might imagine from its name that it is another big rock shelter similar to Old Man's or Ash Cave. But, it is more like a real cave with some unusual differences. Because of common geologic processes of the area occuring in an unusual fashion, the results have produced a very unusual cavern. The cave itself is approximately 200 feet long, and 20 to 30 feet wide carved in the side and part way up a vertical cliff of Black Hand sandstone near the head of its valley. The marvelous buff browns, warm grays and ochre reds coloring the cliff face are in themselves interesting enough for a visit, but you leave the world of color behind when you step into the interior of Rock House. There is an opening at each end of the cave but its most extraordinary feature is the outside wall of the cave. It has five large openings, giving the interior a peculiar, somewhat spooky, uneven lighting pattern. Since most of these openings are pointed at the top someone has referred to them as natural Gothic Arches after that monumental medieval style.

The entire cave is situated in the soft middle zone of the Black Hand Sandstone and is due to erosion along vertical joint fractures. Such weathering is quite common in hundreds of places in the Hocking Hills but a series of five parallel joint fractures lying almost perpendicular to another joint fracture running along the back of the cave and the cliff face causes this unusual cavern. After thousands of years of weathering these joint fractures that broke through the upper zone of the Black Hand Sandstone began a wider path of erosion when reaching the softer middle zone where wind and water carried away enough of the middle zone to form the cave and its five front openings. The openings at either end were caused by a combination of stream action and other joint fractures forcing back the cliff edge at each end.

When you walk into Rock House you will find the floor mostly dry which indicates that the erosion process within was carried out more by wind than water erosion. Because of this dry floor and rather spooky interior it is easy to imagine all kinds of nefarious activities being committed within. Indians undoubtedly used it and there are enough legends about horse thieves, bootleggers and others outside the law using the cave that it gained the name "Robbers Roost."

The site was so popular that a hotel with 16 guest rooms was built in 1835 on the present site of the picnic shelter house next to the parking lot. This hotel, which

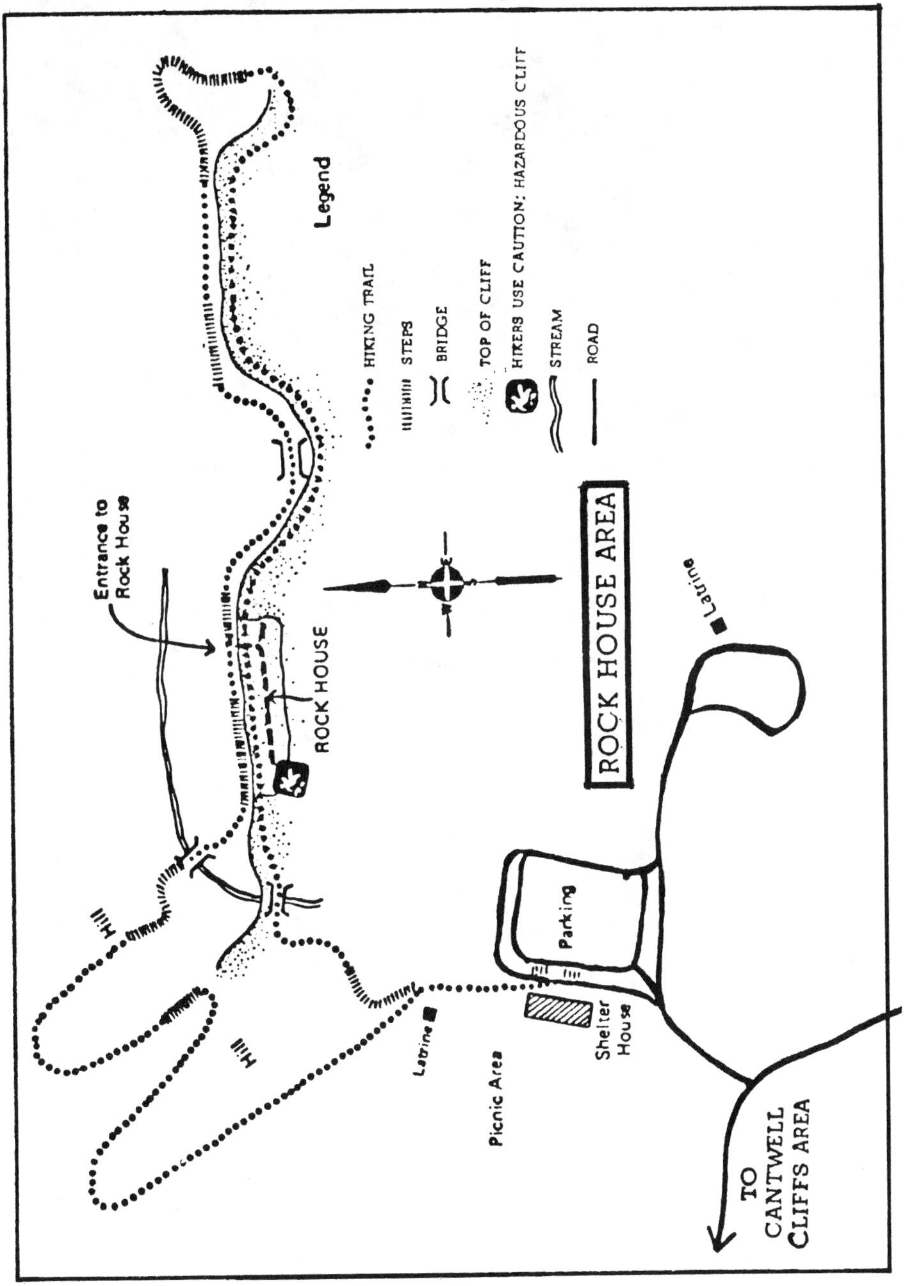
ROCK HOUSE AREA
Entrance to Rock House
ROCK HOUSE
Legend
HIKING TRAIL
STEPS
BRIDGE
TOP OF CLIFF
HIKERS USE CAUTION: HAZARDOUS CLIFF
STREAM
ROAD
Latrine
Parking
Shelter House
Latrine
Picnic Area
Hill
Hill
TO CANTWELL CLIFFS AREA

*Interior of Rock House*

operated until 1925, also had a ballroom so it operated as a successful small resort for the better part of a century.

The complete loop walk is just under ½ mile, and if approximately 200 steps up and down combined are not hazardous to your health, the walk should not prove overtaxing. Much of the trail is close to cliff edges, so keep an eye on the children.

TRAIL DESCRIPTION: To find the trailhead, look for the stone wall on one side of the parking lot. Take either side of the stairway going up the wall which puts you on the drive in front of the picnic shelter, the site of the old hotel. Turn right there and soon the trail angles left off the paved driveway and curves around with the latrine on the left and drinking fountain on the right. You will shortly pass a set of stone steps coming up from the right. A sign to the right there says:

## CAUTION STAY ON MAIN TRAIL

Do not take these steps but proceed straight ahead on the path. These stone steps will return you to this spot on the loop walk. The trail soon switches back to the right and **after a few feet switches back again to the left going down about 22 steps. Before making the turn look straight ahead into a small rock shelter. If rain has been** plentiful, there is a nice waterfall just the other side of the rock shelter, and you can get an excellent view of it from the shelter. But do it with extreme caution because beyond the edge of this rock shelter floor, there is a vertical drop of approximately 70 feet, and a fall here would probably kill you.

Proceeding down the 22 steps, you have a switchback to the right where you get a good view of the cliff that contains Rock House. You go down quite a few well worn steps, cross a bridge near the bottom of the waterfall and face a climb of over 50 steps up to the entrance of Rock House.

From here it is easier to follow the loop around than to return the way you came. When the loop returns you to the rim, there are two paths, one proceeding away from the rim and one that turns right following the rim. Take the one to the right for a few nice views into the gorge and in a short easy walk with a little over 20 steps at its end it joins the original trail just a few feet from the latrine. The trail that proceeds away from the rim once led to a fire tower but it has been torn down and without it there is little of scenic value to make the much longer walk back to your car worthwhile.

## CANTWELL CLIFFS

GENERAL REMARKS: Located some 15 miles from the Old Man's Cave Parking Lot, it is the farthest away of the six major sightseeing areas. Cantwell Cliffs shows many classic examples of joint fracturing in the Black Hand Sandstone and the resultant slump blocks with some that have broken away from the cliff and have slid partway down the hill. One that has moved only inches away from the wall that it was originally attached to, known as "Fat Woman's Sqeeze" is the most famous geologic landmark here. Its gap furnishes a sort of natural fun house walk slightly on the diagonal between the slump block and the cliff. The other outstanding feature is a very large rock shelter or recess cave at the head of the valley of Bush Creek. Not as big as Ash Cave but far bigger than Old Man's Cave, a small creek goes over its rim and drops nearly 100 feet to a plunge pool. This is not a very large stream so unless there has been heavy rain the falls is not much more than a trickle working its way down the back wall of the cave instead of over it. But even if there is no waterfall, the size of this recess cave makes a visit worthwhile. Another striking difference from the other two famous recess caves is its bottom. Since the floor slants rather steeply and a good deal of it is damp or wet from seeping ground water, it is not near as suitable as the others for human habitation. Again this is a high cliff area, so caution is advised. At least two of the loop walks require going up and down over 300 steps, so it is not a good area for those with physical handicaps that inhibit their walking.

TRAIL DESCRIPTION: There are two major loop walks in this area, and both of them have two variations which will be discussed at the junction point. From the parking lot walk past a well maintained log cabin on the left with a sign on it, which says:

## CARETAKERS CABIN

Once past it, walk to the turnaround at the end of the parking lot and follow the trail around to the left of the picnic shelter house and down 59 well maintained stone steps. At this point you can see a trail coming in from both the right and the left as well as one that goes straight down some more steps. The one to the right is the return loop along the rim. The narrow trail to the left, which is rock lined on its right side, has a sign to its right which says:

## DO NOT THROW
## STONES
## OVER CLIFF

If you do take this little trail, make sure no one does throw stones, for one of the major trails of this area is immediately below it. This very short trail of approximately 100 yards in length curves around the top rim of the large rock shelter and ends at the stream, which drops over the lip of the shelter for about 100 feet. If you take this short trail which gives you an excellent but scary view of the rock shelter below use extreme caution for the trail comes up smack to the edge with a sudden drop-off close to a hundred feet, making it an extremely hazardous stretch of trail. Utmost caution should be used with children and if heights make you wobbly it is a good trail to avoid.

The best part of this cliff area is mostly below the rim. To get there follow the trail that goes straight ahead at the junction below the 59 steps which takes you down approximately 70 steps more lowering you into a natural walled area. This is a wide joint fracture and as you walk down it you will soon come to a much smaller one on the right, which is "Fat Woman's Squeeze". Here is the place where you must decide which loop to take.

If you want to do the walk along the cliff base, you can walk through Fat Woman's Squeeze then turn left and walk until the large rock shelter is in view. After you have seen the shelter, turn back walking around the end of Fat Woman's Squeeze and follow the steps and trail along the base cliff. If you wish to take the shortest loop after you pass over two bridges there is a path to the right that takes you to the rim where you turn right. If you want a longer loop which will about double the length of your loop walk, keep following the cliff base trail. You will eventually curve around the bottom of the head of another gorge, cross another bridge and gradually swing around to the right reaching the steps which takes you back to the rim. As you walk back along the rim you pass a well maintained rest shelter complete with a fire place. Unfortunately it is often a place where the litter bums leave their offal. You pass over a well made stone bridge and eventually see the steps coming up from the right where the shorter loop joins the rim trail. Just after passing over a low wooden bridge, the trail forks in three directions. Any of the three will complete the loop back to the parking lot. The one on the far left takes you up past the latrine at the far end of the **parking lot. The middle one takes you up to the parking lot near the caretaker's cabin. The right one continues following the rim until it links up with the original trail at the bottom of the 59 steps.**

The other loop walk is one that takes you down to the gorge floor. After seeing and walking through the squeeze, turn left and walk to the large rock shelter and follow the trail around it which then takes you to the gorge floor and follows the creek. The trail crosses the creek by using a wooden bridge then shortly crosses a second wooden bridge going over one of the tributaries. Just across the bridge about where this trail T's into another, there is a sign facing you which reads:

◄─────── GORGE TRAIL ───────►
RIM TRAIL ↑

This sign is a bit confusing for the arrow pointing away from the L is meant to indicate the trail you have just walked, although it points in the direction of a ravine to the right. If you go up that ravine, it will take you to the rim trail, so if you want the shorter loop you turn right up the ravine until it hits the trail that follows the cliff bottom. When you hit this trail you can either go left for the longer ridge rim trip or right over the bridge until you hit the steps on the left that take you up for a shorter rim walk. Since both trails join, read the previous paragraph at the end of the first cliff trail loop option to see which way you wish to take back to the parking lot.

If you would like to take the continuing gorge trail turn left and in a few feet you will run into another sign facing you which says:

**GORGE TRAIL
.5 MI LOOP ENDS HERE**

Although the scenery is pleasant, there is nothing of a spectacular nature about it so

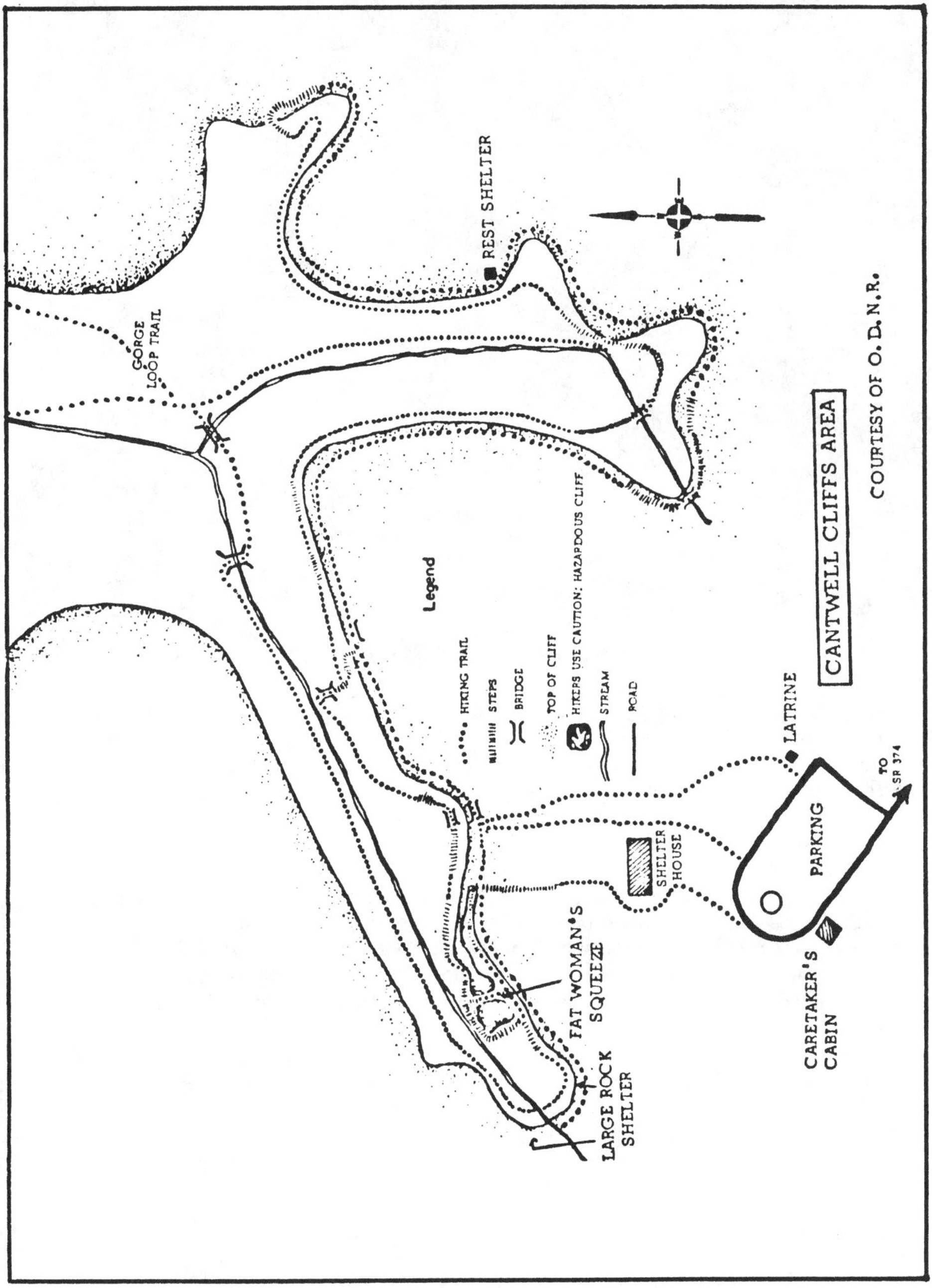
CANTWELL CLIFFS AREA
COURTESY OF O. D. N. R.
Legend
HIKING TRAIL
STEPS
BRIDGE
TOP OF CLIFF
HIKERS USE CAUTION: HAZARDOUS CLIFF
STREAM
ROAD
GORGE LOOP TRAIL
REST SHELTER
LATRINE
PARKING
TO SR 374
SHELTER HOUSE
CARETAKER'S CABIN
FAT WOMAN'S SQUEEZE
LARGE ROCK SHELTER

**Fat Woman's Squeeze at Cantwell Cliffs**

if you feel like stretching your legs a bit, do it. If, however, you are running short of time, you will have missed none of the more scenic parts of Cantwell Cliffs by omitting it. If you decide for the walk, it is generally easy but about ¼ mile longer than the half mile indicated by the sign. Start out passing the sign on the left and you will soon cross the creek, then you will cross another creek about the same size just before they join together. After the third creek crossing the trail curves to the right and T's into another trail. Turn right here to complete the loop, which will bring you back to the sign. I once took a left turn here to see where it went. This path, which is not offical, crosses into private ground and travels through light woodsy country that is **not of high interest. My intention of finding its destination was thwarted when I ran into some low areas with heavy ground water which I plodded through ankle deep.** Since it was December and cold, I gave up and turned back after covering somewhere between one and two miles from the junction.

Once you are back to the sign, follow the trail around to the left up the ravine and follow one of the previously mentioned walks to the rim top and parking lot.

# VESUVIUS RECREATION AREA
## INTRODUCTION AND AREA DEVELOPMENT

When the question arises from novice hikers who want to know where the best hiking trails in Ohio are for putting on some real walking distance with enough bite in the trails to lift them above the Sunday stroll but without feeling that the hikers are climbing the Eiger Wall, where the scenery offers an outstanding vista or two and gives the illusion of being further removed from civilization then they are and where crowds on trails almost unheard of I think of the backpack loops of Vesuvius. Or when an experienced hiker-backpacker wants to know of a trail where a walker can disappear into the back-country walking world for two or three days with climbs that do not lead to exhaustion but with the feeling of a rested gentle tiredness when the hike is over, once again I think of Vesuvius. Although the scenery is not as spectacular as Hocking Hills nor as challenging as Shawnee's demanding climbs, Vesuvius has enough of each in between these extremes with many variations for the day hiker. It also has 24 continuous backpacking miles rarely near a road offering the freedom almost without restrictions where one may camp for the night. The trails here are the most skillfully laid out in the state, for although there are elevation rises of over 400 feet, the climbs are so cleverly accomplished that sometimes the hiker is not aware of climbing at all. Just a few rises could be classified as moderately steep and only one on the Bluegrass Loop that remains steep for any real distance. There are three major trails beginning from this recreation area and they all are within the boundaries of the Wayne National Forest. This makes the Vesuvius Trail and the Wildcat Trail near Burr Oak State Park the only two trail areas in this book that are under the jurisdiction of the U.S. Forest Service. All the rest are managed by the Ohio Department of Natural Resources and lie within State Park and Forest lands.

The name of the recreation area and the development of the Wayne National Forest are, in themselves, unique. When I first heard of the Vesuvius Recreation Area I wondered how it happened to be named after that famous Italian volcano that buried Pompeii and Herculaneum over 1900 years ago. Even with my limited scientific knowledge I know that Ohio's geologic stratas are largely a result of sedimentary deposits and that a report of finding an Adena Culture Indian Village partially preserved under 60 feet of volcanic ash is virtually an impossibility. Since no volcanoes exist in the region, I thought perhaps a large group of Italian immigrants coming to Ironton to work in the once busy iron and steel furnaces might have formed an ethnic community and named it after that famous mountain of their homeland because the belching furnaces they worked in reminded them of it.

Here I was at least partially right, for although the communities have no significantly large population of Italians, there was a very active iron furnace which is still standing with the name Vesuvius Furnace. It sits close to the spillway of the dam that forms Vesuvius Lake and the bottom of that lake was once the location of a village with a population of about 300 where the iron workers and their families lived. This historic relic is a reminder of vivid local economic activity during the nineteenth century and at one time there were over 60 such furnaces in Ohio stretching from Hocking County in the north to the Ohio River and deep into Kentucky. While doing research for my first book, KENTUCKY'S LAND OF THE ARCHES, I found that this area is part of this same iron bearing region and the village of Clay City quite near Natural Bridge State Park was once known as Red River Furnace. The whole area on both sides of the state boundary are known as the Hanging Rock Iron District taking its name from that Ohio River town just downstream from Ironton. It was adopted by the nineteenth century ironmasters who shipped so many of their iron

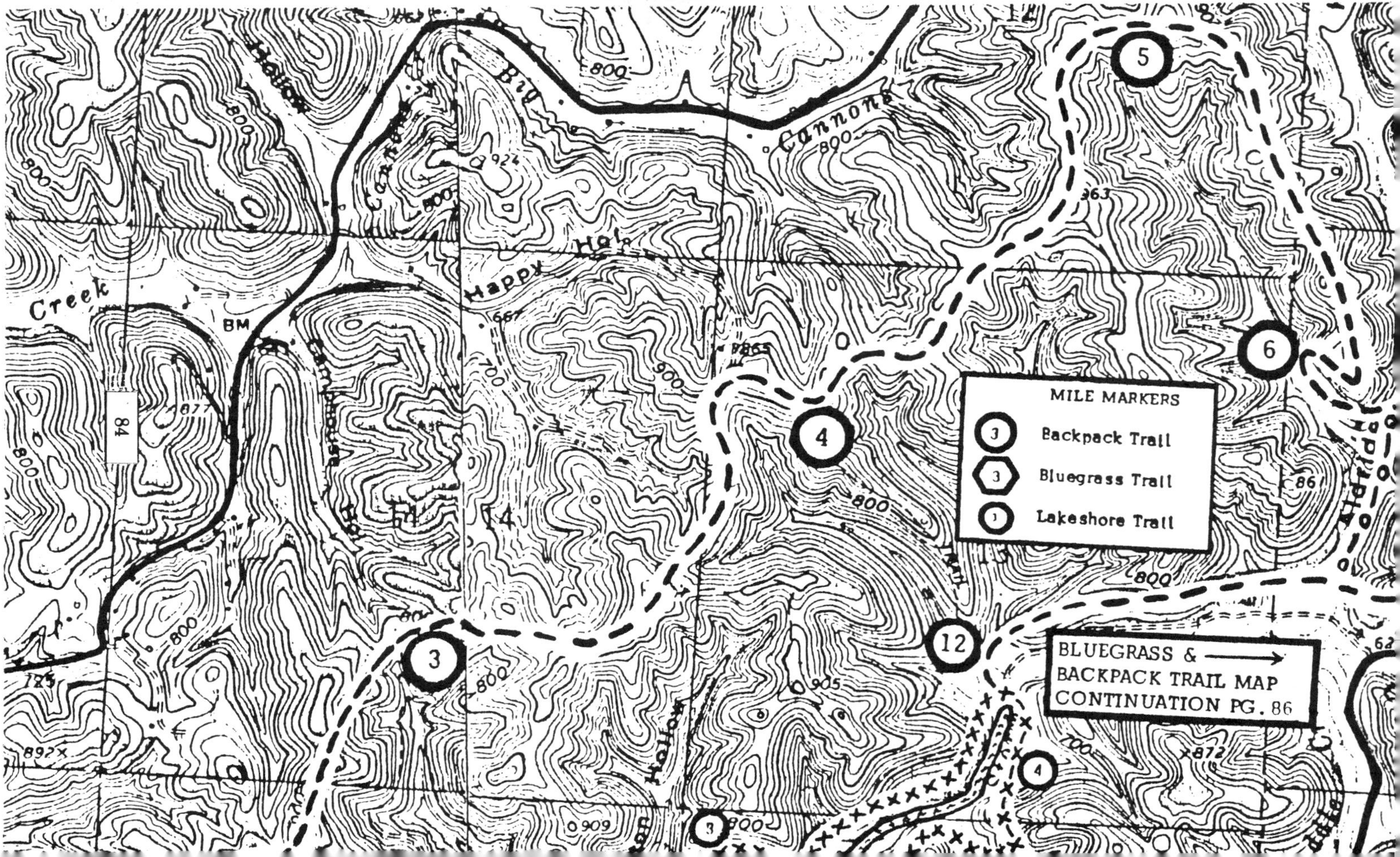
MILE MARKERS
Backpack Trail
Bluegrass Trail
Lakeshore Trail
BLUEGRASS &
BACKPACK TRAIL MAP
CONTINUATION PG. 86
Big Cannons
Happy Hol
Creek
Hollow
BM
5
6
4
12
3
800
900
700
963
924
905
872
909
892

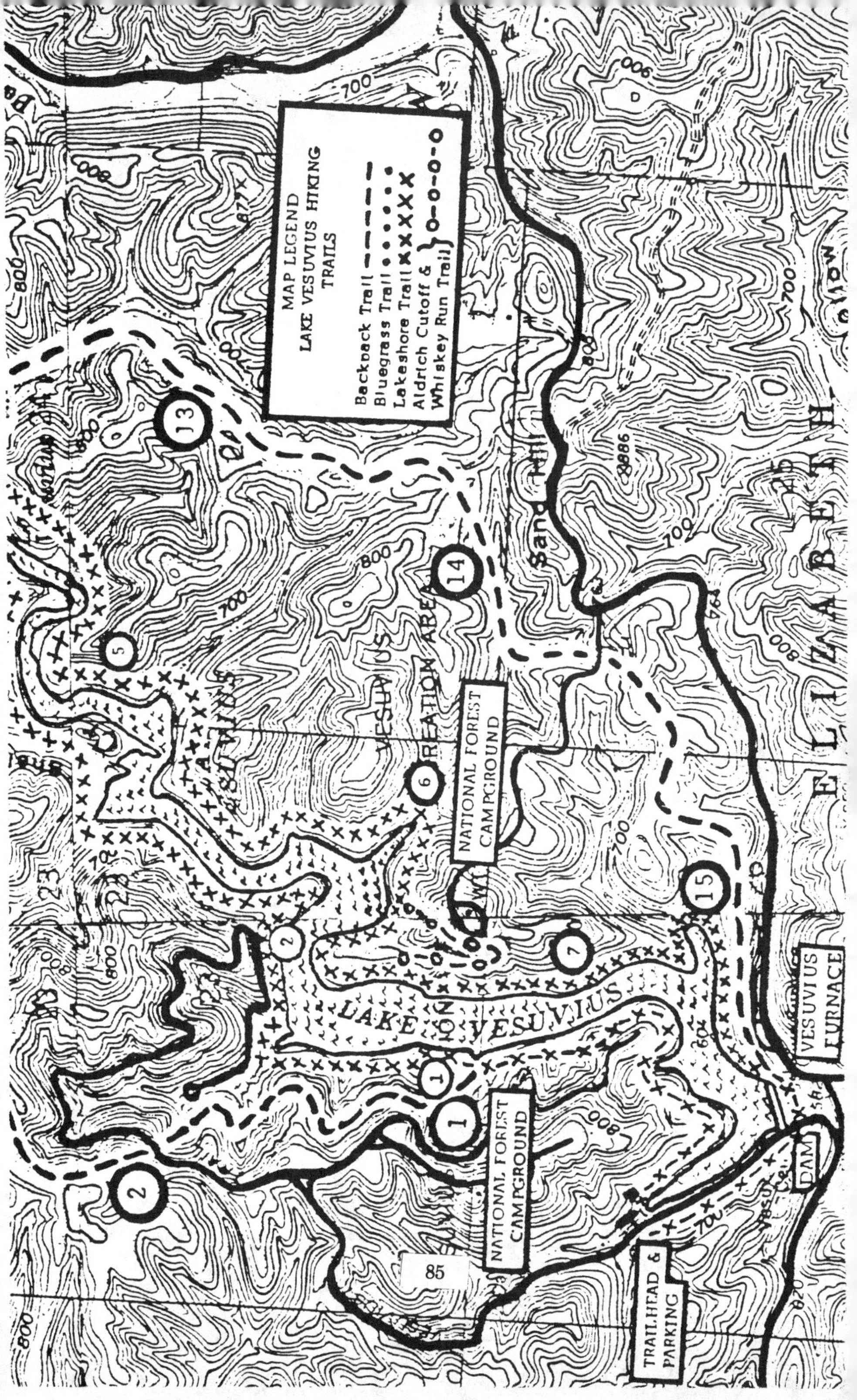
MAP LEGEND
LAKE VESUVIUS HIKING TRAILS
Backpack Trail
Bluegrass Trail
Lakeshore Trail
Aldrich Cutoff & Whiskey Run Trail
LAKE VESUVIUS
NATIONAL FOREST CAMPGROUND
NATIONAL FOREST CAMPGROUND
VESUVIUS RECREATION AREA
VESUVIUS FURNACE
TRAILHEAD & PARKING
DAM
Sand Hill
ELIZABETH

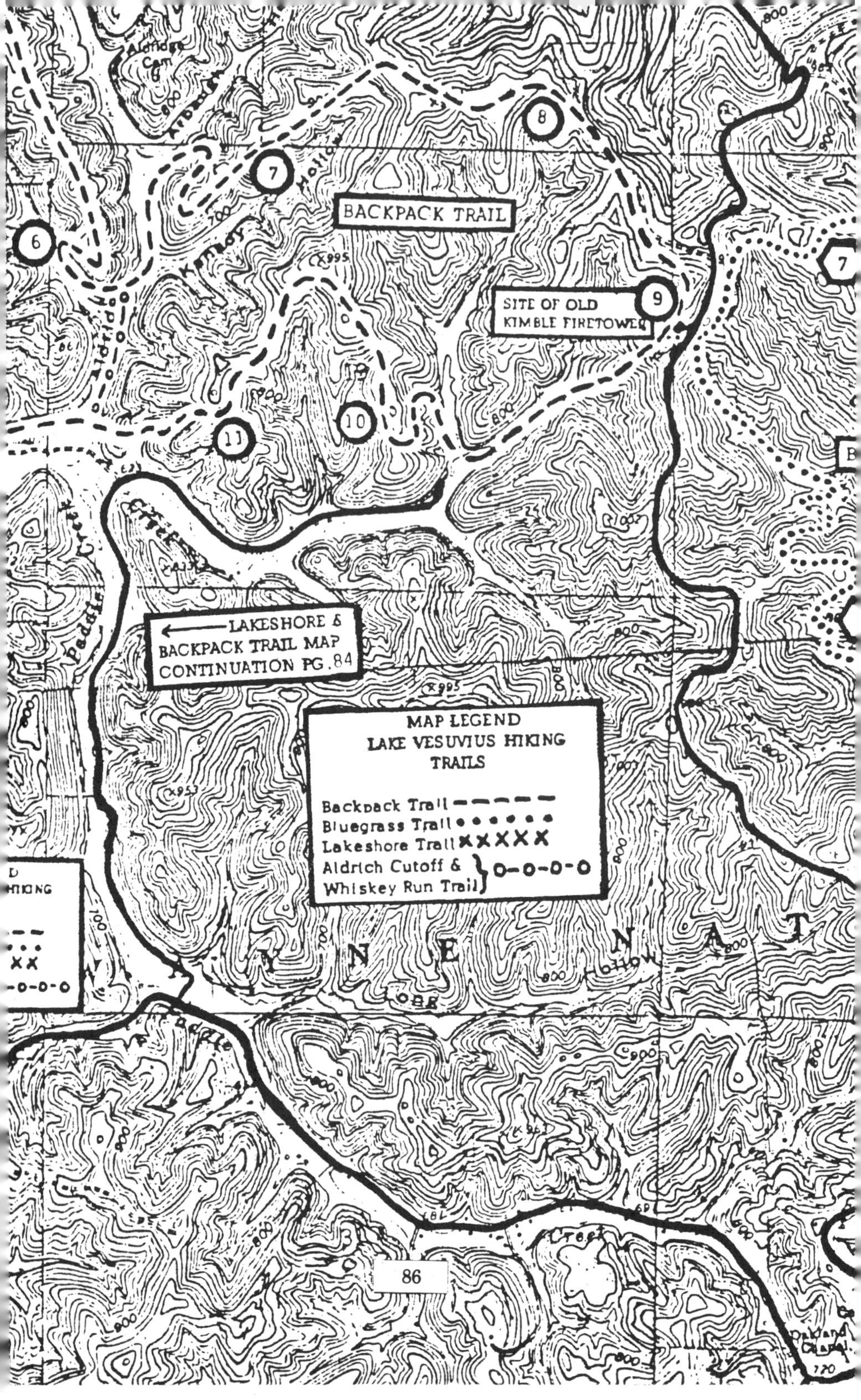

BACKPACK TRAIL
SITE OF OLD
KIMBLE FIRETOWER
LAKESHORE &
BACKPACK TRAIL MAP
CONTINUATION PG. 84
MAP LEGEND
LAKE VESUVIUS HIKING
TRAILS
Backpack Trail
Bluegrass Trail
Lakeshore Trail
Aldrich Cutoff &
Whiskey Run Trail

BLUEGRASS TRAIL

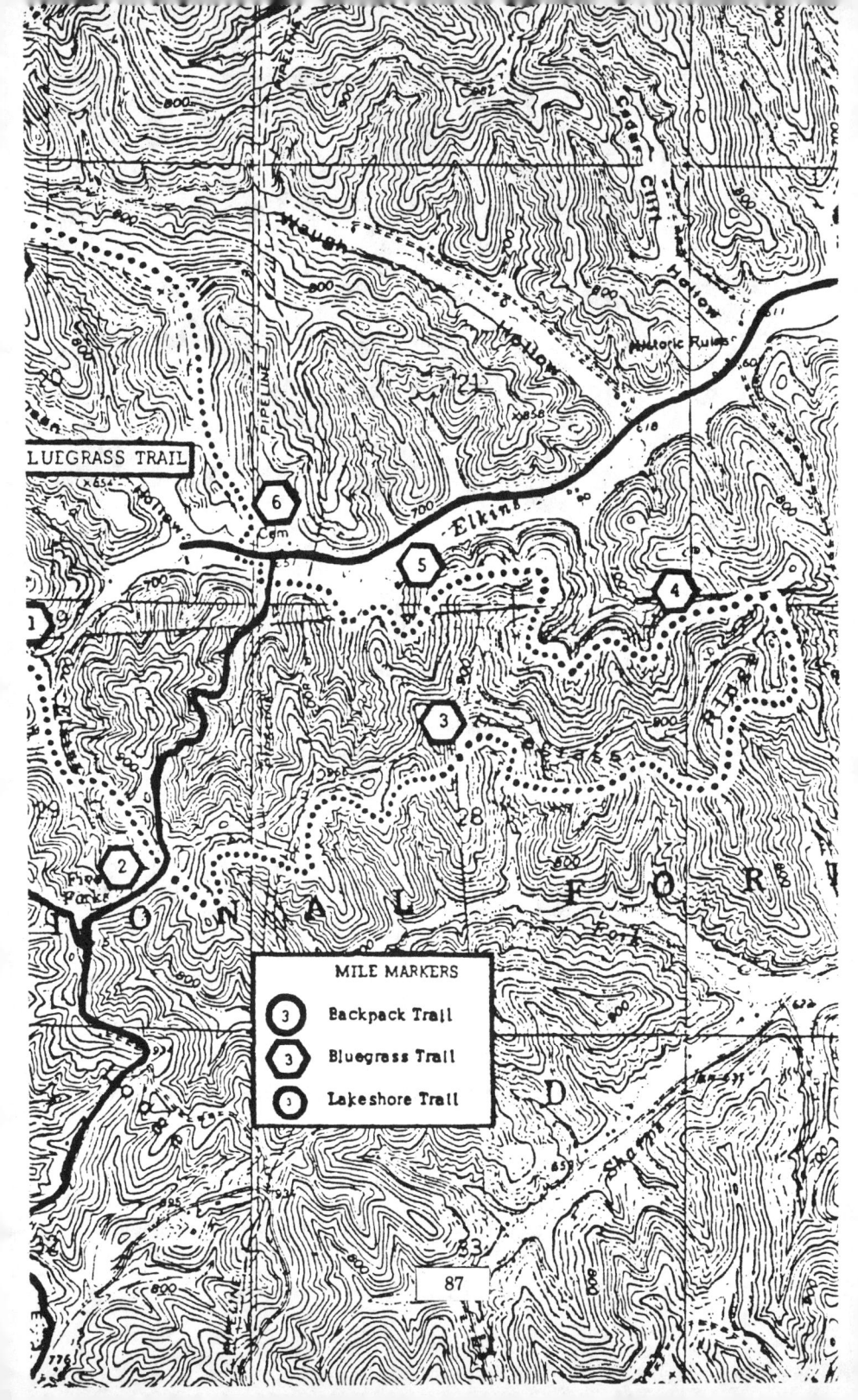

| MILE MARKERS | |
|---|---|
| ③ | Backpack Trail |
| ⬢ 3 | Bluegrass Trail |
| ○ 3 | Lakeshore Trail |

87

*Vesuvius Iron Furnance*

products from that once busy river port.

    The region had two necessary ingredients for the manufacture of pig iron of that time. Many of the beds of sandstone were rich in iron ore and there were thousands of acres of hardwood trees from which charcoal could be made to fire the furnaces. There are several antique furnaces still standing in Ohio and Kentucky including one that was also named after another well known Italian volcano, the still active Mt. Etna. Unlike the two Italian volcanos, these two ancient iron furnaces are just a few miles apart. Another one in Vinton County stands right at the trailhead of the Zaleski backpack loops. As the hardwood forests necessary for charcoal manufacturing gave out, techniques for using coal and coke developed and much of this Hanging Rock District contains coal deposits quite close to the surface that were easily reached by strip mining. But most of the coal extracted was not used by these old iron furnaces, for they had largely fallen into disuse partly because new techniques had obsoleted them and partly because the discovery of the huge iron deposits in the Mesabi range in northern Minnesota made mining of the lower grade iron ore in Ohio and Kentucky too expensive. The Vesuvius Furnace was able to operate longer than most of this type, for it started its fires as early as 1833. It managed to continue operations until 1906. The Ohio Historical Society has recently restored one of these types of furnaces called the Buckeye near Wellston Ohio.

    With the idea of restoring the denuded hardwood forest areas, the Ohio Legislature passed bills that allowed the Federal government to begin purchasing land for establishing national forest areas within the state. Although there was still not a national forest here until long after World War II, the development of the Vesuvius Recreation Area began shortly before that war. The Forest Service designed the present dam which was completed in 1939 by the Civilian Conservation Corps. Once built, the whole basin of Lake Vesuvius was filled in the incredibly short period of a single night during what was called a "gully washer" of a rain. In addition to the dam the CCC's also built the boat dock area, the old beach, the Oak Hill Campground, the **building that now houses both the Interpretive Center and the Lawrence County Historical Society Museum and a beautiful picnic shelter, the remains of which are** located near the end of the Backpack Loop. World War II brought demands for extracting coal from this region in the fastest way possible without regard for the land's future use. During that war over 250,000 acres were decimated by uncontrolled strip mining. In 1951 the Wayne National Forest was established and with the multiple use concept strip miners removed 4½ million tons of coal from the Hanging Rock region but restored the land to conditions where natural habitat could and did return. Various government programs in the 1950's through the 1970's saw further development in the recreation area which included the building of the Iron Ridge Campground, the new swimming beach area and the Backpack and Lakeside loop trails.

## HOW TO GET THERE

Since the Recreation area is just a few miles north of the river city of Ironton, those coming from the southern areas of the state will find that U.S. 52 is a convenient route to use. When the limited access of that highway passes to the north of Ironton, one should turn off on State Route 93 and head north away from Ironton. In a little over six miles on that route you will see a green sign indicating a right turn into the Vesuvius Area. Continue on for about 1/10 mile until you see a large yellow and brown wooden Forest Service sign that says:

## WAYNE NATIONAL FOREST
## RECREATION AREA
## LAKE VESUVIUS

Turn right onto a paved road and follow it to the junction of the recreation road just before the dam.

**Another easier way has recently developed for those living in the Cincinnati and Dayton areas.** From the eastern side of I-275 follow State Route 32 east which will eventually change to State Route 124. When that highway crosses State Route 93 turn right on 93 then follow the directions for coming from the Columbus area which are immediately below.

If you are coming south from the Columbus area on State Route 93, after crossing the railroad tracks at the south end of the small hamlet of Pedro in less than 2 miles you will come to an Ohio State Rest Area on the right side of the highway. Just beyond it, on the left, you will see the large yellow and brown forest sign mentioned in the paragraph above. Turn left in front of the sign on a paved road.

## WHERE TO STAY

There are two campgrounds within the Vesuvius Recreation Area, the Oak Hill campground and the newer Iron Ridge Campground. Both campgrounds are maintained by the U.S. Forest Service and follow federal regulations for such campgrounds. Each site in the campgrounds is pleasantly situated with a black top parking strip, fire grate, and picnic table with both running water and pit toilets nearby. Oak Hill also offers a limited number of flush toilets and cold water showers. Although Iron Ridge does not have these last two mentioned facilities, it is my favorite of the two for the campsites are in a prettier setting and are more secluded.

There are no electrical hook ups at either campground but the maintenance of each campground is of the highest order. Iron Ridge Campground is open the year around while Oak Hill is usually open from May through September. A camping fee is charged during the seasonable months. The campgrounds are on opposite sides of the lake but neither is in sight of it. Iron Ridge does have a short trail (Whiskey Run) connecting it with the Lakeshore Trail.

There are no cabins, lodges or motels in the immediate vicinity; the closest location for such facilities is found in Ironton.

## THE VESUVIUS LOOPS AND THEIR VARIATIONS

**TOPOGRAPHIC MAPS:** Pedro, Ironton, Sherrts and Kitts Hill quadrangles.

**TRAIL BLAZES.** None but backpacker signs with arrows and mile markers indicate turns on the trail.

The loop trails and their backpack variations ........................ see below
Day Hikes .............................................................. 91
Finding the trailheads for the Backpack and Lakeside Loops ................. 91
Finding the former site of the Kimble Fire Tower ............................ 92
Vesuvius Backpack Loop Trail Section 1 from the
trailhead to the Adlrich Hollow cut off ....................................... 93
Section 2 from Adrich Hollow to the Kimble Fire Tower site .................... 95
Section 3 from the Bluegrass-Backpack Trail junction site to the
headwaters of Lake Vesuvius ................................................ 97
Section 4 from the Backpack-Lakeside Trail junction at the
headwaters of Lake Vesuvius to the Boat Dock Parking Lot ................... 99
Aldrich Hollow Cut Off ..................................................... 102
Bluegrass Trail ............................................................ 102
Lakeshore Trail ........................................................... 108
MAPS .................................................................. 84-86

## THE LOOP TRAILS AND THEIR BACKPACK VARIATIONS

The Backpack Loop Trail of 16 miles, the Lakeside Trail of 8 miles, and the Bluegrass Trail also of 8 miles offer many excellent possibilities for both the backpacker and the long day trail hiker. At this writing these trails are not blazed but are marked with mile posts and occasional direction signs at junctions. Both the backpack loop and the Lakeside Trail are well marked and defined so losing the trail is not a serious problem. Not so for the Bluegrass loop. It simply isn't walked enough to be well defined. There have been discussions about changing its status from a hiking only to an all purpose trail that would open it to horses and off road vehicles, which because of its narrowness, means motorcycles. This, to me, would seem tragic, for not only does this trail have one of the most beautiful overlooks of any trail in this book, but its marvelous isolation in deep forests is also one to be treasured by the hiker which the presence of dirt bikes would surely destroy. I am in hopes that the publication of this book will make more hikers aware of its existance and an increased number of walkers will save its present designation.

Another drawback for the backpacker is there is no supply of drinking water on any of the trails. If you are planning a longer hike, there is the possibility of caching water at the old Kimble Fire Tower site before the hike for use on either or both the Backpack and Bluegrass loops. See page 92 for road directions to the site.

There are several possibilities for backpacking trips of different lengths. The first would be to do the 16 mile backpack loop itself. A longer version would be a 24 mile double trip of the Backpack and Bluegrass trail since the two trails junction near the Kimble Fire Tower site. A shorter version would be to start out on the Backpack loop taking the Aldrich Cutoff over to the return section of the loop making a loop trip of about 12 miles. A third and easy backpack trip would be to use the Lakeside Trail to the end of the lake, follow the backpack loop from the junction at the end of the lake in the opposite direction until you find a nice place to camp, returning to and finishing the Lakeside Trail the second day.

## DAY HIKES

Both the Lakeside and the Bluegrass Trails make good single day hikes of 8 miles each. The Backpack Loop can be divided into two day hikes if you have someone who can drive you to or pick you up at the Kimble Fire Tower site. The hiking distance from the trailhead to the Kimble site is 9 miles leaving 7 miles for the return.

I have divided the trail description of the Backpack loop into four separate sections to aid in their location for those wishing to use them in the various possibilities for both day and overnight walks. This should not confuse the hikers who are doing the entire loop, for the sections are presented in linking sequence.

## FINDING THE TRAILHEADS FOR THE
## BACKPACK AND LAKESIDE LOOPS

When you turn into the county road that goes east from Route 93, you will travel just under a mile on this paved road before you come to an intersection with a paved road coming from the left where a sign post between the two roads contains many small distance signs. Turn left on this paved road. Once you make the turn you are no longer on a country road but on one maintained by the federal government. Proceed about a half mile after making the left turn. With the lake on your right you will soon see a little harbor and boat dock area. Turn right into the parking lot immediately behind the harbor. From the parking lot walk toward the water and pass the front of the concesson stand on the left. About 30 feet beyond the concession stand, there is a wooden map of the backpack trail and beside it you can see the trailhead for both the Backpack and Lakeside Trails. Just to the right of the trail a sign facing you says:

## LAKESIDE TRAIL ↑
## BACKPACK TRAIL ↑

If you are planning to backpack for a night or two the Forest Service people suggest a different parking place for your vehicle. Although it is quite legal to leave it in the boat dock parking, your car will be safer, if, after unloading your gear, you drive back to the intersection of the Forest Service Road and the county road that you followed from Route 93. Turn left on the county road and immediately you will see a brown house on the right with a driveway to the left of the house where a sign says **PRIVATE DRIVE**. Turn into the drive passing another house on the left into the garage maintenance site for the recreation area where most of the buildings are on the right. Park on the left side off the road and far enough away from the buildings to give the Forest Service trucks and other equipment easy access to their garages and workshops. It's an easy walk back to the trailhead. This also aids you when you complete a loop for once at the dam hikers can avoid the less interesting road walk past the dam and spend the time examining the Old Vesuvius Furnace while the driver walks the short distance to the vehicle. Those only hiking for the day should leave their cars at the boat dock parking lot.

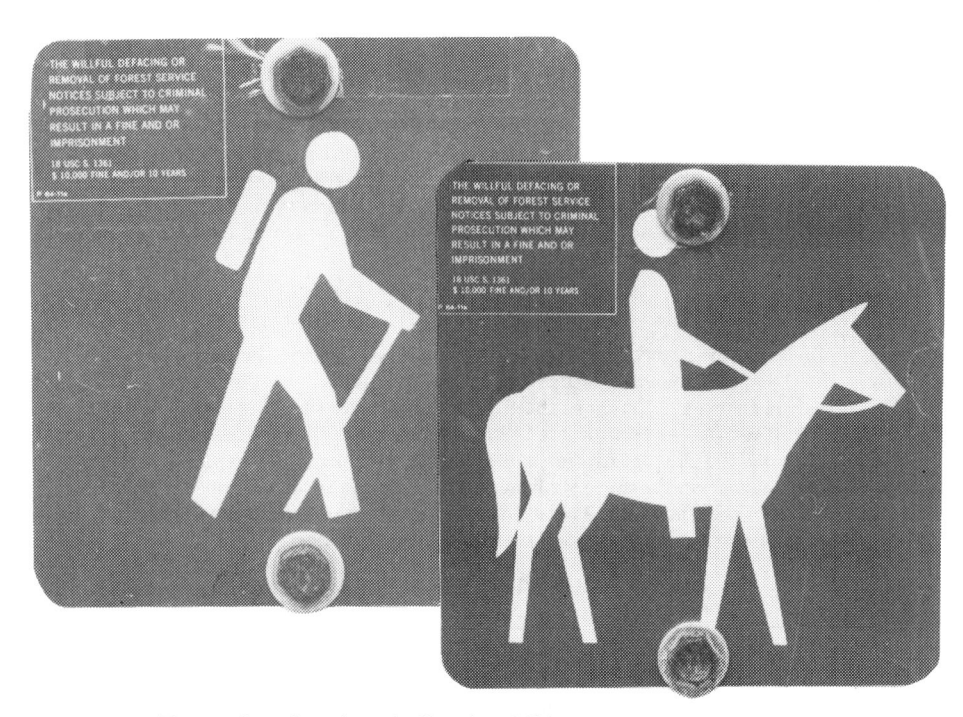

*Forest Service signs indicating hiking trails or bridle paths.*

## FINDING THE FORMER SITE OF THE KIMBLE FIRE TOWER

Since the Backpack and Blue Ridge loops junction near this point the access to the **trails is in a favored location to cache water or supplies for a longer trek or to park a** vehicle for a day loop walk on the Bluegrass Trail. It is not the safest place to leave an automobile overnight, for there have been incidents of severe vandalism here. One of the reasons for tearing the tower down was the almost constant attacks and partial destruction of the tower by these unruly humans. Day walkers and middle of the week hikers have less to fear for most of the mischief seems to occur on weekend nights.

To find this location stay on the rough paved county road that you followed from Route 93 passing the old iron furnace on your right. From the furnace it is just under 10 miles to the tower site. Follow the road uphill and you will pass the Iron Ridge Campground entrance on your left about 1.8 miles from the furnace. In a little under 3½ miles beyond the Iron Ridge Campground entrance the county road T's into another narrow paved road. On the right, at this intersection, there is a wooden house and in front of it close to the road there is a smaller building which once was a combination market and gas station. Turn left at this intersection and proceed up the hill. When the road reaches the top of the ridge, it soon turns to gravel and makes a left turn into the forest with a refuse dump on the left side. The first gravel (not dirt) road to the left, a distance of about 1½ miles from the left turn at the road T, is the turn off to the Kimble Fire Tower site. This is a narrow but well maintained gravel road suitable for normal highway vehicles and in almost exactly 2 miles you can see a cleared area on the left with a small gravel road heading toward a level rise about 50 yards from the road. The rise is the site of the tower and just to the right before the rise there is a small parking area. To find the junction of the Backpack and Bluegrass trails walk up the rise until you can see the old foundation blocks. Turn left and you will see a path taking you into the woods. Follow it and in a few feet you will arrive at the junction.

## VESUVIUS BACKPACK LOOP TRAIL

As was mentioned earlier I have divided this loop into four separate sections. The entire 16 mile loop is a moderate to strenuous single overnighter.

### VESUVIUS BACKPACK LOOP. SECTION ONE.

**From the trailhead to the Aldrich Hollow cutoff.**
Distance: 4 to 6¼ miles
Hike: Moderate to strenuous.
Walking time: 2½ to 3 hours.

**GENERAL REMARKS:** Starting from the trailhead the first half mile of this trail is possibly the most scenic lakeside walk in this book. Once the Backpack Trail splits from the lakeside walk it has the most taxing climb in the entire loop with an altitude gain of about 300 feet in just over a mile up to the ridge top. Then the walking becomes easy again with one marvelous overlook before a very easy descent into Aldrich Hollow.

**TRAIL DESCRIPTION:** The trail ascends briefly and easily into a forest of man planted pines and follows around the end of a small peninsula where the dam is readily visible across the lake. Once around the point there are excellent views of the lake with a large bare sandstone boulder quite visible on the opposite shore. Those who are walking the lakeshore loop or take the option of switching from the Backpack to the Lakeside Trail for the return segment of the longer Backpack Loop will walk directly behind that stone edifice near the end of the hike.

As the trail gradually descends down to the lakeshore, where there are several metal posts sticking out of the lake near the shore, one can see a couple of old narrow dirt roads to the left that junction near the lake. This is the site of the old bathing beach built by the C.C.C. over 40 years ago. It is no longer in use, but if you look up the lake a little more than a half a mile away, you can see the new beach area with the bath house facing you.

If it's a hot day and you feel like a quick dip resist the temptation here or any other section of the lake except the present recognized beach area for if you are caught you will get a free trip to Portsmouth where a federal Judge will relieve you of $30 plus costs. From the old swimming beach follow the trail that continues right along the lakeshore.

You will soon pass a brown wooden building on your right which until 1980 was the pump house for the park water supply. From there you can look out in the lake and see a cement structure with metal climbing rings on its side which once served as the intake for this now unused water system. From the building the trail angles away from the the lakeshore, and, for a short distance joins an old road which soon crosses a small wash. About 100 feet beyond the usually dry small stream is the point where the Backpack and Lakeside Trails part. The Backpack trail forks left and goes rather steeply uphill while the lakeshore trail proceeds straight ahead. A sign between them says:

⟵ LAKESHORE TRAIL ↑
⟵ BACKPACK TRAIL

This is an easy turnoff to miss if the sign is missing and due to the close proximity to roads it has been destroyed or defaced by vandals a couple of times in the past. If you should get to mile marker 1 and you are still along the lakeshore you have missed the turnoff for the Backpack loop. Retrace your steps a few feet and look to your right to find the beginning of the first real uphill section of the Backpack Trail. For those who are following the Lakeside Trail see page 108.

After parting company with the Lakeshore Trail the Backpack Trail has a short, moderately steep section with mile marker 1 on the right side. The trail then turns directly away from the lake and climbs at an easier rate toward the ridge. But before reaching the crest the trail turns right and parallels the ridge top. There is now about a half mile of fairly level walking crossing a few small washes and cutting left around the head of a side ravine. When the trail cuts left a second time into another side ravine there is a steady climb up to the paved park bathing beach road with one short steep section of about 10 feet part way up. The trail goes directly across this road where a backpacker's sign indicates a right turn. This puts you on an old trace road which quickly rises above the paved road and parallels it briefly. As you gain the ridge top, which is just a short distance from the park road, you will pass mile marker 2 on the left side of the trail.

If you feel slightly winded at this point, you can console yourself with the fact that the next 4 miles of this trail is easy ridgetop walking and you are now about 300 feet in elevation above the lake. You will stay on this trace road for almost 2 miles. It has a few less visible old roads that occasionally join it but signs and heavy growth of underbrush on these other roads makes it easy to stay on the trail.

The first junction with another well used trail occurs at a horse trail crossing. A sign to the right facing you at this point says: **BACKPACK TRAIL** indicating that you continue straight ahead on the ridgetop.

Just beyond a point where the ridgetop deteriorates and the trail curves slightly to the right followed by a gentle uphill section, you will find mile marker 3 on the right side of the trail.

The trail passes its first open section since leaving the lake which is only on the trails' left side going uphill from it. If you temporarily leave the trail and walk up about 40 feet you will find a small pond above and out of site of the trail. This is the first of three such ponds that you will encounter. At first I thought that these ponds might indicate former locations of old homesteads since they are all obviously man made but I found these ponds are recent additons made by the Forest Service to furnish the wildlife with a reliable water supply. Beyond this open section another trace road V's in from the left joining the one you are on. Just beyond this junction the road begins a definate descent down the ridge where the trail no longer follows the trace road but turns off to the left and parallels the ridge top which is slightly above and to the left of the trail. A couple of times the trail comes up to the ridge top and you can see that there is another trace road on the ridge top. Although the trail parallels this road for more than a quarter of a mile, it does not join it until the trail cuts sharply left and crosses it. Just before going over the ridge top and the trace road crossing you should find mile marker 4 on the right. After crossing the F.W.D. type road there is a backpackers sign indicating a left turn. For a short distance the trail parallels the road on the opposite side and in the opposite direction you have been walking but soon begins a gradual swing to the right away from it.

You will again cross another F.W.D. road and if you look right as you cross it, you will see the second of the three ponds below you. Not long after this crossing you should arrive at mile marker 5 on the left side of the trail. Shortly after passing the mile marker you will be able to see ahead of you a backpacker's sign indicating a right turn. When you get up to the sign you will see that the trail has turned right on another logging road. Almost immediately the road takes you into the first open area on both sides of the trail. It crosses a large clear cut tract that opens an excellent panoramic view of Shelton Hollow below you. Rapid growth of underbrush is beginning to restrict the view but it should be visible for a few more years especially if you climb up on some old logs that give you a little elevation above the foilage.

After the road and trail cross this area and go back into the woods they will cross two more smaller clear cut tracts with the third small pond to the right of the trail just as you cross the last of these three clear cut areas.

The road becomes less evident as the trail continues along the ridge top until the ridge itself begins to deteriorate. The trail then drops left off the ridge top, then swings right doing a U-turn as it curves over the top of the ridge and begins to angle down the opposite side of the ridge in the opposite direction from the ridge top walk. As you angle easily down you will soon pass mile marker 6 on the right side of the trail. Shortly beyond the mile marker there is a short log fence that parallels the trail on the left and just beyond this fence the trail switches back to the left. The fence was obviously put there by the Forest Service but I couldn't figure out why this little isolated fence should be there. Tom Eaches of the Forest Service told me that years ago this was part of a horse trail and the fence prevented the horses from making an abrupt left turn short cut before the switchback causing serious erosion problems. Horseback riding is no longer allowed on this trail and the fence will, with time, eventually rot away.

The trail continues to angle gently down hill into Aldrich Hollow and just before reaching the small stream at the bottom of this flat and pleasant hollow there is a backpack sign that indicates a left turn. Just a few feet beyond this turn the trail crosses the creek. If you elect to do the shorter loop using the Aldrich Cutoff described on page 91, you will notice at the left turn sign that you can look right and see a distinctive trail following the creek downstream. This is the Aldrich cutoff trail. (For trail description see page 102.)

## VESUVIUS BACKPACK LOOP. SECTION 2

### From Aldrich Hollow to the Kimble Fire Tower site.
Distance: 2 ¾ miles
Hike: Easy to Moderate
Walking time: 1½ to 2 hours.

GENERAL REMARKS: The only slightly difficult part of this section is walking out of the hollow back up to the ridge top, an altitude gain of about 250 feet, but the trail is so beautifully engineered that even with a pack on, it never is either steep or strenuous and if you are traveling light, during much of the gain, you will hardly be aware of going up at all. As you reach the ridgetop you will cross some large open grass fields which offer delightful changes of scenery.

TRAIL DESCRIPTION: After crossing the creek at the bottom of Aldrich Hollow the trail bears left in an attractive wooded section of the hollow soon crossing a tributary of the main creek. You can see from the opening between the trees that at one time this was an old road. You soon see a backpacker's sign which indicates a right turn although the trail proceeds straight ahead. When approaching the sign you will understand its original purpose for there is another distinct old rut road that veers off to the left but the rapid growth of foilage on this left road makes the right fork the obvious choice. Just beyond this point the trail and road begin a gentle climb. You will notice a steep trail coming down from the ridge joining the official trail from the right. Walk beyond it and you will soon see that the side trail is a short cut, for the main trail switches back right just before arriving at a gully and continues to climb at a slightly steeper grade. You will soon find the trail makes a rounding curve-like switchback left as it continues its moderate rise uphill and soon reaches the crest of a ridge finger with mile marker 7 on the right side of the trail. At this marker you have climbed about 200 feet above Aldrich Hollow in a little over a half mile showing an excellent bit of trail engineering which not only minimizes the exertion of the hiker but also avoids any serious problems of erosion. There are some uphill sections beyond the mile marker as the ridge gently descends. As the trail tops out on the ridge you will see a backpacker's sign which indicates a right turn just in front of an F.W.D. dirt road that runs along the ridge top. You turn right on the road and it soon takes you across the first large open field then returns to the woods. The road again hits another open meadow that contains grass in contrast to the weed covered first one. As the road climbs to a high point in the middle of the field that is just under 1000 feet you get a marvelous panoramic view of the surrounding countryside in several directions. While in this area it is worthwhile especially on a beautiful fall day to leave the road and walk left to a point at the edge of the field for a view of the valley below. I missed this marvelous section the first time I walked this trail for the old official trail used to cut right leaving the road just before it entered the field then swept left around the lower edge of the field. All markers have been removed from the old route including the mile marker 8 sign that was on it. The last two times I walked this section there was no mile marker 8 on the road that crosses the middle of the field or the old trail that goes around it. When I asked Tom Eaches which way was now the official trail he said that no decision had been made for the official right of way. He told me that the field was leased to a local farmer. I asked him if that prevented hikers from crossing the field on the road. He said no, that the dirt road was a right of way and anyone could use it. If the official trail is again routed around the field I would opt for the road not because it is the shorter way, which it is, but for the exceptional panorama that is offered by, in effect, taking the high road. The new and old way join as the road leaves the field and soon approaches a saddle in the ridge where trail and road go rather steeply down the saddle then climb up again at a moderately steep grade. Right at the bottom of the saddle, on the left side of the road facing you, is a sign that says: **BACKPACK TRAIL**. It is at this point that a horsetrail comes up to the road and crosses it. For some reason this sign seems to be a target for local vandals for it has been torn down several times in the last couple of years.

Once out of the saddle, the road swings right where another lesser used F.W.D. road joins it from the left. Then the dirt road turns into a gravel road although it is still not a road designed to accomodate vehicles other than the F.W.D. type. Look for a backpack sign on the left side of the road that indicates a right turn off the road into the woods on a true footpath. Once the turn off the road is made the trail descends slightly then levels off. When the trail begins a moderately steep uphill section with a single switchback, you pass mile marker 9 almost immediately to the right of the trail before coming into the clearing at the old Kimble Fire Tower site. The former tower was on the high ground to your right. You will see a small dirt road coming from the left leading up to this high ground. With this road on your left walk up to the rise where you will see the four cement foundation posts that at one time supported the legs of the old tower. Walk just to the right of the two foundation posts on the left and just beyond the far left one you will see a path that goes back into the woods in a rather straight line that is usually mowed to make a wide and easily seen trail through a weed patch and into the trees. In about a hundred feet you will come to the Backpack-Bluegrass Trail junction where a sign on the right of the trail facing you reads:

◄─── **BLUEGRASS TRAIL**  ↑
    **BACKPACK TRAIL**  |

It is easy to miss the turn off from the F.W.D. road into the path that leads you to the tower site. You can stay on this F.W.D. road which soon takes you back into the woods. In less than 1/10 mile the F.W.D. road runs into an improved all vehicle gravel road. Turn right on this road and in less than a quarter mile you will see the rise for the old fire tower and the short road that leads to it on the right.

If the sign is down at the Bluegrass, Backpack trail junction, a left turn off the main trail just about 100 feet beyond the fire tower puts you on the Bluegrass loop while proceeding straight ahead keeps you on the Backpack loop. If you are opting for a long backpack trip that includes the Bluegrass loop you turn left at this point and will return to the Backpack loop at this same place. Remember that most of this loop is on or near ridge tops so make sure you are carrying an adequate supply of water. The trail description for the Bluegrass loop begins on page 102.

## VESUVIUS BACKPACK LOOP. SECTION THREE.

**From the Bluegrass-Backpack Trail junction near the Kimble Fire Tower to the headwaters of Lake Vesuvius.**
Distance: 4 miles
Hike: Moderate
Walking time: 2 to 2½ hours.

GENERAL REMARKS: From the Bluegrass junction the Backpack loop drops into the head waters of Storm's Creek which is the main stream flowing into Lake Vesuvius. After climbing out of this valley, it goes up and follows segments of a ridge top before again dropping into Storm's Creek Hollow following it to the lake. It's a pleasant segment with a bit of up and down with an unusual natural chapel - like grove of pines just off the trail.

TRAIL DESCRIPTION: From the junction the trail begins a long downhill stretch taking you down into Storm's Creek. Most of the downhill section is at an easy grade but there are two steep portions which go directly down the ridge in contrast to the usual easy switchbacking. At this writing the trail soon passes through a section of many dead trees killed off by the severe winters of 1977 and 78. The last steep section which has now become a runoff gully takes you into the hollow bottom which has a combination of small open areas and groups of small trees, many of them pine. The water runoff is less efficient here so you may find parts of the trail rather mucky if the recent weather has been wet. The original trail cuts left into a beautiful copse of young pines but the trail has now eliminated this left cutoff and soon joins an old timber road. There is a horse trail that comes in from the right and turns right at this point while the Backpack Trail turns left and, for a very short distance, follows a small dirt road alongside a tiny wash. In just a few feet, a backpacker sign indicates a right turn over the creek. There is a little wooden footbridge there that at this writing was in a state of disrepair but the crossing is so simple the bridge really isn't necessary. But before making the right turn look left and notice a trail going into a copse of small pines. Follow it back a few feet and it will take you into a beautiful stand of man planted pines with an aisle straight through the middle of the trees where the original trail ran.

If the tall larch grove in Ohio's oldest tree plantation on the Zaleski trail qualifies as a natural cathedral (see page 132) this quiet little area of the Vesuvius trail can rightly be called the chapel.

When you return to the official trail, the little stream you cross over is the diminutive Storm's Creek which will rapidly grow in size as it flows towards Lake Vesuvius and when you cross the same stream at the end of this segment you will see that it has enlarged considerably. If you miss the turn over the creek the dirt road

***Camping in the Vesuvius Chapel of Pines***

soon joins the end of a larger road where there is a picnic area with pit toilets to the left.

Once across the creek the trail begins a moderate, and occasionally moderately steep climb as it angles up the ridge. After a gradual curving switchback to the left the trail continues angling up the ridge in the opposite direction, then swings right again placing you on a lower section of the spine of an inclining ridge. You will soon pass mile marker 10 placed on the left side of the trail. There are several minor up and down sections on the ridge top as the trail very gradually and almost unnoticeably swings to the left, and before you start down into the hollow, mile marker 11 is on the right side of the trail.

You will pass a solitary sandstone boulder which is about eight foot long just to the right of the trail. After swinging right around this rock the trail starts a moderately steep angling descent into the head of Aldrich Hollow. The trail has a curving switchback to the left and continues angling down the ridge until it is almost to the bottom of the hollow where a backpackers sign to the left of the trail indicates a switchback turn to the right. When you reach this point you can see that there once was a distinct trail proceeding straight ahead but it has now fallen into disuse making the right turn more obvious.

You soon are on the bottom of the hollow where the trail crosses a small wash and comes to a junction point with a sign on the left side of the trail facing you which says: **BACKPACK TRAIL** ↑ . As you proceed past the sign you can see a horse trail coming from the right which turns and joins the trail you are on. This is the only time that the Backpack and Horse Trails are briefly one and the same on this loop. The trail soon drops down and crosses the main stream in Aldrich Hollow then cuts right briefly paralleling the stream before angling left and crossing an old road. Just before the road there is a double sign which reads:

HORSE TRAIL ↑<br>
BACKPACKER TRAIL ↑

indicating that both trails do not turn on the road but cross it. This is the point where the Aldrich Cutoff Trail comes down the road from the right and rejoins the main backpack loop. The trail proceeds into a vine thick copse of pines many of them dead or dying and is now on the right side of the main hollow formed by Storm's Creek and its tributaries. It follows along the right side sometimes in the hollow bottom and other times a little ways up the ridge for about ¾ miles. The two trails hit a F.W.D. road which goes off to the right and a sign facing you on the left side of the trail says:

BACKPACK TRAIL ↑<br>
HORSE TRAIL ⟶

indicating the trails split at this point with the horse trail turning right into a dirt road while the Backpack Trail crosses it. Almost immediately after crossing the road the trail curves to the left and heads straight toward Storm's Creek. About 50 feet beyond the curve you will pass mile marker 12 to the right of the trail. In just a few more feet as the trail comes out of the trees, it crosses a well defined F.W.D. type dirt road. To the left facing you there is a sign that says:

BACKPACK TRAIL ↑

indicating that the Backpack Trail crosses the dirt road and immediately crosses Storm's Creek just before that stream enters Lake Vesuvius. On the same post that holds the Backpack sign there is another sign that faces the road on the right which says:

LAKESHORE TRAIL ⟶

This is the junction of the Lakeshore and Backpack Trail and the two run together for about a half mile.

VESUVIUS BACKPACK LOOP   SECTION FOUR

**From the Backpack-Lakeside trail junction at the headwaters of Lake Vesuvius to the Boat Dock Parking Lot at the Trailhead.**
Distance: 4 miles
Hike: Strenuous
Walking time: 2 to 2½ hours.

GENERAL REMARKS: When the Backpack and Lakeshore trail split, you have the option of finishing your hike on either trail since they again join at the lake dam and are one and the same from there to the trailhead. The Lakesore Trail is far more scenic and only slightly longer at this junction than the Backpack Trail. Most of the attractive parts of the Backpack Trail are behind you; therefore many hikers opt for the Lakeshore Trail for this section is indeed one of the most attractive sections of the trail in this book and it also has less climbing than the Backpack Trail. But if solitude is your thing, you will find that there is far more human activity along the lake during the summer months while the Backpack Trail traverses far more isolated country. At this junction you have a half mile to cover before you come to the point of decision.
TRAIL DESCRIPTION: When you cross Storm's Creek you can see that it is now a far bigger stream than the first time you crossed it near or on the little wooden bridge two miles back. Normally it is still an easy stream crossing but with heavy rains it

might require some real wading if it is crossable at all.

After crossing the creek the trail turns right into an open weedy area and briefly follows alongside Storm's Creek on your right. The trail soon takes you back into the forest and to a fork in the trail. The left fork goes up another side hollow but a backpacker's sign and some dead tree trunks across the left fork indicate that the right fork is the continuation of the official trail which skirts along the edge of the forest. As the trail again takes you out of the forest, mile marker 4 for the Lakeside Trail is on your left. You can occasionally see that Storm's Creek on your right has become the upper narrow section of Lake Vesuvius.

The trail then angles left away from the river-like lake and back into the woods where the trail soon parallels a small wash on the right side then comes to a sign post facing you on the left which reads:

LAKESHORE TRAIL →<br>
BACKPACK TRAIL ↑

The Lakeshore Trail turns right and crosses the wash while the Backpack continues straight ahead up the hollow. If you decide to follow the Lakeshore Trail, see page 110 for the trail description.

In just a couple minutes of walking up this hollow bottom the Backpack Trail cuts right, crosses the wash and begins climbing in earnest. Just after the crossing, as you start up the finger of a ridge, you can look left and right and see washes on both sides of you. The trail swings right and then left as it angles partway up the ridge in a moderately steep climb. It then angles around the head of a small hollow on the left as it hangs on the side of the ridge before making a short abrupt climb to the ridge top.

After gaining the ridge top it tops out on a knoll where it makes a sudden left turn off this high point. In just about a minute's walk after the knoll you pass mile marker 13 on the ridge top to the right of the trail. Shortly beyond you will pass a large wooden sign to the left of the trail which is beginning to look a little weatherbeaten. It says:

> TIMBER HARVEST AREA. THIS REGENERATION CUTTING WILL PRODUCE ANOTHER CROP OF OHIO'S FINE HARDWOOD TREES AT THE SAME TIME PROVIDING A VARIETY OF WILDLIFE HABITAT FOR DEER, TURKEY, OTHER SMALL GAME AND SONG BIRDS.

This is a nice way of saying you are about to enter an area that has been clear cut for timber. There are arguments both for and against clear cutting but the hiker must remember that these State and National Forests were originally set aside as tree plantations and these areas are now used in the multiple use concept which gives the hiker many more miles of trail in or near forests.

When you walk into the cleared area the trail makes a left turn indicated by a backpacker's sign. This leads you into a rather straight corridor about 10 feet wide and about a half a mile long which crosses the recently cut area.

It has quickly regenerated into very thick underbrush on each side of the trail with some new trees already 20 to 30 feet high. The thickness of the underbrush shows that it is an excellent habitat for rabbits and birds and makes one glad that the Forest Service keeps this path cleared for it otherwise would be a tangled horror to get through.

After you cross the area the trail V's into the horse trail. A sign that says: **BACKPACK TRAIL→** indicates that you turn right joining the horse trail for a short distance as it skirts along the perimeter of the clear cut area on your right. In less than five minutes of walking a sign to the right of the trail says:

**BACKPACK TRAIL ⟶**
**HORSE TRAIL ↑**

indicating the Backpack Trail turns right leaving the horse trail. If this sign should be down, you will note that the horse trail curves left and returns to the woods. If you reach that point you are just beyond the cutoff point. Retrace your path a few feet back and you should see the Backpack Trail branching off to thé left.

After making the turn the trail goes through an area where selective timbering has been done. Since more sunlight gets through here the weeds are noticeably higher.

The trail then begins a gentle descent on an old trace road which follows the declining finger of a ridge back into heavy forest.

At the bottom the trail crosses a wash and parallels it along the hollow bottom soon passing mile marker 14 on the right between the trail and the wash. Just beyond the mile marker a small wash on the left joins the wash you have been following. At that **point the trail goes down to the creek bottom and follows it downstream for about 15 feet. Then it abruptly cuts left and leaves the stream bed. The trail swings left and** begins angling uphill and almost starts down to the little wash that had come in from the left. At that point the trail switches back to the right soon curving left again and after a couple of easy climbs it hits and crosses a paved road. This road is the Iron Ridge Campground road and you can look right and see the camp bulletin board and the first campsite just beyond it.

After crossing the paved road a backpacker's sign indicates a left turn and the trail parallels the road for a short distance. There is a short easy climb which puts the trail on an old trace road. As it reaches the top another old road comes in from the left. A backpacker's sign indicates you continue right staying on the trace road you have been following. From this point you follow this old trace road which stays on the crest of the ridge going gently downhill almost all the way to the dam. You will pass a large **cement tank on your right which was once part of the Recreation Area's Water System. After passing this block you can look down to the right and get occasional** glimpses of Lake Vesuvius through the trees below you. Mile marker 15 is not far beyond the cement tank on the right side of the trail.

As the ridge narrows the trail passes to the left of two beautiful stone fireplaces complete with chimneys and a flagstone floor between them. The workmanship is of high quality and was originally built during the late 30's as a shelterhouse by the C.C.C. It is quite close to the county road making it easily accessible to vandals who often tore down parts of the building to burn in the fireplaces. It was rebuilt several times but its destruction would begin almost immediately after the job was finished so the Forest Service people tore it down because of the expensive rebuilding costs. The floor and fireplaces remain as mute testimony of the ruthless destruction of public property by the thoughtless mob. You can see a path here that goes down to the **paved road on the left but the official trail stays on the ridge top soon passing some cement floors and walls still containing some pipes on the left. These were once the** comfort stations of the shelter house. There soon is a fork in the trail. By following the right fork you will soon encounter and go down three sets of wooden steps of eight, eleven and three steps each. There are a lot of little trails running in a number of directions but the general idea is to bear to the right leading you to seventeen more **wooden steps that take you down alongside the dam spillway and rejoin the Lakeshore Trail again. Turn left walking next to the dam spillway until a set of 52** cement steps takes you down to the level of the Vesuvius Iron Furnace which is clearly visible across the road. The trail follows alongside a chainlink fence that lines the creek and about 100 feet from the spillway there is a backpacker's sign that indicates a right turn and crosses the creek. Although this crossing is usually easy I encountered it in flood one day after heavy rain when it would have been a real swim in fast moving water. Just a little further downstream is a road bridge that eliminates fording the creek if you happen to hit the creek during flooding.

After the crossing the trail follows the tree line angling up the side of the grass covered dam until it hits the paved road. Turn right on the road and follow it back to the harbor and the trailhead.

## ALDRICH HOLLOW CUTOFF

For general remarks of this cutoff see page 91. To get to the cutoff follow the first section of the Backpack Trail to Aldrich Hollow.

Distance: 4/10 mile.
Hike: Very easy.
Time: 10 minutes

TRAIL DESCRIPTION: When you approach the backpack sign that indicates a left turn on the Backpack Trail which leads to a crossing of the wash in the bottom of Aldrich Hollow, you don't turn left but proceed straight ahead on an easily seen and followed trail that runs parallel to the wash. It is an easy level walk that goes right down the flat hollow with the branch always on your left. The only problem is finding the junction point where you rejoin the Backpack loop. After you cross an open grassy area and enter a grove of small pine trees, keep looking left until you see a horseback trail sign with an arrow pointing up facing the trail you are on. At this point the Backpack and horse trail are running together and cross the trail you are on from left to right. Turn right here and you are back on the Backpack Trail.

If you miss the turnoff the trail soon leads you to a small cement auto bridge. You can either back track to look for the turnoff or you can turn right on the F.W.D. road and follow it about 3/4 of a mile almost to the headwaters of the lake where the Backpack Trail crosses it and the creek. For continuing trail description of the Backpack loop, see page 99.

## BLUEGRASS TRAIL

Distance: 8 miles
Hike: Moderate to strenuous.
Walking time: 4 to 5 hours.

**GENERAL REMARKS:** Although this trail is the only one that comes close to houses on the Vesuvius loops most of it is in such isolated areas that if you want to get away from the madding crowd this trail will lead you into splendid isolation. The number of hikers are so few that in certain areas during the rapid growing seasons some parts of the trail seem more of an idea than a fact. On my first time around, there were stretches where I was not sure if I was on the trail or not and I just plain lost it more than once. This trip made me feel that it would be to great advantage if the trail was blazed. I've since changed my mind for most of the trail is visible enough and with this guide plus a little bit of the old Daniel Boone common sense dead reckoning it adds a little spice to the adventure. As I mentioned earlier because of the comparative low number of hikers the Forest Service is considering changing its designation to an all purpose trail opening it up to horses and off road motor vehicles. So help us save the tranquility of this trail from the roar of trail bikes by hiking it and tell your friends to hike it for the Forest Service doesn't want to change the designation any more than most of us would want it changed. We can keep it by simply using it. Starting from the Kimble Fire Tower site it makes for a good day loop, an easy overnighter or a longer backpack walk by linking it with the Backpack loop.

One drawback is since most of the trail is high there is no safe supply of drinking water and places where water is occasionally found in wet seasons should be considered unsafe unless treated.

This hike has a good variety of scenic changes, first going down and then up and out of a hollow followed by almost 3½ miles of fairly easy walking skirting out one side of the Bluegrass Ridge curving around its end and then bending back again on its other side. **There is a marvelous panoramic view at the end of the ridge close to the halfway point of the trail which is just about tops on my list of favorites.**

You will find that the trail is not at all hard to follow for the first four miles but once around the ridge there are some tryingly vague areas. Once on the return side of the ridge if you did completely loose the trail all you would have to do is walk right down the ridge until you hit the gravel road, turn left and follow the road until there is a bridge crossing Elkins Creek where you again can pick up the scent. There is a pretty stiff climb from Elkins Creek, but it is engineered well so the elevation rise is a gradual one. Camping is allowed anywhere along this trail except the short distance that it follows a public road in the vicinity of the Elkins Creek Crossing. If you happen to have the very good Forest Service map of the Vesuvius trails a rare and not serious error is the 10 mile length they list for the trail when it is only 8.

TRAIL DESCRIPTION:   To find this trailhead by road see page 92. At the junction of the Bluegrass-Backpack Trails the Bluegrass Trail turns left off the Backpack Trail about 100 feet from the Kimble Lookout tower and crosses an all weather gravel road. Just before the road there is a mile marker 8 on the left indicating that this is the end as well as the beginning of this trail and if you complete the loop you will have walked a complete 8 miles. About 30 feet beyond the road crossing you come to the loop junction with a sign facing which says:   **BLUEGRASS HIKING TRAIL. HORSES AND MOTORCYCLES FORBIDDEN.** You turn right at this point to begin the actual loop with the return trail coming in from the left. Look left to see how grown up it is. If the underbrush is pretty thick, you might want to consider an alternate return discussed later in this description. After turning right the trail starts gently down a declining ridge with a hollow developing on the left. Upon reaching the hollow bottom, the trail crosses a wash then turns right and follows alongside the wash in the hollow bottom for almost a half mile. A backpacker sign facing you indicates sharp right turn recrossing the stream where the wash makes a decided curve to the left. After crossing the branch the trail moves directly away from the stream before curving gradually to the right as it passes a side ravine on the left and begins angling moderately up the ridge. A backpacker's sign indicates a switchback to the left as the trail continues angling up then gradually swings right around the hub of a ridge and crosses over a ravine near its head. Again the trail curves gently right, passes mile marker 1 and starts easily down again toward the bottom of a hollow turning left on a declining ridge finger. Just before running into another wash below the path the trail again turns left and angles down to the branch crosses it and follows alongside it downstream taking you down to the bottom of another hollow where the wash eventually empties into another stream which is the headwaters of Elkins Creek. Here the trail turns right and follows Elkins Creek upstream in a narrowing hollow. When it crosses the stream (usually dry) the trail continues upstream for about only 40 feet before it cuts left and begins angling up the ridge. Gradually the trail swings right as it climbs going around a couple of ridge humps and around a couple of small ravines until the trail climbs to the ridge top paralleling a road to the left. Just before the trail climbs to the ridge top and crosses this narrow all weather gravel road mile marker 2 is to the right of the trail. The trail is now on the top of Bluegrass Ridge and will follow this ridge usually just below its crest to its end a distance of almost two miles. It then swings left cutting over the top of the ridge and returns just below its crest. This means you have about three miles of trail that is on or near the ridge top.

When reaching the road you can look left and see an F.W.D.type road leaves the improved road about 20 feet up from the road-trail junction. The trail does not go to that road but continues directly across the gravel road and, in about 100 yards distance, crosses the F.W.D. road, with a backpackers sign to the right of the trail indicating you do not turn right on the F.W.D. road. After crossing this road you may come to a sign which says:

## HIKING TRAIL HORSES AND MOTOR VEHICLES PROHIBITED

On my first walk on this trail I decided to have a snack here, sitting myself down on a handy log. I rested my pack against the sign and to my amazement the sign fell over. As far as I can recall except for some callous teen-age days of my youth which are best forgotten, this is the only time that I was responsible for vandalizing a sign. But my guilt was eased a bit for time and nature had done a real rotting job on the post. When I rewalked this trail the sign was still there propped up against a tree just as I had left it a year and a half before. At this point the trail turns left and begins skirting along just below the ridgetop which is to the left. It crosses a narrow cleared area which once was a timber road but is so grown up today that no vehicles could use it. It is not long before the trail reaches another wide open section which is about 50 feet across but runs lengthwise out of sight. The trail goes directly across this open section until it junctions with a horse trail which follows along the edge of the cleared section. The trail turns left on the horse trail and follows it uphill along the perimeter of the forest for about two hundred yards. After topping one little rise, you will see another higher rise beyond it. You climb about half way up this second rise and on the right hand side of the trail there is a sign facing you which says:

## HORSE TRAIL ↑

When you get up to the post you will find another sign on the same post facing the trail which says:

## HIKING TRAIL ↑

indicating a right turn for the hiking trail which immediately leaves the horse trail and returns to the forest.

As you continue, with the ridge top on your left, the trail comes quite close to the ridge top where it dips in a saddle and not far beyond, mile marker 3 is on the right side of the trail. After passing the mile marker, the trail climbs with a gentle grade up and over a side ridge finger where it hits another old logging road, turns left on this road for about 10 feet then turns right going back into the trees.

For the second time the trail comes quite close to the ridge top where there is an old logging road, but the trail does not reach either for just as it looks as if it will continue up to the road it runs into a downed tree which looks like it has fallen across the trail blocking your way to the top. But right in front of the tree the trail switches back to the right and begins angling down the ridge. It doesn't go down far before it hits a steep embankment of a wash below the trail and switches back to the left putting you back in the original direction. After passing two rock outcroppings which may be hard to see during the spring and summer months, the trail starts a long easy climb up to the ridge top where it curves left and soon hits the logging road on the top of the ridge. At this writing there is a dead fall across the road and the trail follows the dead fall across the road back into the forest. This is the eastern end of Bluegrass Ridge and from this point the trail swings back and returns on the other side of the ridge. But before proceeding on the trail, turn right on the old logging road which, in a few feet, brings you into a large open field, once a central point for some extensive logging operations. From this point you have a wide panoramic view of ridges and valleys in at least three directions, and, if the weather and seasons are favoring you, you have one of the grandest hunks of scenery that the trails in this book can lead you to.

When returning to the trail, if the dead fall across the road would be removed, you will be able to find the returning sections of the trail by locating some cattails in a little swampy area of the open section quite close to the woods. From the cattails moving away from the open area, you walk about 35 feet on the old logging road and you should see where the trail leaves the road on the right. The trail climbs easily and crosses over a ridge finger with an old logging road on top of it. After crossing the road there is a backpacker's sign which indicates a left turn where the trail starts angling part way down the ridge and soon passes mile marker 4 on the right.

As you come to a small open area, the trail looks as if it might proceed straight ahead, but it takes a right turn returning to the trees heading downhill. It gradually swings left holding onto the ridge about the same altitude taking you through an area of groups of small trees, many of which are pines. Because there are gaps between the groups and the trees are not yet very tall, much sunlight reaches the ground often making the grass grow quite high which sometimes makes the trail quite hard to follow. After going through the copses of small trees, you will come to a second grassy area with the trail skirting along its left edge before again returning to the trees. It soon enters another grassy area about 30 feet across completely surrounded by small pines. On my first walk it seemed that the trail just died in this little opening and after a half hour's search I still wasn't sure where the trail continued. I eventually followed what seemed to be the most logical place that the trail would go. It turned out that I was right, but I wasn't sure of it for almost a quarter of a mile because the trail was so faint. If the trail is still not distinct here walk directly to the opposite end of the grassy area turn left and proceed uphill. There is a beautiful stand of pines on your right as you walk almost up to a huge dead fall where the trail goes right into the pine forest.

There is one more grassy area to cross before the trail returns to a mature forest and for the next mile it is easy to follow, occasionally topping out over a few little side ridges. During the leaveless season you will soon be able to see a mobile home down in the valley quite a ways below you on the right. This is the first time that an inhabited dwelling is visible from the trail on any of the three Vesuvius loops. Shortly beyond this sighting you will pass mile marker 5 on the right. Just after the mile marker the trail cuts left to go around a wash in a side ravine. After it curves right around and over the wash, the trail gently swings left and goes down into the flat bottom of a large side hollow and immediately crosses the wash on its floor. Once across the wash the trail angles left up the ridge in the upstream direction briefly before turning right and leveling off heading back toward the valley. Once again it curves around a knob then gently descends into a second side hollow which is wider and flatter on the bottom than the last one. Again the trail crosses the branch at the bottom but this time cuts right leading you out of the forest into a large cleared area. You are now in **the valley of Elkins Creek and on a F.W.D. type road. You will soon see and extremely steep trail coming down from the left which joins the road you are on. A sign just before this junction and to the left of the trail facing you says HIKING TRAIL→** to make sure you don't turn left up that ultra steep trail. That trail is for horses and it joins the trail you are on with the two running concurrently for about a half a mile.

The combined trails then cross a small wash and turn right on a modern gravel road. Aside from the last quarter mile from the dam to the boat dock at the end of both the Backpack and Lakeside trails, that is the only section of any official trail at Vesuvius that is on a public highway and it is not on it very long. It is also the only section that brings you momentarily close to rural homesteads.

The road soon crosses a cement bridge taking you over Elkins Creek which, although still a small stream, is decidedly bigger than when you crossed it the first time near its headwaters better than three miles back.

Immediately after the bridge crossing, the trails turn left on another gravel road and proceed toward a house that is easily seen on the left side of the road. But before reaching this small wooden home, a combined horse and backpack trails sign indicates a right turn off the road and begins angling up the ridge with one of the longest uphill sections in the Vesuvius area. The path is quite wide, swinging left, continuing a steady uphill grade which will eventually raise you 300 feet above the **bridge crossing at Elkins Creek.**

**For awhile both trails run just below the ascending ridge top on the left and it is here** that you will pass mile marker 6 to the left of the trail. Shortly after the marker both trails climb to the spine of the ridge and continue the climb. It looks as if both trails will climb another hundred feet in a rather straight line up to the top of the ascending ridge but the hiking trail makes an abrupt right turn going off the ridge top and separates from the horse trail at a point where there is a sign to the right which says:

HORSE TRAIL ↑
HIKING TRAIL ⟶

Just after making the turn you will see another sign prohibiting vehicles and horses. After the turnoff the trail is less distinct as it drops off the ridge but soon turns left and continues to climb just below the ridge top on the left. It reaches the top of a connecting ridge to the right of the one you have been paralleling. The top is narrow and open and the feeling here is that it will follow the ridge top to the right, but it soon **turns left off the ridge top and cuts left again and follows another finger of the ridge on the right of it a few feet below its crest. It was in this section that I ran into the first** serious problem with a briar patch. On my first hike it was nearly impossible to get through. On the next two visits the situation was much improved. If you have to detour and work your way around a briar patch, don't drop too far down into the hollow but tend to stay fairly close to the ridge top for in less than a half mile the trail climbs up to the ridge top and crosses it.

On the ridge top it again junctions and crosses the horse trail which is on a F.W.D. road that also serves as the horse trail. A sign across the road and facing you says:

HIKING TRAIL ↑

indicating that the trail does not turn on the road with the horse trail but crosses it and returns to the forest. The last two times I passed this point I had a good example of why my decision to explain the exact location and direction of the signs had been a good choice, for someone had pulled the sign post out of the ground; then turned the sign around and replaced it in the ground making it appear as though the hiking trail turned left and went down the descending ridge top. The last time there I had a couple of hefty hikers with me and we were able to lift the sign out of its rather deep hole and turn it to the proper orientation. But who knows when the hooligans will be back to repeat their mischief.

Although physically not demanding, the last mile of trail from this point is often an extremely exasperating one to cover, for it is the least distinct section and crosses

*Hiking the Lakeshore Trail*

bramble patches where the trail may totally disappear. The worst of these patches is located almost at the end of the loop. On my first hike on this section, I would have given up and retreated to the road on the ridge top had I not been determined to complete the official trail for the information necessary for this book. I made it with torn clothing and my vocabulary of cuss words exhausted. This stretch has been in a little better condition on my later hikes but the Forest Service has a running battle keeping this area open because of the rapid growth and the low volume of hikers. This may result in some difficult going especially in the summer and early fall. You may recall that at the beginning of the Bluegrass loop just a few yards from the trailhead I suggested you look left to see what kind of condition the return trail was in. If, in your opinion, it looked like a briar-patch jungle you might consider this option. Turn right on the horse trail road and follow it up the ridge to an improved gravel road. Turn left on the road and in less than a half mile the second rutted road to the right returns you to the Kimble Fire Tower site.

If you wish to complete the official loop and avoid the road walking, in less than a minute's walk beyond the horse trail junction mile marker 7 is on the right. The trail continues curving gently to the left close to the ridge top on the right staying mostly level and never descending back down to the hollow bottom. The trail goes easily up and over two ridge fingers. Neither requires any serious uphill climbing. You may hear an occasional automobile for the gravel road is running parallel above you out of sight on the right. The bad bramble patches occur about 100 yards from the end of the loop. If the trail has been consumed in briary vegetation, simply climb up the short distance to the ridge top on the right. When you reach the maintained gravel road, turn left and follow the road until you see the rise for the former Kimble Fire Tower on the right.

If you can slither or hack your way through the brambles, you will soon be back at the loop junction where a sign on the left facing the trail says: **BLUEGRASS HIKING TRAIL. HORSES AND MOTORCYCLES FORBIDDEN.** Turn right here, cross the road and you quickly pass mile marker 8 on the right just before the junction with the Backpack Trail.

## LAKESHORE TRAIL

From Boat Harbor to Boat Harbor loop hike around Lake Vesuvius.
Distance: 8 miles
Hike: Moderate to strenuous
Walking time: 4 to 5 hours

GENERAL REMARKS: This is one of two trails included in this book that is either on or close to a lake for the complete loop (the other is the Burr Oak Trail). The scenery is often more than pleasant, and it makes for a good day hiking possibility with a couple of drawbacks. Some of the most picturesque locations along the water (and there are several) are too often turned into rubbish dumps by thoughtless boaters who litter the bank with the garbage of their picnics and fishing excursions. On one hike I heard a woman cry out "Why doesn't the Forest Service clean up this mess." They do -- over and over again, hauling out what seems like tons of human offal many times each season but this effort, plus arrests for littering, do not seem to slow down the tide of debris. Although this trail does not have an over abundance of hikers, its close proximity to the water means that people are seldom far away so if you are after an isolated walk it will seldom seem so during the busy seasons.

When I first walked this trail it was impossible to do a legal overnighter and stay on the trail since the entire shoreline area was in the restricted camping area. This boundary has changed somewhat and an overnight stay is now legal starting about half way between mile marker 2 and 3 to mile marker 5 on the other side of the lake. Because of the human traffic both on and around the lake, it would be wise to move back into the woods out of sight of both lake and trail if you plan an overnight stay.

TRAIL DESCRIPTION: To find the trailhead see page 91. The first mile of this trail runs concurrently with the Backpack Trail. For this description see page 93.

After passing the dividing point for the two trails you will soon pass mile marker 1 on the left. The trail continues to follow close to the shore line cutting left just before arriving at the bath house and swimming beach where the trail goes over a wooden foot bridge and follows the chain link fence around the other side of the bath house. Beyond the bath house you will pass a large rock outcropping to the left of perhaps 60 feet in length before the trail climbs moderately and angles up the side of the ridge. Since you are going out around the end of a peninsula, there is one brief section where the ridge is low enough that you can see the lake both to your right and your left. Just beyond this view you will pass mile marker 2 on the left side of the trail. After swinging left around the head of that peninsula, you will soon be able to see a swampy area developing to your right on the left shore of the lake. As you get closer to this area, you can see a small and quite low peninsula jutting out from the left shore that almost cuts the lake in half. As the trail angles down close to the lake level and swings inland going back up a hollow for a short distance it crosses the outer boundary of the Vesuvius Recreation Area. This means you are still on Forest Service Land but out of the restricted area.

As you are crossing the wash in that hollow, the trail goes up a small embankment. There is a big rounded rock to the left of the trail which is about the shape and size of a military pill box and as you pass it you can see it has natural slits in the rock which suggest gun posts making the illusion even more plausible.

**Just beyond the rock the trail passes a small pond which is between the trail and the lake.**

Then the trail climbs slightly and ambles along and near the lakeshore going through several sections of man planted pines. If you look carefully you may find many evidences of beaver in this area containing both slicks toward the water and beaver cut trees. You will also go over the top of a rock outcropping with the lake directly below the edge about 30 feet straight down. If you have small children with you, caution is advised here for the dropoff is sudden. Not far beyond this outcropping **you will pass mile marker 3. From there the trail climbs slightly to the top of a deteriorating ridge and turns right on it heading towards the lake. The trail appears** to go straight down to the lake shore to the end of another small peninsula and there is such a trail, but after turning right on the ridge top the official trail goes only about 40 feet on the ridge before abruptly turning left and drops off the ridge almost to the shore. Once down, the trail remains close to the lake level until you are well on the return leg of this trail on the other side of the lake. The trail parallels the lake which looks like a narrow deep creek at this point and soon passes two large boulders to the left of the trail. Just after passing them look across the lake and see a grove of evergreens which have long lower branches that almost span the width of the lake that are just above a rock outcropping on the opposite shore.

Then you pass another rock wall on the left that parallels the lake and trail for about 100 yards. As you come to the end of this rock wall you will see that the trail is now on a F.W.D. road which you follow to the crossing of Storm's Creek at the headwaters of the lake. Just after you cross a small wash, you should see a sign on the right side of the trail facing you which says:

### LAKESHORE TRAIL ⟶

On the same post but facing the trail is a sign that says:

### BACKPACK TRAIL ↑

**which indicates that the Backpack Trail comes in from the left and crosses the road while the Lakeside Trail turns right leaving the road and joins the Backpack Trail.** Both trails almost immediately cross Storm's Creek. If the sign should be down you can identify this turn by looking left where a far less prominent rut road comes in from that side, and you can look right and see the Storm's Creek Trail crossing. If you follow the road until you see a small rock cliff on the opposite bank of the creek and a steep wooded hill rising above it, you've missed the turn. Retreat, keeping a sharp eye to the left to find the trail crossing of the creek.

**For the description of the joint trails from the Storm's Creek Crossing until the Backpack and Lakeside Trail separate see page 99.**

## LAKESIDE TRAIL Continued From the trail division of the Backpack and Lakeside Loops back to the trailhead.

From the trail division the Lakeshore Trail turns right crosses the wash, climbs part way up the ridge, levels off, where you can see that the lake looks like a small river below you. Again the trail drops to cross another wash, then has the first uphill climb which is a little more demanding than moderate. Mile marker 5 is passed to the left of the trail shortly followed by a swing to the left going around another inlet in the lake. At the end of the inlet, the trail goes down and crosses two washes, climbs out again, and passes over a rock outcropping where a beautiful vista of the lake is seen. After another wash crossing the trail again swings left to get around another much longer inlet. Shortly after swinging around this inlet, you will see a trail coming in from the left with a sign facing you that says:

◄──── WHISKEY RUN ────►
LAKESHORE TRAIL

This short loop trail leads up to a large rock shelter which once held a moonshine still. If you don't mind a rather stiff climb, you can take the trail up to this cave-like rock overhang and follow the loop back to the Lakeside Trail. There is also a short trail from the shelter that leads up to the Iron Ridge Campground near Campsite 35.

If you stay on the Lakeside Trail, you swing around a land point where you will be able to see the bathing beach on the other side of the lake. After passing into a pleasant pine forest the return junction of the Whiskey Run Trail comes in from the left. It is not long before the old swimming beach is visible on the opposite shore and a group of sandstone outcroppings rise up on the left side of the trail containing one small rock shelter which is big enough to shelter you on a rainy day. Just beyond these outcroppings, you will pass mile marker 7 to the left of the trail and not far beyond the mile marker another large rock shelter, marred by the unfortunate blight of paint spray can messages, is on the left. Just beyond this shelter the trail comes quite close to the lake swinging round a cliff face on the left which is plainly visible and one of the most scenic landmarks you saw if you started this hike at the trailhead on the other side of the lake.

After swinging round this rock face the trail moves away from the main lake body to circle the last side inlet before the dam. At the end of the inlet, the trail goes over two washes and climbs slightly. The trail then descends almost to the lake level and passes by an interesting rock cliff on the left. The stone surfaces are naturally cut in such a way that they resemble Paul Bunyon-like building blocks, and you can look right and see slump blocks that broke away from these surfaces centuries ago now lying on the hillside with one well out in the lake.

Just after passing the giant blocks the trail appears to go behind one of the boulders that is quite close to the shore but the official path goes in front of the rock. If you walk behind the boulder this trail almost immediately ends in an old small cement foundation.

Soon the trail comes up to the cement dam spillway, turns left following the spillway alongside a chain link fence then drops down 53 cement steps bringing you to the level of the old Vesuvius Iron Furnace which can be seen across the road. From here the trail follows alongside Storm's Creek but a backpacker's sign soon indicates a right turn where the trail crosses the creek. Once across, the trail follows alongside the trees on the left angling up to the dam and reaches the top fairly close to the paved road. Turn right and follow the road back to the boat harbor.

*Hikers Crossing the open field on the Vesuvius Backpack Loop near the Kimble Fire Tower site*

# THE ZALESKI TRAILS

## INTRODUCTION AND AREA DEVELOPMENT

The Zaleski backpack loop, like all other major hiking areas in this book, begins near or on a man-made lake, but Zaleski is different in two ways. It is the only loop on state forest land where the name of the state park (Lake Hope) and the state forest surrounding it (Zaleski) have different names. It is also the only one that does not have a loop that circles the lake.

It is an excellent hiking area, both scenically and historically, with many loop possiblities for both the backpack and day hiker. These are some of the reasons that it is hiked by many people and is, perhaps, the most popular in the state. Oddly enough it was named after a man who was never in the area. But when reaching the attractive and interesting ruin of the old iron furnace you may have the suspicion that the name Zaleski and that furnace must, in some way, be connected. And indeed they are. This area was once the location of two highly important industrial activities of the nineteenth century, both relying upon natural deposits and growths that were exploited for the industrial requirements of the century. Indeed, one of the important geologic deposits was put to use hundreds of years before this area was ever seen by a white man. A very durable flint, now called the Zaleski black flint, was of such high quality for the manufacture of tools and weapons that the moundbuilders of the Adena culture were quarrying it over 1000 years ago, and arrowheads and spearpoints from this source have been found as far south as Portsmouth. Two of the earthworks of this ancient society are found on the backpack trail.

With the coming of white settlers during the latter part of the eighteenth century, Vinton County saw little growth in permanent settlement for its rugged hills made it far harder to farm than more desirable and easily obtainable land in nearby counties. But a German immigrant miller, whose name was probably Musselman, discovered a layer of flint in the area much softer than the Zaleski black flint and worthless for arrowheads but composed of more open cell-like structures which was almost identical to a famous stone found in France that was highly prized for making millstones. With the need of grinding grain by water power growing rapidly as the Midwest was settled by thousands of immigrant farmers, the demand for millstones was high and the possibility of profits was extremely good. A thriving millstone business developed and marketed under the name "Racoon Millstones." By 1814 a settlement grew up on the land that is now on the bottom of Lake Hope numbering over 50 families and this business prospered for over 30 years. As the economic importance of millstones began to diminish the slack was taken up by the growth of the iron industry. In 1854 the Hope Furnace began operations and by the time of the Civil War the region around the present Lake Hope was like a smaller version of Pittsburg. This development of Ohio's iron industry is discussed in slightly more detail in the introduction of the Vesuvius section area of this book. It is also at this time the name Zaleski enters the scene. Count Zaleski, for whom the town and forest were named, never visited any part of the region. He was a Polish exile who fled to Paris and became active in the banking business, forming the Zaleski Mining Company largely from investment monies he received from other Polish emigres. In 1856 the present town of Zaleski was laid out, and another furnace built just north of that town did the majority of that company's smelting. At that time the abundance of nearby hardwood forests, necessary for making charcoal used in these types of furnaces, were in abundant supply. The local deposits of limestone and iron ore were not in enough volume to supply the demand and were supplemented by other deposits nearby shipped in by rail. With six of the active furnaces of almost seventy in Ohio located in Vinton County, the booming industry produced more iron than the market demanded and financial ruin faced most of the furnace owners. However, the demand for iron, particularly for casting cannon, skyrocketed during the Civil War bringing a booming wartime economy. By the end of the war, depletion of the hardwood forests and new smelting techniques doomed this local industry, and the Hope furnace stopped operations in 1874. Its original site was chosen because of its close proximity to 4000 acres of hardwood forest along Sandy Run and part of the Zaleski loop trail is on a portion of the old wagon road used to haul logs to near the furnace site for the making of charcoal. There was once a railroad spur that ran from the furnace south on the land that is now Route 278 to a junction with the B & O Railroad. The old industrial town of Hope is now at the bottom of the lake and only the furnace and the graveyard at Olds Hollow are left as reminders of that once busy time.

A later economic activity that has left many unattractive visible scars in the region was the strip mining of the many coal veins lying close to the surface in the surrounding area during the earlier part of this century. This left much of the countryside a veritable wasteland with no thought of reclamation, and the hiker can view some of the remains of this ecological disaster, for the trail briefly passes over some of these old sites and crosses and follows streams that are still actively polluted by these old mines. Over 25000 acres of this once denuded forest and mining sites have been incorporated into the present Zaleski Forest. Parts of this forest date back to experimental tree plantations planted around the beginning of this century and are the oldest of this type in Ohio. Almost all of the forested trail areas here are of secondary growth, but they've been growing for a long time. When the dam was built forming the 120 acre Lake Hope over the site of the former town the area became a prime location for development of recreational facilities. Begun by the State Forestry department over three thousand acres, mostly surrounding the lake area, were developed into what is now known as Lake Hope State Park.

## HOW TO GET THERE

For those coming from Dayton or from northern Cincinnati, take Route 35 east from I-71 following the bypass around Chillicothe and taking U.S. Route 50 east through Mac Arther to Route 677. Follow 677 north to the town of Zaleski where you will pick up Route 278. Follow State Route 278 north until you pass Lake Hope on the left, and just a little over a mile from its dam you will see the Old Hope Iron Furnace on the left and the backpack parking lot on the right.

For those coming from the Columbus area there are two major ways. For the first you follow U.S. 23 south to Chillicothe then follow the same directions on Route 50 east as given in the previous paragraph for Dayton and Cincinnati. The other way is to follow Route 33 southeast past Logan until Route 328 is reached. Go south on 328 to route 56. Turn left and follow Route 56 to Route 278. Turn right and follow 278 south approximately 4½ miles until you see the Hope Furnace on the right and the backpack parking lot on the left.

## WHERE TO STAY

The state Class B Campground in Lake Hope State Park has 223 campsites with heated washhouses during the season and pit type latrines but no electrical hook ups. The road to the campground is a left turn off State Route 278 just 3/10 miles north of the backpack parking lot.

MAP LEGEND
ZALESKI BACKPACK TRAIL

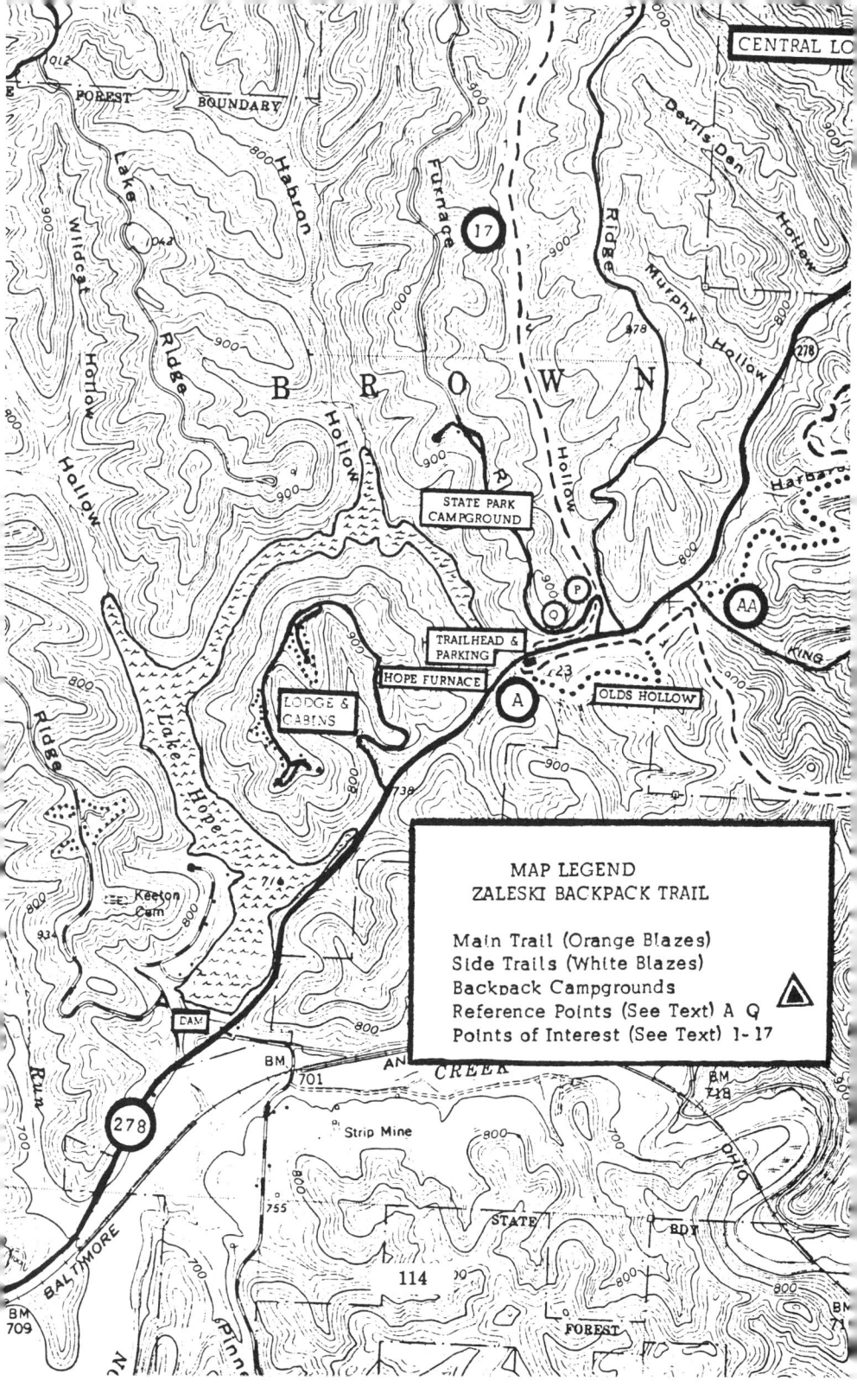

Main Trail (Orange Blazes)
Side Trails (White Blazes)
Backpack Campgrounds
Reference Points (See Text) A-Q
Points of Interest (See Text) 1-17

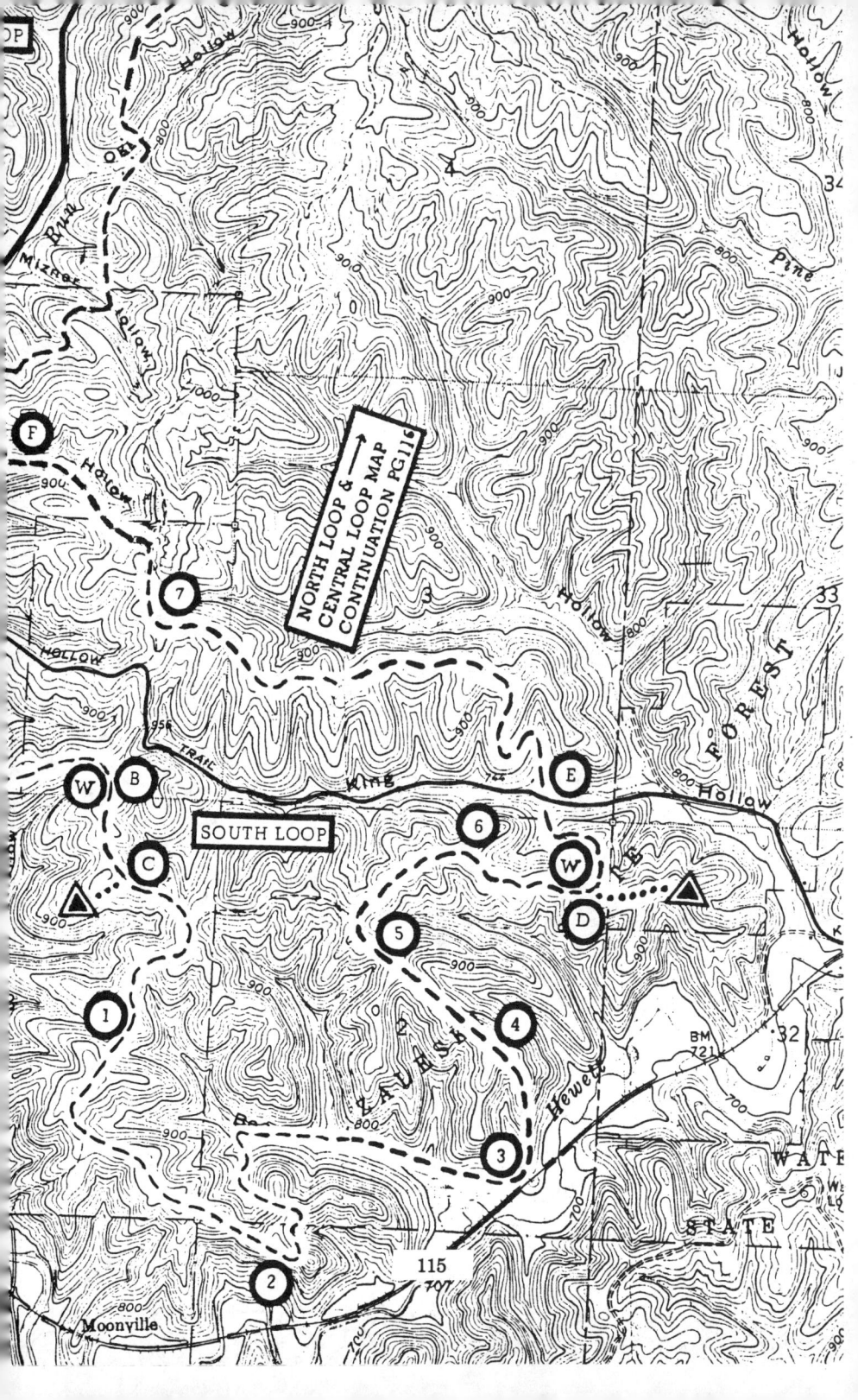

NORTH LOOP &
CENTRAL LOOP MAP
CONTINUATION PG 116

SOUTH LOOP

115

CENTRAL LOOP

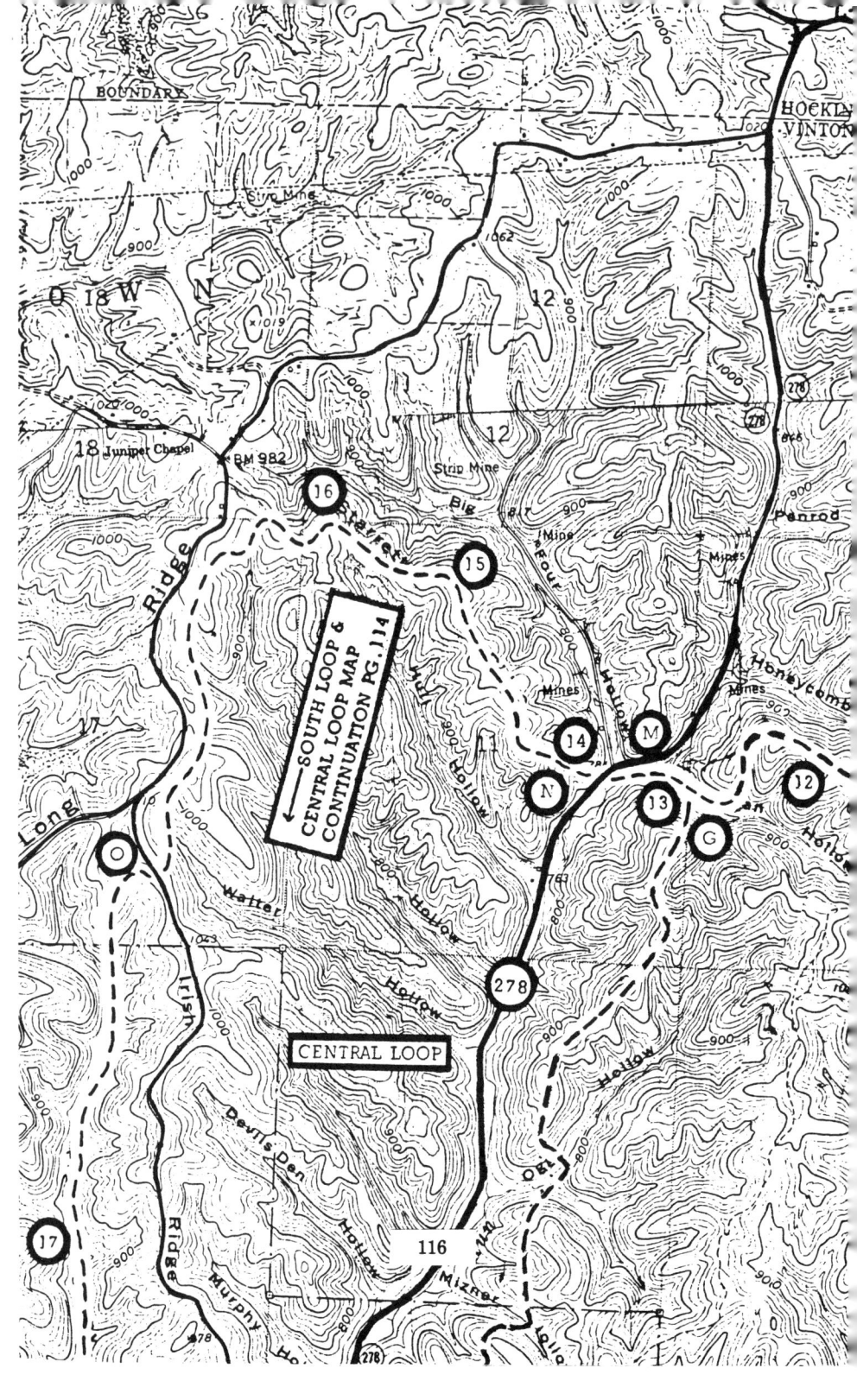

**MAP LEGEND**
**ZALESKI BACKPACK TRAIL**

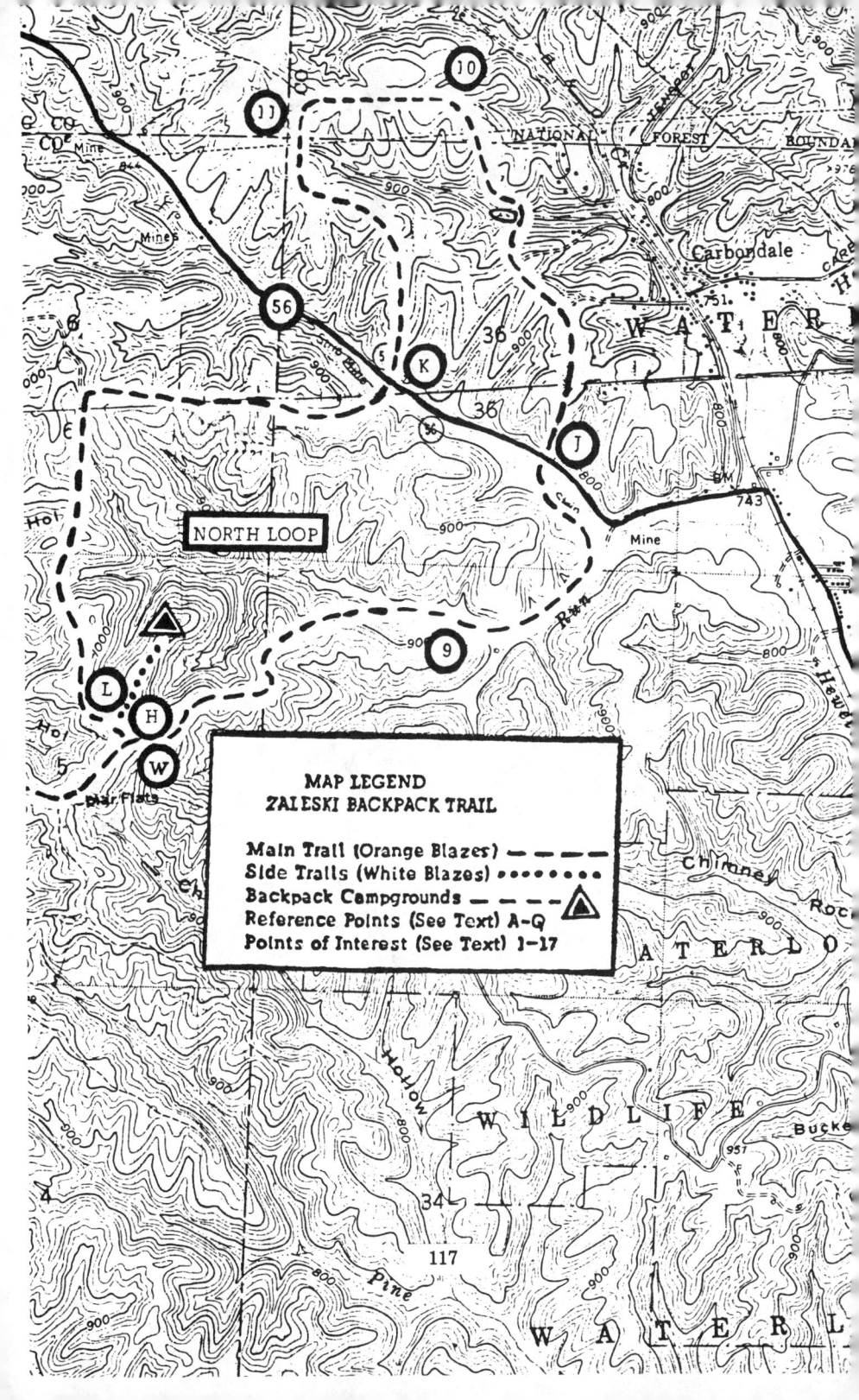

Main Trail (Orange Blazes) — — —
Side Trails (White Blazes) • • • • • •
Backpack Campgrounds — — — ▲
Reference Points (See Text) A-Q
Points of Interest (See Text) 1-17

117

*Examining an old rail bed that once ran from a strip mine*

*Gravestone in the Olds Hollow pioneer cemetary*

Twenty five deluxe housekeeping cabins are also located in the state park with two bedrooms, full bath and kitchen that can accomodate six people and are open the year round. There are also 21 housekeeping cabins that are open during the spring through the fall seasons as well as a dining lodge. For information or reservations write:

Lake Hope State Park
Zaleski, Ohio 45698
Telephone (614) 596-5253

## HIKING THE ZALESKI LOOP TRAIL AND ITS VARIATIONS

**TOPOGRAPHIC MAPS:** Mineral and Union Furnace quadrangles

**TRAIL BLAZES:** Main Trail: orange. Side Trails: white.

Backpack and day hike loop possibilities ................................................... see below
Finding the Trailhead ....................................................................... 122
Backpack Trail, South Loop to Point F ................................................... 122
Backpack Trail, Central Loop from Point F to G ........................................ 127
The North Loop ............................................................................. 129
Central Loop from Point G to Point A .................................................... 134
Side Trail from Point AA to Point F ...................................................... 138
Side Trail from Point F to Point AA ...................................................... 140
Olds Hollow Trail ........................................................................... 141

## MAPS

South Loop ................................................................................... 114
Central and North Loops .................................................................. 116

## BACKPACK AND DAY HIKE LOOP POSSIBILITIES

This is one of the trails that requires that you register yourself at the trailhead. There are three water taps on the trail that are kept supplied by the state forest personnel, so carrying enough water for more than one day is not necessary except in extremely cold weather conditions.

I have divided the main Zaleski backpack loop into three smaller loops which can be used in a variety of ways in different loop hikes. If you have the excellent O.D.N.R. Zaleski trail map, usually available at the trailhead, neither the names for these loops nor Point AA are found on it for they are additions I made on my map and in my text for reasons of clarity. All other points and numbers I have used are the same as the current O.D.N.R. map. If you have the first map issued by the state you will notice that the numbered stops are different from the curent O.D.N.R. map and mine although everything else is the same. The three loops are:

**1. The South Loop:** Starting at Point A hiking the main trail to the side trail junction near Point F - following the side trail to Point AA and back to A. Approximately 10 miles in length.

**2. The Central Loop:** Starting at Point A of the main backpack loop to Point AA -Then left on the side trail to the junction with the main Backpack trail near Point F, turning left on the main trail at the junction to the junction at Point G. A left turn at Point G to M and on back to Point A. Approximately 10 miles in length.

**3. North Loop:** Starting at Point H back to Point H in a counter clockwise direction. Approximately 6 miles in length. All these loops are described on pages 121-122.

*Ruins of the Hope Iron Furnace*

In various combinations there is a possibility of six different loop hikes starting at Point A. Three of these are possible as day hikes and three others would require overnight stops. All but the shortest are demanding enough that they should be attempted by only those hikers in good physical condition who can take a moderate amount of uphill - downhill stress. Each is briefly discussed.

**Olds Hollow Loop** This easy hike of a little under two miles is really shorter than any other hike in this book except some at Hocking Hills and falls way under the 8 mile length I usually used for what would and would not be included. Since on the longer treks, hikers have the option of using either the main trail or the Olds Hollow Trail I have included it. The Olds Hollow Trail is just slightly longer than the main trail when measured from their two junction points and has a moderate hill climb that the main trail largely avoids. But it takes one through the old "Pioneer Cemetery" which really isn't a pioneer cemetery at all for the grave dates are a good half century later than the time of the first settlers in the area. The graves, mainly dating from the middle of the nineteenth century, are still of historical interest. The other point of scenic interest is the "Olds Hollow Cave" which again is not a cave in the usual sense but a rock shelter at the head of narrow and attractive small gorge with a waterfall eroding a hole in its roof. One can return by the main trail through some lovely man-planted pine groves back to Point A. For trail description see page 141.

**The Main Trail.** At just under 22 miles with three campgrounds and three water hydrants, there are a number of ways this worthwhile hike can be made by seasoned, experienced backpackers. It can be done as a very demanding two full days of hiking with an overnight stop at the campground at Point H which almost evenly divides the hike into two eleven mile segments. For those who have over estimated their ability, the very interesting North Loop could be skipped, saving about 6 miles the second day. Other complete loops on the main trail can be worked out by using more days and one of the two campgrounds on the South Loop for the first night. The campground at Point C is in a good location for those getting a late afternoon start for it takes only about an hours walking time to reach it. If you wish to hike to the campground at Point D, although it is less than 5 miles from the trailhead, this trail has a couple of good climbs and much of scenic and historic interest so you should allow 2½ to 3 hours to get there.

**South Loop Hike.** Starting at Point A and by taking the Olds Hollow trail on the outward leg returning on the side trail from Point F to AA, then following the Main Trail back to the parking lot the hiker will only be repeating less than ¼ mile of trail in an opposite direction during this ten mile walk. This can be done as a long day hike or as an easy backpack overnighter with two campsites and water sources. Since the climbs are not overly demanding and the campsite at D is almost at the halfway point of the loop, it is one of the best loops in this book for the beginning backpackers for a good break-in overnighter, testing both legs and equipment over a moderately short trail. The South Loop is scenically the most attractive with one marvelous overlook and several points of historic interest along the way. The biggest drawback of doing the South Loop is that it is quite busy during the seasonal hiking weekends. It is the most frequently used backpack loop in the state, so unless you like a lot of company, hike it in marginal weather or during the off season.

**Central Loop Hike.** Like the South Loop the Central Loop can be done as a long day hike of about 9½ miles or as a single overnighter of about 10 miles utilizing the campground near Points L - H for the overnight stop. This divides the overnighter almost in half with less than 5 miles each day and only two climbs of any consequence. Although the walk is quite pleasant, it is not as scenically interesting as the South Loop, but it avoids the hiking crowds and leaves one pretty much alone during most of its 10 miles.

**South and Central Loop Hike.** Combining these two loops together, eliminating the F - AA side trail, gives the hiker a combined distance of a little over 17 miles. This distance excludes it as a day hike for everyone except supermen but makes a nice, single overnighter with a tough, long first day of close to twelve miles to the campground near H. If the 12 miles seems a bit much it can be done as a double overnighter with the first night spent in one of the campgrounds on the South Loop and the second at the campground near Point H.

**Central and North Loop Hike.** The North Loop is walked even less than the Central, which means many hikers miss many of the most fascinating sights on the Zaleski Loops for it includes a beaver dam, an auger mine, a strip mine and one of the most beautiful groves of very tall pines I have ever seen in an isolated setting. If you happen to reach this grove when the weather is pleasant, it is one of the most beautiful places of the living world I know for silent meditation. Although the trees were man-planted over seventy years ago, I have felt here a unity between man and his natural world that almost becomes a kind of religion.

This hike of about 16 miles can be done as a lopsided overnighter with less than five miles the first day to the camp near Points L - H and a long, second day of about 11 miles that is far from being easy in several places. It could be made into an easy double overnighter by staying two nights at the campground near L-H, splitting the three days of walking into about 5 miles the first day, 6 miles the second on the North Loop and 5 miles the third day finishing the South Loop. But the fly in the ointment is that the state rules specify no more than one night may be spent in the same backpack campground.

**The North Loop Day Hike.** If you read the first paragraph of the Central and North Loop hike, you know that this is an area of high interest. The distance of 6 miles makes it ideal for a leisurely day hike, but it is the only one of the loop walks that does not begin at the trailhead at Point A. If you wish to do this as a separate day hike, drive north on Route 278 from the backpack parking lot at A until it junctions with Route 56 in just over 4½ miles. Turn right on Route 56 and go about 1.2 miles. Look for an unimproved road on the right with a bridge that is still useable with galvanized guardrails that crosses the creek paralleling Route 56. You will see the unimproved road goes uphill. That is Point J. See pages 134 and 129 for trail description. Your car is usually safe here during the daytime, but don't use it for overnight parking for the risk of having your car vandalized is high.

## FINDING THE TRAILHEAD

When you are in the backpack parking lot directly across State Route 278 from the Hope Iron Furnace, you will notice a small shelter on the south side of the parking lot where the O.D.N.R. Zaleski map is usually available which is also the self registration point for the backpack trail. After filling out your permit, when facing Route 278, turn left and cross the highway bridge that takes you over Sandy Run. Often the stream is quite wide here for it is the headwaters of Lake Hope. Just beyond the bridge Point A is on the left side of the highway where a sign says:

## OLDS HOLLOW TRAIL
## ZALESKI BACKPACK TRAIL

Immediately behind the sign is a metal footbridge with wooden handrails that carries you over a swampy area and starts you on your hike.

## BACKPACK TRAIL SOUTH LOOP
**From Point A at the trailhead to the junction with the side trail at Point F.**

DISTANCE: 7.8 miles

HIKE: Strenous

WALKING TIME: 4 to 5 hours

GENERAL REMARKS: If you decide to use the Olds Hollow Trail on this loop you will pass both the pioneer cemetery and an interesting rock shelter. The rest of this segment includes two primitive campgrounds, one of the best overlooks from any trail in this book, walking through the main street of a town that has almost totally disappeared and a small ceremonial ring made by ancient Indians many hundreds of years ago. There are three climbs on this segment which gain almost 300 feet in altitude apiece. But, for the most part, the gradient is not steep and there is a good deal of ridge top walking between each of the three climbs.

TRAIL DESCRIPTION: Once across the metal footbridge at the trailhead you will see a sign which tells you the bridge was built by the 1974 Class of Hocking Technical College located at Nelsonville, Ohio. Once across the bridge the trail climbs above the swampy terrain by going up 17 square logs implanted in the ground. A short distance

beyond the steps you come to the trail junction where you will see a sign that reads:
## OLDS HOLLOW CAVE

This is the split between the Olds Hollow and backpack trails which again join in a little under a mile. For those who are not in too much of a hurry or who are only doing the South Loop, I suggest following the Olds Hollow Trail. Slightly longer and a bit more uphillish than the backpack route, the "Cave" (which is really a small but interesting rock shelter with a small waterfall coming over its top) and the cemetery make it a more interesting way to go. For trail directions for Olds Hollow see page 141.

The right side of the fork in the trail is the Olds Hollow Trail, the left is the backpack trail. If you continue on the Backpack Trail you will soon be traveling through a magnificent grove of very tall man-planted pines. The grove has a marvelous open feeling within a heavy forest for the large accumulation of pine needles on the ground makes a natural soft carpet which inhibits the growth of other plants. After passing through the pine grove, the trail heads down to a swampy area where a little wooden footbridge carries you across the bottom of this small ravine. Across the ravine the trail climbs easily up to another trail split with a wooden post with a yellow arrow indicating you follow the larger trail to the left. After the trail passes through another attractive pine forest, it then drops down to another small wooden footbridge. As you approach the bridge you can see a small trail that goes straight up a steep embankment from the bridge but the official trail, once across the bridge, turns right and in just a few feet takes you to the Olds Hollow Trail junction. A sign to the left of the trail and facing you says:

| OLDS HOLLOW TRAIL
◄────── KINGS HOLLOW

Turn left here for the continuation of the Backpack Trail. If you wish to see the "Olds Hollow Cave," follow the Olds Hollow Trail just a few yards up the creek and you will soon be in front of that rock shelter.

### FROM OLDS HOLLOW JUNCTION
### TO TRAIL JUNCTION A.A.

If you followed the Olds Hollow Trail to this point, you make a right turn at this junction in the direction of Kings Hollow. The trail soon switches back and starts climbing the ridge. As the trail swings around the end of the ridge, there is a trail division with an orange blaze marker indicating a switchbacking left fork is correct, but you can follow either one for they soon join up again. The trail heads down toward the hollow then swings up again passing a very small rock shelter on the right. As it starts down a second time, you will soon be able to see a stream, gravel road and road bridge to the left just before you reach trail junction A.A.

This is the junction where the return trail from Point F rejoins the backpack trail to complete the South Loop. If you are continuing on the backpack trail to Point B and beyond, the trail turns right and goes up the hill. There is a sign there that is beginning to show its age which reads:

**MOONVILLE TRAIL TO MIZNER RIDGE, BEAR HOL (HOLLOW) AND COPPER SNAKE TRAILS. MOONVILLE 3.8 MILES TRAIL CAMP IN BEAR HOL.**

There is no sign for the trail to the left but it is the end or beginning of the F-AA. side trail. If you are doing only the South Loop, this is the junction where the side trail rejoins the backpack trail.

If you want to bypass the South Loop and do only the middle and North Loops you turn left here going down the hill following the white blaze marks to Point F. For trail description from AA to F, see page 138.

Continuing on the Backpack Trail, immediately after this junction you have your first good steady climb up to the ridgetop with about a 200 foot gain in altitude. Most of the climb is moderate with only one short steep section. Once on the ridgetop you have about two easy miles of ridgetop walking before dropping down into Bear Hollow. The trail starts up an ascending ridge finger which gradually widens, and you will find yourself on an old trace road which prominades you down a marvelous forest boulevard which is either on or near the ridgetop. There are several trace roads that join the right hand side of the trail. Do not take a right turn at any of these junctions but continue either straight ahead or, bearing slightly to the left, stay on the ridge. Shortly you will come to a sign which says:

## POINT B DRINKING WATER

which means you have covered the first 1½ miles of this trail and you can look right and see the water tap below you. On the left you can see a gravel road and turn around that was specially built for the purpose of getting the water truck to the trail's storage tank.

If you get a late start and are planning to spend the night at the Point C campground, you are quite close to that campground because the indicated distance between Points B and C on the O.D.N.R. map is 3/10 mile, but it is much closer than that. It is a minor mistake in an otherwise quite accurate map, for I walked that distance at an easy pace in two minutes. From Point B the trail continues on the old trace road and soon passes the Point C sign. You will see the white blaze marks on a trail to the right which in a very short distance arrives at the campsite complete with privies and a fire ring. Continuing on the old trace road for about a half mile beyond the campground at C you come to Stop 1. Each of the numbers refers to historical data relating to the trail printed on the O.D.N.R. map. In case you do not have this map, I will include these data sometimes in an abbreviated form. The notation for Number 1 says:

1. You are walking on a portion of the original road from Marietta to Chillicothe, which also passed through Middletown (known today as Athens). This road, abandoned by 1870, was actively used by early settlers and by Indians of the Fort Ancient group (this area was an important Indian hunting grounds).

About another half mile beyond Stop 1, the trace road and the trail part company with the road going to the left and trail to the right. Although there is no sign, the division is well marked with orange blazes. Just before the overlook at Point 2, the trail descends down over the top of a rock outcropping then arrives at a panorama known as the "Moonville Overlook." The information for Stop 2 says:

2. The portion of the railroad track in the valley which can be seen from this overlook is purported to be haunted by the ghost of Moonville. At the turn of the century, so the story goes, a brakeman was killed near the Moonville tunnel as he waved his lantern to stop the train. The man was exceedingly drunk, and unfortunately swayed into the path of the oncoming steam locomotive. Reportedly, he was buried in the Moonville graveyard, and if you come here at night, some say you can see his lantern a-glimmerin' and a-wavin', still trying to stop that train.

Down below, as you view the countryside from this excellent overlook during the months of heavy foliage, it is just about impossible to see the path of the train, which was the situation on my first walk through of this area. Apparently anticipating my coming, the B. and O. Railroad had a train pass through just three minutes after my arrival. I saw no sign of the ghost and any time I may pass this overlook in the future I hope that I never entice the poltergist lamp swinger to stage a matinee performance.

After passing the overlook the trail turns left over the ridge, descends slightly as if it is preparing for the drop into Bear Hollow, but soon goes up crossing over another ridge section before it begins another angling descent which curves back and forth a few more times. It then runs into a hillside wash. There it turns left and follows the wash toward the hollow bottom; then it cuts left away from the wash and drops steeply down to the bottom of Bear Hollow and hits an old trace road. The trail turns right on the trace road which soon crosses the stream bed but continues to follow it downstream. The trace road crosses another small wash coming from the left just before the two branches join together. The trail and trace road climb above the level of the stream briefly while still paralleling it; then they return to the level of the stream passing a beaver pond on the right which is full of dead and dying trees. Just beyond the pond the trace road climbs a little and takes you down what was once a thriving street of a nineteeth century village. This is point of interest 3 which the backpack trail map says:

3. You are now traveling down the main street of an early mining town, Ingham Station, which had a store, railroad depot, and was inhabited by several families during the 1870's. It takes a sharp eye to find any evidence of a town that existed over 100 years ago. Notice the old cellar hole on the trail's edge. The entrance to the old Ingham mine is further up the trail and to the left.

About the only easily seen sign of habitation today are some rose bushes and gnarrled apple trees. The trail and trace road angles left at a point that was probably at the end of the village and climbs away from the town and the railroad. You can turn right at this point and walk a few feet over a small rise that gives you access to the modern railroad tracks that served as the lifeline of the once existant town. The official trail does not follow the trace road very far before it takes an abrupt right turn off the old trace road. It goes directly through a heavy weed patch which is often almost impossible to see during the growing season. The only way I could find it the first time I walked this trail was to follow the trail in reverse. If you miss this turn, just follow the old trace road up an exposed sandstone ridge as most people do for the official trail again joins the trace road near the top of the hill. The reason for this short side cutoff from the more direct road is that it passes in front of a long abandoned small coal mine in the side of the hill. If you do pick up the turn, once beyond the weed patch, you will find yourself on another trace road. But an orange blaze soon indicates a left turn off the road, where the trail passes the sealed entrance to the old mine and begins a steep climb up the ridge. Although not long, this is the steepest climb in the entire Zaleski circut. As you begin the climb, you can look below you to the right and see a second small mine entrance. After passing the steep pitch the trail switches back and passes in front of a rock outcropping. Just beyond the rock wall the trail turns right and goes up about 20 dilapidated steps that aid you on the climb. Beyond the steps the trail rejoins and turns right up the old trace road. At the top of the hill, you can see an overlook on the right which is Stop 4. The view is explained in the O.D.N.R. map as follows:

4. The fields and buildings sometimes visible to the east are part of an old town named King Station. This stretch of railroad track from Moonville through Ingham to Mineral is considered by many to be the loneliest in the state of Ohio.

The trail now joins another trace road coming in from the left, and there is about ½ mile of easy ridge top walking beyond the campsite turnoff at D before dropping into King's Hollow.

About a half mile beyond Stop 4, you will come to Stop 5. And by looking just off the trail to the right you will see what looks like a giant doughnut in the ground that is over 20 feet in diameter. The O.D.N.R. map explains.

5. The small donut-shaped mound is a ceremonial ring built and used by the Indians of the Adena who were active in southern Ohio between 800 B.C. and 700 A.D. Notice the chips of black flint in the roadway. This Zaleski flint, which outcrops in portions of Vinton County, was the third most important flint to the Indians of Ohio.

On a couple of my walks I have been alone when I reached this ceremonial ring and it gave me an eerie feeling to stand alongside this ancient mound that was built about 1200 years before our time and predates the great gothic cathedrals of Europe by 500 years. I wondered what scenes and ceremonies took place here hundreds of years before the written word reached this continent.

In less than 15 minutes of walking you will pass Stop 6, which says that the trail is again on the old road that was the main highway between Marietta and Chillicothe until 1870.

Soon thereafter a sign on the left side of the trail says "CAMPSITE" and it points to a side trail to the right (with white blazes) which continues down the old Chillicothe road for a walk of less than five minutes to the campsite.

You are now at Point D. Down to the left, off the main trail, is the drinking water tap. To continue on the backpack trail don't turn but continue straight ahead until you hit the gravel road used for hauling water. Turn left on the road, and almost immediately turn off the road with a blaze marker and a sign at the turn which says BACKPACK TRAIL. You now begin a descent of about 200 feet to Kings Hollow. As the trail comes down the ridge it splits, the left one going down quite steeply but the official trail which continues on the right goes almost to the water-supply gravel road. It then curves around to the left just short of the road staying level for awhile before it cuts right and goes down steeply into a small ravine. There are a few well worn log steps here to aid you as you go down and cross the wash. After climbing out of the little ravine, the trail swings right paralleling the wash and enters an all-weather gravel road named King Hollow Trail near Point E. Turn left on the road and walk about 50 feet. You arrive at Point E where the trail turns right off the road. In case the sign is missing, there are two trees with orange blaze markers to indicate the turn.

I remember my first walk on this section began as solo walk on a hot muggy July morning that threatened rain. The gloomy weather outlook coincided with a "low" in my usual enthusiasm enhanced even more by the fact that it was also Friday the 13th. I envisioned one of the local newspapers publishing a story later in the month that told about a hiker stumbling on my rotting corpse after I had been killed either by a seventeen foot rattlesnake, an enraged Big Foot, an irate marijuana grower or all three. Although the rains came, I plodded uphill in lonely isolation. The forest monsters not only spared me but retreated from my overactive imagination as I reached the ridge top. If one proceeds beyond Point F to Point G, the hand of man is only seen in the blaze markers, abandoned roads and cleared areas now grown up that had once been farms. I encountered no other person that day and the only man-made sound I heard was the lonely wail of a train as it traveled through the ghostly Moonville - Kings Station section. The continuing, gentle rain and the surrounding quiet gradually changed my mood from a lonely despair to a warm and not unwelcome melancholia.

After leaving Kings Hollow trail road at F the trail climbs up the ridge at a moderately steep grade. There are evidences of decayed log steps in some of the steeper sections, but they are so deteriorated that they offer little help. The trail hits one of the fingers of the inclining ridge in about a half mile. As the trail reaches the major spine of the ridge, it turns left on an old logging road until it runs into an improved dirt road at Stop 7. The O.D.N.R. map says.

7. Most of the area that you have traveled thus far and will travel for the next four miles is known as the Zaleski Turkey Management Area. As the sign nearby indicates, this is a cooperative effort by the Divisions of Forestry and Wildlife to provide suitable habitat for propagation of wild turkey.

There is a large sign alongside the road that identifies the surroundings as the "Zaleski-Waterloo Wild Turkey Management Area." The trail goes directly across the road and after about five more minutes of walking hits another primitive road used for a gas well. Crossing this road diagonally about 20 feet to the left, you have only another 60 paces to cover before the trail takes a sharp left. This is the old Point F and the original routing of the Backpack loop continued straight ahead at this junction, while the day loop return took the trail to the left. The Backpack loop now follows what once was the beginning section of the F-A.A. day side loop return trail and the new Point F is now to the left at the bottom of Harbarger Hollow. After this left turn, the trail follows the top of a descending ridge finger for about five minutes walking time. It then leaves the ridge top and angles easily down its right side until it reaches the rather flat bottom of Harbarger Hollow. Just after passing a rock wall on the left that contains a small recess cave, you arrive at the new Point F. On the right side and parallel to the trail a sign says:

POINT F<br>
POINT G ↑

Just beyond the sign you can see a trail to the right which is the continuation of the Backpack Trail.

Looking straight ahead you will see a sign facing you which reads:

DAY LOOP<br>
RETURN TO<br>
POINT A.

If you are doing only the South Loop, you proceed straight ahead from this junction. For this side trail description see page 140.

**BACK PACK TRAIL CENTRAL LOOP.**<br>
**From the Junction at Point F to Point G**

DISTANCE: 2.7 miles
HIKE: Moderate
WALKING TIME: 1 1/2 to 2 hours

GENERAL REMARKS: Since most hikers lean toward doing only the first loop the more adventuresome backpacker will find this loop narrower, much less traveled, but still easy to follow. If you had previously walked the old F to G segment you may remember that it was an easy ridge top country stroll. This new routing is a bit testier with one arduous hill climb but you will find that it traverses a more isolated area, crossing several pleasant ravines and side hollows in an attractive forest setting.

TRAIL DESCRIPTION: The trail immediately crosses the small main branch of Harbarger Hollow and begins a short steep climb up the side of a small tributary of that stream. When the trail crosses that small wash the grade eases as it swings

*Beaver cut tree on North Loop*

left then curves to the right over the top of the declining ridge. After crossing a small side ravine, the trail comes to a little knob where you can look right and straight ahead of you into an attractive wild ravine. There, the trail turns left, then climbs slightly before descending down to another small wash. When the trail comes down into a rather wide hollow, turns right and follows the branch upstream, you are in Mizner Hollow. After turning left and crossing the stream, the trail then partly reclimbs and hangs onto the side of the ridge.

There are a couple of more small side hollow crossings before you come to a moderately steep descending section of trail which curves right down to the flat and wide bottom of Ogg Hollow. The trail then follows the wash of the hollow upstream before crossing it diagonally and continuing briefly in the upstream direction. When the trail turns left away from the stream, get ready for a long steady climb up the inclining ridge. You will gain about 250 feet in altitude on this steady moderate climb, which should take you less than five minutes. Although never really steep, it is long enough that you will find it a taxing climb if you are carrying a well ladened backpack. Once up, you follow the gentle up and downs of the ridge top for several minutes until you reach a high knob where you can look down in every direction. The trail makes a sharp left off the knob still following the ridge top. When the trail makes a rounding curve to the right, it is only a short walk on one of the ridge fingers before the trail slants down the deteriorating ridge into Morgan Hollow. When you reach a rounding switchback to the right you have a short moderately steep section before reaching the hollow bottom. You will find that just after crossing the branch that the trail T's into another at Point G. A sign paralleling that trail and facing you says:

<pre>
            POINT G
            POINT L  ──────▶
    ◀────── POINTS M.Q
</pre>

To your left, paralleling the trail, is a sign that reads:

### POINTS F-A

If you are only going to do the Central loop, you turn left here. Before the trail was rerouted, the distance from G to M was 6/10 mile. Now you only have about a minutes walk before crossing Sandy Run and a weed patch before arriving at Highway 278, which is a far shorter distance than the 1/10 mile indicated on the states' revised map. The Point M sign is to the right of the trail about 30 feet short of the paved highway. For the trail description from Point M to Point A see page 136.

### BACK PACK TRAIL

From Point G to Point L linking the Central and North loops.

DISTANCE: 1.1 miles
HIKE: Moderate
WALKING TIME: 30 to 45 minutes

GENERAL REMARKS: This section linking the Central and North loops is the only segment that you will walk in both directions if you walk the entire Backpack Trail. One good moderate climb is ahead of you before you reach the campsite at Point H.

TRAIL DESCRIPTION: After a right turn at Point G, the trail follows the bottom of the hollow for a couple of minutes walking before it begins an angling climb up the ridge. Although never steep this moderate steady climb raises you over 200 feet in altitude in a relatively short distance. If you are carrying a backpack and are tiring you can console your sore muscles with the thought that this is the last climb between you and a possible overnight rest at the Point H Campsite. Once on top it is only about 3/4 mile of easy ridge walking to that junction.

After about a five minute walk along the ridge top you will come to the sign for Stop 12 to the right of the trail. The state map tells you that:

> The road that you are now walking was used during the 1860's to haul charcoal to the Hope Furnace. Charcoal, which was used to fire the iron furnace, was made in the forest by piling wood in large stacks, covering it with wet earth and leaves, and burning it for 10 to 12 days.

Not far beyond this point in a small open area the trail turns left. This is the old Point G and the original routing of the trail came in from the right here. The rest of the walk to the junction at L is an attractive, level one on a narrow road which takes less than five minutes and it is a delightful way to end the day's walking if you plan to spend the night at the campground. You will soon reach and walk on a gravel road with a turnaround to the left used by the water trucks. Walk down the road for a short distance and a sign to the left paralleling the trail says:

<pre>
            POINT L
            POINT J  ──────▶
</pre>

*Old Auger mine at Stop 9 on North Loop*

Right across the road from this point there is another sign that says DRINKING WATER. Just below it on the right is a short steep drop to the water tap.

If you are planning an overnight stop at this point, turn on the trail to the left that leaves the gravel road. You will pass a well defined trail to the right which is a shortcut back to the camp. You can take it or walk a few feet farther to Point H where a sign facing you says: CAMPSITE. Turn right and follow the trail to the fire ring and privies. The O.D.N.R. map indicates a distance of 1/10 mile from L to H when in reality it's about 50 feet. A sign on the same post but parallel to the trail identifies this campsite junction as POINT H.

## BACK PACK TRAIL NORTH LOOP
### From Point L to Point H

DISTANCE: 6.3 miles
HIKE: Strenuous
WALKING TIME: 3½ to 4½ hours.

GENERAL REMARKS: Of the three major loop walks at Zaleski the North Loop has more areas of high interest both scenically and historically than the others, but is the part most frequently left out by hikers. On it one passes beaver dams, an auger mine, the blighted areas of strip mines, over mounds of their tailings and, in direct contrast to these man created blights, a walk down a corridor of possibly the most magnificent forest in Ohio. It is part of the oldest tree plantation in the state.

Although just a little over six miles in length, it is an area that does not lend itself to fast hiking. The climbs are not severe but the up-and-down sections are frequent enough that many hikers will find this the most tiring loop at Zaleski. It is also very easy to lose the trail in several locations, for it often has sudden turns that are not obvious. Although, in most cases, these turns are clearly blazed in orange, it is the general terrain that sometimes makes them hard to see. But the rewarding enviroment through which this trail passes is so different and enlightening that many hikers will find it well worth the effort.

TRAIL DESCRIPTION: From Point L with the water tap on your right, proceed down the gravel road for about 60 paces. There, the trail turns left off the gravel road which is indicated by a post with an orange blaze. This segment is not on any type of road and it stays on or near the top of a declining ridge for several minutes of walking before making a decided left turn over the ridge top. It then cuts around the head of a hollow, climbs slightly up and over another ridge finger zig zagging along its top before it begins to angle down the side of the ridge. On the way down the trail switches back twice, goes over a small wash with some deteriorating logs making a quasi-bridge and then drops down to the hollow bottom of Trace Run, a drop of about 200 feet from Point H. Turning right, near the bottom, the trail passes a beaver pond to the left complete with a lodge. On my first walk this pond was still active evidenced by some trees recently cut by beaver and several slicks down the hillside into the water, and a well-maintained dam. A year later however the beaver had moved elsewhere for the slicks had grown up and the dam was leaking in several places.

Just after passing the dam, the trail drops slightly, crossing a small wash where the surrounding ground can be quite mushy before climbing a rise on the other side. Here the beaver played a colossal joke on the hiker for they cut and felled no less than twelve trees with deadly accuracy right across the trail. It is almost as if the beaver were not too politely telling us to move the trail somewhere else away from their territory. When I rehiked this section of trail a year later, the trunks were still there. I suppose some day a trail crew will cut a path through these fallen trunks, but it would be nice if they didn't for, although they are a little difficult to get over when carrying a pack, I aways find myself laughing at this unintended prank that the paddle tails engineered so nicely, creating a natural road block.

Not far beyond the former beaver pond you come to Point 9 on the right which is an old auger mine. If you look at the rock wall on the right, you can see a thin vein of coal under its sandstone cap which was not wide enough to easily remove with the usual methods. The miners used a large auger leaving several round tunnels in the vein. For some unknown reason the point number was moved from this spot further down to a strip mine which isn't an auger operation at all and it is not long before you walk into the ground of this old strip mine with a large pile of trailings and a section of an old mine railroad. Most of the rails are gone but the ties are still pretty much in place. Although it is sort of inviting to follow the old rail bed, the trail turns left away from it. There is a post there with an orange blaze mark on it right next to the railbed, which also has the Stop 9 sign on it at this writing, which isn't Stop 9. If you look left you can see a rock with an orange blaze mark on it, and as you walk toward it you can see a small stream on the left. Cross the creek and climb up the mine tailings where you will see a narrow stone road that once was used by the miners. Follow the road moving away from the mine. You follow this old road until it fords a small stream. You can look across the creek and see that the road runs into State Route 56, but you do not cross the stream here. When the creek and the highway are in view, look left and you will see a large rock surrounded by mine rubble. Just to the left of that rock there is a break in the trees and the trail goes up that break. This turn is an easy one to miss and the way I originally found it was to walk this section of trail in the opposite direction from Point J. If you miss the turn you can walk to the paved highway, turn left and follow Route 56 until you come to the first F.W.D. road on the right which goes up a steep grade. That is Point J and you turn right into that road off the highway. The walk on Route 56 is only 2/10 mile and if you are falling behind schedule it's a little faster than following the official trail. If you follow the official trail, after making the left turn off the strip mine road you climb through the break in the trees which brings you to a level area on top of old mine tailings. You turn right, walking through a rather scrubby forest of small trees. When you come to another open area you will see that you are paralleling both the creek and State Route 56. Just before you reach the line of trees, the trail cuts right and goes steeply down over some large rocks to the creek. When you get down to its banks look upstream for a telephone pole on the opposite shore which should have an orange blaze mark on it. Cross the creek and make for the pole. Just beyond the pole the trails turns right away from the creek. The trail is not too distinct in an area of brush and high weeds, but fortunately the blaze marks are frequent and you soon reach Point J at State Route 56.

To continue on the J-K section cross the paved highway and begin following the steep dirt road uphill which is directly on the other side. This J-K stretch has many tricky turns and it is very easy to miss them. Since this is the least walked section of all the Zaleski loops, it is very easy to lose the trail, but the scenic rewards in a huge pine forest make it well worth the effort. As you go up the steep jeep-type road, you can see that bricks, stones and other objects have been mixed in the dirt to give vehicles better traction. Even so, it is so steep a F.W.D. vehicle would be the only type most likely to make the climb and even that would be chancy in wet weather. Except for a little grunting, hikers should have no difficulty. The road soon reaches a crest where a sign says:

## PRIVATE ROAD
## NO TRESPASSING

At that point the trail turns left off this dirt road into another smaller, narrower and less prominent road which is no longer used by vehicles for erosion has made it impossible. The side road leads to an open area with some old fruit trees and other man-planted shrubbery now gone wild suggesting that houses once stood on the left. I once met a fine old gentleman and his wife walking in this area. After living many years in Columbus he had retired and moved back to the area of his childhood. He told me my assumption about the houses was correct and he had been born and raised in one of them but they were torn down many years ago. He also told me a great deal about the days when the mining activities were in full swing.

The trail and road cross under two separate sets of telephone poles and wires. After passing under the second set the road soon forks as it will shortly do a second time. Take the left road at both forks. Just beyond the forks where an old trash pile is seen on the right, you will see that the road is now covered with grass. You will come to a very large oak tree on the left side of the trail and an even larger oak a little farther on the right with a diameter of at least four feet. Shortly beyond this point watch for blaze markers on the left side of the road which indicate a left turn off the road and into the forest. This is an easy turn to miss and if you're still on the road when it starts downhill you have missed the turn. Once into the forest the trail begins to descend with a series of switchbacks down about 150 feet to a small pond. When I first saw the pond in the distance I thought it might have been engineered by beaver but when reaching it, I discovered that the dam forming the pond is man made. The old man later told me it had been built by a mining company as a water supply for their steam engines. He said when he was a boy the water was crystal clear and it was a favorite swimming hole for him and his boyhood friends over 50 years ago. Today the pond is full of algae as well as other growths leaving a murky brown water which looked anything but inviting for a summer dip.

The trail turns right, skirting alongside the pond and then turns left and crosses the dam. On the other side the trail briefly follows the pond then begins climbing the ridge. On the way up it crosses a steep gully made by the stream that flows into the pond. Except for this crossing the grade to the ridge top is moderate. As you approach the top the hardwood forest gives way to conifers leaving the forest floor in a blanket of pine needles. Soon the trail crosses a cleared area about 50 feet wide then veers slightly to the right. Shortly after the trail returns to the forest there is a large wooden gate on the right complete with high post and a board across the top giving the impression that it is an entrance to a western ranch. Just beyond the gate the trail makes a left turn staying on top of the ridge, and not long after you walk into a conifer forest which is one of the highest and most beautiful in Ohio. This group of larches planted over seventy five years ago, are at Point 10, which says:

> You are now entering a mixed coniferous planting known as the Doolittle, Enderlin, York, or Carbondale Forest. This plantation has been of interest to botanists because it is one of the oldest unmanaged plantations in southeastern Ohio. The forest is composed of conifer plantings with an understory of woody and herbaceous plants. A total of 197 species of vascular plants were collected, identified, and deposited in the Bartley Herbaruim of Ohio University during a 1964-65 ecological study of the forest. The planting started in 1906 and continued for nearly 30 years. Over 200 acres were planted, of which about 60 remain.

There is a bronze plaque mounted on a cinderstone base that identifies the huge trees as European Larch planted in 1908 by M.H. Doolittle and named after Richard Enderlin who founded the forest.

When I first saw these straight rows of large tree trunks that have grown so very high, it reminded me of a similiar emotional experience that I felt years ago when I first walked into one of the great religious stone edifices in France known as the Gothic. The upward and soaring thrust of the trees seemed like living wooded counterparts of the nave's tremendous piers. As I walked down the corridor of trees with the stone pointed arches replaced by sky, I felt the quiet strength of their unspoiled magnificence for I was standing in a natural temple which in part expresses to me what God really is. I have been there several times and, as it turned out, I was always alone. Despite its large area this is the kind of place where two people would be a crowd. Reflectively I have often thought of the hiker who hurries on because miles covered and speed are the most important things, who passes this grove hardly looking up, never knowing a good reason why he passed this way at all.

Once through the corridor of this pine basillica there is a fork in the trail where blaze marks indicate that one takes the right fork which leads to another rather straight walk through a second stand of magnificient pines. The trail then turns left and skirts though other patches of pine forest and gradually becomes part of what was once an active logging road. Watch the blaze marks carefully for the trail takes an abrupt left turn off the road. Although the blaze is prominent, the feeling of wanting to follow the road makes it an easy turn to miss. Heading down toward a small ravine, which is fairly steep on the approach side, the trail then climbs gently up the ridge where you will soon pass a fascinating tree on the left side. This oak has a trunk that was bent until it is parallel to the ground, and from it two new trunks have grown up making it look like a squared U. I thought at first it may have been an old Indian signal tree but it doesn't seem to be quite big or old enough. Just beyond the U tree the trail again crosses a cleared section for power lines. Crossing the cleared area, the trail joins a dirt road to the left; however if you look to the right in the other direction along the dirt road about 100 feet up the road and still in cleared area, the sign for Stop 11 is located. This indicates that a surveyor's mark close by marks a common point for the counties of Hocking, Vinton and Athens. Since I've never had an overwhelming desire to stand in three Ohio counties at the same time I only made a cursory attempt to find the location with no sucess. Most of this loop is in Athens County with a little over a third of it in Vinton County. The road into the woods showed a great deal of heavy use the first time I hiked this trail in 1979 for the tractor lugs of heavy logging equipment used in near by timbering operations had really chewed up the road. But walking the same section a year later, I was surprised how quickly nature was covering many of the scars. Watch closely for another abrupt left turn off this road. If you miss the turn you will soon walk into the timbered area. Some small trees remain and you will see how quickly shubbery and other plant growth reclaim the area. This timbered area begins in about 50 paces beyond the left turn. As you continue on the trail after making this left turn, it again joins an old and narrower trace road where you can also see the ridge is narrowing. You follow this ridgetop narrow old road until the trail makes an abrupt turn to the right leaving the road and soon starts steeply down and you will begin to see glimpses of Route 56 below you. The trail turns left paralleling the road, then drops down to Point K at Route 56. The K. H. section continues on another small road directly across Route 56. All of this 1.6 mile segment follows various types of F.W.D. and trace roads, but only the very beginning could be used by normal highway vehicles. In many places evidence of roads is almost non existant and you never have the feeling of walking down a well used public highway.

After crossing Route 56 the trail follows a non-maintained rutted road first using a bridge with a galvanized steel railing and it then starts uphill passing the tailings of an old strip mine to the left of the road. There are some refuse dumps on both sides of the road and it becomes more rutted and difficult for motor vehicles as it climbs. Although the grade is moderate the elevation gain is more than 200 feet in a little over a half mile which is enough to make most hikers very aware of the gain.

Almost at the base of a huge oak tree which is hollow in the lower trunk, the road forks with the trail following the right fork. The road then goes over a crest which was once lined by a very ancient split rail fence. Unfortunately, it has since been removed by persons unknown. There is a section of about 100 yards where the trail follows a less prominent road but soon again returns to the more prominent one. In one location the road makes a definite right curve with a little trail going straight ahead. The official trail does not go on it, however, but continues on the road. Shortly beyond the curve, the road crosses a much older wagon road now rapidly disappearing into the natural scheme of things. Just beyond the crossing, the road curves to the left and splits into two segments on a higher point of the ridge. The road to the left is the correct one, and it soon leads you to a large sign announcing that this is a Turkey Management Area and motor vehicles are prohibited. Beyond this point both trail and road were very faint during the times I have walked it, and the blaze marks are very helpful. Just before you reach the crest of the ridge you can see where a couple of trees have grown enough to have the remnants of an old barbed wire fence going right through their trunks. The trail goes gently downhill through a grove of very high poplar trees until it skirts the head of a hollow to the left and climbs easily to another ridge top. After skirting along the side and top of the ridge you will see a sign on the left side of the trail facing you which says:

◄────── **CAMPSITE**

*Former drift mine entrance at Stop 14. Now sealed shut*

 

A sign on the same post but paralleling the trail on the left identifies this junction as POINT H. You can see the beginning of the campground is immediately to the left. If you desire a little more seclusion for your overnight stay, you can turn left and walk further on back, for the campground extends quite a distance in that direction. If you don't turn here and proceed straight ahead, you arrive at Point L near the water stop in less than 50 feet.

If you are walking the entire backpack loop you will probably have already walked the G-L segment of 1.1 miles in the opposite direction. If you haven't, you will find that the L to M segment starts as a very easy walk that follows an old wagon road along a narrow declining finger of a ridge. You have hardly begun this segment when you come to Stop 12 on the left side of the trail.

It is not long before the road drops off the ridge top to the right but the trail proceeds ahead staying on the ridge. Shortly thereafter the trail falls off the left side of the ridge and angles easily down to the bottom of Morgan Hollow. As the trail parallels the stream you may notice that if there is water in it the stream runs quite clear. This is in direct contrast to the color of Sandy Run into which it soon empties, for the bottom of that stream has a bright orange color caused by mineral pollution from an old mine site upstream. Once in the hollow bottom, you only have a couple of minutes walk to Point G, and by proceeding straight ahead at this junction, another minutes walk brings you to the crossing of Sandy Run and Point M.

# CENTRAL LOOP

**From Point M to Trailhead at A.**

Distance: 4.9 miles
Hike: G to N easy, N to O strenuous, O to A easy.
Walking Time: 2 hours 15 minutes to 3 hours.

GENERAL REMARKS: This is the only part of the trail that has two short sections that briefly follow a public highway. They occur almost at the beginning and right at the end of the trail and they both are on the same highway. With only one area of steady climbing occurring immediately following Point N., the rest of this section is more or less level and downhill which is a nice thing to think about if you are tired. It also has the only section that follows a hollow bottom for any appreciable distance, which makes a nice contrast toward the end of the hike from following ridges and crossing hollows.

TRAIL DESCRIPTION: Arriving at the paved highway, you turn left on Route 278 for a short 1/10 mile along this well traveled road to Point N. On the left side you soon come to a small building with corregated iron side and in front of it sign post number 12 which says:

> The structure that you see is a metering station, utilized in the Lake Hope mine sealing demonstration project. The building contains instruments that monitor water quality and flow. The objective of this project is to prevent acid mine drainage from entering the area.

When you see a gravel road coming in from the right you are close to Point N, where the trail leaves the highway. Just past the gravel road (Four Hollow Road) on the right side of Route 278, there is a cable guard rail along the highway. Cross the highway and walk to the end of the guard rail where you can easily see a trail going rather steeply uphill. This is Point N. On the first part of the walk from N to O you face an elevation gain of about 200 feet but once you are up you have mostly ridgetop walking to Point O and this is the last climb of any significance on the rest of the hike. You are hardly started up this first climb when you come to sign post number 14 which will probably be eliminated sometime in the future for it is no longer visible. On the Zaleski maps published at this writing marker 14 said:

> This is an old drift mine. The vein of coal, exposed by natural drainage, was extracted by hand and cart. The vein was mined wherever it drifted, thus its name.

When I first walked this trail there was a classic example of this type of mine on the ridge side of the trail. By looking into its narrow interior, you could see there was still timber shoring up the ceiling and even a vein of coal was visible. The included picture gives you some idea. But on one walk I encountered a crew closing the front of the mine. This was a federally funded project to inhibit the drainage pollution caused by old mines and today there is no indication of where the old mine was. I had a very ambivalent feeling about the whole matter. I'm all for cleaning up as much as possible the ecological mess made by the mines but on the other hand, this little mine was such a classic example of its type that it would have continued to be an enjoyable stop for the many hikers that pass yearly.

Not far beyond the site of the drift mine the uphill grade becomes more gradual and as the trail climbs up the ridgetop you may be aware that a long time ago this was probably a country road. Soon, you come to Stop 15 confirming this impression for it says:

> You are now on an old township road, used until around 1920. It was during this period that the last of the farms on what is now Zaleski State Forest were being abandoned.

As you can see, the remnant width of the road was only wide enough for a model T type motor vehicle and steep enough that some pushing from the passengers was probably needed.

Stop 15 is almost at the crest of the ridge, so your hike from here has many short ups and downs but the steady climbing is mostly over. The trail stays on the old township road for perhaps a half mile up to a high point on the ridge. As it descends again, blaze marks indicate a right turn off the old township road where the trail begins to climb. It soon arrives at Stop 16. The trail note for that stops says:

> This is the site of a former farm. Be careful not to fall into old wells and cellars. Some clues to former habitations are foundations stones, old fence rows, and ornamental, shade and fruit trees.

This site is now well grown over and almost no visible evidence of the old homestead is left.

Just past Stop 16, you can look left below you and see you are paralleling another old road where a few strands of barbed wire left from the days of the old farm are still visible. The trail gradually climbs and skirts an area that once was a farm field, but small trees are reclaiming the land for the forest. The trail drops down, momentarily rejoining the old road, but only for a few feet before the trail turns left off to the road and in less than 50 feet hits another trace road and turns right on it. Soon the road comes to a small open area on a high point on the ridge. The road soon starts down curving to the right but as it does so, the trail turns off the road on the left side and soon crosses another trace road. Now the trail wanders through the woods going over small washes and it is evident that this part of the trail was never part of a trace road. The trail hits still another trace road turns left on it for about 15 feet then turns right off of it where you will encounter some easy up and down sections as it meanders through the woods. This section T's into a wide, straight, well-defined trail with no indication of which way you should turn. If you look right, you can see that this trail soon ends on a maintained gravel road. But you turn left on this trail and walk about 12 feet where you see a smaller trail leaving the more established one on the right. Like the first turn on the wide trail, this second turnoff was not marked during the times I walked it, but I was reassured, for after I made the right turn I found a blaze mark about 20 feet from the junction. From here it is less than a ten minute walk to Irish Ridge Road, a maintained all weather gravel road at Point O.

Since you are about to begin the last lap of the loop you may find a miscalculation of time or speed will make you reach the Backpack parking lot at Point A much later than you wanted. If you wish, you can turn left on Irish Ridge Road and in 1.9 miles it dead ends into Route 278. When you turn right on the paved highway another 1/3rd mile takes you to the parking lot. Both the road and trail walk are about the same distance but the road is faster, easier and much less attractive. But for reasons of health or impending darkness the road alternative is there to use.

It will probably take you a little over an hour if you go from O to A by the trail, and it is quite different from any of the preceeding sections for most of it is in or near the bottom of the rather long Stoney Hollow. The elevation drop is about 275 feet, but only the first part is at all steep.

The O. P. segment begins directly across Irish Ridge Road. Just to assure you there is a square wooden sign with an orange blazer and next to it a NO HUNTING sign complete with bullet holes.

The trail starts out fairly level on a finger of Irish Ridge that is lightly timbered with a few open areas. As the trail begins a gentle descent down this ridge finger the forest becomes much denser with larger trees. There is a moderately steep section near the bottom of the hollow which should be negotiated slowly with a backpack. The trail then levels off, cuts sharply to the left and goes steeply down into a side hollow. There are some log steps in the steep part, but they have deteriorated and are of marginal help. Once down in the side hollow, the trail crosses a usually dry tributary, turns right and takes you into the main hollow, turns left and follows the creek in the hollow bottom downstream. Most of the trail from here on is fairly level but don't relax yet for the trail climbs part way up the ridge on the left, hangs on the side of the ridge then returns to the hollow floor three times with a couple of the ups and downs steep enough to be a bit testy. You cross the main stream at least eight times and for one short stretch it is right smack up against the creek, which is five feet directly below. Except during runoff periods, the stream is small and sometimes dry so the crossings are easy.

About 3/4th of the way along this stretch the trail leads you to an attractive sandstone rock shelter near the left bank which is about 100 feet long and has an overhang of about 25 feet. Unlike most rock shelters this overhang remains fairly high so one can walk almost to the back of the shelter without stooping down. It would be a dandy place to wait out a rain storm for it is more than deep enough to keep you well out of the weather. Another interesting natural phenonoma is a small tree that began its growth just under the lip of the shelter. When it grew enough to reach the top, it bent its way out from under the top and around it.

Three more stream crossings brings you to Stop 17, which says:

> Notice the old slab piles across the creek, an indication that this area was cut over at one time. The logs were sawed by portable mills set up throughout the area. These slabs resulted from a selection cut that was made in the early 1950's

Unlike the closing of the drift mine by man this shows how nature is reclaiming what was once an easily seen landmark for it is now almost impossible to spot the slab piles since they are now covered over with rapidly growing vegetation.

After a few creek crossings there is one easy climb that takes you between a rock-facing and slump-blocks that slid away from it, then the trail quickly returns to the hollow bottom. One more easy climb that takes you above a sweeping bend in the creek is the last one, and it is located close to the road at P.

When reaching the hard surfaced campground road at P, your woodland walk is over. A right turn here would take you into the campground, but you turn left and walk the short distance to Route 278. Turn right following the road and once over the crest of a rise you can see the Hope Iron Furnace to the right and the parking lot on the left. Road walking isn't much fun but the distance from Point P to the parking lot is only 3/10 mile.

I remember my first completion of this trail came on a warm afternoon on July 14. Bastille Day in France, I thought, and I half expected to see waving tri colors and dancing in the streets as I had once witnessed in Paris several years ago. But even though the parking lot was quiet and deserted, I decided to drive to the nearest sidewalk cafe and have a glass of Vin Ordinare to celebrate the fall of the Ancient Regime. More realistically, however I settled for a beer from the cooler in my car trunk which wasn't all bad and my mind reflected back to the double pleasure of that memorable day in Paris and of the lovely hike I had just completed.

*Olds Hollow Cave*

## SIDE TRAIL

### From Point AA to F

DISTANCE: 7/10 mile
HIKE: Easy
WALKING TIME: 20 to 25 minutes

GENERAL REMARKS: This side trail is used in this direction for those wishing to skip the South Loop and do only the Central Loop or the Central and the North Loop. See hiking suggestions on page 119. To find the trail head and description from Point A to this junction, see page 122. This trail is blazed with white blaze marks.

TRAIL DESCRIPTION: From the AA junction the trail goes left down the hill with the first white blaze mark about 20 feet down the trail which, despite the lack of signs at the junction, lets you know that you are on the side trail. Very quickly the trail takes you down across a low wooden foot bridge over a small wash to King Hollow trail a narrow maintained gravel road. The trail continues almost directly across the road into the weeds. There is a sycamore tree about 70 feet from the road that has a white blaze on it just above the weed level. Once the sycamore is reached, you return to the woods and cross a small wash and you soon see Sandy Run Creek on the left. The trail then swings away from the creek and climbs gently over the top of a rock shelter, swings left over a little wash and left again which now puts you on the opposite side of this little ravine and gives you a good look at the rock shelter you just passed over. The trail is momentarily close enough to Route 278 that the traffic is audible and occasionally the road itself can be seen to the left.

Moving away from the road, the trail switches back once and crosses a small wash which has cut a pretty miniature gorge in the rocks. The trail then swings gradually right around the end of the ridge and into Harbarger Hollow. But before reaching the hollow there is a rock outcropping on the right which contain two small narrow rock shelters that are still big enough to shelter you during a rain squall. The first one has two tiny arches about 1½ feet high.

Soon the trail is in the flat bottom of Harbarger Hollow, following it in the upstream direction. As you drop down to its bottom you pass a rock shelter on your right and go by a sign facing the trail in the other direction. Just past the sign, which tells walkers coming from the other direction that this is the side trail back to A, you arrive at Point F. A sign paralleling the trail on its left side says:

**POINT F**
**POINT G** ↑

For continuation of the Central loop see page 127.

### SIDE TRAIL F TO AA

DISTANCE: 7/10 mile
TIME: 20 to 25 minutes
HIKE: Easy

GENERAL REMARKS: This side trail is used as a link returning you to Point AA if you wish to do only the South loop.

TRAIL DESCRIPTION: From the junction at Point F you proceed straight ahead passing the sign facing you which says:

**DAY LOOP**
**RETURN TO**
**POINT A**

Heading in the downward direction of the hollow the trail begins to climb the left side of the hollow, curving to the left around the end of a ridge. There are rock outcroppings to the left with two small rock shelters in the rock wall. These two shelters are large enough, however, to shelter you from a rain shower and one of them has two tiny natural arches a little over a foot high. The trail continues to swing left up another small hollow then turns right across a small wash that has cut a miniature gorge just below the stream crossing. Soon the trail switches back once, heading back out of this ravine. As the trail swings left, both Sandy Run and Route 278 are below at your right and automobiles are frequently heard.

Again the trail swings left into a small side hollow and by looking to your right, you can see a good-sized rock shelter below you on the hollow's other side. Then the trail curves right over the wash and across the top of the rock shelter you just saw. Shortly after this, you will be able to see Sandy Run below you on the right. As you pass a big sycamore tree, the trail takes you out of the forest and through a weed patch about 70 feet across, ending at a narrow maintained gravel road called King Hollow Trail. Cross the road going slightly left for the continuation of the trail which almost immediately goes over a low wooden footbridge crossing a wash. Then you begin a short climb to A.A., and only about a minute's walking from King Hollow Road, you should arrive at the junction.

At the junction do not take the trail to the left uphill but the Moonville Trail sign should be enough to tell you that is the way you came. Since you have most probably covered this trail in the opposite direction a description here is unnecessary; however, when you get to the first stream where you can see a low wooden bridge across it, you are at the Olds Hollow Trail junction. The trail to the left going into a little ravine is the Olds Hollow Trail. If you haven't walked it, there are enough interesting spots on it for you to consider the walk. It is slightly more difficult and a hair longer than the backpack return but it takes you to "The Cave" and the old pioneer cemetery. If you came that way, you will follow the Backpack Trail back to A. The trail is easily followed and needs no description here.

## OLDS HOLLOW TRAIL

DISTANCE: .6 miles one way, 1.1 mile for loop walk.
HIKE: Easy
WALKING TIME: 15 to 20 minutes to Backpack Trail Junction. 30 to 45 minutes for short loop walk

GENERAL REMARKS: This short section can be used as the first part of the backpack loop, a very short loop walk or a return alternative for those doing the south backpack loop only. It is more scenic and historically interesting than the segment of the south backpack loop which it almost parallels for it passes through the remnant of the burial ground for the town of Hope and walks through an attractive short gorge containing a small recess cave at its beginning with a trickle of waterfall.

TRAIL DESCRIPTION: This trail begins running simultaniously with the Backpack trail from Point A. Once across the bridge and up the 17 steps, about a minutes more walking time takes you to the separation point of the two trails. The trail branching to the right with nine easily seen wooden block steps has a sign to its left facing you which says:

### OLDS HOLLOW CAVE ⟶

After taking the right fork you will see that the trail skirts to the right of a beautiful stand of man-planted pines and begins working up a little hollow before it easily drops down and crosses the wash at the bottom of the hollow by means of a low wooden foot bridge. The trail then switches back to the left quickly followed by one to the right as it climbs out of the hollow. After the last switchback there is a short moderate to moderately steep climb before the trail enters another stand of man-planted pines. As the trail enters the conifer forest it crosses a little boggy area on ten split logs and immediately crosses what looks like a wash but was most probably an old wagon road. The trail turns right and parallels this old road briefly before swinging away from it and out of the pines. An easy gentle climb soon brings you into what was once a cemetery for the town who's location is now at the bottom of Lake Hope. A sign there calls it a "Pioneer Cemetery," but the remaining few graves on which dates can still be read show most of the interred died in the 1850's, about 50 years after the original settlers had put up their cabins. There's one larger stone which attracted my attention for its eroded surface seem to reveal that he died at the age of 79 in 1855. His birth then would have been in the same year as the beginning of the American Revolution. But I had misread his age on the weathered surface and he had actually been born in 1796. Still visible on his tombstone is one of those morbidly beautiful poems that are frequently found on graves of the 19th century.

> Remember man as you pass by
> As you are now once was I.
> As I am now so you must be
> Prepare for death and follow me.

The town in which he lived now too is buried, lying beneath Lake Hope. The fires of his iron making livelihood have been cooled for almost a century and the furnace a crumbling ruin at the trailhead. His once upright grave now broken at the base, lies upon the earth directly above him. Soon erosion and perhaps sooner vandalism will erase the only remaining monument of his existance. But this variation of a well known tomb poem written by no one we know will survive. This may establish a mood of introspection that often may be felt on the long loop at Zaleski perhaps more than any other trail in this book. For as the hiker passes through town and farms that have all but disappeared, the ceremonial ring and grave mounds of the ancient Adenas, a walk through the desolation of the strip mines and the glory of walking through the Cathedial like pines in the old tree plantation, he may be affected by the visible and often transitory effects of man of his enviroment. Whether those before us ruthlessly exploited or tried to protect and enrich their surroundings, they have all passed from the scene, soon forgotten, the marks of their existance survive or perish by forces beyond their control.

As the trail leaves the pioneer cemetery there is a curve to the left followed by another to the right before beginning the drop into the head of Olds Hollow. The rather steep decline to its floor is made easy by over 30 wooden steps which take you to "The Cave" and its little waterfall. Once you have viewed this small rock shelter you turn left and follow the small gorge out about 150 feet to the junction with the backpack trail. As you approach the junction there is a sign to the right facing you which says:

⟵ **OLDS HOLLOW TRAIL**
**KING HOLLOW** ⟶

This is the junction with the backpack trail. Those wishing to continue the backpack loop turn right here and go uphill. Those desiring to do only the short Old's Hollow Loop follow the trail straight ahead using the backpack trail to return to the trailhead. For continuation of the backpack trail see page 123.

# BURR OAK AND WILDCAT LOOPS
## INTRODUCTION AND AREA DEVELOPMENT

The double loop hikes at Burr Oak and Wildcat trails offer a dichotomy of things, many good, some bad that are in contrast to other loop hikes included in this volume.

The first of these is that these two connecting loop hikes are the only linking hikes in this book where one loop is under the control of the state government while the other is under Federal government control. The Burr Oak loop is almost entirely within a state park of the same name encircling a large flood control reservoir lake which is rarely out of sight and sometimes the trail is almost in it. The lake, which is in the form of a giant J, heads south from the dam for about 1½ miles before curving northward for another four miles. It was built in a co-operative effort with O.D.N.R. and the U.S. Army Corps of Engineers. The Ohio department purchased the land that the lake and state park now occupy and the corps built the Tom Jenkins dam as a multiple-use reservoir for flood control and recreation. The water level and runoff after heavy rains are controlled by the Corps of Engineers. The trail around it stays closer to water and has some of the best lake views of any trail in this book.

In contrast, the Wildcat Trail is one of two hiking areas that are found in the Wayne National Forest, and most of the walk is located on or near ridgetops with the only water crossings over small streams that hardly qualify as creeks. It is never in sight of any large body of still water passing only one small pond on the entire loop. These two trails are reminescent of the old Scottish song; the Wildcat Trail is the high road and the Burr Oak Trail is the low. The dichotomy existing between these two trails is also evident in their construction. The Wildcat is beautifully laid out with gradients that are usually easy and almost never steep. Most of the trails on the southern end of the Burr Oak loop are also generally well done but the northern sections must have been engineered by someone who hated hikers, loved soil erosion, had little or no knowlege of how good trail gradients are achieved or simply didn't care. In many of these northern segments some of the descents are frighteningly steep and quite hazardous for a load carrying backpacker. In every case the dangerous descents could have been eliminated by some easily engineered switchbacks. Some unofficial switchbacks are becoming evident, for prudent backpackers seeking more sensible routes, have simply caused them to come into existence. Contrary to the usual policy of this book, to encourage hikers to stay on official paths to keep from making soil eroding shortcuts at switchbacks and other segments, thus avoiding a muddle of confusing unofficial paths, it is prudently suggested that the wiser choice is to ignore this policy on several climbs and descents of the northern parts of this loop and follow the safer deviations.

## HOW TO GET THERE

From the Cincinnati, Dayton area follow the same directions for Hocking Hills given on page 46 until you are on Route 56. Follow Route 56 east until you reach Route 278. Turn left on 278 going north until you reach Route 33 at Nelsonville. Turn right on 33 for a short distance to Route 78. Turn left on Route 78 and follow it north, then east into the town of Glouster and there turn left where Route 78 joins Route 13. As you leave the town of Glouster Routes 13 and 78 split. If you are doing a winter hike and are going to start at the winter park headquarters at Point J as is suggested by this writer, turn right on Route 78, and in about 4.2 miles you will see the large sign for the lodge and cabin areas. Turn left here and follow the lodge road a brief distance until it splits going in two directions with a left turn leading to the lodge and a right turn taking you into the cabin area At this junction is a parking lot in front of the nature center and winter park headquarters.

143

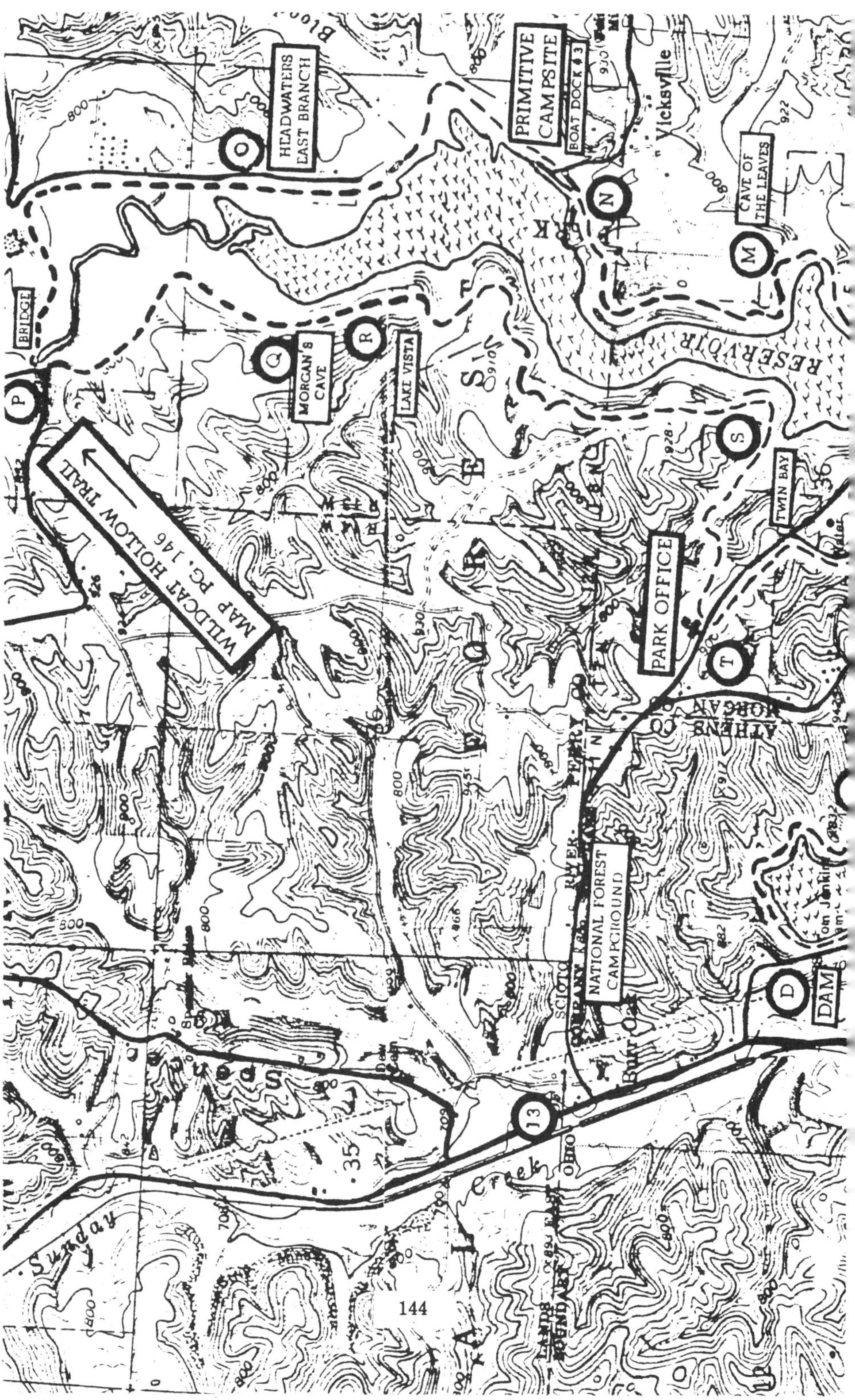
HEADWATERS LAST BRANCH
PRIMITIVE CAMPSITE
BOAT DOCK # 3
Vicksville
CAVE OF THE LEAVES
BRIDGE
MORGAN'S CAVE
LAKE VISTA
RESERVOIR
TWIN BAY
PARK OFFICE
WILDCAT HOLLOW TRAIL
MAP PG. 146
NATIONAL FOREST CAMPGROUND
DAM
ATHENS CO
MORGAN
PERRY
Sunday
Creek
OHIO
13
O
N
M
P
Q
R
S
T
D

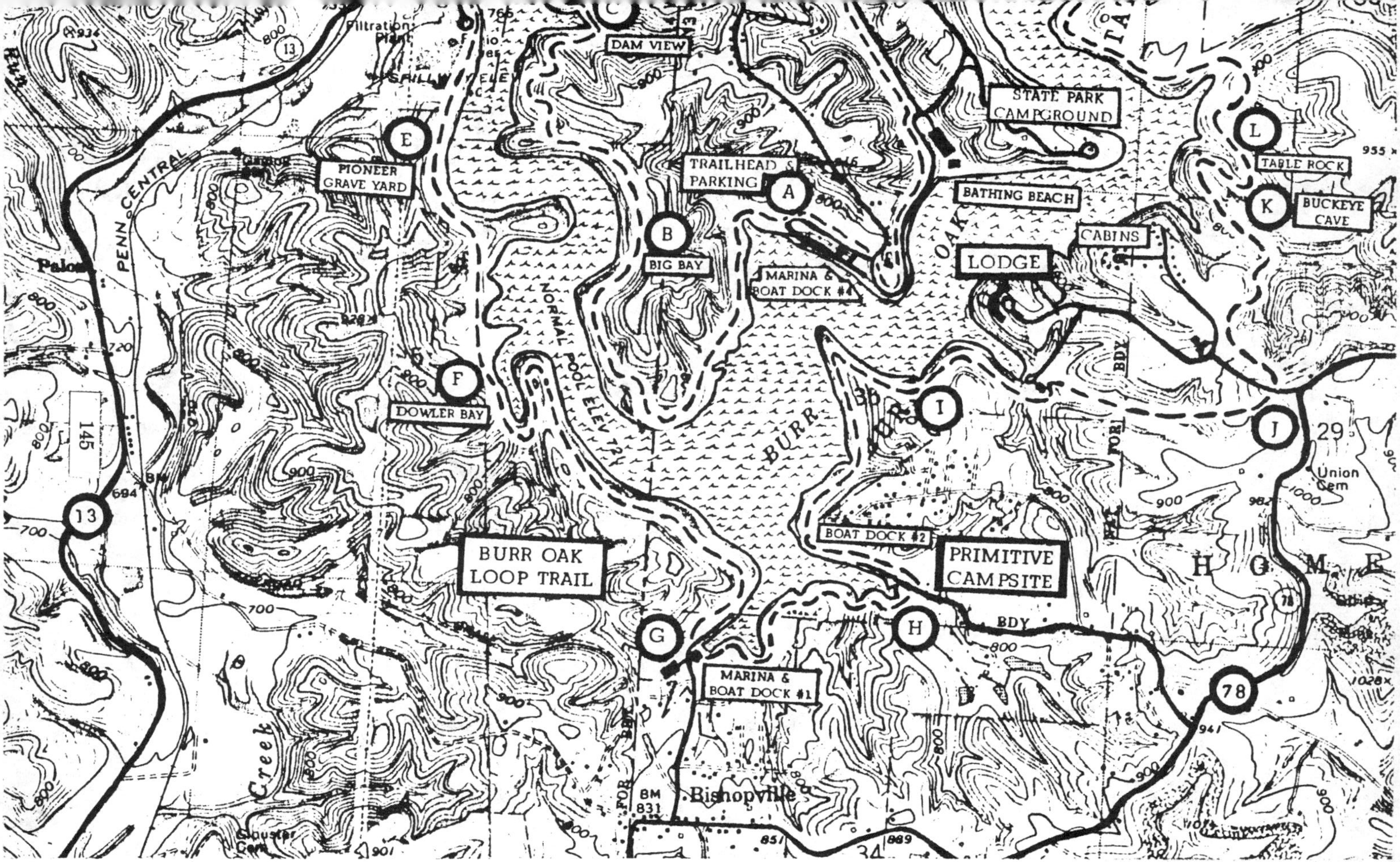
DAM VIEW
STATE PARK CAMPGROUND
PIONEER GRAVE YARD
TRAILHEAD & PARKING
BATHING BEACH
TABLE ROCK
BUCKEYE CAVE
CABINS
LODGE
BIG BAY
MARINA & BOAT DOCK #4
DOWLER BAY
NORMAL POOL ELEV 72
BURR OAK
BOAT DOCK #2
PRIMITIVE CAMPSITE
BURR OAK LOOP TRAIL
MARINA & BOAT DOCK #1
PENN CENTRAL
Creek
Bishopville
Union Cem
A
B
C
E
F
G
H
I
J
K
L
13
78

Sunday
East Branch
Creek
Sunday
San Toy
MORGAN CO
PERRY CO
Creek
PIONEER HOMESTEAD
4
5
6
7
Creek

147

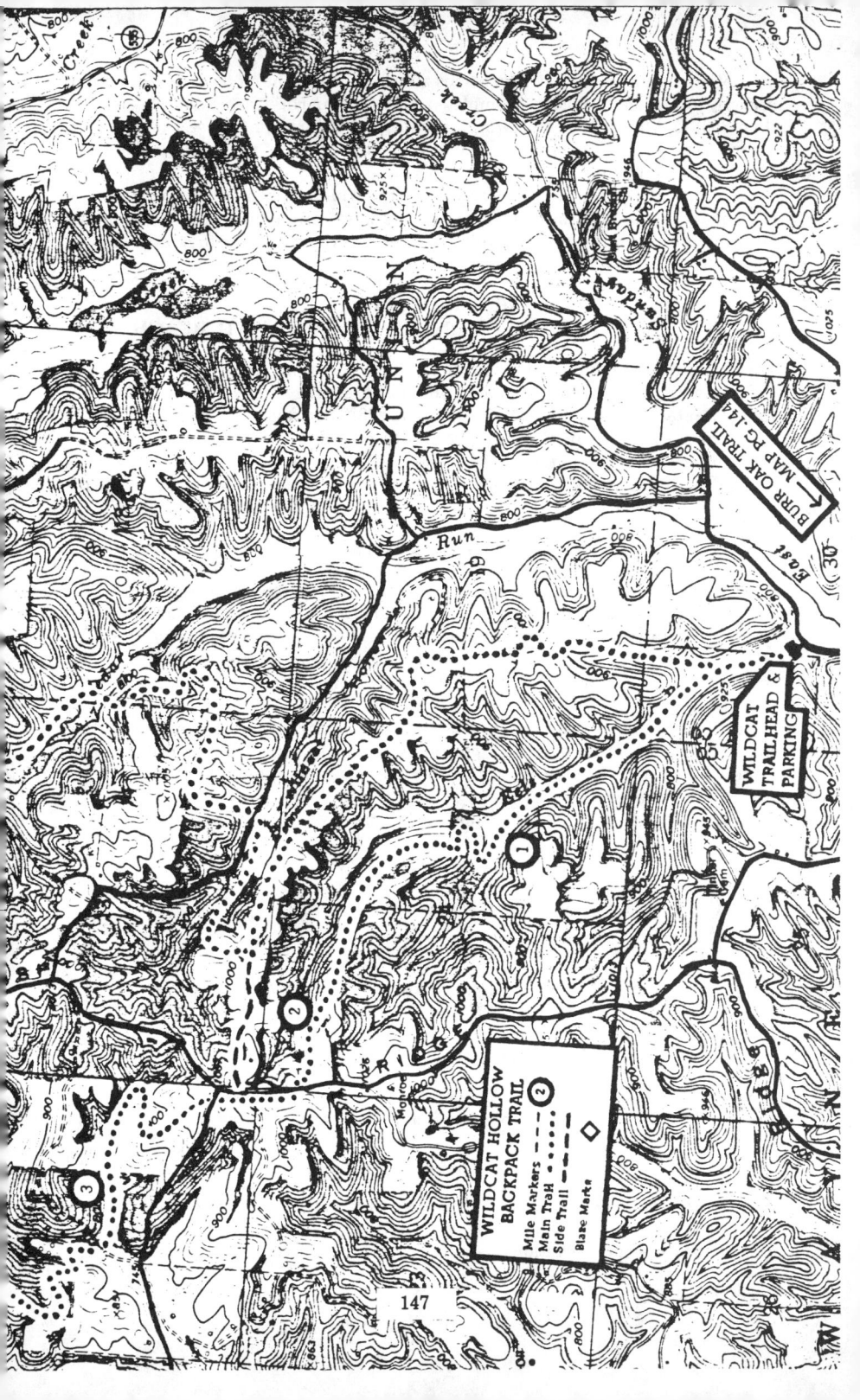

Another simpler way may now be possible for people coming from the Cincinnati area. By following the recently completed Appalachian Highway (Route 32, then 124, then 346) to Athens then following Route 13 north through Glouster much of the meandering around appears to be eliminated. I haven't tried this route yet but it is a way I'll try on my next trip.

If you wish to go to the campgrounds, or the trailhead at Point A, turn left and continue on Route 13 passing the Tom Jenkins dam entrance on the right. Just under a half mile beyond the Tom Jenkins Dam turnoff you will come to a large sign on Route 13 which says:

## BURR OAK STATE PARK
## PARK OFFICE, BOAT RENTAL, CAMPING AND BEACH.

Turn right here and follow directions for finding the trailhead at A.

For people coming south from the Columbus area there are two choices. One is to follow Route 33 south to Nelsonville to Route 278. Then follow the directions for the Cincinnati, Dayton route that are given in the preceding paragraphs.

The other is to take Interstate 70 east from Columbus to State Route 13. Turn right and go South on Route 13. About seven miles beyond Corning, Ohio you will reach the campground road on the left.

## WHERE TO STAY

There are both Class A (without electricity) and primitive campsites at the Burr Oak State Park Campground on the park road off State Route 13. There is also the "Burr Oak National Forest Campground", another primitive facility on the same road. You also will find primitive campsites at Boat Dock #2 and #3 off Route 78 as well as a private campground along the same highway. All of these campgrounds are closed during the off season.

Burr Oak is one of two hiking areas included in this book that have large state lodges accommodating overnight guests. It is one of four areas included that also have cabins to rent. The Burr Oak facilities are open year round but reservations are almost always necessary.

Address:  
                        Burr Oak Lodge  
                        Route 2, Box 12  
                        Glouster, Ohio 45732

Toll free phone for reservations: 1-800-282-7275

## HIKING THE BURR OAK - WILDCAT TRAILS
## AND THEIR VARIATIONS

**TOPOGRAPHIC MAPS:** Corning and Deavertown quadrangles.

**TRAIL BLAZES:** Burr Oak - Yellow.  
                    Wildcat - White squares

|  | Page |
| --- | --- |
| Finding the trailheads. Point A | 151 |
| Finding the trailheads. Wildcat Trail and Point P on the Burr Oak Loop | 151 |
| Finding the Winter Burr Oak trailhead near Point J | 143 |
| Back pack loops and variations | 151 |
| Day Hike possibilities | 152 |
| High water hikes | 152 |

## THE BURR OAK AND WILDCAT LOOPS

Burr Oak Map ........................................................................ 144
Point A to Point D.................................................................. 153
Point D to Point G.................................................................. 154
Point G to H ........................................................................ 156
Point H to J ......................................................................... 157
Point J to N ......................................................................... 159
Point N to P......................................................................... 162
Point P to T ......................................................................... 165
Point T to A ......................................................................... 168
Wildcat Trail........................................................................ 168
Wildcat Trail Map.................................................................. 146

    This is the only general hiking area in this book that has two separate trail maps issued by different governmental agencies. One is a federal map issued by the Forest Service for the Wildcat loop; the state map is the Burr Oak lakeside loop. The Wildcat map issued by the U.S. Department of Agriculture is quite accurate in both direction and distance with a couple of minor exceptions. A marvelous improvement in the Burr Oak map over earlier O.D.N.R. hiking maps was to print it on a waterproof type paper so it will not dissolve into pulp if one is relying on it during heavy weather. Unfortunately the vagueness and inaccuracies on this otherwise fine attempt are frequent enough to lead to some colossal misinterperations.The trail still does not have signs at the reference points that are found on the O.D.N.R. map. Many of these points like Point A and Point D are obvious and need no signs. But there are several of these locations that are obscure and I have never been able to find some of them like the cemetery at Point E and the Cave of the Leaves at Point M.

    Many years have passed since the issuing of this map and the signs are still not up at this writing. This shows a serious breakdown between intent and accomplishment. Possibly the critical financial condition of the state, which obviously made budget cuts necessary, caused the erection of these signs to be put on the back burner. I have included these signs on the map in this book and in the trail text. I guessed as best I could where the locations of the ones that I could not find might be.

    There are also places on the O.D.N.R. map that do not exist like the campground near Point P. The mileages given between points are often wrong by a wide margin usually indicating distances that are quite longer than they actually are and, in one case only, shorter than the actual distance. In a recent conversation with Bob Stoncel, the park's assistant manager, I learned that plans to put up signs have been scheduled and delayed several times because of pressing emergency work. The signs are still a high priority item and may be up by the time this book is in print. The mileages I used in this text when they differ from those on the O.D.N.R. map were determined partly by older mileage signs, walking times and, in one case, by automobile speedometer. If not dead on, they are pretty close, but I have indicated both the mileages I feel are correct and those on the O.D.N.R. map at the beginning of each hiking unit. However, if you want to feel like Superman, believe the mileages on the O.D.N.R. map especially between points J and N.

    The location of the trail itself on the O.D.N.R. map is often in general terms only and is sometimes quite a ways from where the trail actually is. In one case the original trail layout was changed by hikers who followed another path and used it so often that it has been incorporated as an official part of the trail.

    Other markings that have been changed by time are several beaver lodges shown on the map, for they are no longer visible from the trail. But in any case the map in this book should suffice.

    Blaze marks on the Burr Oak Trail are painted yellow and from Point D to Point P the Buckeye Trail follows the Burr Oak so there are additional blazes along that stretch. The blaze marks on the Wildcat Trail are made of small white squares affixed so one corner of the square points to the ground.

There are several places where the Burr Oak Trail crosses low lying poorly drained swampy areas which become a sort of Rousseauian jungle nightmare of high weeds where the trail seems to disappear into a soggy mush during the growing seasons and crossing them can be an adventure all by itself. Although sometimes quite frustrating, these crossings are not dangerous and by late fall with the demise of the weeds the trail is easily seen across them. Most of the Burr Oak loop is well marked and easy to follow. On the Wildcat Trail you will find it well blazed, even easier to follow with the added feature of mile posts.

Those planning to do the Burr Oak Loop should be aware that this lake was created partially to collect runoff water during heavy rainfalls, holding the surplus to be drained away more slowly to prevent flooding and serious erosion on the streams and lands below the dam. This often means that after heavy periods of rain several parts of the Burr Oak Loop Trail are under water, and hiking them, except for the aquatic or by making difficult detours is often impossible. This frustrating deterrant has happened to me on two different occasions. When the water level in the lake is high, it usually takes days, not hours to drop to the pool stage. The Wildcat Trail, however, is unaffected by serious flooding, and if you don't mind mucking through a few muddy spots during or after rainy spells, it is almost always walkable.

If you are going to do the complete Burr Oak Loop hike between March and November, the parking lot for Boat Dock 4 at the marina next to Point A is a good place to leave a vehicle. At this writing there is no self registration, so it is best to leave a note on the windshield so the park rangers will know that it is not an abandoned car. From November 1 until March the boat dock is closed and the danger of vandalism to your car increases. During that period the ranger patrol headquarters is moved to the other side of the lake near Point J next to the Nature Center just off the Lodge Road. The parking lot just in front of the building is a safe place to leave your vehicle during the winter months. Drop in to the station to let them know the car is yours, or if no one is there, leave a note on your windshield.

Another nice feature of these two loop trails is that they do not suffer from overhiking. The Wildcat Trail is pleasantly deserted much of the time, rarely comes close to any occupied human dwelling and even the few roads it follows or crosses are dirt or gravel in remote areas. Although, by contrast, the Burr Oak Trail is quite near many areas of summer population, it is in or close to these areas only briefly and the only segment that suffers from being tramped by hundreds is the very short one mile stretch from the vicinity of the lodge to Buckeye Cave. Some may find the serenity of their lake walk being interrupted by the sounds of outboard motors for the lake is heavily utilized by fishermen. But since motors can be no more than 10 horsepower one will not be disturbed by roaring aquatic monsters throwing rooster tails or pulling bevys of wave jumping water skiers. I've found that these less noisy and generally slow power boats almost add to the tranquility of a lazy summer day and remind me of my boyhood vacations in Minnesota.

One of the most appealing times to do this lake loop would be during fall's full color burst for the combination of the lake and the high density of hardwoods along its shore must make for some spectacular viewing. All my hikes here have been in the winter or summer and I'm looking forward to my fall initiation.

A word of caution for hay fever sufferers: During the late summer and early fall many of the low areas have many pollen producing plants which could bring some real suffering for those who have an allergic reaction to these plants.

## FINDING THE TRAILHEADS
## POINT A

Following the campground road from the junction of State Route 13 and the campground road follow the campground road east. Soon the small primitive "Burr Oak National Forest Campground" is passed on the right. Don't confuse it with the larger state park campground as I did on my first arrival in the midst of a late night cloudburst in August.

About 7/10 mile beyond the campground there is a paved road that goes off to the right with a large sign in between the roads telling which direction to take for various locations in the state park. Either direction will take you to the trailhead, but I prefer to proceed straight ahead, for it not only leads to the park headquarters and the campground but it gives you a better orientation for the trail and the option of starting at Point T or Point A. Soon you will pass the park headquarters on the left which is Point T, and although at this writing there are no signs to indicate it, this road is the T - A segment of the loop trail. Shortly beyond the camp office the road divides again with the left turn going into both the Class A and primitive areas of the state park campground, but to get to the trailhead, follow the main road straight ahead downhill until you see a large parking lot and the bath house for the bathing beach at its end. Just as you reach the parking lot there is a stop sign. Do not go into the parking lot but turn right on a road which takes you to the lake's edge, following it briefly where you can look across the water and see the Burr Oak Lodge on the opposite shore. As the road swings right and starts uphill, you can look to the left and see the marina and Boat Dock #4. Turn left and follow the road that parallels the marina and continue to the far end of the boat dock area and turn into the parking lot. There you will find the trailhead leaving the marina along the lake shore at its far end.

## FINDING THE WILDCAT TRAILHEAD AND POINT P ON THE BURR OAK BACK PACK LOOP

From the junction of the state park campground road (Athens Co #107) and State Route 13 head north on State Route 13 for just under a half mile and turn right on the first paved road. Almost immediately after the turn you pass another road to the left. Go beyond it until you hit the second road on the left where a sign identifies it as Irish Ridge Road. Turn left on Irish Ridge Road and follow it until you come to the first paved road on the right which is Dew Road. Turn right on Dew Road. It will eventually curve left by some houses and starts downhill where the road surface turns to gravel at the Morgan County line. When the road gets to the bottom of the hill it swings left. If you look straight ahead at that point you will see a small cement bridge that once served as part of a driveway for some buildings that were torn down long ago. That is the continuing trail from Point P. For trail description see page 165. For the Wildcat Trail continue on the main gravel road for about 2/10 mile and you will see a forest service sign on the left at the entrance of the parking lot for the Wildcat Loop. For trail description see page 168.

## FINDING THE WINTER TRAILHEAD NEAR POINT J.
See Page 143.

## BACK PACK LOOPS AND VARIATIONS

There are at least three good ways to use these two loops for backpack trips of one to four days in length. I've found that the Burr Oak Loop of approximately 23 miles works out well as a double overnighter but the legal campgrounds aren't ideally situated for dividing the hike into a reasonable amount of miles between stops nor are they very pleasant areas to camp in. If one starts at Point A you have a reasonable distance of 7 miles to the first campground at Point H or a hideously tough walk for one day of 13½ miles to the second campground at Point N. By stopping at the first campground on a double overnighter you have an easy 6½ mile day to the campground at N then a tough but manageable hike the last day of about 9½ miles back to A. It would be nice if the once proposed horseman's campground near Point P would become a legal backpacking campground near Point P, for the campground on the O.D.N.R. map near that point simply doesn't exist. Even though the proposed horseman's camp is not an official campground, park personnel have assured me that camping there by backpackers is permitted so the second day's walk from Point H would be lengthened to about 9 miles and give the hiker an easier last day of about 7 miles. If one wants to do this loop in the winter months, starting at the suggested departure near Point J, the backpackers who wished to use official campgrounds only on a double overnighter would spend the first night at Point N just 4 miles away. But the second day would require a gargantuan walk of 16½ miles around better than half the lake to the next legal campground at Point H. The last day would be a mercifully short walk of 2½ miles. But by using the proposed horseman's camp the mileage spread becomes much more manageable with about 6½ miles the first day from near J to that camp still leaving a long second day of about 10½ miles to Point H.

With the Wildcat Trail only 2/10 mile away from Point P, a long double loop hike of 36 miles is possible with a nice contrast of ridgetop and lakeside walking. With its length of 13 miles the Wildcat works out as an ideal single over-nighter, especially good for beginning backpackers for the grades are easy to moderate and the trail is easy to follow. It also has the advantage of the hiker picking his own campsite almost anywhere along the trail wherever the land on each side is owned by the federal government. Its one drawback is there is no safe water supply on the trail so water must be carried. This also becomes a problem for those doing the Burr Oak Loop between November 1st and March, for the water is shut off in the campgrounds but since there are roads to all four boat docks as well as to Point P, water drops before the hike are easily accomplished.

## DAY HIKE POSSIBILITIES

Because of the length of this lake loop, day hikes at Burr Oak are pretty much of an impossibility. Only the 13 mile Wildcat Loop might be done in a single day by experienced hikers in superb condition. But for those with transportation and someone who can drop them off or don't mind walking both directions on segments of the lake loop, the possibilities are almost endless. There is a unique situation at Burr Oak for people having boats. Prearranged pick-ups and drop off points are easily reached at the boat docks at Point A, G, H, N and near Point I. There are road accesses to all these points as well and others at Points D, P and T.

## HIGH WATER HIKES

As previously mentioned, after extended periods of heavy rains many segments of the Burr Oak Loop are under water, sometimes for days. Such conditions pretty much eliminate doing the lake loop in a single hike but the Wildcat Loop is not only high and, if not dry, it still can be covered in a soggy condition. Also day hikes along the lake in certain areas are almost always possible. These following areas are usually above water but in some cases require back tracking on the same stretch. Point D almost to Point G, Point H to beyond Point L. Point T walking in reverse almost to Point P. To find anticipated water levels of the Burr Oak Lake at the Tom Jenkins Dam one might call the Cincinnati or the Huntington offices of the Corps of Engineers. The Cincinnati phone number is (513) 684-3072. The Huntington number is (304) 529-5604. The normal pool stage for the lake is 721 feet.

# THE BURR OAK LOOP

**Point A to Point D.** from the trailhead at the marina at Boat Dock #4 to the Tom Jenkins Dam.
Distance: 3.5 miles. O.D.N.R. Map 4 miles.
Hike: Easy to moderate
Walking time: 1½ to 2½ hours.

GENERAL REMARKS: This section of the trail known as the "Lakeview Trail" was built many years before the backpack loop was planned. It is mostly in mature forests with some excellent views of the lake particularly in the area of the Tom Jenkins Dam. There are a few climbs but none of them are particularly taxing.

TRAIL DESCRIPTION: For finding the trailhead see page 151. When leaving the parking lot at the east end of the marina you can see that the shoreline is frequently used by bank fishermen for the surrounding shore has obviously been walked on a great deal. After crossing a small stream the trail cuts left and you begin to pick up the first yellow blaze markers. It isn't long before you can look left and slightly to the rear for a view of the marina area. The trail leaves the shoreline and crosses three small wooden bridges that take you across three small streams that enter the lake. Although you will cross many similar streams on the Burr Oak Loop, there are only three other crossings that have the luxury of a bridge. Be careful of these bridge surfaces when they are wet, for they can become treacherously slippery.

Staying close to the shore, the trail swings around a point of land and begins a moderately steep uphill section. Once up the hill there is some easy ambling up and down in this section which is now some distance above the lake with the trail crossing a few small washes that offer no real difficulty. Somewhere in this area is Point B which is called Big Bay, and as you get glimpses of the lake through the trees you'll find that Big Bay is not particularly big.

After making an easy climb to a hillcrest the trail makes a decided right turn away from the lake. It won't be long before you will be able to see a square cement tower on the opposite shore of the lake which is the water control intake for the dam. The trail again turns right and begins to drop at an easy grade until it is almost at the lake level at the end of a small bay. There it crosses a wash, rises slightly and curves left over another creek at the headwaters of this bay where you have a nice unobstructed view of the south end of the dam. This is Point C on the O.D.N.R. map called "Dam View". Once across the creek, the trail climbs moderately steep for about 20 feet and turns left then follows the other side of this small bay. As the trail leaves the water's edge you may notice a short side trail to the left which in about 50 feet takes you to the end of a small point of land where there is a very pleasant vista of the lake and the dam. I had an enjoyable lunch stop there one warm July day surrounded by the forest and a multitude of wild flowers. The only sour note was the offal scattered along the bank, most probably left by fishermen.

Back on the main trail it soon crosses another small wash and swings out of this little bay area and moves right around a bend in the lake where you will find your first unobstructed view of the entire earthen dam. The trail follows right along the shoreline, paralleling the dam on the opposite side, then cuts away briefly from the lake shore to cross some washes that empty into another inlet. Just after crossing these washes the trail T's into another well defined trail and turns left on it. There you may notice some old blue blazes on the trees for this was the original path of the Buckeye Trail, but it has been rerouted and now shares the same path as this trail on the opposite side of the lake.

As you approach the dam you will find public restrooms with flush toilets to the left of the trail maintained by the Corps of Engineers and open in all but the winter season. You will pass a sign facing the trail on the right side which says:

**LAKEVIEW TRAIL ⟶**
**ENDS DOCK AREA 4   3.5 MI**

with the arrow pointing in the direction you have just come. There is a shelter house also on the right which is a nice place to sit and view the dam while possibly enjoying a trail snack. During the summer months there is a water hydrant and drinking fountain at the far end of this shelter. Just beyond the shelter the trail hits the paved dam road which is Point D.

**Section D to G** from the Tom Jenkins Dam to the Marina at Boat dock #1
Distance: 3 miles
Hike: Easy.
Walking time: 1 hour 15 minutes to 1 hour 45 minutes

GENERAL REMARKS: This rather easy and quite pleasant segment has much diversified scenery from the Dam and spillway to splendid lake views. All up and down sections are minor and should cause no problems except for the inept, out of shape or physically handicapped person.

TRAIL DESCRIPTION: Once the trail hits the paved dam road it turns left and follows the road across the dam. It is here that the new routing of the Buckeye Trail joins the Burr Oak Trail and from this junction you will see both the blue blaze marks of the Buckeye and the yellow marks of the Burr Oak Trail all the way to Point P. Although there are other segments of trail in this book at Tar Hollow, Hocking Hills and East Fork that are also part of the Buckeye Trail, this 13 mile segment is by far the longest.

Once across the dam there is a turning circle for autos with two openings in the guard rail around it that are crossed by a single length of chain. Walk over to the left opening which is closest to the lake. Keeping the cement water intake building on your left, drop down the embankment from the left opening toward the lake. As you go down you will notice a row of large evergreens that parallel the lake in a grassy area that is kept mowed by the Corps of Engineers. Walk alongside this magnificent line of trees, keeping them and the lake to your left which will soon take you past the cement dam spillway on your right. This emergency overflow is 19 feet above the pool stage of the lake, so it would take a colossal cloud burst to bring the water level that high.

Just the other side of the spillway the forest begins again and there are two trails going into the woods. The most obvious one is close to the lake shore and shows evidence of being well used. It looks like the right one, and I took it on my first walk, but it is just a bank trail made by fishermen. The official trail goes into the woods a little closer to the spillway than the lake with both blue and yellow blazes assuring you that you are on the right trail. In this section there are a good many easy up and downs with the lake usually in sight below you on the left. The lake will disappear for awhile for you will be walking past a penninsula that juts out in the lake. Not long after passing this headland the trail comes into a quasi-open area which served a few years ago as farm fields but is now being reclaimed by heavy brush and small trees. It is in this area somewhere that the old pioneer cemetery at Point E is located. My attempt to find it in the high weeds ended in frustration. I had optimistically hoped that some friendly spirit of Revolutionary days would, by gentle osmosis, lead me to the last of his worldly remains, but such was not to be. The assistant manager of the park later told me that, although he grew up in the area and remembered playing near the cemetery as a child, he couldn't find it either until he got some help from a person who had relatives buried there.

This open area is divided by a thin line of trees which is quickly crossed. When the trail returns to the woods it dips down to cross a wash where a pipe spans the depression made by the wash. If you look left you can see a back part of the lake

*Author recording trail notes on a trail along east shore of Burr Oake Lake*

known as Dowler Bay, and is Point F on the O.D.N.R. map. As the trail crosses another creek it cuts left and skirts the finger of land that creates Dowler Bay. At the end of this point the trail begins to follow an old trace road that skirts along fairly close to the lake shore. After you have walked a few minutes in this section you will be able to look left across the lake and see Boat Dock #4 where you may have begun your hike. This trail then T's into another trail and turns right on it which takes you back to the bay that contains the marina at Boat Dock #1 and Point G. On one spot on your walk back to Point G where the trail is on the edge of the lake and about 10 feet above it, you can look across the bay and see another boat dock. You might assume it is Boat Dock #1 at Point G and your immediate destination, but it isn't for it is Boat Dock #3 at Point H. Almost immediately after sighting this dock the marina at Boat Dock #1 does come into view and a short walk brings you to the paved end of the marina. The trail does a big U right around the harbor basin, and as soon as you hit the paved turn about for autos, there is a water hydrant and drinking fountain that is on during the spring summer and fall months. At the curve of the U there is a concession building with flush toilets around the back. This concession is open from the spring through the fall where boats may be rented, snacks and cold drinks purchased. I have stopped there several times and talked to the manager Mr. J. Douglas Reys who gave me valuable information on the trail and told me an interesting story about an unusual boat rental. One of the long distance hikers became quite sick on the trail and was unable to continue. His companions walked to the marina, rented a canoe, rescued their sick friend and paddled him back to the marina. Little did I realize then that about a mile from this location a year and a half later I had my only serious trail walking accident in thousands of hiking miles and I almost needed the same kind of rescue technique.

**Points G to H.** From Boat Dock #1 to Boat Dock #2 and Primitive Campground.
Distance: ½ mile.
Hike: Strenuous.
Walking Time: 25 to 45 minutes

GENERAL REMARKS: Although only a half mile long this is perhaps the toughest and the most frustrating half mile in the entire loop. The trail is sometimes quite hard to follow, and there are no less than four crossings of swampy inlets in this short distance.

TRAIL DESCRIPTION: Leaving the marina building at Boat Dock #1 you walk past the boat launching ramp and follow the harbor around on a gravel walk. When you get to the end of the harbor there is a sign facing the trail on the right side which says:

◄——— **BACK PACK TRAIL**

The trail swings right staying so close to the shoreline that it is almost in it due to the soil erosion of the bank. The footing becomes unstable and the trail tilts towards the water. Then the trail moves back from the lake into a swampy area with a creek. A trail division here has one trail going down to the swamp and another to the right. The right fork is correct and it soon climbs into a narrow but long open area with some lovely man-planted pines along its edges. The trail does not stay in this open area long, for in about 50 feet the trail cuts left into the trees and descends with a moderate grade down to a small wash and crosses it and a high weedy flat area. If the weeds are not too high you can look right and see some summer cottages. Once across the flat area the trail angles left and begins a moderate climb above the other side of the backwater you have just walked around and joins an abandoned road for a short distance toward the lake where the walking is easy. As the road and trail come into the open there are excellent views of the lake, and you can see the marina and Boat Dock #4 at Point A which is just under a mile away by water but almost 7 miles by trail. It is the longest view across water you have on the entire loop. As you curve around the end of this rounded ridge to the right and begin moving away from the main body of water, keep a sharp lookout for a sudden left turn out of the open section which drops very steeply down about 30 feet to another small backwater area of the lake. After crossing a small stream the trail skirts the edge of this backwater area very close to the level of the lake. Then the trail again climbs above the lake level but close to the shore on the top of a steep embankment and slowly curves around to the right, back towards another inlet. As you make this right swing you can look across the water and see the docking facilities at Boat Dock #2. The trail then heads back away from the lake towards another inlet and again takes you steeply down to the flat bottom of another hollow. With the lake shore about 40 feet to your left, you cross this flat area and its creek and start climbing straight ahead up and over a declining ridge. Finally, the last inlet between you and the boat dock comes into view as the trail cuts right and parallels it. From your higher vantage point you can see there is a sizable swamp below, so this ridge side walk goes back quite a ways before it angles gently down into the hollow. About 20 feet across this flat area the trail comes out of the trees into an open area where the weeds are quite high during the summer months. If you lose the trail in the weeds, just walk straight across to the trees on the other side and walk up to the ridge until you hit a paved road where you should turn left. If you are able to follow the trail it takes you to a creek on the far side, immediately crosses it and starts angling to the left up a small ridge in the general direction of the lake. When on top, the trail again becomes tricky to follow, for it seems as if one should go straight ahead, but the trail turns right and follows the left side of the ridge for about 30 feet then turns left, goes down across an abandoned road and continues over to a paved road about 30 feet away. Turn left on the paved road for the brief walk to Boat Dock #2 at Point H. As you approach the docking area there is a bulletin board to the right and next to it a water tap and drinking fountain that are on from early spring until November 1. There is a short gravel road to the right which is along the primitive camping area. One look at the camping location and all dreams of a beautiful wilderness site alongside blue lapping waters quickly vanish. Since there is a road access this spot is shared by trailers, big tents and motorhomes. That in itself isn't bad, but the whole area has a trashy look and the john stinks to high heaven from over use. If you had intended to camp here but feel you might pull on to the next primitive camping area for a better location, stay where you are for that next camp is still 6½ miles away and no better than this one.

**Point H to J** From Boat Dock #2 to The Burr Oak Lodge Road.

Distance:   2 miles. O.D.N.R. map 2.5 miles
Hike:   Easy to moderate
Walking Time:   50 minutes to 1 hour 15 minutes

GENERAL REMARKS:   This segment comes in delightful contrast to the rather rough half mile preceding it, for there are no swampy inlets to cross. This stretch consists of an easy walk out to a point of land which has a nice panoramic view followed by a ridge walk in a mature forest before coming to the lodge boat dock briefly following an attractive hollow then covering a mostly open and moderate climb to Point J.

TRAIL DESCRIPTION:   To get on the trail follow the paved road with the docking facilities on your left until the pavement ends. As you leave the road there is a sign on the right side of the trail facing it which says:

```
        ←———RAVINE TRAIL
     ENDS LODGE MARINA 1.5 MI
        ←———BACK PACK TRAIL
```

As you walk out the gravel path you will soon be able to see Boat Dock #1 to the left. In its first sections this segment is right at the lake's edge and little landslides have forced a few short detours uphill. The trail then takes you into the woods but remains close to the lake shore and will remain in the woods until it reaches the lodge boat landing. There is one pleasant little open spot near the water where someone has illegally made bonfires, for one will find black smuges of fire rings there. The trail goes easily out to a point of land with a very pleasant vista. Even though the trail is flat and easy, it is here that disaster struck me one December day.
There had been some snow, then a very light rain. My right foot hit a slick spot and slipped under me with my left foot tripping over my right. I fell with a twisting motion which played havoc with my right ankle. When I unscrambled myself I realized that my right ankle was, at least, badly strained. Fortunately it was one of the few times that I had someone with me in the hundreds of miles I have walked for this book. I even had the right sized individual for Steve Wareheimer, my companion on that backpack trip, is a big bear of a man that makes even a six footer look like a shrimp. I found that I could hobble along with my hiking stick, and he carried both backpacks with little difficulty. Fortunately our car was parked at Point J so we had only a little over a mile to cover and I went right on checking my field notes. X-rays later confirmed that I had broken my right ankle, the first broken bone I suffered in better than fifty years of life. But the whole thing struck me as ironic. I have jumped scree piles for long distances on several occasions in the Wind River Range in Wyoming. On this same hike Steve and I had covered the northern section of the Burr Oak trail with some hazardous segments with no more problems than a few slides. So where do

I break my ankle? On a dead flat level stretch of trail that a baby could walk. Oh well, I had one friend break his ankle stepping off the curb in front of his house. My recovery was sufficient enough that I'm back on the trail and many of the last parts of this book were researched since the break. I still occasionally hike alone but it sure is nice to have the security of a friend along. Despite my unfortunate encounter here, the area around the point is delightful with excellent lake views in three directions. If you are there on a bright day it's a nice place to have lunch or a snack break. There was a picnic table there the times that I have walked it but how long such an amenity will remain there is very problematical.

After leaving the point the trail begins climbing up the spine of an inclining ridge. It remains high above lake level for several miles with a brief exception at the Lodge's boat launch. As you climb you soon run into a trail division, the left fork falling off the ridge with the right continuing up the ridge with a large oak between the two trails. Take the right fork and you will soon pass five magnificent burr oaks that line the left side of the trail like sentinels. Then the trail drops off the top but hangs on the left side of the ridge where you can see several other large oaks to the right including one that seems to be growing right out of a boulder. It is somewhere in this vicinity that I believe Point I is intended. This indicates "Halfway" on the O.D.N.R. map. Don't misconstrue this to mean that you are halfway around this trail, for you are in for a big let down since it is less than a third of the distance from Point A. I asked the assistant manager of the Park what it meant, and he wasn't sure either, but we both agreed that it probably means the halfway point between Point H and J. The trail eventually crosses a couple of ravines which are easy to cross. The second one has an interesting rock shelter to the right which will always be impressed on my mind with the vision of Steve Wareheimer carrying my pack balanced on his head as he walked along the top of a large log in front of the shelter.

Just past the rock shelter the trail cuts right and parallels an inlet to the left, but hangs on the ridge side about 2/3rds of the way up. The inlet contains the lodge boat ramp and docking facilities. In the summertime when you walk through this deeply wooded stretch you may hear a great deal of splashing and happy chatter to the left of you for on the far side of this inlet where it joins the lake and mostly out of sight from the trail is the bathing beach for the lodge and cabin patrons. Just as the boat docking area comes into view the trail begins to decline at a moderately steep grade. Part way down there is a fork in the trail with one trail turning back toward the lake. The official trail continues to move away from the lake and soon comes down to a small wooden footbridge which furnishes an easy crossing over a deep ravine. This is the first bridge crossing since the three close to Point A and there are only two more on the entire trail. Once across the bridge the trail crosses an open field to a parking lot for lodge patrons with boats. There is a trail that goes off to the right, but stay left to the parking lot. If you walk this section during the summer and early fall you will be surrounded by Joe Pye weed growing to heights over eight feet. Just before the trail hits the parking lot there is a sign to the right facing the trail which says:

⟵ RAVINE TRAIL ⟶
ENDS DOCK 2-1.5 MI.

When you hit the parking lot you can look across it and see a sign facing you which says:

⟵ BACK PACK TRAIL

As you cross the parking lot you can see the boat ramp and dock to the left. Also to the left is the paved parking lot road which goes rather steeply uphill. If you wish to go to the lodge for meals, a wash up in the public restrooms or just to see this very attractive facility, follow it until it T's into the Lodge Road. Turn left and follow the signs to the lodge. But if you wish to continue on to Point J on the backpack trail, do not follow the road even though the backpack trail sign points in that direction. Near the point where the road joins the parking lot there is a trail that goes off at about a 45° angle between the road and the parking lot which starts uphill. That is the continuation of the backpack loop. There is a sign between the road and the backpack trail that says:

⬅——— NATURE CENTER .4 MI.
RED FOX TRAIL .3 MI. ———➡
CHIPMUNK TRAIL .3 MI.———➡

Almost immediately after returning to the forest the trail crosses a small stream. From here you have a 200 foot altitude climb to Point J but the climb is nicely spaced out making it gradual most of the way. This is also the first time the trail takes you quite a distance from the lake and will be out of sight of it for over 1½ miles. You will soon cross a stream where you can see you are in the bottom of a hollow. You will have two more creek crossings before the trail turns right, climbing from the hollow bottom at a short, moderately steep grade. Then the trail hits an open corridor between the trees and stays in mostly open country to Point J and beyond. The trail briefly follows an old trace road but soon turns left off the road, crosses a small wooden bridge over a wash and again enters a short forest stretch just before reaching the paved lodge road at Point J.

**Points J to N.** From the Burr Oak Lodge Road to Boat Dock #3 and Primitive Camping Area.
Distance: 4½ miles — O.D.N.R. map 7½ miles
Hike: Strenuous
Walking time: 2½ to 3 hours.

GENERAL REMARKS: Shortly beyond Point J the one mile walk to Buckeye Cave at Point K is the most used segment of the trail for hundreds of the lodge and cabin guests make the walk to this moderate sized and interesting rock shelter. Many believe that it is the usual type cave, for a question frequently asked at the Lodge and nature center is whether it is necessary to carry a flashlight or lantern to explore it. If you walk the segment to the cave in nice weather on a popular weekend, you are likely to witness some real human suffering for the walk is not easy and there are some moderately steep trail grades for this altitude gain and loss is about 150 feet during the round trip of about 2 miles. It is not that taxing for a conditioned hiker, however, and I expected it to be far worse than it is. On my first round trip walk to the cave I passed a number of exhausted, almost panic stricken walkers on their return journey. Their only walking excercise probably consisted of covering the ground between a parking lot and supermarket. They had badly underestimated how far a two mile walk really is and having no idea at all of what it is like to climb a 100 feet or so in altitude. I remember two obese ladies who looked seriously ill and were possibly in great physical danger whose every step was one of obvious agony. They were both with groups of people who were helping them as best they could. The difficulty of the overweight ladies did not surprise me but what did were the large number of people I encountered who otherwise appeared in excellent health but looked like an Everest climber in the last phases of oxygen exhaustion. I was warned by three young men who looked like they could have been the backfield of a high school football team that I was undertaking a walk that had exhausted them and that maybe I should back off from doing it. When I informed them that I had already covered 6 miles that day carrying about 20 pounds of equipment with little discomfort and intended doing 4 miles more they looked in astonished disbelief apparently guessing that I was either a cronic liar or an elder superman. Neither, of course, is true. I was reasonably fit but still handicapped with fifteen pounds of flab. Hikers in superior condition could and

*Rock Shelter called Buckeye Cave*

often do leave me in the dust.

Once beyond the cave the trail population falls off considerably for few of these day hikers go on to Table Rock at Point L. Probably many people are discouraged from visiting this rock of moderate geologic interest because the O.D.N.R. map has the distance between Buckeye Cave and Point L as 2 miles when actually it is just over an easy half mile away.

On the other hand, it has the prettiest lake shore walk in the entire loop and other lake vistas well worthwhile. Physically, it is one of the most demanding stretches on the entire lake loop but the difficult sections are spaced out nicely giving one time to catch his breath.

TRAIL DESCRIPTION: From Point J you cross the Lodge road, turn left and skirt along the edge of the trees paralleling the Lodge road. There is no defined trail here, but it is an easy walk through the grass towards the Nature Center. As you approach the Nature Center you will see there is a paved road that runs in front of it. Turn right and follow it in that direction. For those starting their hike from the Nature Center, with that building at your back turn left on the road in front of it.

As soon as the paved road curves to the left there is a jeep type road that proceeds straight ahead. Between the two roads there is a sign facing you which says:

## BACK PACK TRAIL

Follow this unimproved road and you will soon pass a sign on the left facing the road you are on, but the printing is on the other side to be read from the paved road which says: **BUCKEYE CAVE TRAIL .8 MI.** Follow this little dirt road into an open area where the trail turns to the left into the trees and junctions, with another well defined trail which turns right. Because of its heavy use the trail is wide here and easy to follow. Heading downhill with some moderately steep grades the trail drops about 150 feet down to a hollow. After crossing the streams in its bottom the trail then climbs up above the creek level, swinging right around the end of a ridge where, during the winter seasons, you can again see the lake and the State Park Campground on the opposite shore. After completing a long U around the edge of the ridge the trail heads down steeply into another hollow with more than 50 log steps to aid you to its bottom. There, on the right, is the rock shelter at Point K known as Buckeye Cave which is about 30 feet deep and about the same distance wide. Its most interesting geologic feature is that a stream flowing over its lip has cut a long narrow hole in the ceiling.

To continue, cross the wash at the bottom of the hollow and turn left, angling up the hollow side. Shortly after crossing another smaller wash, the trail T's into another. The trail then turns left at this junction. It swings right to go around the head of a smaller ravine then swings left again soon crossing two small washes, the second one having a solid rock bottom. Table Rock at Point L is on the left and quite easy to miss. Look for it just as the trail begins a definitely steeper grade downhill.

From Table Rock the trail descends into a flat-bottomed hollow and crosses a creek about 25 yards away from the lake shore. The trail crosses the hollow then begins ascending at a moderately steep grade almost to the crest of a ridge, turns left then goes over a ridgetop which is between two small inlets of the lake and soon goes down to the second inlet. After crossing it the trail again climbs at a moderately steep grade giving you a nice view of the lake below. Then it angles down at a moderately steep grade until you are right along the lake. This is a very attractive section, paralleling the wooded shore for the hand of man is usually not visible here and I have had the illusion in this vicinity of being much farther removed from civilization than the geographic realities. If you hit this stretch on a pleasant day it's a nice place to have lunch or just doze and daydream for awhile.

At this writing you will arrive at a place where blaze marks somewhat vaguely indicate that the trail drops a little to the left, then continues along the lake shore. There is also another trail with no blaze marks that heads rather steeply uphill. If you follow the official trail you will find it on a steep eroding slope offering treacherous footing with a great deal of vegetation that you have to fight your way through. It's difficult to keep your balance, and if you lose it there's a good chance you'll end up in the lake. This is one of the rare exceptions where I prudently suggest that you avoid the official trail. Follow the trail to the right uphill. After nearing the ridge top it skirts it for awhile then goes steeply down and links up with the official trail again. Although it's a bit of a climb, it is both easier and safer. Possibly when the blazes are repainted they will mark the trail to the right and make it the new official way. I've done the trail both ways, and like many hikers before me I found the one to the right to be a sensible detour. It may no longer be a detour by the time you get there. The trail then gradually swings right as it prepares to go around the east section of Twin Bay. The name is used because there are two moderate sized bays directly across the lake from one another with the east one being the larger of the two. The trail hits and crosses the flat section at the head of the bay. In the summertime this can be a really tough section to find your way across for the blazed trees are necessarily small and almost impossible to see among the high weeds, but they are easily seen during the winter months. I had a sneezing attack here one early September day for a high percentage of the weeds are goldenrod.

As you walk away from the lake along the forest fringe of this low area look for a small tree at the edge of the field with a blue blaze. Then look across the field and a little to the right where another small tree is visible about halfway across it. Make for that tree which also has a blue blaze. From there look to the woods on the other side and you may be able to pick up another blue blaze on a tree on the fringe of the woods. When you reach it you will see there is a creek that flows into East Bay just beyond the tree line. The trail immediately crosses the creek but you might have to go upstream a bit to make a dry crossing.

If all signs of the trail are lost in the weed patch, cross the field heading slightly to the right until you hit the woods and creek. If you've gone to the right far enough you can turn left following the creek until you pick up the blaze marks.

Once across the creek the trail begins to angle uphill in the general direction of the lake at a moderate grade, and soon you will have a good view of the east side of Twin Bay on your left. There is a short steep section down to another wash where the trail turns left and follows the wash almost to the lake. But about 10 feet short of the shore the trail turns right following the lake shore and begins to climb paralleling the lake only to be followed by another extremely steep drop down to the lake shore. There are some nice open spots here but are somewhat marred by refuse left by thoughtless boaters. The trail climbs joining an old trail road heading to the ridgetop, but before the top is reached, the trail turns left going back into the woods and around the head of a small ravine. Staying close to the ridge top, the trail ambles up and down through the woods with one nasty uphill section which, fortunately, lasts only about 10 feet. It is in this area I believe Point M on the O.D.N.R. map was meant to be located called "Cave of the Winds", my guess is that it is probably a rock shelter but I have never been able to find it. After staying close to the ridgetop mostly in the forest the trail has only one more descent to the lake level, then climbs out again before finally dropping down to Boat Dock #3. When the trail angles down again almost to the lake shore and crosses a small wash, you know you have only one more climb to go. After crossing this small wash the trail climbs over a small rise, drops and crosses a second slightly larger branch. If you look left at the crossing you can see where the first wash joins the second. This small creek is in a narrow ravine. The official trail goes directly up away from it which can only be described as a "bitch of a climb". Here is another good place to break the rule of following the official trail because hikers with better trail engineering sense than whoever laid it out have prudently hiked a switchback into the steep ravine side. Look left and you should be able to see it, and having tried both ways with packs on, I vouch for the switchback. A stiff uphill grade takes you to a ridge crest where you can look through the trees and see Boat Dock #3. At first the descent is gradual but suddenly the trail makes an abrupt left turn with the most ridiculous descent on any trail described in this book. It drops like an airplane in a stall for almost 50 feet. Again an unofficial trail is the wiser choice. It goes right, angling down into a ravine. Once down don't follow the trail to the right, for it leads away from the boat dock, but bear left until you hit the black top at Boat Dock #3 and Point N. Unfortunately, the primitive campground here, like the one at Point H, is more like a slum than the usual idea of an isolated clearing in the woods away from it all. It's not the fault of anybody for the facility suffers more from overuse than abuse. With its road access it was primarily designed for the use of fishermen, not for backpackers and the new multiple use concept fits in badly with the isolation that most backpackers seek as well as getting lost among the larger mobile camping units.

You may notice that the map shows a town quite close to Boat Dock #3 called Vicksville alongside the road that connects Route 78 with the campground. Some may feel that the nearby location might be a good place to stock up on a couple of forgotten essentials or the luxury of a cool soft drink. But Vicksville is a collection of mostly summer homes named after a farmer who's surname is Victor, the land once being part of his farm. This small hamlet of summer residents has no store.

**POINT N TO POINT P.** From Boat Dock #3 to the crossing of the East Branch of Sunday Creek near the headwaters of the lake.
Distance:   3 miles. O.D.N.R. map 3.5 miles
Hike:   Moderate
Walking Time:   1 hour 40 minutes to 2 hours 15 minutes.

GENERAL REMARKS:   The first part of this segment can often be frustrating and unpleasant during the growing seasons and the underfooting can be quite soggy if the weather has been wet. Scenically it doesn't compare with the lower sections for the upper end of the lake is shallow, mostly flat and a good deal of the walk is through weedy swampy terrain making parts of this trail frustratingly difficult to follow. My first walk here occurred during early September after a long rainy spell. I lost the trail so many times it took me almost three hours to cover 3½ miles. When I finished I looked like I was wearing rusty chain mail, for my arms and my body were covered with hundreds of nettles and my legs and feet were coated in gray muck. Summer day hikers looking for a pleasant excursion and those with small children best look elsewhere. But much of this can change with the seasons. I once covered this section during the winter after a long dry spell and found the walk pleasant, physically easy and the trail baby simple to follow.

This section also includes the only section of trail before Point T that follows a paved road. It's not a fast moving public highway but a rather interesting straight stretch with a group of summer homes lining the road on the right. The O.D.N.R. map has a primitive camping area near Point P which doesn't exist and, although one may be added later, it will never be where it is located on that map for it would be in an extremely swampy area. There is a nice camping area near Point P with latrines and completely isolated, offering much of what the backpacker is looking for. It was originally designed to be a camp for horseback riders but was never used for that purpose. Since it is right alongside the trail, it would be ideal for backpackers so I suggested to Bob Stoncel, the assistant manager of the park, that it should be made an official primitive campground. It has not beeen so designated at this writing but Mr. Stoncel assured me it was quite legal for backpackers to camp there if they wished.

TRAIL DESCRIPTION:   Walk through the dock area with the lake on your left and you will soon pass a sign facing you on the right which says: BACK   PACK TRAIL ↑ This immediate area of the trail along the shoreline is often an unpleasant mess for many bank fishermen have a nasty habit of leaving their beer cans, bait containers and other refuse scattered along the shore. The trail then moves into a large swampy area and turns away from the lake skirting the bottom of a hill on the right until a creek comes into view on your left. Walk alongside the creek for about 30 feet and watch for a yellow blaze that indicates a left turn across the creek. Once across, with the creek at your back, walk out of the trees into the open field. In the late fall and winter months the trail will be obvious, but in the summer you may have to make your own path and plow through the weeds and head toward a section of small trees. When you reach the trees look for the blaze marks taking you through the narrow grove of trees and brambles angling toward the right for the swamp has moved in from the left. As you leave the trees the trail follows the edge of the swamp and the walking is often through muck and standing water. Once beyond a group of cattails the trail slowly swings to the left passing through heavy brush and small trees, finally arriving at a good stand of larger trees. Once in these trees you cross the second creek in this flat area, after which the trail turns left and follows the creek briefly, then turns away and goes through another small area of high weeds and small trees. The trail again may be mucky as it skirts an area with a hill on the right and a bog on the left. Soon you can see the inlet of the lake on your left close to where the creek you just crossed enters the lake. The trail then follows the lake shore where you can see Boat Dock #3 on your left. As you walk along the lake shore you can see you are headed for another point of land. The lake has eroded much of the trail here, making the path narrow with difficult footing. Just about the time the trail here, swing easily left following the shoreline out to the point it leaves the shoreline going into another mucky area, and gradually bends right where you will see a large fallen dead tree to the left of the trail. Just beyond this an abandoned road begins and to the right of it facing you a sign which says:

## BACK PACK TRAIL ↑

As you come up over a little rise on the road there is an abandoned farm on the right. Passing the driveway into the farm, you will see that the road you are on becomes paved and maintained. On my first hike along this road with cottages and a man-made pond to the right, I kept looking for yellow blaze marks for I was not sure the trail followed the road. Twice I followed paths to the lake shore to make sure I had not missed a turnoff that would have taken the official trail down and along the lake shore. I covered half the distance of the road with no sign of a blaze mark and wondered if I had made a mistake. Then it dawned on me to 'look down'. I did and there on the road surface were large yellow arrows. As you get near the headwaters of the lake Point O is somewhere in this area for this shallow area is called, "Headwaters East Branch".

The road climbs and curves to the left in front of an attractive A frame house then curves around the back of the same house. As the road curves right there is a sign on the far side of the road facing you which says:

## ←——— BACK PACK TRAIL

Here the trail leaves the paved road and begins to follow an unmaintained dirt road to the left. The rutted road eventually swings right leading into an open field with two privies on the far left. This is the location that was once to be designated as a horsemans camp, but now can be used as a good primitive campground for the backpacker.

The official trail does not make the right curve into the field but proceeds straight ahead, still continuing on an old road which is not quite as well defined beyond the curve. The trail and the road gradually decline as they curve slowly to the right until they reach the flood plane of the upper lake. In wet weather this can be another waterlogged area with inches of standing water in many places. At first the trail follows along the base of a hill on the right but gradually swings away from the hill heading toward East Fork Creek which flows into the lake. Just before reaching the creek there used to be a sign on the right side of the trail which read CAMPSITE ↑
I looked through the area and could find only high weeds and no evidence of anyone camping there. It really is a dreadful location because the flat land is often flooded, remaining saturated with water long after the flood waters receded. Any camp-ground at this end to remain functional should be on higher ground. The O.D.N.R. map has a campground marked further south on the opposite side of the creek in an even worse location. It simply never existed nor ever will in the spot indicated for it is in the middle of a swamp.

The trail soon runs into the creek with stone foundations for a non-existing bridge. When I first walked this area one August afternoon there was a beautiful rustic bridge across the creek that had been built by Boy Scouts. The span was made by two long trunks of Sycamore trees with smaller branches laid across and attached to the two trunks for the path. As pretty as it was I knew it wouldn't last long and by December of that year it was unusable. It has been replaced by a less attractive but far more practical metal floating bridge with pontoons that rise and fall with the level of the stream. It is about 50 feet upstream from the site of the old bridge. The last few years saw this bridge working very well but the last time I saw it some of the pontoons had developed leaks and it was in danger of being destroyed. State budget cutbacks have necessarily caused much maintenance work to be postponed. Postponing the necessary repairs very much longer on this bridge will likely mean the loss of the whole bridge but I was assured by park personnel that it soon would be repaired. If it

*Boy Scout bridge (now destroyed) that was the original crossing point of East Fork Creek at the headwaters of Burr Oak Lake*

should be gone or sunk and the water is at a moderate level just go upstream until you find a place easier to cross.

When you cross over the bridge you are at Point P. If you are continuing the Burr Oak Loop read the trail description from Point P to Point T for directions. If you are going to do the Wildcat Loop in the Wayne National Forest, make a right turn after crossing the bridge and walk toward the maintained county gravel road passing a low cement bridge on the left that once served as a driveway entrance for a no longer existent home site. When you reach the gravel road turn right and in 2/10 mile you will see a parking lot and a sign that indicates the trail on the left which is the trailhead. For trail notes of this 13 mile loop see page 168. The Buckeye Trail also parts company with both trails here although it follows the road past the trailhead for the Wildcat Trail.

**POINT P TO POINT T** from the bridge crossing of East Branch of Sunday Creek to the State Park Office and campground - beach - marina road.

Distance: 5 miles. O.D.N.R. map 7 miles
Walking Time: 2½ to 3½ hours.
Hike: Strenuous

GENERAL DESCRIPTION: Although there are many short up and down sections with the hardest single climb on the Burr Oak Loop on this segment it is, in this writer's judgement, the most rewarding. Except for the very beginning the trail crosses no low-boggy areas. Even though the trail never follows along the lake shore, the lake is still often in sight and from the higher elevations most of the best lake vistas are from this side. This side is high most of the way in contrast to the many low areas the trail crosses on the opposite shore. Even when the lake water is fairly high only the beginning of this segment is ever under water. The Indian Signal tree found alongside the trail gives it another spark of interest. The yellow blaze markers are often a bit thin or nonexistent across the open areas, but the crossing of the open sections are far easier for they do not have the very high weed growth found on the other side of the lake.

TRAIL DESCRIPTION: At this writing the first part of the continuation of the loop trail from Point P is not too obvious but fortunately becomes much easier to follow once the first quarter mile is behind you. From here on you will only have the yellow blaze marks to follow. Once across the floating bridge at Point P turn right in the direction of the maintained county gravel road and you will see a low cement bridge on the left which is quite close to the county road. It once served as a driveway back to a former homesite. Turn left and cross the bridge and follow the path between the trees that was once a road. When you pick up the yellow blazes this old drive goes quite close to the creek but the trail follows it only briefly. Look for a yellow blaze and arrow that that the trail makes a right diagonal turn off the road, leading you through an often mucky area with many small dead trees. After crossing this area the trail goes between the dead trees on the left and a little rise on the right about 15 feet high which was once the foundations of a house or barn. The trail then crosses a small open weedy area on slightly higher ground out of the mucky flood plain, crosses a small wash, rises over a small finger of a ridge, drops down again and crosses a second wash. After this crossing the trail starts the first moderately steep climb. It doesn't take you quite to the top of the ridge but hangs along its side. You will cross an open section where you can look across the lake below you and see some cottages on the far shore. Except for occasional drops to cross ravines and hollows the trail is never near the lake level but skirts along the side or top of a ridge to Point T. When the trail returns to the woods you will run into a section of old fence that lies in the general direction of the trail. The trail passes from one side of this fence to the other several times.

Along this section you will pass a rock outcropping about eight feet high paralleling the trail on the right. I once noticed a set of painted initials here that I found in a couple of other locations as well as carved into the trunk of a beech tree. Apparently our natural world must suffer the scars brought by the torrid passions of young love. Beyond the outcropping the trail descends and crosses a flat hollow in the woods. The O.D.N.R. map's Point Q, which is called Morgan's Cave, is somewhere in this vicinity but I have never been able to find it. After two creek crossings in the hollow, the trail begins the second moderately steep climb on this segment, again going part way up the ridge, then hanging on its side. This is a lovely wooded walk with the lake shore about 100 feet below. The trail breaks out into the open on a finger of a side ridge that turns left and heads toward the lake which gives you a lovely view across the lake where a white house is visible, high on a distant ridge. This is one of the better views from this side of the lake, and I think the O.D.N.R.'s map Point R called Lake Vista is meant to be here. The trail descends gradually partway down this declining ridge, and as it returns to the forest makes an abrupt right turn away from the lake and skirts around a ravine and comes to a sign which says: PORTERS DROP. I was told this sign was put up by a youth work crew because there is a drop beyond the sign over a rock outcropping. Although not high, one of the participants in the program fell over it and broke his arm.

From the sign the trail turns right, drops quite steeply down to a flat hollow bottom, crosses the creek and cuts across an open section on the hollow bottom. Just as you are about to enter the trees again the trail turns right moderately climbing up to and across an open area. When the trail returns to the trees the going gets very steep and finally climbs to another open section at the top of the ridge. It cuts across the field without the aid of blaze marks and once back in the trees, again cuts right away from

*Indian Signal Tree*

the lake where a deep ravine develops on the left. The trail drops down steeply about 15 feet to the wash in the ravine, crosses the wash, then turns left and follows it downstream for a short distance. It then cuts right and climbs steeply out of the ravine then turns left following the ravine for awhile before gradually swinging right. Soon the trail passes the Indian Signal tree on the right. These trees were bent when saplings by Indians to indicate tribal and hunting ground territories and there are several of them still in existence in various parts of Ohio.

Once past the signal tree the trail turns right going up the side of a ravine and in about 100 yards the trail angles down to its wash, climbs out and heads in the direction of the lake. Then the trail turns right, away from the ravine, and into an open field where you can easily see a barn on a hill across the lake.

Once across the field and back into the trees, the trail immediately crosses another small wash steeply going down then up about 20 feet across its ravine. Shortly after the crossing, the trail turns left and starts gently downhill towards the lake, cuts right, crosses another wash, then climbs easily to the ridge top. Here the trail follows along the ridge top crossing back and forth between sections of the old fence and across several washes. Watch for one very abrupt turn to the right where the blaze arrow is painted on a rock that is fading in the natural growth of lichens on the rock surface.

Finally the trail begins to angle down gently toward a land point in the lake between the main body of the lake on the left and the west side of Twin Bay on the right. This is where I believe Point S called "Twin Bay" is located on the O.D.N.R. map. The trail then veers to the right, angling down and away from the lake where the west side of Twin Bay is now on your left and continues to angle down beyond Twin Bay into the hollow at its head. Almost on the hollow bottom the trail crosses a series of four side branches before coming down to the hollow bottom. Once on the bottom the trail proceeds up the hollow until it cuts left, crosses its main streams and goes directly across the bottom of the hollow. On the other side the trail splits and the yellow blazes go in both directions. The left direction will eventually lead you into the State Park Campground but the loop trail turns right and begins a long steady climb until it passes the Park Offices on the right and brings you to the paved road at Point T. You will see signs along the left side facing the trail which says: YACC EAST BRANCH TRAIL, and another which says:

CAMPGROUND TRAIL ENDS
◄──── CAMPGROUND ONE MILE

The East Branch Trail is, of course, the one you have just completed.

**POINT T TO POINT A** from the Burr Oak Park Headquarters to the trailhead at the Marina at Boat Dock #4.
DISTANCE: 1.3 miles. O.D.N.R. map 1.5 miles
WALKING TIME: 25 to 40 minutes
HIKE: Easy

GENERAL DESCRIPTION: This section is an easy downhill walk entirely on paved road. At this writing this section is not blazed but it is quite easy to follow. Unlike the other paved road which the trail follows on the northeast corners of the lake, this road may have a great deal of traffic during the warmer months of the year so it is best to walk alongside the road, or face the traffic if you prefer the added speed that walking on pavement gives you. If you started your loop walk at A and your car is in the marina parking lot, you might have the most chipper of your group shed his or her pack, quickly hike to the car and drive it back if the members of your party are very tired, especially carrying packs. If you are packing the trail during the winter with a start at Point J, this civilized part of the walk is easy, and you'll soon be back off the road and into the woods beyond Point A.

TRAIL DESCRIPTION: Turn left on the paved road in front of the park office and in a little less than 2/10 mile the road forks. The left fork, as the signs indicate, goes into the campground while the right fork that you follow heads towards the beach and picnic area. From there you follow the road downhill about a half a mile until you reach the parking lot for the beach area. At its entrance there is a stop sign. The trail does not go into this parking lot but turns right on a road just beyond the stop sign. This road goes through part of the picnic area to the shoreline of the lake, curves right where you have a good view of the lodge across the lake. As the road continues around, you will soon see Boat Dock #4 to your left. There is a backpack sign there that indicates the left turn. Walk to the opposite end of the marina and you will be at Point A.

# WILDCAT TRAIL

DISTANCE: 13 miles
HIKE: As an overnight backpack trip. Moderate. As a single day walk. Strenuous.
WALKING TIME: 6 to 8 hours.

GENERAL DESCRIPTION: This hike, entirely in the Wayne National Forest, is possibly the finest overnight loop for beginning backpackers in this book. The climbs on well engineered trails are easy but there are enough of them to let one know if clothing and equipment are wearing well or are ill fitting. Most of the trail is on or near ridge tops but it has no outstanding overlooks. It is just long enough to show how well one's body is prepared and despite its isolation it has enough road crossings that if serious trouble does occur, the trip could easily be abandoned in several places. It is also pretty enough that experienced backpackers may enjoy it too, especially as the seasons first easy shakedown walk.

Much of this trail crosses a primitive weapons hunting area, so during legal seasons you may run into hunters with bows, arrows and muzzle loaders. I've found these hunters sensible and cautious, and they do not pose the threat that the hiker faces in hunting areas where modern weapons are permitted. For more information on this trail read through the introduction on page 143 and the parts relating specifically to the Wildcat Trail in HIKING THE BURR OAK WILDCAT TRAILS on page 150. Directions for finding the trailhead are on page 148.

TRAIL DESCRIPTION: This fine trail has a delightful beginning directly into a pine forest where the ground is entirely covered with pine needles. You will soon see the square white blaze is fastened in such a way that two of the square's points are perpendicular to the ground. In the next few minutes you will go in and out of these groves and cross the stream called Eels Run four times as you work your way up its hollow for almost a mile. After the first stream crossing, you will come to a backpack sign facing you on the right side of the trail with an arrow pointing straight ahead and another arrow pointing right. This junction is where the return part of the loop comes in from the right and rejoins the main trail. For the outgoing part of the loop proceed straight ahead. The trail reaches a point where the large hollow splits into two smaller ones and the creek also splits into two tributaries. Here the trail crosses the left fork, follows it close to its bank, then crosses it again. Just a short distance beyond this crossing mile marker 1 is on the right side. The trail then recrosses this branch for the last time, heads up a rise and appears to dead end in front of a ravine. It doesn't, for it switches back to the right and continues to climb. Another switchback followed by three rounding switchbacks has the trail curving left around the end of the ridge then climbs at a gradual and moderate grade up to the ridge top. Although there is over a 100 foot rise, it is engineered so well that on my first walk I was only vaguely tested physically although I was carrying a pack weighing 40 pounds. Following along the ridge top the trail comes to an open field, passing mile marker 2 on the right. The area is nice and level and could be a good camping site for those who began their hike late in the day.

Returning to the woods, the trail passes over several little gullies. You may notice, down to the right off the trail, a huge barrel attached by pipes to a shed. It is the site of a once operating oil well. This is the first of many you will see along the trail, and you won't miss much if you observe this one only from the trail.

Coming up alongside a maintained gravel road the trail follows alongside it for a short distance before crossing it. This is Irish Ridge Road. At the point where the trail hits this road, there is a narrow primitive road to the right which serves as a connection between the outgoing and return segments of the Wildcat loop. It is designed for those who wish to take a shorter loop day hike.

To continue on the main loop turn right on Irish Ridge Road and follow it a short distance until another road comes in from the left. You can look beyond the junction to the left of Irish Ridge Road and see the old country school house that is no longer used but named on the government trail map. When you approach this junction you can look across the road on the left and see a sign facing the road which says:

⬅——— PERRY COUNTY ROAD 70<br>
⬅——— WATER WORKS ROAD

You cross the Waterworks Road close to the intersection where the trail leaves the road, turns left, parallels it briefly then turns right away form it. As the path crosses a cleared area for power lines there is a path that goes to the left, but the official trail proceeds straight passing under the lines into a grove of small pines. You will soon have a switchback to the left, then one to the right as the trail passes through

*Oil well sheds along Wildcat Trail*

partially open country with small groves of young evergreens. The trail is now going towards the head of a ravine seen on the left, makes a left turn, dropping steeply to its bottom then turns left following its branch. The times I've covered this trail, right after this turn I've seen an interesting hollow log lying to the right and by looking across the creek at this point you can see where recent selected timbering has taken place on the hill behind it. The trail follows the wash going down at a moderate grade until it has a short moderately steep drop down to the banks of the stream and crosses it. The trail turns left following in the direction of the wash as the ravine widens out into a hollow. You will soon pass an oil well site on your left with a shack that once covered the motor that ran the pump. As you walk pass this site you will see that the trail joins a dirt F.W.D. road which soon leads you into a more mature forest of conifers. On this section you will pass mile marker 3, which is on the right. Just beyond this marker the trail comes to a point where two hollows join to make a larger one and as you approach an oil well shed you can look left and see a whole group of these oil well sheds with various connecting rods, pumps and pipes that comes close enough to look like housing for people that it has the suggestion of a pioneer village.

    The trail swings to the right heading up the other small section of hollow. It soon passes under a large cable where you can look left and see a dirt F.W.D. road. The trail goes to the road, turns right on it and crosses a creek. If you look ahead you can see another oil shed up the road, but before you get to it there is an oil pipe that crosses the road high enough that vehicles can pass under it. The trail angles off to the left of the road and passes under the pipe and goes to the fringe of the woods. Just before the trail returns to the trees a sign facing the opposite direction says: WILDCAT HOLLOW —BACK PACKING TRAIL. Once in the woods the trail curves around to the left which is soon followed by a curving switchback to the right and begins angling up the ridge at an easy grade. About 100 yards up, the trail seems to dead end but really takes a sharp switchback to the left, and, within 30 feet, it switches back right again then gradually curves to the left up the side of a hollow. As the trail climbs near the ridge top it gradually swings right, going through a pine grove and hits a F.W.D. dirt road and turns right on it. The trail follows this road up to a saddle. Close to where the road hits the top of the saddle there is another dirt road going off to the left but the trail goes to the top of the saddle then turns left on the ridge top which grows increasingly narrow. While following this ridge top, you pass a ruin on the left which is marked on the forest service map as "Farmhouse". It is the interesting remains of an old log cabin complete with a store cellar. This location is so isolated that it must have been a homestead built in the last century and now has that aura of romance about it that makes one think of people dressed in home-spun, deerskin and coonskin caps carrying hexagonal barrel muzzle loaders. It is not far beyond this site that you will pass mile marker 4 on the left side of the trail.

While still following this ridge top, you will come to a location on the left side of the ridge where recent timber operations have taken place. The ridge beyond this point becomes an F.W.D. timber road which can be very mucky in wet weather. It is easy to follow this road until it dead ends into Irish Ridge Road, but look for a turn to the left off the timber road where the trail becomes a woodland path again. If you miss the turn, when you get to the maintained gravel road turn round and walk back and in about a two to four minute walk you will come to the turn you missed to the right.

After leaving the lumber road the trail circles around the head of a hollow on the left of the trail and crosses several small washes and then has an easy climb up to a maintained gravel road. Just before you get to it there is the standard sign prohibiting vehicles and horses facing the opposite direction. There are several log steps implanted in the embankment to help you down to the road. When you hit the road turn right and walk about 100 feet before turning left. You will notice that as the road goes uhphill it makes a curve to the left. The trail's left turnoff is just before that curve. A short distance after leaving the road, mile marker 5 is to the left of the trail.

After crossing several small washes, some with culverts draining to the left, the trail T's into another trace road and turns left on it. When it begins going downhill you get one of the rare views of a wide expanse of the countryside on this trail before it drops into the trees as it heads toward the bottom of a hollow. As it goes steeply downhill, curving to the right you can see a white pipe with an orange top sticking out of the ground on the left. This is part of the pipeline operated by the Columbia Gas Company. You will see many more of these white pipes before finishing the loop. You leave the road here and the trail heads in the direction of the pipe. Just before it reaches the pipe the trail turns right and goes down to the head of a small wash, turns left on the other side of it and goes diagonally away from it.

There are some easy switchbacks down to the main creek in this hollow where the trail reverses direction and follows it downstream, crossing it three times. The last crossing is easily seen, for just beyond the crossing is another orange topped white pipe where the trail begins angling up the ridge at a moderate grade. You can tell that the trail is close to the gas line for you will pass a whole series of the white pipes on the right side of the trail. When the trail almost reaches the ridge top it makes a curving switchback to the right and climbs up the backbone of an ascending ridge. This climb is gentle and long, gaining about 100 feet in altitude and passes mile marker 6 on the right. When the trail reaches a maintained gravel road you have your second and last crossing of Irish Ridge Road. Turn right and go about 75 feet up to the first telephone pole on the left, and just beyond it up to the crest of the hill a sign on the left facing you is a backpack trail sign indicating a left turn off the road. As the trail continues on the ridgetop you will pass mile marker 7 about 100 yards beyond the road. The trail swings right as it drops down to the bottom of a hollow, crosses a creek with a slight steep short climb up its bank. This area has oil wells indicated in this location, but if they are there they are well hidden in the trees for I have never seen them. With the creek on the left the trail starts angling gently uphill moving diagonally from the stream, crossing some small washes before coming into an open area where there is a definite V in the trail. The trail follows the right fork leading away from the main hollow before crossing a wash with the aid of a culvert where it turns left and heads towards the main hollow again. As you approach another large hollow in front of you the trail switches back to the right and climbs the only moderately steep section of trail on this entire loop which lasts about 50 feet. This is followed by a very gradual climb as the ridge ascends until the trail enters a pretty grove of man-planted pines with a small attractive pond on the left built by the forest service as a water hole for the wildlife of the area. Just beyond the pond the trail is on an old narrow trace road which is soon paralleling a modern gravel road on the left. Soon the trail reaches the gravel road.

The original routing of this loop turned right here and followed roads for the last five miles back to the trail head. Now the official trail no longer follows roads but is a woodland path all the way to the end. This new route is a little longer and more demanding with some interesting clear cut overlooks. It also descends and climbs out of two hollows with easy grades.

From this point the trail crosses the gravel road diagonally to the right where you will find some log steps to help you up a low embankment. You will soon cross a swath cut in the forest for a gas line with red topped white pipes visible. The trail soon goes directly across another gravel road. There is a dirt road that T's into the gravel road at this point and it is easy to assume that the trail follows this side road, which it doesn't. The trail continues about ten feet to the left of the road and soon passes a small pond which you will see on the right. This is one of the small watering holes the forest service maintains for wildlife.

After crossing a few small ravines, the trail parallels a wash to the left of the trail, going downhill for a minute or two. It then crosses the wash and briefly continues to follow it downstream before swinging left, climbing up to and skirting alongside a large clear-cut area that rises on a hill to the left. About a five minute walk beyond this point brings you to a second clear cut area in the shape of a large U. The trail cuts across the bottom of the U. Look directly across to the forest fringe on the left for a blaze mark on a tree. As you walk across the U and approach this blaze mark, you can see one on the forest edge on the other side of the U above a large fallen tree. The trail returns to the woods just to the right of that deadfall.

A few more minutes walking will take you to a third clear cut area that is narrower than the first two. The trail goes slightly to the right of a direct crossing and returns to a light forest covering for only about 50 feet before making a sharp left turn into a fourth clear cut area that is even narrower than the last one. Again, the trail goes almost directly across the cut area and a little to the left where once back in the woods it joins an old trace road. The temptation is to follow the road, but after a couple of minutes on this road the trail makes a sharp left turn away from it. You now have about a mile of pleasant woodland walking, crossing several small washes, skirting little ravines and around rolling ridge knobs before arriving at the last and largest clear cut area before dropping into Cedar Run Hollow. As you enter the clearing you may have the feeling that the trail should go downhill to the right but it doesn't. If you look across the lumbered area, you will see slightly to the right, a few solitary trees that escaped the chain saws. The tallest of these has a blaze mark. Walk to it but pass it slightly to your right. When you are alongside that tree, turn left and walk a few feet to the top of a rise where you will come to a recently used logging road. Looking left here you can see where about 100 feet of scrap logs have been laid across the road which looks like a rat's nest of broken branches as a deterrant for off road vehicles. Follow the road to the right into a small and rather thin patch of forest. When through this little clump of trees, the weeds can often be quite high. If the path is non-existent, just follow along the narrow ridge top until the ridge starts dropping at the fringe of the woods.

There you should be able to pick up a blaze mark where the trail turns right skirting the cleared cut area on the right. This is soon followed by a curving switchback to the left where the trail begins angling down the side of the ridge at a moderate grade to the hollow bottom. Turning right, the trail crosses Cedar Run with the aid of a two log bridge, which is a very small stream at this point. Moving directly across the hollow, you soon come to a second small stream which has a four log bridge. Just beyond the crossing, the trail goes up a brief moderately steep section then turns left and follows a little table on the ridge side in the down stream direction. You are not on this level section very long before the trail makes an abrupt right turn which is very easy to miss where it begins the climb up to the ridge top. If you miss the turn, an unofficial trail soon leads to a point with a steep drop back down to the creek made wide at this point by a beaver dam. Retreat about 30 steps and you will see the trail to the left that takes you up the ridge.

It is a moderate climb up this ridge finger with one brief moderately steep section. After a switchback to the left a right curve puts you on top of the ridge. This easy ridge top walk takes you almost to a large fenced in field which is part of a farm. Just before reaching the field the trail turns left away from it and begins following the side of a ravine on the left until you see another ravine on the right. The trail then briefly follows the ravine on the right upstream before crossing it then following it in the downstream direction. You now have an easy descent into the hollow that gives this trail its name until it comes out of the woods and crosses a maintained gravel road.

Turning right, the trail proceeds up Wildcat Hollow staying fairly close to the road. It then turns left and, as it crosses the hollow bottom, you can see a large bare patch of small stones to the right. Passing to the left of those stones the trail climbs a bit then turns right and passes above the stony area. Here, you will be able to look down and see a swamp area below you as well as an old shed and storage tank.

Continuing an easy angling climb up the ridge the trail takes you back into the forest. When you pass another small oil shed on the right and you are helped across a creek by many small logs, you have a moderate climb that should take less than five minutes up to the ridge top.

The trail then T's into a grassy lane where you will see white blaze marks going in both directions. This old narrow road, which is kept clear by the forest service, is the connector trail for a shorter loop walk from the vicinity of Irish Ridge Road. You turn left here and you will soon come to a fork in the old road. Follow the road to the left which skirts an open area to the right where you can look down and see Wildcat Hollow below you on the left.

You follow along the left side of the ridge until the trail turns right into a quasi-open area and crosses an old cement floor. After crossing this meadow the trail returns to the woods for a brief few minutes before entering and crossing a second open area. You will again find that this trail briefly follows another old trace road on the left side of the ridge. It turns right off this road into a third open area and proceeds right down the middle of it.

When the trail returns to the woods, it begins an easy angling descent down the right side of the ridge to the hollow bottom. It follows alongside the wash in the downstream direction and soon T's into another trail. This is the outgoing section of the trail. Turn left here, and, after one crossing of Eel's Run and a short walk through a pine forest, you arrive at the trails' end.

# SHAWNEE STATE PARK AND FOREST
## INTRODUCTION AND AREA DEVELOPMENT

Shawnee, Ohio's big one, the largest in the area has the longest and most difficult trails with the highest climbs and longest descents. Like Tar Hollow, Zaleski, and Hocking Hills, its trail head is in a state park surrounded by a state forest. But in Shawnee it exists in far larger proportions. Like Vesuvius and Tar Hollow, much of Shawnee's development was due to the recovery work planned and executed by the Federal government to help end the Great Depression of the 1930's. It is a marvelous example of what can be done with land that once was considered of little practical value. Because the area's topography contained quite high ridges with few wide hollows, most of it was not particularly suited for farming. The rugged slopes and narrow hollows were ruthlessly and extensively timbered, as well as ravaged by forest fires. There were no serious thoughts of reforestation or fire control through the late nineteenth and early twentieth centuries. It wasn't until 1922 that the first government land purchase of 5000 acres became the beginning of what is now the largest state forest in Ohio with a present area of about 60,000 acres. In that same year, other land acquisitions began for the purpose of establishing a game preserve named after Teddy Roosevelt, who had died in 1919. He was the first U.S. president to do outstanding work of conservation of public lands during his administration. Most visitors to the area mistakenly presume, as I originally did, that Roosevelt Lake was named after his famous cousin, Franklin, whose federal legislation had so much effect in establishing and preserving recreational areas in the United States. Little development of this area was carried out until the 1930's. At that time no less than six separate Civilian Conservation Corps' Camps were established in the locale. The Corps' work included building many of the roads that now traverse the forest as well as the dams for five small lakes which includes Roosevelt Lake, Bear Lake on the Silver Arrow trail and Pond Lick close to the South Loop of the Backpack Trail and next to the presently active C.C.C. Camp.

When Ohio developed its own Department of Natural Resources in 1949, the picnic and camping areas adjacent to Roosevelt Lake were turned over to the Division of Parks. Today the park area has been enlarged to over 11,000 acres, which includes the larger and newer Turkey Creek Lake, the large Shawnee Lodge and 25 housekeeeping cabins. In 1951 the rest of the Roosevelt Game preserve became the Shawnee State Forest. Although the parking lot for the Shawnee Backpack Trail is in the state park, practically all the mileage of the backpack and Silver Arrow loops are in the state forest managed by the Division of Forestry and Wildlife. When backpacking became a popular pastime in the 1960's under the concept of multiple use of forest areas, this large reforested area offered a prime location for laying out long hiking trails. The first was the Silver Arrow Boy Scout loop starting at Camp OYO. Then in 1973 the North Loop of 22.8 rugged miles was laid out. The longer South Loop and its wilderness side trail of almost 40 miles was added in 1974. Except where forest fire damage deems it necessary, the present policy is to harvest little or no timber near the trail leaving it enclosed in deep forest.

Shawnee is often called the "Little Smokies of Ohio" because of the panorama offered from the three existing fire towers as well as from a few roadside overlooks. These views show the series of high ridges that are somewhat reminiscent of their higher mountain cousins to the south. Unfortunately there is not one good overlook on either backpack loop that allows the hiker to see the type of terrain that the trail passes through, although the Boy Scout Silver Arrow trail has two such locations. The maintenance of the backpack loops, the many signs, and the primitive camping areas are carried out by the Shawnee State Forest personnel of the State Division of Forestry and Wildlife with their local headquarters at Friendship Ohio. The Silver Arrow trail is mostly maintained by the Scioto Council of the Boy Scouts of America.

## HOW TO GET THERE

With the completion of the divided highway on State Route 32, most people coming from the Cincinnati-Dayton area will find the seemingly more direct State Route 125 a torturously slow, very twisty highway that threads its way through many time-consuming towns. Equally frustrating is following U.S. Route 52 east from Cincinnati along the Ohio River with even more towns to slow you down. Some may prefer this route, however, for it does follow the Ohio River and there are some excellent river views of our southern border. If you opt for the river road, follow U.S. 52 until State Route 125 dead ends into 52 from the left at Friendship, Ohio. Turn left on 125 and go approximately seven miles to the large sign which indicates a left turn to the Shawnee Lodge. After making that turn, you will find the parking lot for the Backpack Trail is immediately on your right. The quickest, and by all means the most unscenic route follows State Route 32 east from its junction with I-275 until you meet State Route 247 near the town of Seaman. Turn right on 247 and follow it south to the town of West Union. Turn left on State Route 125 and follow it about 22 miles until you see the large sign indicating a right turn to the Shawnee Lodge. Turn right there, and immediately take another right turn into the parking lot for the Backpack Trail.

For those coming from the Columbus area, follow State Route 23 south until you come to State Route 348, which comes in from the right at Lucasville. Turn right on 348, and in less than two miles, there is a junction with State Route 104. Turn left on State Route 104 and go south into the town of West Portsmith where you will turn off on Route 339 on the right until it junctions with US 52. Follow 52 southwest through the town of Friendship to where State Route 125 dead ends into 52 from the right. Turn right on 125 and in approximately seven miles you will see a large sign indicating a turn to the left Shawnee Lodge. Turn left. Then immediately turn right into the parking lot for the Backpack Trail at Point A.

## WHERE TO STAY

If you are plannning to do some of the day hiking possibilities that are suggested beginning on page 184 you may find overnight accomodations at the Shawnee Campground, in the Shawnee Lodge or housekeeping cabins. All three are open year round. The campground, situated almost next to Roosevelt Lake with its entrance less than two miles east of the backpack parking lot on State Route 125, has 107 sites. Rated by the state as a Class A camping facility, it has electrical hook ups at all sites and a camping fee is charged. There are no primitive camping areas in the state park. The Shawnee Lodge has 50 guest rooms with the nightly fee a bit on the expensive side but the whole facility is a beautiful one. The 25 housekeeping cabins have complete cooking facilities and can easily accomodate six people. Reservations for the lodge and the housekeeping cabins are made through the lodge and are almost always necessary. For information or reservations call or write:

SHAWNEE STATE PARK LODGE
State Route 69-A
Portsmouth, Ohio 45662
Phone: (614) 858-6621

# HIKING THE SHAWNEE BACKPACK LOOPS AND THEIR VARIATIONS

**TOPOGRAPHIC MAPS:** Otway, West Portsmith, Buena Vista, Pond Run and Friendship quadrangles

**TRAIL BLAZES:** North and South backpack loops - orange. Side trails - white.

176

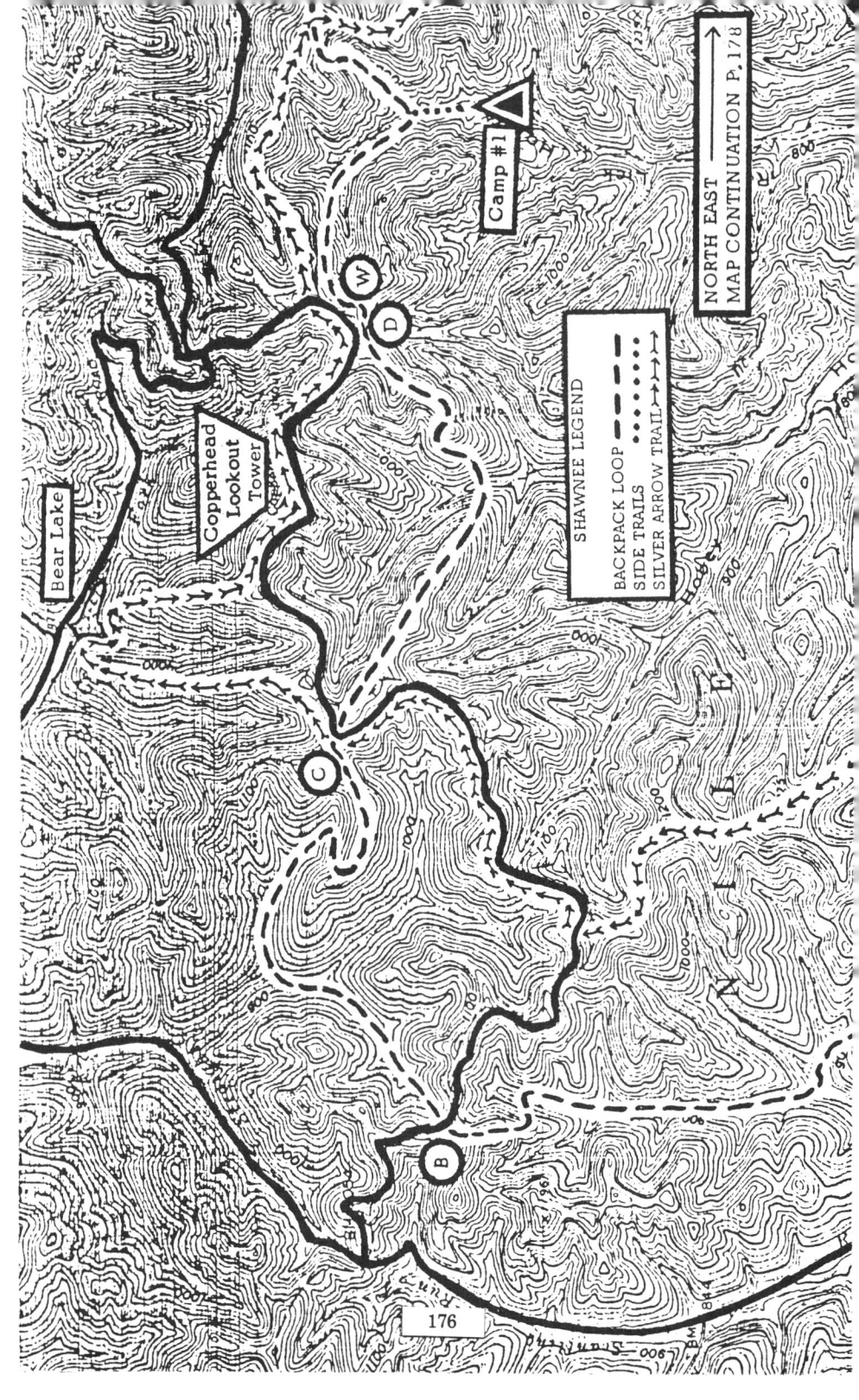

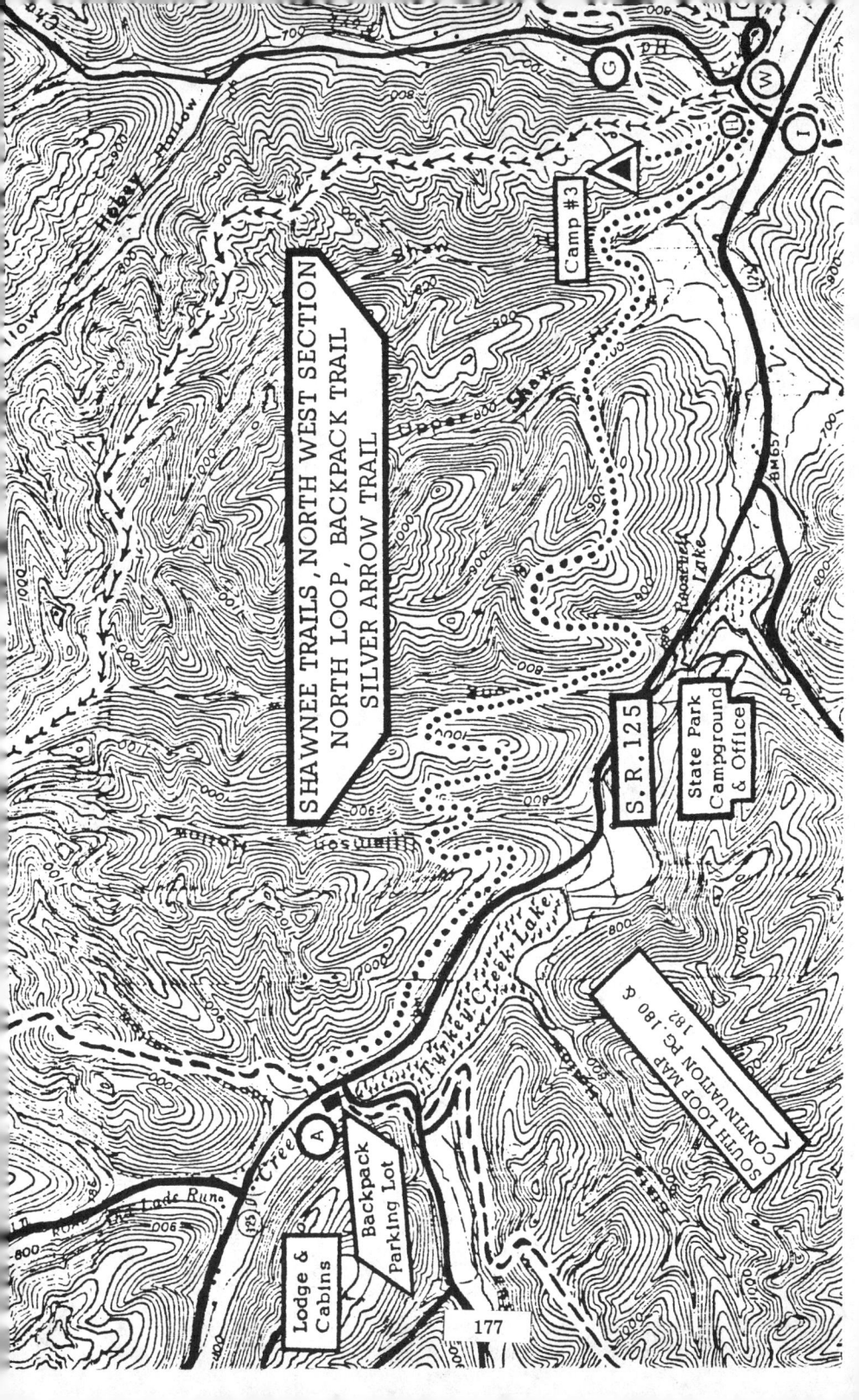

SHAWNEE TRAILS, NORTH WEST SECTION
NORTH LOOP, BACKPACK TRAIL
SILVER ARROW TRAIL

178

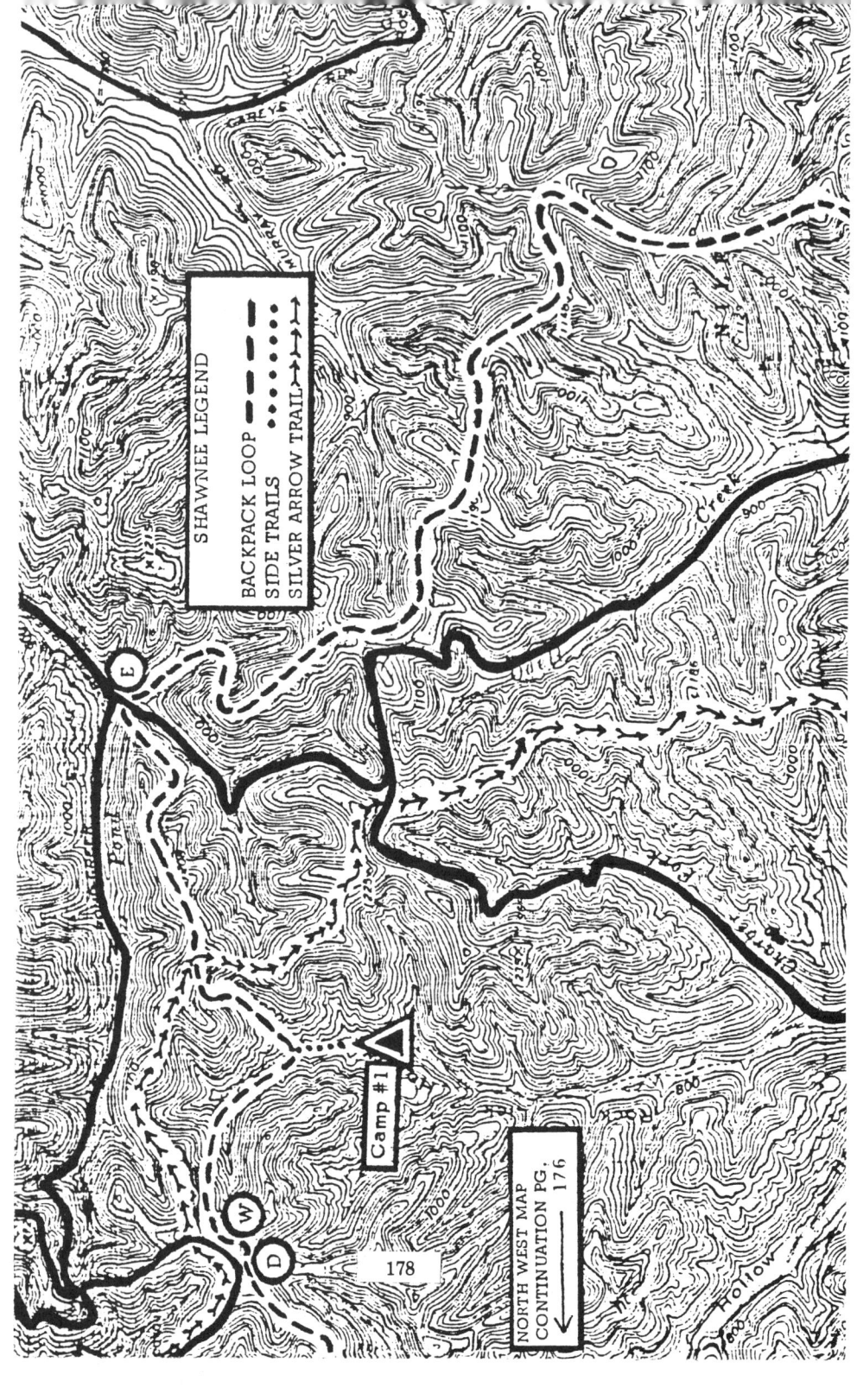

179

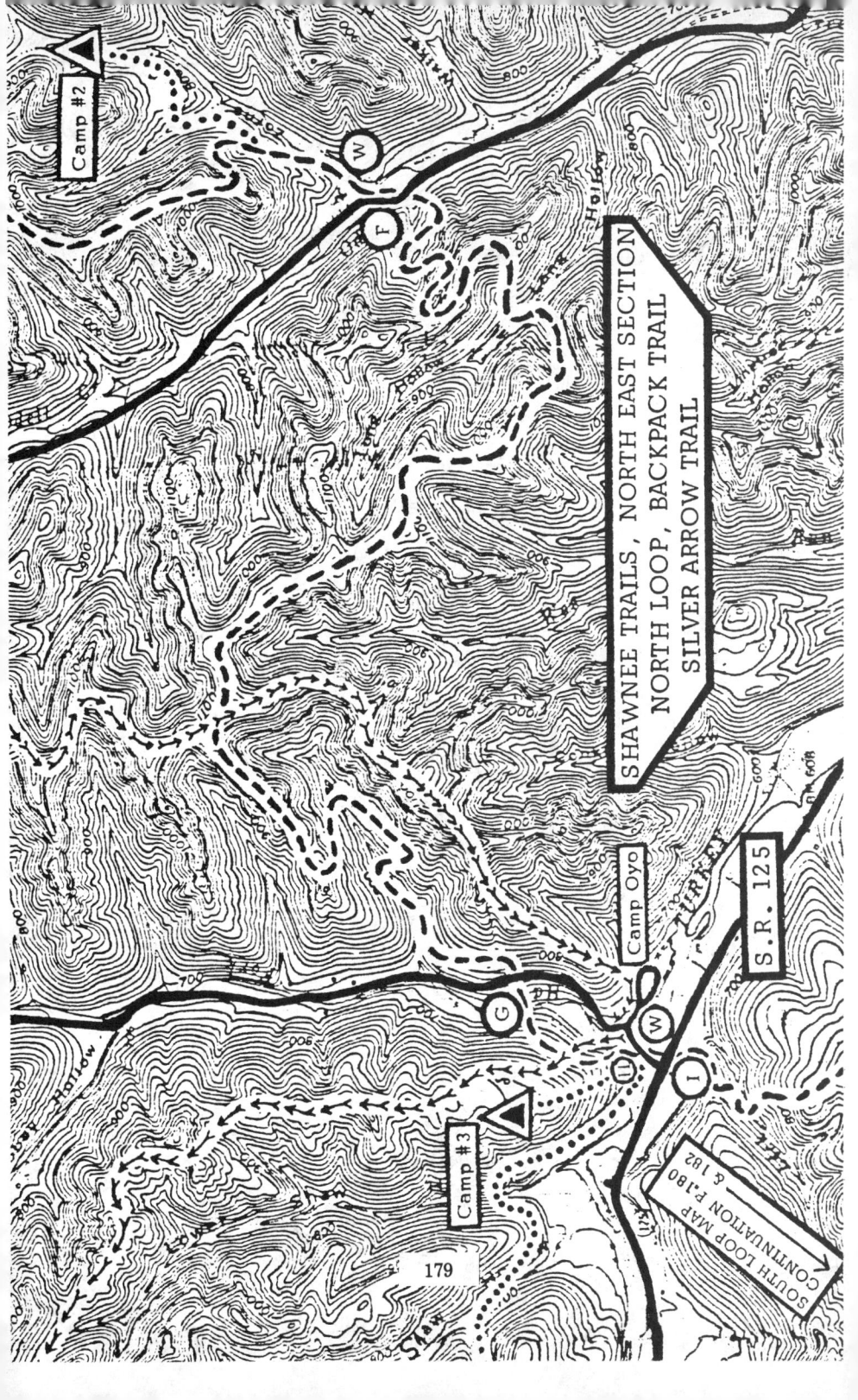

180

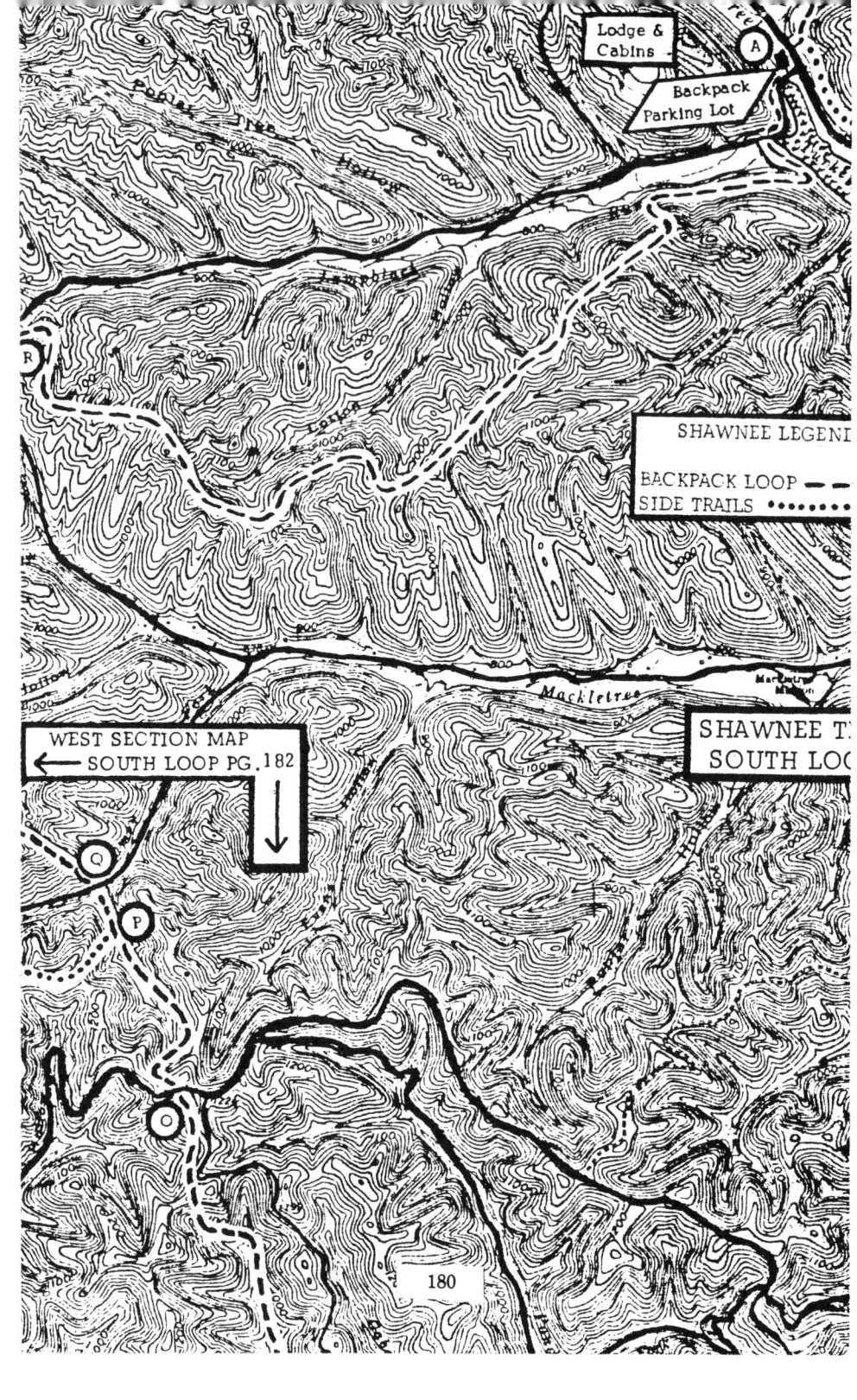

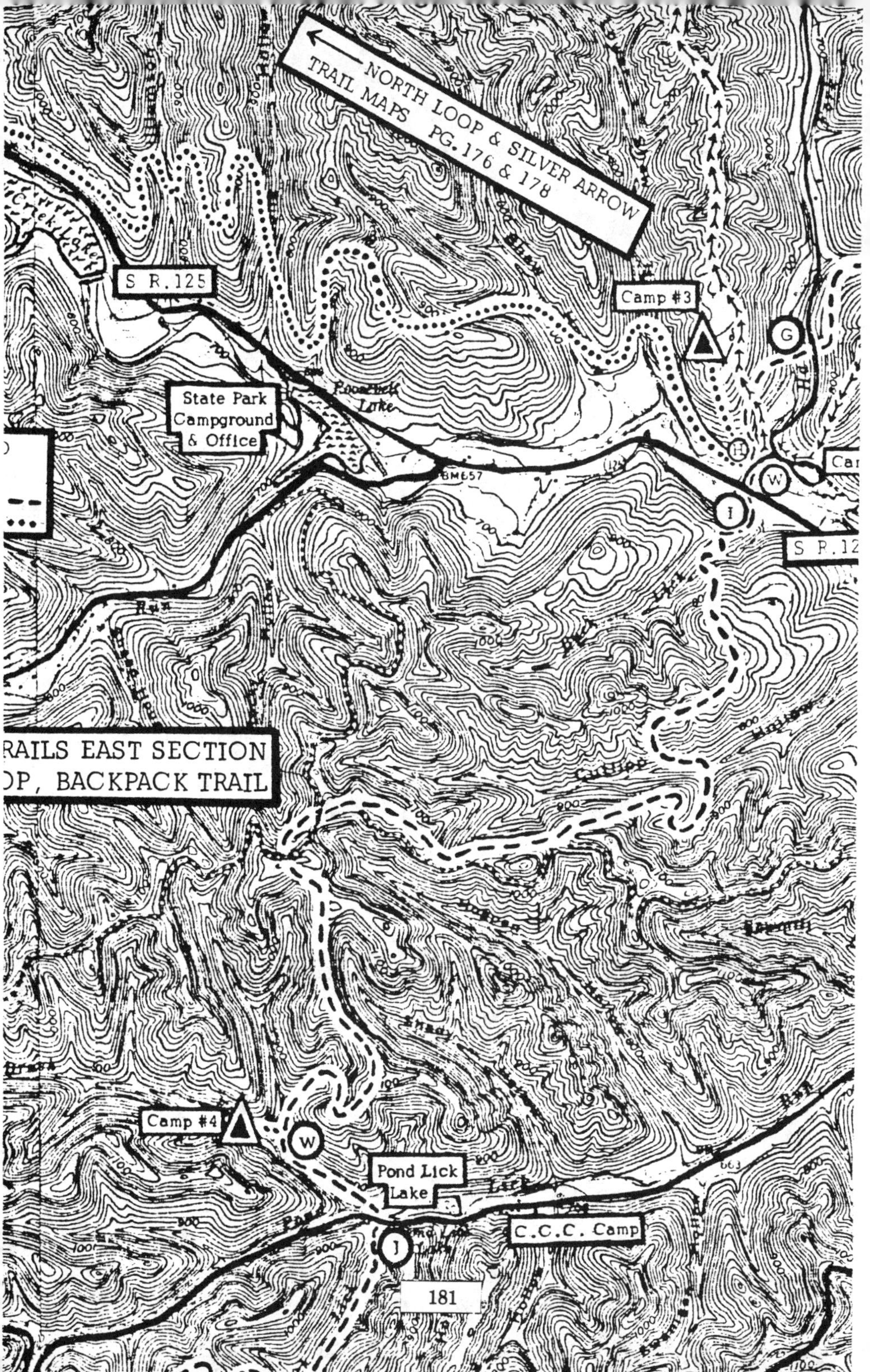

NORTH LOOP & SILVER ARROW
TRAIL MAPS PG. 176 & 178
S R.125
Camp #3
G
H
W
State Park
Campground
& Office
BM657
I
S R.12
RAILS EAST SECTION
OP, BACKPACK TRAIL
Camp #4
W
Pond Lick
Lake
C.C.C. Camp
J

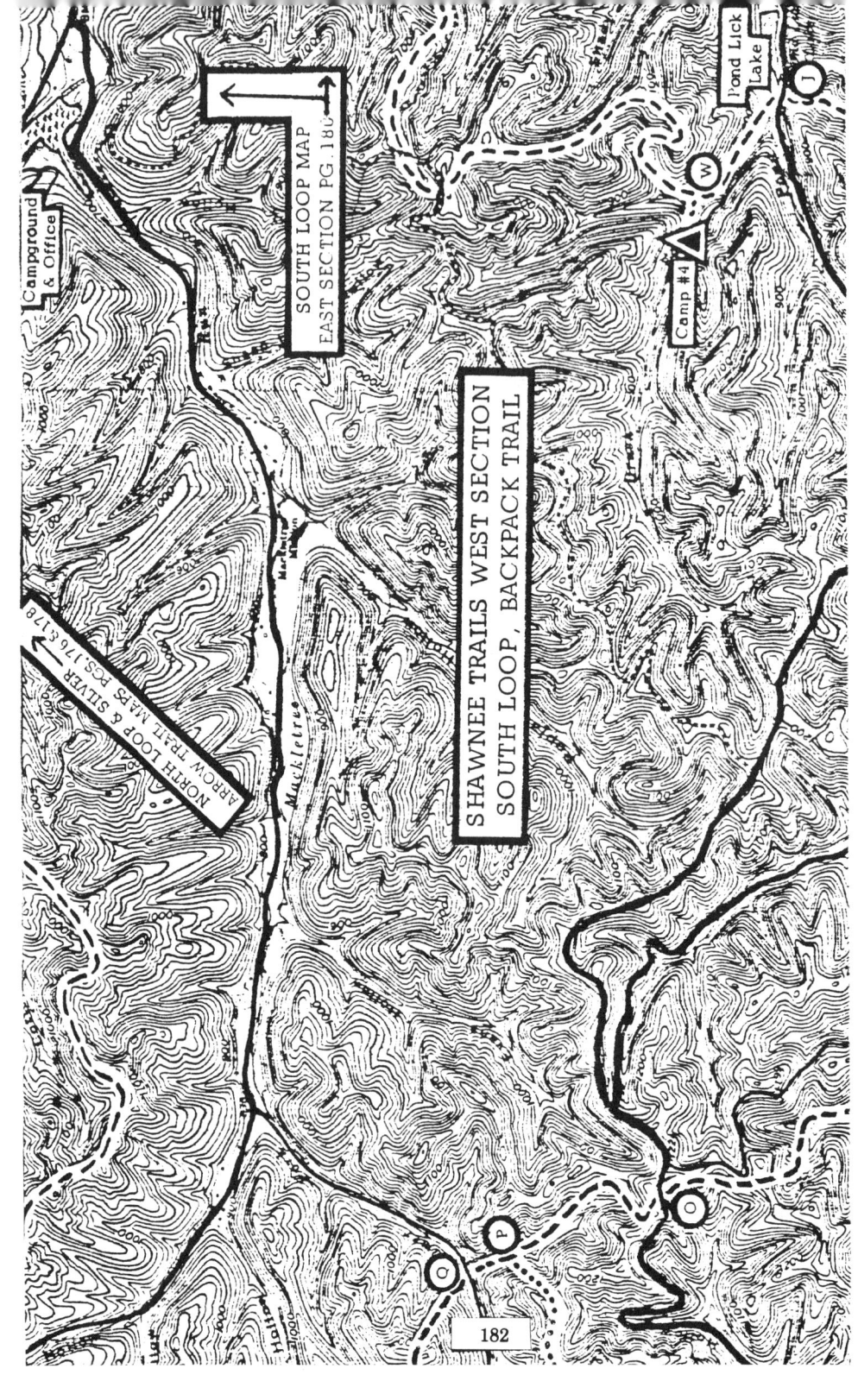

SHAWNEE TRAILS WEST SECTION
SOUTH LOOP, BACKPACK TRAIL

SOUTH LOOP MAP
EAST SECTION PG. 180

NORTH LOOP & SILVER
ARROW TRAIL MAPS PGS. 176 & 178

Campground & Office

Pond Lick Lake

Camp #4

Mackletree

182

## SHAWNEE LEGEND

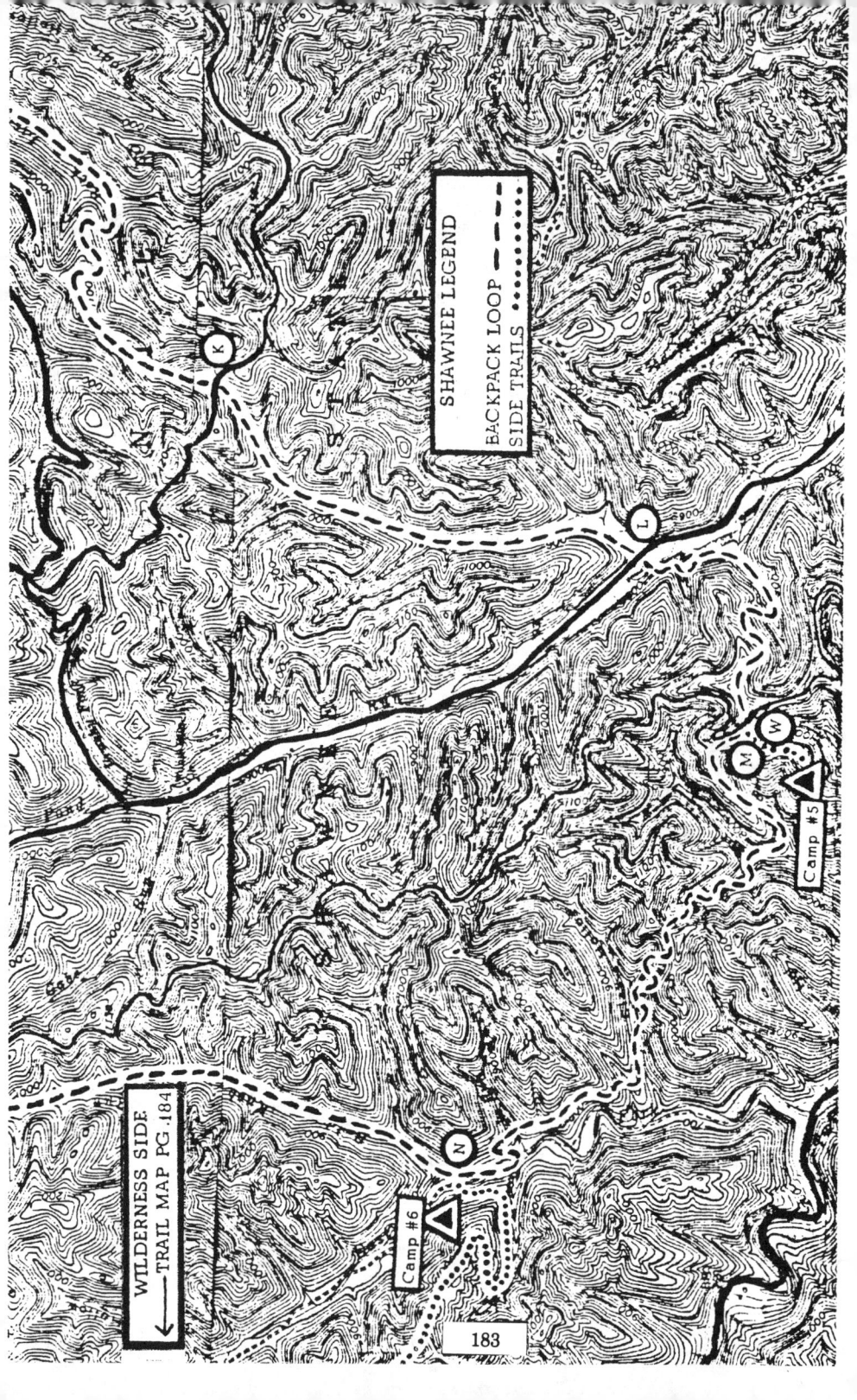

BACKPACK LOOP — — —
SIDE TRAILS • • •

K

L

M W
Camp #5

N
Camp #6

← WILDERNESS SIDE
TRAIL MAP PG. 184

183

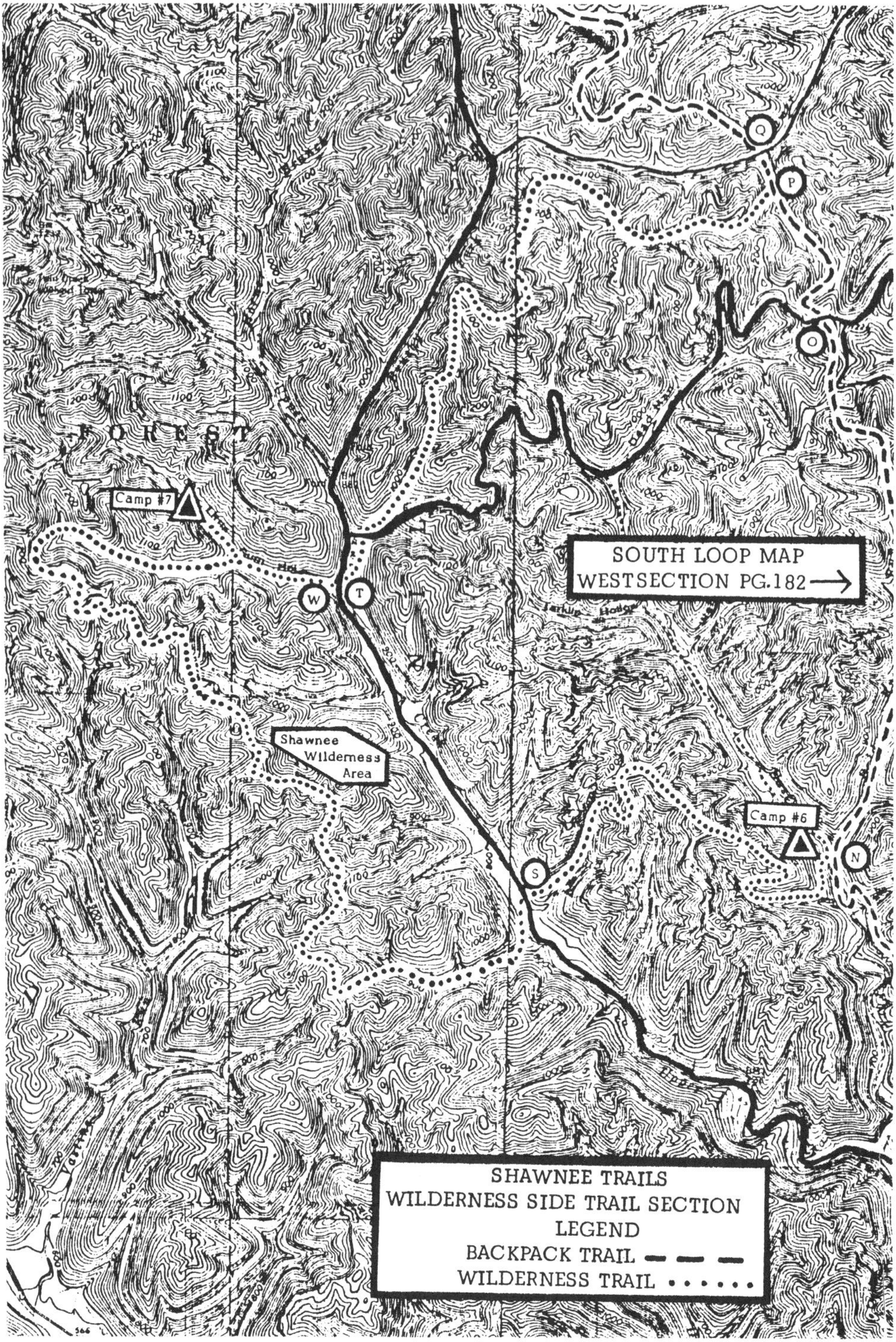

FOREST
Camp #7
W
T
Shawnee Wilderness Area
S
Camp #6
N
O
P
Q
SOUTH LOOP MAP
WESTSECTION PG.182 →
SHAWNEE TRAILS
WILDERNESS SIDE TRAIL SECTION
LEGEND
BACKPACK TRAIL
WILDERNESS TRAIL

*View from Copperhead Fire Tower*

Silver Arrow trail - painted silver arrows.

|  | **Page** |
|---|---|
| **GENERAL TRAIL INFORMATION** | 175 |
| Hiking the loops | 188 |
| Single night backpack loops | 189 |
| Day hikes | 190 |
| Finding the trailheads at Point A | 192 |
| **North Loop Backpack Trail** | |
| Segments A through H | 192 |
| Side Trail H to A | 199 |
| **South Loop Backpack Trail** | |
| Segments A through A | 200 |
| Wilderness Side Trail segments N through T | 215 |
| Silver Arrow Trail | 220 |
| **MAPS** | |
| North Loop | 176 & 178 |
| South Loop | 180 & 182 |
| Wilderness Sidetrail | 184 |

## GENERAL TRAIL INFORMATION

With over 70 miles of marked and maintained trails the hiking possibilities for the backpack loops are many but if you are new to the backpack world and are just starting your trail adventures, Shawnee is far from the ideal location to begin. The physical demands made on the hiker are extreme and the backpacker covering either of the two major loops is facing the most difficult and demanding walks described in this book. I remember talking with Stan Richards, the manager of Shawnee State Forest, who told me "If they're inexperienced backpackers please tell them to do their first hikes at Vesuvius or Zaleski, for those loops are far better suited for the novice hiker than Shawnee." Having hiked all the trails in these three areas at least twice, I wholeheartedly concur.

But Shawnee also offers some options that are not quite possible in other areas. If you are planning a strenuous hiking trip over several days (possibly along the Appalachian Trail or many of the long and often difficult trails of the western U.S.), Shawnee is there to test your mettle and your equipment. It will get you in shape for the long haul. This is the only loop trail mentioned in this book where the hiker can have an extended trip of several days. Not only will the repeated up and down sections of this longer trek cause some aching muscles, but also it will bring out other such possible discoveries such as an inadequate or ill-adjusted hip belt rubbing your hipbones raw, boots you thought were well broken in producing blisters in new places, and the pack you felt was just a mite heavy at the trailhead after three days of carrying it lightened by the consumption of edible provisions, now feels as if it were loaded with cannon balls. If you run into a couple of days of heavy rain you might also find that calling your boots waterproof was a misnomer, that putting up or taking down a tent, as well as cooking, and eating in heavy weather places a great strain on human tempers and reveals the flaws that begin to show in your personal equipment. I once used a tent of a major and respected brand. I was assured by a salesman that I trusted that it would not leak. It didn't, at least from the top, but water readily seeped through the bottom until the tent's interior was like a partially-filled bathtub. When I returned home, the guarantee was honored but that didn't save me from a miserable night on the trail and from cancelling the last night of that trip. It's much better to find out about such problems at Shawnee than it is on some mountain pass 30 miles from the trailhead and 2000 miles from home. You might also find out that your favorite weekend hiking pal has some annoying habits that multiply on longer trips until they are driving you right up the wall. Shawnee gives one the advantage of prematurely terminating a long trail hike at a handy road crossing. Making such harsh discoveries way back in the booneys a few agonizing days away from the nearest pavement of civilization can expose you to not only great discomfort but real danger from the elements.

The map of the Backpack Trail printed by the Ohio Department of Natural Resources also includes trail tips which are as follows.

## TRAIL TIPS

1. Shawnee Backpack Trail crosses rugged terrain, requiring moderate levels of skill and endurance. Sturdy footwear, proper clothing, and good equipment are essential.

2. Respect the solitude sought by other backpackers and practice good camping etiquette.

3. The main trail is marked with orange blazes and side trails with white blazes. If

you become lost, follow water courses downhill to a road, usually within a mile. Carry a map and compass.

4. For safety, hike with a companion. Disabling injuries are very dangerous when you are alone.

5. The only drinking water supplies will be close to road crossings, as shown on your map. Supply is limited—please use wisely. They may not be serviced in winter due to bad road conditions. Laterines are provided at each campground for your convenience.

6. Beware of poisonous snakes. Both rattlesnakes and copperheads inhabit the forest. High leather boots or heavy leggings afford good protection. Watch where you sit and put your hands, especially in rocky areas. If bitten, seek medical aid immediately.

7. Select and repack your food so that you will have a minimum of awkward and disposable containers. A portable stove is recommended. Supplies of wood fuel may not be readily available.

8. Extinguish all smoking material carefully. Scrape away all leaves and duff to mineral soil. Be especially careful with campground fires and smoking during March, April, May, October and November, the forest fire danger periods in Ohio.

9. If you discover a forest fire, hike the trail to the nearest road immediately and report it to the forest or park headquarters.

10. For your protection, park your car only at the trailhead. Cars parked in the forest may attract vandalism.

11. CAUTION: Campgrounds situated in valleys may be flooded and stream crossings may be impassable due to rapid runoff following a severe storm.

12. Hornets and yellow jackets may be encountered particularly during late summer.

I have some personal comments to add to this excellent list. I have found the orange blaze markers on the major trails are frequent and easy to follow but the white markers for the side trails are a little thin especially on the N to P wilderness trip. The signs, which number close to 60 along the trail, suffer the usual destruction by vandals, but the forest service people at Friendship do an outstanding job in replacing those that are destroyed. Usually the signs that suffer the worst are those close to a road with the interior signs left in good shape. I have noticed that interior signs far from the roads suffer far more damage at Shawnee than in other areas. I have seen several that have been butchered by axes miles into the forest. The only plausible explanation for this odd phenomenon is that the damage was carried out by inexperienced hikers who, having found physical demands of the trail were far beyond what they expected, take out their frustrations on the signs in their exhausted condition.

Generally, you can count on water being delivered to the seven water locations the year round. Only once on one frosty November walk did I find one empty. The assistant manager of the forest told me that particular one was always running out far sooner than the others and suspected some prankster was trying to make life difficult for both the backpackers and the forestry department. The culprit, however, turned out to be a leaking tank which has since been replaced.

Park your car only at the trailhead as suggested or at Camp OYO or the CCC Camp for any overnight hike. Vandalism is severe on the more isolated roads of the forest. In one instance, a car was picked up and heaved over the ridge of a hill. It is usually safe to park in these more isolated areas for day hikes because the majority of the vandalism seems to occur at night. The warning about Yellow Jackets reminded me of a personal trail incident that happened when I was making my initial hikes for this book. My younger daughter, Barbie, who was about 10 years old at the time, and I were attacked by a swarm of Yellow Jackets during a July day hike who repeatedly dive bombed our heads. In a matter of seconds I was stung on the top of my head about five times and Barbi received about eight. We had to return the way we came and as we passed the location of the attack with our extremeties well covered and in great haste, I discovered a large hornet's nest in a very small tree right alongside the trail. I inadvertently hit the tree with my hiking stick when we passed the first time, which set them off.

Shawnee is an especially bad place to hike in shorts, for the abundance of poison ivy and brambles alongside the trails can really chew up your legs. Walking in tennis shoes or other light footwear is also a bad choice for not only are you more susceptible to injury on the rocky terrain, but also, there is a remote chance that a poisonous snake might strike at you and such footwear offers little protection. Weather is harder to predict on these longer hikes and if you walk a day or two in soggy tennis shoes, you'll soon wish you hadn't. I remember three young men passing me in high spirits one sunny August day that were so attired. I happened to catch up with them later in the day after a light rain had fallen. One of the them who looked quite bedraggled with badly scratched legs and sopping tennies, told me, "For God's sake tell people in your book not to wear tennis shoes or shorts on this trail." And so I have.

## HIKING THE LOOPS

There are three hiking loops that are suitable for overnight stays of one night up to a week that vary in length from 14 to 50 miles. The shortest is the Boy Scout Silver Arrow Trail that begins near Camp OYO, (For the description of this trail and finding its trailhead see page 220) but most hikers come to do one or both of the Shawnee Backpack Loops. The two loops plus the side trails A.H. and N.S.T.P. make a total mileage of 58 miles with eight laterine equipped primitive backpack campsites, all but one having a treated water supply nearby.

If you are going on one of the longer hikes, make tentative plans for the campground you wish to stay in each night. But keep those plans flexible enough that you can adjust your overnight stays to accomodate the many unforeseen things and occurrences that may delay, or more rarely, speed up a trip. The general trend for hikers planning a trip is to widely overestimate the distance they can do in a single day and the amount of weight they can comfortably carry. Keep your pack weight down as much as possible but carry enough protective clothing to shield you against nasty changes in the weather. I once took a four day hike in December with a balmy temperature the first day in the high 50's. The morning of the last day the temperature had fallen into the middle teen's and it was snowing hard.

## THE NORTH LOOP

Of the two loops, the north one is the most popular and a high percentage of the approximately 1200 hikers that fill out hiking permits annually attempt only this loop because it's shorter than the South Loop by about 5½ miles making it a good length for a two night 2½ day weekend trip. It is also better known, for it was completed in 1973 just a year before the South Loop. But, in my estimation, its climbs are more demanding and it is not quite as scenic as its southern neighbor. It has the advantage of starting off from Point A directly away from State Route 125 soon leaving the road noises behind, while the first section from A to H on the South Loop is often close enough to that highway that one is often in hearing range of the traffic. There are three overnight camps and treated water sources on the North Loop with an average of about 6 rugged miles between camps. Many try to hike from Camp 1 to Camp 3 in a single day, a walk of almost 13 seldom-easy miles. Only seasoned young backpackers should try it. Most hikers will find that the location of Camp 2 is welcomed at the end of the second day. Don't start out too late in the day from Point A to Camp 1 for it's a slow walk of over 6 miles and you should plan to reach camp well before dark. Notes for finding the trailhead and trail descriptions begin on page 192.

## SOUTH LOOP

Because of its length many hikers stay away from the South Loop for weekend trips. Indeed, to cover almost 30 miles on a long weekend makes it more of an endurance test than an enjoyable trek. But, never-the-less, the South Loop has several advantages. There is better overall trail engineering on the South Loop, which is almost never very steep and only one segment there is really difficult. The trail is seldom easy, but is without the exhaustingly steep climbs found on the North Loop.

One way to shorten this distance and put the South Loop in the time frame of a three-day two-night hike is to eliminate the 4.6 mile A - H section and start at Point I. After registering your hike at the backpack parking lot at Point A, drive east on State Route 125 approximately 2.2 miles until you come to the first paved road on the left with a sign for Camp OYO. At the intersection, there are some mail boxes on the right side of State Route 125. About 30 feet beyond them where a path has been cut through the thick rose bushes that line the highway is Point I. If you have only one car, unload your gear there and have the fastest hiker return the car to the parking lot at A. Then hike the fast two miles back to Point I. A good hiker without gear can cover this fast road walk in less than 40 minutes. This leaves a South Loop hike of about 25 miles-making it a good distance for a double overnighter for experienced hikers in good condition.

This would exclude the very lovely side trail loop N.S.T.P. that takes you into the wilderness area which has a distance of 10.5 miles. This only adds about 7½ miles to the hike since it eliminates the N.O.P. section of trail. By adding the wilderness loop and starting at Point I, the South Loop walk becomes better than 32 miles long, pushing it above the limit of all but the young super hikers in the time frame of a weekend. But, if you have more time, the whole loop starting at Point A and including the side trip starting at Point N, is about 37 miles with six overnight campgrounds and five watertaps to accomodate you.

## HIKING BOTH LOOPS

If you have the time and include the wilderness area side trip you can have a continuous trip of about 50 miles, the longest backpack loop hike on marked trails through a rugged semi-wilderness forest over hillly terrain that I know of in Ohio. Only the A. H. and N.O.P. segments are missed on this hike. Neither is remarkable for its scenery and the A. H. segment is hampered by road noise. Road crossings are few and the brief H to I segment is the only part of the trail that briefly follows a road.

### SINGLE NIGHT BACKPACK LOOPS

If one looks at the O.D.N.R. backpack trail map it appears that the Shawnee area offers no easy possibility of a one-night backpack loop. But there are at least two. The first, which can also be done as a very long day hike, is the Boy Scout Silver Arrow

Trail that is described on page 220. Another overnight loop of approximately 15 miles may be taken on the South Loop starting and returning to Point J, leaving your car parked at the C.C.C. Camp close to point J. This does require about 4 miles of road walking, but it is mostly on a backwoods gravel road in pleasant surroundings with almost no traffic and offers one magnificent overlook. Follow the trail from Point J (see description on page 204) through Point O with an overnight stop at either Camp 5 or Camp 6. If the weather is pleasant my choice would be Camp 6 since it is approximately halfway and is in a prettier setting. On the other hand Camp 5 has drinking water close by. When you get to Point O turn right on the gravel road. After turning you will find that there are two roads that branch off to the right. But stay to the left which is more or less straight ahead and you will soon pass the excellent overlook areas on your left. After a walk of about 2¼ miles the road comes to a three way split. Take the left one, which is paved. In about two miles, it takes you back to the C.C.C. Camp.

## A TWO DAY ALTERNATIVE

If you are looking for a nice double night hike which encompasses almost all of the above loop, you can add the side wilderness trail (See description on page 215) from N to P spending your second night at Camp 7. This hike is about 24 miles in length. At Point P you would turn right to get to Point O then turn left on the gravel road. If you wish to do either of these hikes, after filling out your trail permit at Point A, drive southeast on State Route 125 for slightly less than 4½ miles until you pass the Turkey Creek Freewill Baptist Church on the right. Just beyond the church turn right on Pond Lick road and in just under 2 miles you will see a large C.C.C. Camp sign on the left. Directly beyond the sign on the left side of the road, there is a log cabin which is part of the C.C.C. complex. Park your car in front of the log cabin, for this area is lighted at night and is patrolled. There is another parking area further on in the C.C.C. Camp but the director explained to me that the space in that lot is often taken by visitors and official purposes and he prefers that the area in front of the log cabin be used by hikers. At this writing the camp is open all year; thus parking there is relatively safe. But the cutting of government subsidies could foreseeably close the camp during the winter months. If this occurs, the risk of parking there would increase tremendously. If you park at the log cabin, be sure you don't block the heavy equipment area just to the right.

To find Point J, follow the road through the camp and pass the small Pond Lick Lake on the right. At the far end of the lake, there is a gravel drive going down to the creek just before it enters the lake. There, you should see a sign indicating the J.K. section of the trail. To find the J.L. section, continue up the paved road for about ten feet and you will find the trail leaving the road to the left where there should be a J.K. trail sign.

## DAY HIKES

Both the Silver Arrow and the J. O. loop can be done in a single day, but they should only be considered by very experienced hikers in excellent condition who are used to walking over rugged terrain and by fools. Somewhat less challenging but still above the class of a Sunday stroll, one of these following walks may be the kind of hike you wish to do. If you have only one car and no one to drop you off, you can walk the S.T. wilderness section of 4 1/2 miles and 1 1/3 miles of pleasant and rather isolated gravel road walking back to your car. The middle section of this walk, which follows an abandoned ridge top road through the wilderness area for approximately 2 miles, is one of the pleasantest walks at Shawnee. Read on for directions to the trailhead.

If you have someone to drop you off, you can walk the last rather easy segment of the South Loop from Point R back to the parking lot at Point A. This last link in the loop has the advantage of starting at an elevation well above Turkey Creek Lake making most of the hike a gentle downhill walk. Although there are several short uphill sections, none are really strenuous. Of the many short downhill stretches only one is really nasty, but it lasts but a few yards. This makes a delightful walk of just under 5 miles which is a good distance for those not totally out of shape but have some trepidation towards the more challenging and longer segments. If you want to add a few more miles to this walk with some demanding uphill sections which also includes walking through an area devastated by a forest fire, you can add segment Q.R. to the R.A. section giving you a total distance of about 8½ miles. The directions to find the trailhead of the S to T wilderness hike take you right by the starting point for these other two walks, so the directions to the starting point of these three walks are included together as follows: From the backpack parking lot at Point A, drive south away from State Route 125 on the lodge road, passing Turkey Creek Lake swimming and picnic area on the left. About 6/10 of a mile from Point A the road curves to the right and another smaller road that looks like a driveway to a maintenance building goes off to the left. Make a left turn off the paved road. When you pass the maintenance building, you will see that the drive is actually the beginning of a gravel road. Follow this gravel road until it climbs up to a ridge crest almost exactly 3 miles from Point A. You can look to the right here and see a one-lane rut lane. Directly across the gravel road at this point you can see a trail to the left of the road. That is where the R. A. segment begins and it should have a sign to the right of the trail about 25 feet from the road that says:

BACKPACK TRAIL<br>SEG. R.A.

See trail description on page 214. To find Point Q, continue on past this point and soon the road comes down off the ridge crest, curves to the left and passes several houses. It then curves left into another road. Turn right onto the new road. Almost exactly 2 miles from Point R or 4 miles from Point A, there is a small dirt pulloff to the left about large enough for one car. Directly across the road from it the Q. R. segment of the trail begins. There should be a sign there that says:

BACKPACK TRAIL<br>SEG. Q.R.

See trail description on page 210.

For the S to T segment of the wilderness loop, continue beyond this point for about another mile until this road dead ends into another gravel road. Turn left on this road which will ford a creek twice. Just after the second creek crossing the road T's into another road where you turn left. About a half mile from the left turn the road goes over a culvert, and if you look carefully, you can see a trail coming down to the road on the right. That is Point T where you will leave the trail and walk back on this section of road to complete the loop. Keep driving on this road which is paralleling Twin Creek to the left. When the road crosses Twin Creek it can be done in two ways. By going straight ahead, the road fords the creek. By going left, there is a road bridge going over the creek. This is Point S. If the water is not too high go across the ford and you will notice a large flat rock that runs for several yards along the right bank of the creek. Pull your car up on that flat rock and park it. Follow the flat rock on foot downstream until it ends. Look to the right and you will see where a trail has been cut through heavy underbrush moving away from Upper Twin Creek. That is the beginning of the S to T segment. For the trail description see page 216.

The Silver Arrow Trail may also be split into two single day hikes of about 7 miles each. For directions see page 220.

# FINDING THE TRAILHEADS AT POINT A

If you are traveling east on State Route 125 you will come to a large sign which indicates a right turn off the highway onto another paved road. This road takes you to the lodge and the bathing beach on Turkey Creek Lake. If you are traveling west on State Route 125 your turn will be to the left on the lodge road just after passing Turkey Creek Lake. Whether you are coming from the east or west, once you have made the turn you immediately make another turn to the right into a paved parking lot. On the right side of the parking lot, you will see a small wooden shelter with a water pump underneath. A sign near this shelter says:

## SHAWNEE FOREST BACKPACK TRAIL PARKING

On this shelter there is a sign that says.

## SHAWNEE BACKPACK TRAIL
## INFORMATION
## HIKERS PLEASE REGISTER

Below the sign are two wooden boxes. The one on the right holds the trail maps. If there are maps take one per group. If there are none the maps in this book should be more than adequate. A box to the left holds the trail permits. Fill one out and deposit it in the slot below before you begin your hike.

To find the trailhead for both the A.B. segment of the North Loop and the A.H. segment of the South Loop, stand with the parking lot at your back. While facing the small shelter, look left between the shelter and the parking sign to an embankment on the other side of State Route 125. You can see 13 log steps leading up the embankment. These steps are the beginning of the trails for both segments. About the time you enter the forest the trail divides. A sign on the left says:

## SHAWNEE
## BACKPACK TRAIL
## SEG. A. B.
↑

The fork to the left is the A.B. segment. If you follow the fork on the right, you are on the A.H. segment and a sign about 6 feet from the junction says:

## SHAWNEE
## BACKPACK TRAIL
## SEG. A. H.
↑

For trail notes for A.H. segment and the South Loop see page 194.

# NORTH LOOP

Map for the North Loop is on page 176 & 178.
**Segment A.B.** from State Route 125 at A to Forest Service Road 6
DISTANCE:   3.1 miles
HIKE:   First half, very strenuous, second half, moderate.
WALKING TIME:   1 hour 20 minutes to 2 hours.

GENERAL REMARKS:   The first segment starts off with a vengance with a stiff 300 foot climb followed by a rather steep decline. It, at least, lets you know right away if you are in condition to do the North Loop.
TRAIL DESCRIPTION: Following the left fork at the A.B. - A.H. trail division, the trail swings right, going up the side of a small ravine before dropping down and crossing a wash at its bottom. There is a slight climb over a hump that is between this

small ravine and the next one known as Hosler Hollow. Working its way up this small hollow, the trail parallels the wash before crossing it and starts angling up the ridge. This begins the first real climb of the trail, gaining better than 300 feet in altitude in about a half mile. It begins rather steeply, but moderates occasionally as it climbs. You will soon pass a place on the right where two washes join together. Just after this junction the trail crosses the left one and continues climbing between the two. Near the ridge top the trail swings to the left and angles at an easier grade up to its crest. If you are carrying a pack of significant weight, it will probably take you the better part of a half hour to reach the top from the trailhead.

If you are comparatively new at backpacking, it is here that you might pause momentarily to make an assessment of your level of hiking ability. Almost everyone carrying a heavy pack will find this climb a bit of a lung buster. That in itself is no reason to quit, but if you suffered real agony, feeling that this climb has pushed you over your level of endurance and you wished to God you were someplace else you're probably not ready for this trail, for you have only come ¾ths of a mile on about a 23 mile loop hike. Several climbs lie ahead that are just as taxing as this one if not more so.

The trail crosses the ridgetop and again gives you another challenge, for the trail immediately begins to drop into another hollow, angling steeply to the right. This is one of the meanest downhill sections on either loop, for the descent is often steep and sometimes very steep with many areas of unsure footing as it zig zags down. After the trail crosses one wash where the trail swings left, now following alongside the new stream bed. The trail crosses this wash three times. After the third crossing the trail passes over two smaller side washes then turns right just in front of a third side wash before it empties into the large branch.

Following this new wash upstream the trail soon crosses it then turns right on an old trace road. The walking is now easy as you proceed up a rather flat hollow. You will find this second ridgetop climb is far easier than the first one. The trail follows near or alongside the streambed. When the trail again crosses the usually dry stream, it starts steeply up the ridge and on my first hike here I assumed that this was the place the real climb out of the hollow began. But the trail only climbs steeply about 25 yards, then veers left, hanging on the side of the ridge paralleling the wash which is below on the left. The trail slowly angles back down to the hollow bottom. Once you are down again, the blaze marks are quite helpful, for the trail goes in and out of the wash, crossing the wash and its tributaries many times as it proceeds up the hollow.

When the trail starts angling up the side of the ridge on the left side of the stream with two quick rounding switchbacks, it signals the beginning of the climb from the hollow to the ridgetop, a climb that is relatively easy and short. Once on top you quickly reach the gravel road at Point B. To find the B.C. segment, turn right and walk at an angle across the maintained gravel road about 40 feet where a sign alongside the road says:

S B P TRAIL<br>SEG. B C

There is a tree at this trailhead with a prominent orange blaze on it to reassure you if the sign is missing.

### POINT B TO POINT C

DISTANCE: 1.6 miles
HIKE: First part easy, second part very strenuous.
WALKING TIME: 45 minutes to 1 hour.

GENERAL REMARKS: This short trail section of just over a mile and a half has an easy walk down to a hollow bottom, which eventually starts easily up a side hollow. When it leaves the hollow bottom it begins one of the steepest climbs on the entire loop going up about 250 feet in about a quarter of a mile.

TRAIL DESCRIPTION: The trail goes rather directly, quickly and easily down to the wash at the hollow bottom and follows it downstream sometimes on one side, then on the other, and occasionally in the stream bed itself. The trail gradually turns right and begins moving up a side hollow. You may not be aware of the turn until you see that you are now following the wash upstream where the walking continues to be easy. When the trail leaves the stream bed and begins to angle up the ridge you are at the beginning of a short but very steep climb with one brief level section in which to catch your breath. When you mercifully reach the ridge top, the trail turns left and follows along the ridge crest. It's about a ten minute walk along the ridge top to the maintained gravel road at Point C. The trail proceeds directly across the road where a sign says:

## BACK PACK TRAIL
## SEG. C.D.

**SEGMENT C.D.** From State Forest Road 6 to water stop at D.

DISTANCE: 1.6 miles
HIKE: very strenuous.
WALKING TIME: 45 minutes to 1 hour

GENERAL REMARKS: This segment of about 2 miles drops about 300 feet into one of the main branches of Hobey Hollow then turns and climbs another 300 feet right out again. Neither the downhill or uphill sections are easy, for the descent and climb combined take less than a mile.

TRAIL DESCRIPTION: Immediately after crossing the gravel road there is a short steep uphill section of about 20 feet where there is a fork in the trail. The right fork is correct and the orange blaze marks assure you this turn is correct. It takes you along the ridge top heading toward the end of the ridge. Somewhere along this ridge, the trail reaches an altitude of about 1270 feet making it one of the highest elevations of the trail and 500 feet higher than the trailhead at Point A. When the trail starts down the end of the ridge it is so direct and drops so fast that water erosion has made a gulley out of the trail and the footing is occasionally rather unstable. Near the bottom the slope becomes more gradual, until it reaches the main wash, crosses it and hits an F.W.D. road with telephone poles that run alongside the creek. Going directly across the road, the trail reenters the forest where it swings left and climbs quite steeply for about 50 feet. From there the climb moderates a bit, but continues a steady uphill rise to the top which is never easy. When you hit the only switchback on this section, you are fairly close to the top.

Continuing along the top of a ridge finger, the trail climbs slightly just before arriving at an intersection. There, it Ts into an F.W.D. road which has a fallen tree across it to the right to discourage the illegal passage of off road motor vehicles. The trail turns left on this road which comes immediately into a small open area which is Point D. The road is maintained for the use of the water truck, and, as you approach the area, you can look right and see a galvanized pipe with a padlocked metal top sticking straight up out of the ground. This is where the truck fills the tank below. By turning right here, you will see a sign that says DRINKING WATER with its dispenser just off the trail to the right. This is the closest water supply to Camp #1 still 1.1 miles away so fill up if you are planning an overnight stay there. It's downhill most of the way.

If you started from Point A early in the day with more than ample time to reach camp before darkness, you might want to make a short side trip to see the marvelous panoramic view from the Copperhead Fire Tower about a half mile away. If you so decide, with the water intake on your right, walk the water tank truck road out to the maintained gravel road. Turn left on the road and walk until you see the tower on your right. If the weather is cooperating, once you climb the tower's eight platforms and over 70 steps, you will be able to view several ridges showing you the kind of terrain the trail covers.

**SEGMENT D. E.** From the water supply at Point D To Camp #1 and Point E.

DISTANCE:  to Camp #1 1.1 miles, D to E 1.8 miles.
HIKE:  to Camp 1 easy. From Camp #1 to E very strenuous.
WALKING TIME:  To Camp 1 - 20 to 30 minutes, D to E - 50 minutes to 1 hour 10 minutes.

GENERAL REMARKS:  The hike to the campground requires little effort, but the climb out of the hollow is a stiffer matter. After the climb, you have an easy walk down to the first paved road crossing.

TRAIL DESCRIPTION:  From Point D the trail passes between the drinking water intake on the left and the dispenser on the right dropping rather steeply for a short distance before skirting around the head of a ravine on the right. There are about ten minutes of level walking before the trail turns right and begins to drop down to a wash where the trail turns right and follows it down, crossing it several times and often is in the stream bed itself. It soon joins another wash coming in from the right. You will see a V in the trail near an old fire ring. The trail to the right that continues down the ravine is the campground trail, and following the white blaze marks, it is an easy walk of about three minutes to the camp. There should be a sign there pointing the way but the last time I was there it had been mutilated.

By following the left fork and the orange blazes the trail starts up a side ravine easily at first but then gains almost 350 feet in altitude in a little over a quarter mile, which is a bit of a shocker if you've just finished off a heavy pancake breakfast at Camp #1. The grade goes from moderate angling to steep a couple of times, crossing one branch before it tops out.

Once up, the trail hits another well defined trail that follows the ridge top. This is the Boy Scout Silver Arrow Trail and if you are doing that loop with a side trip spending the night at Camp #1, turn right here and follow the ridge top. (For the continuing trail notes for the Silver Arrow Trail see page 218.)

The Backpack Trail crosses the other trail bearing to the right but still stays left of the Silver Arrow Trail. There is a big orange blaze on a tree at the intersection to help you. After this intersection the trail follows a deteriorating finger of the ridge downhill with some moderately steep sections until a paved road can be seen ahead. The trail swings left and eventually angles down to the road at Point E. The continuation of the trail is directly across the road. A sign there says:

S. B. P. TRAIL<br>
SEG. E. F.<br>
↑

**SEGMENT E.F.** From Shawnee State Forest Road #1 to Odell Creek Road.

DISTANCE:  To Camp #2 4.6 miles. To Point E 4.6 miles.
HIKE:  First part strenuous, remainder moderate
WALKING TIME:  2 hours 15 minutes to 3 hours.

GENERAL REMARKS:  This segment has its only serious climbing almost at the beginning and this 300 foot climb is spread out enough that it is not overly difficult but with enough bite to it that you'll surely know its there. Once up you have one of the longest ridgetop hikes on the backpack loops before it easily descends into the wide flat valley formed by Odell Creek.

TRAIL DESCRIPTION: Once across the paved road the trail immediately crosses a stream that parallels the road and goes easily up a hollow where it crosses right over the crest between two hollows and starts up the side of this new hollow on the right. After one left switchback and a gentle curve to the right the grade eases off with the trail soon reaching the top where there is a small clearing.

In the early part of the ridgetop section the trail drops down a little ways to the left side of the ridge, and although it never descends down to a hollow bottom it does drop enough that it crosses several little side ravines which keeps the walking from being easy.

After one moderately steep uphill stretch which places you almost on top of the ridge, the walking becomes and stays fairly easy right to the end of this segment and is on or near the ridgetop for some distance.

You may encounter some definite white blaze markers going off to the left. Since the side trail to Campground #2 is also blazed white, some may think this trail leads to the campground from this ridgetop location even though there are no signs. It doesn't, for that turning is much further along and comes after you have partially descended the ridge. At this writing the blaze marks are quite conspicuous although there is no worn path in the direction that they lead. When I first encountered them I knew they had not been there on my first walks in this area and I followed them for nearly a mile to make sure this was not the work of some prankster. Convinced they were put there for some intended purpose, I later asked about these blazes at the forest's headquarters at Friendship. Ben Hamilton, the Forest's assistant manager, told me that someone in officialdom had decided that there should be a hiking link from Riverside Park on the Ohio River between Friendship and Portsmith to the loop trail. The forest service personnel were ordered to blaze this proposed eight mile trail which they did. But the rest of the plans for the trail fell through. Thus this blazed section is not maintained nor is it designated as an official trail.

There is still a considerable distance of ridge top walking to be covered before arriving at the Camp #2 trail junction but you know when you are getting close to this side trail, the water stop and Point F when the trail drops off the left side of the ridge and switches back twice as it goes down. A short distance after the switchbacks, you will find the turnoff to the campground and on the left a sign facing the trail on the left side says:

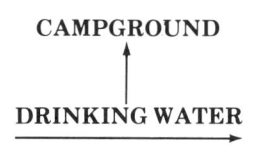

**CAMPGROUND**
↑
|
**DRINKING WATER** →

If the sign is down this well worn trail to the left is easy to locate. Walking to the campground is neither short nor easy and the distance between the camp and the drinking water is well over a half mile. If you are staying the night at Camp #2, it might be easier to drop your packs at this junction and continue on the main trail to the water hydrant to get a fill up before walking back to the camp.

From the junction it is between a 15 to 20 minute walk to the campground. Its trail takes you up a little ravine with a switchback lowering you to its bottom. The trail crosses the wash, angles right, going up another small ridge, curves to the left as it crosses over its top, and starts up a second ravine. It soon reaches the wash at the bottom where the campground is found directly on the other side of the streambed.

When you continue on the main trail from this junction, the trail is quite easy. In about 5 minutes of walking, and just before the trail breaks out of the woods into the flat valley of Odell Creek, there is a sign on the left side of the trail which says: DRINKING WATER. If you look down to the left, you will see the rut road used by the water tank truck. Just below it is the water tap. After a fill up, it is not necessary to return to the point where you left the trail. Turn left on the rut road which soon takes you to the open field where the official trail joins it.

If you don't go down for water you will find the main trail entering an open field where it joins and turns right on the water tank road for the short distance to a maintained gravel road at Point F. To find the beginning of the F.G. segment turn left on the gravel road walking over a wooden road bridge that goes over Odell Creek. About 50 feet beyond the bridge, the trail leaves the road on the right where a sign facing the road says:

### BACKPACK TRAIL
### SEG. F. G.

**SEMENT F TO G.** from Odell Creek Road to Hobey Hollow Road.

DISTANCE:   4.5 miles
HIKE:   First part very strenuous, last part moderate.
WALKING TIME:   2 hours 15 minutes to 3 hours.

GENERAL REMARKS:   There are a couple of deterrants to this otherwise long pleasant ridge top section, but they both occur on the first part of this segment. The initial one is a stiff climb of over 300 feet in less than 1/3rd mile which is a rather grim beginning for the day's hiking activities if you have spent the night at Camp #2 or an agonizing obstacle if you are trying the big hop from Camp #1 to Camp #3 in the same day. Adding to all this exhaustive frustration is the unpleasant fact that you are hardly on the ridgetop long enough to catch your breath before you begin a descent to a hollow bottom and climb out all over again. Two facts that may brighten these formidable realities are that you will find the second climb far easier than the first and all the struggling parts of this segment are behind you in the first hour.

TRAIL DESCRIPTION:   Leaving Odell Creek Road the trail returns to the forest and you have an easy walk until you cross the first wash. From there, the climbing becomes arduous and the struggle for altitude has begun. After crossing the stream the trail turns right and follows it upstream with steep, very steep and a few relenting level sections. It finally switches back left away from a side ravine and continues to climb steeply. One more switchback and the trail soon reaches the ridgetop where it turns left and gives you about a five minute breather before it falls off the ridge to the right. There it begins angling down at a moderate grade. It soon switches back and continues the moderate downward angle almost to the hollow floor, where it turns left and follows alongside and some times in the downstream direction of the wash at the bottom. Be wary of the flat sloping rocks along this section, for they often are deceptively slippery. When you cover a short and extremely rocky stretch in the stream bed, just before it joins another large wash, the trail turns right and crosses the major stream course following it briefly downstream. Then the trail begins the gradual climb to the ridge top. The ascent is longer and more gradual than the proceeding one and it wanders back and forth much more on the side of the ridge as it makes its way up. Once there, you have an easy ridgetop walk of about 1½ miles. Just about the time you have completed the first mile you will junction and cross the Silver Arrow Trail.

When the trail drops off the left side of the ridge the beginning of an easy descent has almost begun. After a short distance the trail again joins the ridge crest with no climbing because the ridge drops to the trail's level. The trail then climbs to a knob on the ridge then makes a U turn to the left as it drops off the ridgetop and starts downhill in the opposite direction. The walking here is tricky, for although there is only one short steep section, the trail is not deep enough into the ridge side to allow for firm level footing.

The trail now heads up a small ravine but soon cuts right, drops down moderately steep to the wash then up again on its other side. The trail now hangs on the ridge side, undulating across several small side washes and knobs as it works its way toward the end of the ridge before angling down. There is a switchback to the right which carries you almost to the bottom of this steep downward section which soon levels off as it parallels the creek on its right.

Twice the trail crosses the creek, and after the second crossing, you can look down the hollow and see Hobey Hollow Road ahead. Turning left away from the creeek, the trail parallels this paved road before dropping down to it at Point G.

To find the beginning of the G.H. segment on the opposite side of the road turn left and walk about 10 feet where a sign there says:

### S B P. TRAIL
### SEG. G H

For possible options at this point read the general remarks for this next segment.

**SEGMENT G to H** from Hoby Hollow Road to the Junction at H for continuation of either the North or South Loop or trail to Camp #3.

DISTANCE: .6 mile
HIKE: Moderate
WALKING TIME: 20 minutes to ½ hour

GENERAL REMARKS: Even though this brief trail section brings you to a major trail junction it is not quite as easy as it looks on the map and other options might considered. Those people making a weekend hike on the North Loop may find that this hike used up more time than they estimated. Completing the G.H. - H.A. segments of over 5 miles back to the parking lot may make their departure for home far later than they wish. If so, the hiker can turn left on Hobey Hollow Road and walk the 4/10 mile to Route 125, turn right on 125 and walk for 2.8 miles more back to the parking lot. A little over 3 miles of road walking isn't fun, but the H.A. segment section is not easy and if you're very tired and short of time, the asphalt may be the better choice.

Another problem that can occur here is the crossing of Harber Fork, which, during periods of heavy runoff, can be difficult or impossible to cross. If this occurs and you are making the complete North South loop circuit and are not planning an overnight stop at Camp #3 you can go right to Point I by turning left on Hobey Hollow Road and walking the 4/10 mile to Route 125. Cross it. Turn left and, in about 30 feet past the mail boxes, you will reach Point I.

If you want to get to Camp #3 and the creek is too high there is another way you can try. Turn left on Hobey Hollow Road. When you pass the entrance to Camp OYO, on the left you will see a paved drive on the right that goes down to Harber Fork and crosses it using both a culvert bridge and a ford on its top. Unless the water is terribly high you can cross the stream there and follow this paved drive a short distance till it ends. You will see a one-lane rut road on the right (water tank road). Follow it a very short distance and just before it begins to curve to the right there is a trail to the left. Follow it briefly across the corner of an open field back into the woods, and in about a minute you will arrive at Point H.

TRAIL DESCRIPTION: After leaving Hobey Hollow Road, the trail drops down and crosses Harber Fork. Once across the trail crosses a wash, then divides. The fork following along the bank of Harber Fork downstream is the most pronounced, but is incorrect. Take the easy to miss right fork which begins to climb the ridge. It angles up about half way, then hangs onto the side of the ridge and continues to head in the direction of Turkey Creek until it begins to swing around the end of the ridge. Just after you round the ridge end, there is a prominent uphill, downhill trail that crosses the Backpack Trail. This is the Silver Arrow Trail. Once in this area the traffic along Route 125 is noticeable. Not long after this trail turns left and goes easily downhill to Point H. When you hit the junction, you will see a large sign to the left facing the trail which says:

        ⟵
      SEG H.G.
      SEG H.I. ⟶
⟵ CAMPGROUND
      WATER ⟶

If you are going for water or continuing the H.I. section don't turn. Go straight ahead. The H.I. trail directions for continuing on the South Loop begin on page 195. There are two trails with white blaze marks here. If you want to complete the North Loop, the H. A. segment goes to the right of the trail you are on at about 90°. The trail that is closer to you and is between the H. A. segment and the one you have just completed, is the Camp #3 trail. If you are staying the night there, you have about a 10 to 12 minute climb which raises your altitude about 200 feet. It's a long way back for water so it might be wise to follow the H.I. segment for about a minute to the water tap to fill up before the climb to the campground.

**SEGMENT H to A** from H trail Junction to the Parking Lot at A.

DISTANCE: 4.6 miles
HIKE: moderate to strenuous
WALKING TIME: 2½ to 3 hours

GENERAL REMARKS: This segment, which has the distinction of being the only trail at Shawnee that is described in both directions, completes the North Loop in one direction and begins the South Loop in the other. Although it has some attractive sections, its often close proximity to Route 125 means that it suffers from traffic noise far more than any other segment at Shawnee. Remember its blaze marks are white.
TRAIL DESCRIPTION: This trail starts fairly level but as it swings right into Upper Shaw Hollow, the hillside slope gets steeper. After walking about 10 to 15 minutes you will pass over a side wash which is distinguishable from many others by its extreme rock strewn bottom. The trail continues up the hollow, gradually heading toward the wash at its bottom. Just before it reaches the stream, it has a rounding switchback to the left where it joins an old trace road. The trail and road cross this streambed and follow it downstream but soon the trail cuts right off the old road and begins angling up the ridge going over its hump then gently moves into Upper Shaw Hollow and angles easily down and crosses its wash. The trail continues upstream with the wash on the right, soon crossing a side ravine and small wash and follows this ravine uphill. The trail crosses the little ravine a second time with a short steep section on the opposite side then it takes an abrupt left turn, moves away from the ravine and switches back to the right.

Now there is a deep wooded ravine on your right as the trail gradually climbs to the ridgetop. Crossing over its crest, the trail stays near the top going over two washes before it swings downhill in the direction of Route 125. As the trail approaches a clearing cut for telephone poles, it turns right and skirts along the edge of this clearing for a short distance before swinging right going back into the woods, and angling down to the wash at the bottom of Long Hollow. If you want to walk out to the campground at Roosevelt Lake, before you cross the wash you will see a faint trail that follows the usually dry wash downstream out to Route 125 and the campground entrance.

Continuing on toward Point A, the trail crosses the stream and climbs part way up the ridge moving up Long Hollow. The trail then hangs onto the side of the ridge for a long, straight and level section, a kind of unusual level step in the ridge side, broken only by a couple of gullies and a walk around a deadfall. This section is followed by a short and sometimes steep angular climb up to the ridgetop. Once the top is reached, it swings left going off the ridgetop, switches back to the right and heads to the bottom of Williamson Hollow. You cross two washes at its bottom just above the point where the two branches join together. The trail then starts angling up the ridge in the direction of State Route 125, comes around its end, and parallels the state route. Here you are entering an area of about 5 acres that suffered a human-set forest fire in 1981. Although many of the trees survived, you can see the ugly charred scars left on their trunks. You will also notice that this wooded area is far more open and covered with weeds caused by those missing trees. Occasionally you may get a glimpse of Turkey Creek Lake to the left, after walking out of the burned area. You will cross three washes before the trail joins the A. B. segment, drops down to the left, and crosses 125 to the Parking lot at Point A.

# SOUTH LOOP

For general description of the South Loop see page 189. The trailhead directions are found on page 186 and the map of the South Loop is found on page 180 & 182.

**SEGMENT A.H.:** From the trailhead at Point A, backpack parking lot alongside State Route 125 to trail junction at the North and South loops and path to Camp #3 at H.

DISTANCE: 4.6 miles
HIKE: moderate to strenuous
WALKING TIME: 2½ to 3 hours

GENERAL REMARKS: This is the only segment on either loops that is used by both loops and although it is seldom in sight of State Route 125 it is the only segment that parallels a major road for any appreciable distance with the noise from motor traffic tending to detract somewhat from the feeling of leaving civilization behind.

TRAIL DESCRIPTION: Remember from the A.B., A.H. fork you will be following the white blaze marks to H. After crossing three dry washes, the trail passes through an area devastated by a forest fire deliberately set by persons unknown on March 15, 1981. It burned almost 5 acres and, although many trees are still standing (often with badly charred trunks), the open weedy areas attest to the many trees that were totally destroyed.

Just beyond this burned area, the trail turns left, starting up the side of Williamson Hollow and angles slowly down to its bottom. It crosses two washes just upstream from the point where these two usually dry streams join. Once across, the trail briefly continues in the upstream direction on a rather wide path uphill, but soon turns towards Route 125 with a rounding switchback to the right. Climbing the hill at an angle, there is a switchback to the left. As the trail continues upward at a moderate grade, it finally crosses the ridgetop and begins angling down again in the downstream direction. It does not go far before it levels off hanging on the ridge for a rather unusual long level stretch on a kind of ridge platform, broken only by a walk around a dead fall and a couple of washes. The trail eventually falls off to the left of this level stretch and angles down to the branch at the bottom of Long Hollow, where there is a large flat rock to the left of the trail. As soon as you cross the stream bed, you will see there are two paths, one angling uphill and another following the wash downstream. The trail going uphill is the continuation of the A. H. trail, while the other leads to Route 125 at the entrance of the campground near Roosevelt Lake. Angling up the ridge, the official trail takes you close enough to the highway that you can see it through the trees then it reaches and skirts along a clearing for power lines and telephone poles before making an abrupt left turn back into the woods and begins climbing again. Coming to a rounding switchback to the left, the trail then curves back again to the right which puts the trail on the top of an inclining ridge, following it up at an easy grade. The trail swings gradually right and goes across a couple of side washes that are near the top of the ridge. The walking is easy, gradually gaining and crossing the ridgetop wth a deep heavily forested hollow coming into view below on the left. The trail drops off the ridgetop, switches back to the left, and about the time it looks as if the trail is going to the bottom of the ravine, it turns right and parallels it. There is a trail that turns and goes down to the wash which was once the official trail, but now deadfalls have caused a rerouting. The trail continues to parallel the ravine before a new left turn covers a short steep section down to the wash and crosses it. Continuing downhill, the trail stays fairly close to the wash until it crosses it a second time. From there, you can look left and see the major branch of Upper Shaw Hollow. Easy walking takes you down across the main wash. Once across, the trail angles up the ridge in the downstream direction, swings over the hump of the descending ridge, swings left, and angles down into Lower Shaw Hollow where it hits an old trace road and follows it. The trail and road pass some small rock outcroppings on the opposite side of the branch before both cross the stream bed. But once across, the trail then leaves the road and climbs steeply about 30 feet with a rounding switchback to the right where the grade becomes much easier. After briefly paralleling the stream at this higher elevation, the trail swings left and begins angling further up the ridge. The trail passes an interesting flat rock that juts out almost into the trail with a tree growing from its top that reminds one of a small shallow rock shelter. Just beyond it, you cross a small wash which has an unusually heavily strewn rock stream bed. As the sloping hillside levels out, you are close to the trail junction and soon you will come to a large sign facing you which says:

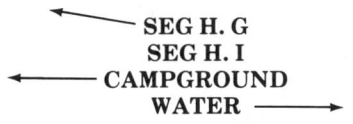

```
       ←——— SEG H. G
             SEG H. I
    ←——— CAMPGROUND
             WATER ———→
```

Since there are about five more miles to cover before reaching Camp #4, many who got a late start or are breaking into their hike slowly will wish to spend the night at Camp #3. Its trail is on your left at about a 45° angle, also with white blaze markers. You must gain about 200 feet in altitude which will take you ten to twelve minutes walking time. If you need water, get it before the climb by briefly following the H.I. segment.

If you are continuing on the South Loop or you wish to replenish your water supply before trudging up to the campground, turn right at the sign.

**SEGMENT H.I.** from the major North South Loop Trail and Camp #3 trail junction to Point I on State Route 125.

DISTANCE:  .3 mile
HIKE:  very easy
WALKING TIME:  10 to 15 minutes

GENERAL REMARKS:  This segment has three features that distinguish it from all the rest. It is the shortest, the only one that follows sections of paved road and physically the easiest. Despite its brevity, without directions it can be a bummer to follow. The first time I tried it all signs were down and I wandered around for a good ¾ of an hour before I stumbled on what had to be point I.

TRAIL DESCRIPTION: Follow the orange blaze markers south from Point H. In about a two minute walk, there is a sign on the left which says: **WATER**. This sign heads you to the water tap.

Just beyond the water sign, the main South Loop Trail enters a small open field. It curves left across the field, and runs into the gravel road for the water truck. Turn right on the gravel road and it shortly hits a narrow paved road, which will take you down across Harbor Fork on a combination ford and culvert bridge and up to Hobey Hollow Road, where, just to the left you see the entrance to Camp O.Y.O. Turn right on this wide paved road which almost immediately takes you over Turkey Creek and dead ends into State Route 125. Cross the state highway and turn left toward the mail boxes. You walk about 30 feet beyond them where you will see a narrow path cut through the heavy rose bushes that line the highway. This is Point I and a sign there reads:

**S. B. P. TRAIL**
**SEG I. J.**
↑

**SEGMENT I. J.** from State Route 125 to Camp #4 and Pond Lick Road.

DISTANCE: 5.2 miles
HIKE: Strenuous
WALKING TIME: 2½ to 3½ hours

GENERAL REMARKS: Of all the segments on either loop, this one has the highest altitude gain. From its lowest point on the State highway it climbs about 600 feet to its high point on a ridge above Cutlipp Hollow then drops about 500 feet to Pond Lick Lake. Spread out over 5 miles the excellent trail engineering has managed this greatest uphill downhill section so effectively that the gradient is almost never steep and does not reach the severity of several climbs on the North Loop.

TRAIL DESCRIPTION: Once through the thick bramble patch that borders Route 125, the trail goes directly across an open field. Just before the trail returns to the woods there is a second barrier of rose bushes with a path cut through for the trail. Once under the trees, the trail goes up and over an abandoned road before dropping to a shallow pond which has a small rock cliff on its opposite shore. The trail skirts around the left end of this pond, then curves right and begins to climb steeply above and close to the edge of this rock face before it switches back to the left, moving away from the cliff and the pond below. In a few more feet, it curves right and starts up the middle of an inclining ridge finger on a well-defined path. It then parallels a hollow that is below on the left before dropping down to the top of another rock outcropping, where there is an excellent view of this very pretty hollow formed by Buck Lick. Turning left, the trail goes down to the stream, crosses it and turns right following it briefly upstream before it begins to angle up the ridge. There are two quick switch backs as you climb and later as you approach the top there are two more switchbacks. The trail briefly follows an old wagon road, but leaves it on the left and drops off the top of the ridge slightly. It passes over three side ravines up toward their beginning, then angles down to the bottom of Cutlipp Hollow and crosses its branch. There, the trail turns left and goes in the downhill direction of the stream, but, as the creek drops rapidly below you, the trail swings right into a side ravine and follows its wash upstream. Then, angling away from the wash, the trail begins a steep climb. After a switchback to the right the grade moderates a bit as it continues up to the ridgetop. Once there you can see that the spine of the ridge drops rather steeply to the right but the trail turns left and follows the ascending ridgetop. The trail then drops to the right of the ridge crest, where it switches back twice before entering a magnificent grove of large oak trees with one giant just to the left of the trail, having a diameter of about four feet. Not far beyond this grove the trail hits a saddle on the ridge and enters a one lane gravel road that is maintained for fire control but is not open to other vehicles. Turning right on the road, the trail soon leaves it again on the right in about 70 feet. If you find this isolated road pleasant walking, you can stay on it until another similar road forks into it from the right. If you wish to take this option, read ahead to find the location of the trail's final turnoff from the road.

If you follow the trail instead of the road, it skirts around the right side of a ridge knob while the road skirts it on the left. The road and trail join again at the next saddle but once past the saddle, the trail climbs right, away from the road and goes over a ridge knob which is over 600 feet above the bench mark on State Route 125, the high point of this segment and completes the highest single altitude climb on the Shawnee trail system. When the trail descends from the high point back to the road it joins the road where another fire road forks in from the right. Just a few feet beyond this junction, the trail again drops off to the right, descends for awhile, then ascends to the road, goes directly across it, and leaves it for good. There are orange blaze marks on both sides of the road. So if you followed the road, keep an eye out for these marks and when you see them, turn left off the road and begin the climb up the ridge. Once on top, the trail turns left and follows the ridge briefly. Then, turning right, it drops slightly to an old logging road. All vestiges of this road gradually disappear, as the trail follows along the ridgetop through an area where the forest was either selectively cut or suffered a forest fire for there are many large trees but they have more open areas surrounding them. This has allowed a substantial growth of underbrush with one variety of spiked vine bordering the trail in many places which causes no end of irritation and downright misery for the hiker wearing shorts. Even those with long pants will notice a constant and annoying plucking from both sides of the narrow trail during the growing seasons.

As the trail nears the end of this ridge, it turns right and follows a descending ridge finger at a moderately steep grade. The trail again swings right, off the ridge finger, and angles down the ridge at a moderate grade. After a switchback to the left it angles down almost to the hollow bottom where it switches back right again and heads toward a branch on the hollow floor. Just before the stream the trail T's into another. If you wish to go to Camp #4, turn right here, and in less than a minute you will cross the creek into the campground.

To continue the loop trail and to locate the next water tap, turn left at this T and in a short distance this trail T's into a logging road. By looking right, you can see that the road crosses a branch of Pond Lick, but the trail turns left and follows the logging road. At one time the water for this area was located in a pumphouse next to Pond Lick Lake, but easy accessibility to that spot from Pond Lick Road resulted in severe vandalism. Now the water tap has been relocated much closer to Camp #4. As you follow the logging road look left until you see a curving rutted road joining the one you are on. That is the turnaround for the water truck. For water, turn left on it and in about 20 feet you will see a path to the right which leads to the spigot. There is a sign there that says: DRINKING WATER, but it is often buried from view from high weeds.

As you continue on this road toward point J, you will pass a thick cable stretched across the road and padlocked to keep out unauthorized vehicles. Just beyond the cable, a road that fords Pond Lick comes in from the right, but the trail continues straight ahead on the road that now shows much less use. After a short distance, it does a loop around at its end just in front of Pond Lick Lake. The trail leaves the road on the right just before the turnaround and goes over to and crosses Pond Lick. You can see that there is a short gravel drive on the opposite bank that goes directly to Pond Lick Road, but the trail does not go that way. Once across Pond Lick, it follows a less distinct road to the left which angles up to the paved Pond Lick Road at Point J.

*Pond Run Lake. South Loop*

To find the beginning of the J.K. segment cross Pond Lick Road, turn right and walk about 10 feet where you will see a trail going off to the left with a sign that says:

### SBP TRAIL
### JK

**SEGMENT J.K.** from Pond Lick Road to State Forest Gravel Road 2.

DISTANCE: 1.9 miles
HIKE: Moderate
WALKING TIME: 45 minutes to 1 hour 15 minutes

GENERAL REMARKS: If you have spent the night at Camp #4, you will find these next two segments are going to give you the easiest beginning for the day's hiking found anywhere on this trail, giving you a good chance to get limbered up for the later, more difficult sections.

You will find a non-taxing walk up a side branch before the climbing begins on this segment and, although it does climb over 300 feet, the elevation gain is spaced out nicely and is almost never steep.

TRAIL DESCRIPTION: The trail follows a rutted F.W.D. road into the forest and side hollow formed by Rock Lick. This section of trail is often quite damp and the high weeds during the summer months will make a morning hike even wetter. Still, it is a pleasant walk up this side hollow. But those without water repellent boots will soon have wet feet in all but the driest of seasons. The trail and road cross the stream, putting it on the right side of the trail. You will cross several easy dead falls that lie across the road and left there on purpose to discourage off road vehicles. At one point the trail seems to come down and cross the stream but it only goes down to the stream bed, follows it upstream for about 30 feet and returns to the same bank.

Soon you will see where two branches join together to form the one you have been following. You follow the branch closest to you for about 40 feet, where the trail turns right, crosses the wash, goes over to the other branch, turns left, and follows it upstream-sometimes alongside it and sometimes in it. But when you reach a point where the stream is on your right and the trail makes a sharp right turn across it and climbs a three foot embankment on the right side the climb to the ridgetop is about to begin and the wash is left behind. A series of switchbacks with mostly moderate grades in between take you to the top with only a section or two that are moderately steep. Once the trail reaches the top, it turns left and follows the ridge. In about ten minutes of walking, you should reach the maintained gravel road at Point K. The beginning of the K.L. segment is directly across the road where a sign reads:

SBP TRAIL<br>SEG K.L.<br>↑

**SEGMENT K.L.** from Forest Service Gravel Road 2 to Pond Run Road.

DISTANCE: 1.8 miles
HIKE: Easy
WALKING TIME: 40 minutes to 1 hour.

GENERAL REMARKS: This segment is an easy stroll down Pheasant Hollow. The name is a bit of misnomer, for pheasants don't like the clay soil of southern Ohio and even when released in the area soon head elsewhere. The walking covers either a gentle downhill grade or level walking on the hollow bottom, which gives you a breather for the following two segments are the toughest of the South Loop.

TRAIL DESCRIPTION: Once across the road, you have about five easy minutes of ridge top walking before the trail makes a right turn and drops off the ridge rather steeply. Soon it switches back where it begins to angle gently down. You can see a ravine developing on the right, and soon the trail angles down to its wash, turns left, and follows it downhill. As the ravine widens, the trail crosses its wash four times. Just before this last crossing, the trail turns left near a point where this wash joins another. The two joining ravines widen to make Pheasant Hollow. The trail follows down the bottom of the hollow alongside the rather pretty stream, crossing it and a few side washes several times. When you come to the paved highway, you are at Point L on Pond Run Road named after a stream that you soon will be crossing. To find the beginning of the L.K. segment, cross the road, turn left and walk towards the road bridge that goes over the branch you have been following. When you get to the bridge you will see a trail going away from the road on the right where a sign says:

SBP TRAIL<br>SEG. L.M.<br>↑

**SEGMENT L.M.** from Pond Run Road to Forest Service Gravel Road 5.

HIKE: Strenuous
DISTANCE: 1.2 miles
WALKING TIME: 40 to 45 minutes

GENERAL REMARKS: After the two pleasant and comparatively easy sections from J to L, the next two are the most demanding on the entire South Loop. The distance for these two combined segments is just about 3 miles, but it will probably take you longer to cover them than the last 5. This short L to M segment climbs almost

400 feet in about ¾ of a mile, and parts of the trail offer unsure footing, making for some very slow going.

TRAIL DESCRIPTION: After leaving Pond Run Road, the trail briefly parallels the branch coming out of Pheasant Hollow across an open weedy section. Almost immediately after returning to the trees, the trail crosses Pond Run, a very large creek about 15 feet across which would be difficult or impossible to cross after heavy rains. It runs directly into the Ohio River about 4½ miles from this crossing.

Once up on the opposite embankment, the trail turns left on a wide ledge along the creek and follows it downstream. The trail momentarily departs this level area by turning right, going part way up a side ravine crossing its wash, turning left, and returning to the level area. When the trail turns right up a second side ravine, you leave the area of Pond Run and begin the climb. The trail stays in the narrow V cut by the stream and crosses its wash several times. There are many flat moss covered gray rocks in the bed. Be careful when stepping on them, for they often are as slippery as banana peels. Twice in this area, I've suddenly found myself being dumped unceremoniously in the creek for my lug soled shoes lost traction as fast as slippery ones on these tricky surfaces. Even without this hazard, the walk uphill in the wash is one of the most exasperating, for it is quite narrow and steep banks often make the trail not much more than a treacherous toe hold wide.

Finally the trail cuts to the right away from the wash, and although the trail goes rather steeply uphill, it is still a relief to get out of the narrow bottom of that ravine. You have a switchback to the right followed by another to the left, raising you well above the stream bed. You will have two more sets of switchbacks after these first ones, and once past the third set, you are practically on top. Once on top a couple of minutes of ridge walking brings you to the gravel road at Point M. This is the only point on either loop where two overnight camps are only 2 miles apart. Those two miles, however, are the most physically demanding on the entire South Loop and if darkness is impending, it is a particularly bad stretch to cover in poor light. The further camp is the only designated campsite that does not have a treated water supply. But, on the other hand, if the weather is pleasant, Camp #6 is not only the most isolated, but it is situated in a particularly lovely area beside a magnificent stream with pools big enough to take a refreshing dip on warm days and to supply drinking water if you are carrying adequate purification supplies. If the weather is decidely soggy Camp #6 is a bit gloomy, whereas the ridgetop openess of Camp #5 may be a better choice.

To find the water supply and Camp #5 from the gravel road at Point M look straight across the road and a sign there says:

BACKPACK TRAIL<br>
SEG. M.N.<br>
→

Directly behind that sign there is a path to the left that takes you down to another sign which says:

SHAWNEE<br>
BACKPACKING TRAIL<br>
CAMP NO. 5<br>
↑

When facing the sign look downhill to the left and you will see another sign which says DRINKING WATER with the water tap next to it. Camp #5 is about a five minute walk which stays right on the ridge top all the way and moves directly away from the road.

To find the M.N. segment, turn right on the gravel road if you have just completed the L.M. segment or turn left on the road from Camp #5 or the water location. Follow the road which is in rather high, open country until the road begins to make a definite curve to the right. Just before the curve the trail drops off the road on the left where a sign says:

## SBT TRAIL
## SEG MN
↑

If the sign is not there the trail can be a little hard to locate during the growing seasons, for the weeds are high and the trail drops into some bushes. Just look for the only trail to the left near the road curve.

**SEGMENT M to N** From Forest Service Road #6 to Camp #6 alongside East Fork

DISTANCE: 2 miles
HIKE: Very Strenuous
WALKING TIME: 1 hour 15 minutes to 1 hour 45 minutes.

GENERAL REMARKS: Despite the short distance and the general appearance on the topo map this stretch is a real bear. You must descend over 300 feet into one ravine, only to climb rather steeply out and immediately drop steeply into another before any part of this trail becomes easy walking. I assumed on my first hike here that I could day hike it in both directions with no real problems. I took my ten year old daughter with me, for I felt this would hardly push her to her limits. It didn't but it sure tired her out and I had a very unhappy little girl in the last stretches of the walk. Despite its physical demands, with sometimes almost treacherous footing, it is one of the most scenically attractive segments on either loop.

TRAIL DESCRIPTION: After dropping down from the road the trail crosses a small open area before returning to the trees. On the following segments, you will find several metal signs affixed to trees placed there by a nearby chapter of the Sierra Club. These signs identify many of the natural features of the area. The first ones appear shortly after the trail returns to the forest. Once back in the woods, the trail goes down the top of a descending ridge before dropping off to the left side and going steeply down to a small ravine where it turns right and drops gradually down over 200 feet to a hollow with the strange name of Stable Gut. There, the trail crosses an attractive stream and immediately starts an uphill climb of about 400 feet in a miserably short half mile. After the creek crossing, the trail goes up quite steeply for about 50 feet paralleling a dead fall to the left. When the trail goes to the base of the downed tree, it turns right where you can soon look down to the right and see the stream you just crossed now quite a bit below you. The trail approaches a tributary of that stream, turns left and begins following the wash upstream. Just after you cross over another wash, which is a tributary of the one you have been briefly following, the going gets very steep with two quick switchbacks to aid you in the climb. Once beyond the switchbacks the rate of climb eases somewhat until you encounter another very steep section just before a third switchback to the left which is almost on the ridgetop. The trail then crosses over the ridge crest and immediately starts angling down the ridge to the left at a moderately steep grade. There is one short very steep section that would be very tricky in wet weather. Just beyond that, you hit a pair of switchbacks which end the steep sections for this segment and you have about a mile of easy walking to Point N.

The trail angles down and crosses a wash in the bottom of Blue Clay Hollow quite close to where this side hollow enters the main hollow of East Fork. The large stream is still out of sight on the left, but as you walk up its valley somewhat above its floor you cross over one beautiful side branch which has a solid stone stream bed having just a trickle of a beautiful minature cascade just to the left of the trail. Shortly after this crossing, the trail cuts abruptly left right in front of a tree and starts down to the hollow bottom of East Fork. There it turns right on an old wagon road. You can see

*Along South Loop near Point M*

that this was an active road very long ago for it is far narrower than a modern F.W.D road. Its bed is lower than the surrounding terrain for passing wagon wheels made the ground much more susceptible to water erosion. Through the years, this action wore the road surface down until it now resembles a wide ditch and makes for some decidedly soggy walking in wet weather.

The trail only stays in the road bed a short distance before exiting to the right. After a couple of easy downhill switchbacks, the trail brings you alongside the east fork of Upper Twin Creek and parallels it upstream. The trail comes into the first open section since entering the forest near Point M and skirts this rather small area on the left. It then briefly follows the trace road a second time which soon leads you into a grove of hemlocks. As you enter this evergreen area, there is a fork in the trail with the left one going down to the stream. Take the right fork which still parallels East Fork but keeps you above it. Soon this trail brings you to Point N. A sign there facing the trail says:

**SBP TRAIL**
**SEG NS**
←

### Location of the N.S.A. and N.O. Segments and Camp #6 at Point N.

Although this junction is well marked by signs, I have found that they suffer an unusual amount of mutilation especially since this point is so far from a road. I have never been to this junction when all the signs have been in place as they should be. Since these signs are maintained and regularly replaced by the Forest Division of the O.D.N.R. the only reason I can think of for this destruction is the action of exhausted and immature hikers who take out their frustrations on the signs making life more difficult for future hikers, tired or not. If the N.S. segment sign is up, the rest should be easy. This is the turn for the N.S.T.P. side trail marked with white blazes and this 10½ mile loop is well worth taking if you have enough time and energy left. For description and trail notes see page 209. If you wish to take this trail, and one way of getting to Camp #6, take the path to the left at the sign down to the creek. Turn right and walk upstream about 10 feet. Look across East Fork and you should see a bare brown spot on the opposite shore where the trail continues. Shortly after the creek crossing the trail splits. By going straight ahead you will soon pass the two privies of Camp #6 and the camp itself just beyond. The trail to the left that goes up the hill is the continuation of the N.S. segment.

Another way to Camp #6 and the beginning of the N.O. segment can be found by proceeding straight ahead with East Fork below you on the left. Continue upstream until you almost reach a large tributary of that stream known as Bald Knob Run. There a sign says:

## SBP TRAIL
## SEG. N.O.
↑

The beginning of this segment follows Bald Knob Run upstream. Camp #6 is directly across East Fork at this point. If all signs are down or missing just follow the trail above East Fork until it runs into the junction of these two larger streams where there is also an old fire ring. For the N.O. segment bear right following close to Bald Knob Run. To find Camp #6 turn left and cross East Fork and walk a few feet into the campground. If you wish to continue on the N.S. segment of the side trail follow the trail left, out of the campground. After passing the two privies on the right you should soon see a trail to the right which is the N.S. segment.

**SEGMENT N to O** from trail junction at East Fork to the Forest Service Gravel Road 2.

DISTANCE:  2½ miles
HIKE:  moderate
WALKING TIME:   1 hour 15 minutes to 1 hour 45 minutes.

GENERAL REMARKS:   This segment follows the wide and pretty hollow of Bald Knob Run right to its end. After the struggling sections of the last segment, by contrast this segment is a breeze. Although there is an elevation gain of over 400 feet, most of it is very gradual. Not until the very end of the hollow is reached is there a short uphill section which may cause a little deep breathing.

TRAIL DESCRIPTION:    Bald Knob Run is to your left and you will have three easy crossings of this stream while it is still a fairly large branch. Then the trail stays on the left side of the stream for quite a distance, but as the stream becomes a small wash, the trail crosses it several times. When it finally leaves the stream bed, it curves around the head of the hollow and climbs up the ridge at a moderately steep grade. After a curving switchback, the trail is almost to the top. Once on the ridge, the trail drops a little to the left and hangs just below the top until it reaches the maintained gravel road at Point O. The next segment is directly across the road where a sign says:

## SPT
## SEG. OP
↑

For those completing the shorter loop back to Point J, turn right for your road walk back to your take off point.

**SEGMENTS O.P.Q.** From State Forest Road to Plummer Fork Road.

DISTANCE: 1.1 miles
HIKE: Easy
WALKING TIME: 25 to 35 minutes

GENERAL REMARKS: This short double section runs from one gravel road on a ridgetop to another in a hollow with the junction of the Wilderness trail at Point P in between. From Point O the trail drops gradually for better than 300 feet, which makes for easy walking on these combined segments.

TRAIL DESCRIPTION: The trail starts out by going down the middle of a declining ridge finger, but soon drops off to the left somewhat steeply. Then it moderates a bit, angling down the ridge, swinging right around the head of a hollow until it reaches and parallels the small stream at its bottom. After going over several side washes, it goes left crossing the main steam just before reaching Point P. The side trail comes in from the left and as you pass it you can look left and see a sign that says:

SBP TRAIL
SEG PT
↑

By continuing downstream alongside the wash there is a sign on the main trail which says:

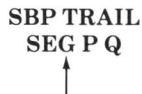

SBP TRAIL
SEG P Q
↑

Just before you hit the gravel road at Point Q, there is a small open weedy section. To find the Q.R. segment turn right on Plummer Fork Road and walk about 50 feet where you will find a trail leaving the road on the left with a sign that says:

BACKPACK TRAIL
SEG Q R

If the sign is missing, follow the road until you see a small parking area on the right side of the road just large enough for a single automobile. The trail begins almost directly across the road from it.

**SEGMENT Q.R.** from Plummer Fork Road to Camp #8 and Forest Service Road #16

DISTANCE: 3.8 miles
HIKE: Strenuous
WALKING TIME: 1 hour 45 minutes to 2½ hours

GENERAL REMARKS: After the easy downhill ambling, the next stretch requires exercising the uphill muscles a bit more than usual, for like the A.B. and the F.G. segments on the North Loop, this trail goes uphill only to come down and do it all over again. But of the double climbers, this trail is by far the easiest and the hard work is all behind you by the time you get to Camp #8. If you are staying there the night, your last and final leg is a gentle walk out of about 6 miles to Point A. If you are making a longer trek with no overnight stop, the last miles at least don't throw Shawnee's version of an Eiger Wall at you as the wells of strength are running dry.

There is another less fortunate but interesting area to be covered in this segment. It stands as a sad testament to the ignorance, vengenance and stupidity that the human mind too often falls victim to. On the third of April, 1981, a forest fire was set deliberately from a near by road which consumed over 500 acres of the forest. Much of the affected area burned over the part of this Q.R. segment. Because of the severe damage, almost 300 acres of forest have been harvested before the wood had completely deteriorated. Cutting such a huge area is never done under normal timber management conditions, but in an effort to control forest disease, insect problems and speed a healthy growth of new timber, this large cut was deemed necessary. Most of the trail from the junction of the Camp #8 side trail and Point R crosses the burned area. At least half of Camp #8 has been necessarily made unusable by the logging operations, but at this writing, enough of it has been left untouched so overnight camping is still possible, if not as cozily pleasant as I remembered it in the days before the disasterous fire.

TRAIL DESCRIPTION: Not 20 feet after leaving the road at O the trail crosses Plummer's Fork, turns left and begins a diagonal climb up the ridge. After a rounding switchback to the right, the trail then gradually swings left again until it is on the center of an inclining ridge finger. It follows this finger left down into a saddle of the ridge then climbs out before again dropping into a second saddle. There, the trail drops off the saddle to the right and angles easily down to the bottom of a side hollow. It follows that wash downstream until it enters one of the many hollows named Long in the area, which is a bit of a misnomer because this particular Long Hollow isn't very long. The trail turns left in Long Hollow and begins following a side runoff before turning abruptly right, crossing the main stream. It then crosses a small trickle of a wash a few times up to a point where two smaller washes come out of their separate ravines and join to make the one you have been following. After crossing both of these tributaries, the trail follows the one on the right and begins to angle up the left side of the ravine. The climb from here to the ridge top is moderate, with one short steep section. Once on the top, the trail follows it to the left then swings right, passing an open grassy area on the left. Continuing on the ridge top, you will know when you are approaching the side trail to Camp #8 when the ridge drops down into a low saddle. An old wagon road once crossed the ridge here at the lowest point of the saddle and the trail to Camp #8 follows the old road to the left. A sign there facing the trail says:

## CAMPGROUND

If the sign is down (as it was the first time I camped here) the trail to the left is fairly obvious and the white blaze marks reassure you that you are on the right path. It's about a three minute walk to the campground. You also turn left here for the water, but it is not at the same site. Nearing the campground you will begin to see some of the devastating effects of the fire and much of this general area has been badly torn up by it and the subsequent logging operation. Following the old wagon road downhill, the trail to the campground soon turns right off the wagon road and shortly ends at the campsite. If you want to get to the water spigot, stay on the wagon road which will soon pass the privies on the left just before the wagon road T's into a logging road. If you want water, you turn left on this logging road and follow it for about a five minute walk. You will know how to find the watertap by looking left until you see a rut road coming downhill from the left joing the one you are on. This spot is the turnaround for the water truck and the watertap is just beyond this junction on the left.

To find the campground or at least part of it, turn right instead of left on the logging road that you hit just after passing the privies, and in a few feet, you will be in the half of the campground that was not wiped out by the fire.

I have a vivid memory of my first overnight stay in this campground, and, if I may digress for a few paragraphs from the usual uphill downhill descriptions of this book,

I'd like to report the happenings. It was years before the fire when this campground was more cozily secluded and the ideas of doing this book were beginning to jell in my mind. Hiking alone, I was subsequently joined early in the day by a short-haired medium-sized brown dog of no particular breed that I knew. As we moved along it was as if we had been close companions doing these walks together for many a year. I could see that he was well-fed and groomed, so I knew he wasn't a stray and the longer he stayed with me the more I worried that I was leading him further from wherever he came and he was becoming hopelessly lost. But soon his own actions relieved my worrying for he would suddenly turn off the trail ahead of me and disappear for long periods. Just about the time that I would begin to think he was gone for good, he would appear again, happily wag his tail, follow along with me for awhile, then again disappear. After several repeat performances, I realized that although his general appearances suggested the kind of dog who would prefer the hearth to the woodland, he was thoroughly acquainted with the forest and probably knew where we were better than I did.

As we walked toward Camp #8 on that November afternoon, an early snowfall made the walk ever more pleasant. As we walked through the gentle stillness of the falling snow I and my sometimes companion watched the autumn brown turn to white and continued on until we arrived at the campground just before night. I barely had time to pitch my small tent and fix a hurried supper before the light was totally gone. I hesitated to feed the dog for fear it would falsely encourage him to stick by me rather than to seek his own homestead. But, strangely he sought no handout. Instead he stayed curled up nearby, snoozing as the snow continued to fall, the snow now partially turning his brown coat to white. I finally relented and fed my companion partly because I felt he deserved it and partly to see if he was hungry at all. He consumed every morsel offered, but his attack on the food was never ravenous.

Before darkness, many of the surroundings of the campground that I could barely make out suggested this area might possibly have been a homesite, at least a half century back in time. As I wondered what the voices at this hour would have sounded like and said inside the existent cabin, if indeed it did exist, darkness enhanced these fantasies until at last, wearily, I crawled into my tent. I did not encourage the dog to follow, for I wanted to do nothing to discourage him from returning to his true home,

Although I was very tired from my day's hiking, sleep was not with me. Thus, I read by candle light for about an hour. When I found it necessary to go and relieve myself, I fully expected to see the dog gone, but he was lying quite near the tent, curled up asleep, again partly covered by the intermittant, lightly falling snow. Even though he looked perfectly content I could feel the temperature was dropping and he obviously planned to spend the night. Worried that my short haired friend might finally become miserably uncomfortable, I invited him inside where he quickly curled up and went back to sleep, and, shortly after, so did I.

Sometime during that dark cavernous night there was a moving clatter the like of which must have been close to the decible range of a panzer division attacking Stalingrad. I thought I was dreaming but, even in that hazy state I was conscious of the noise slowly moving outside the front of my tent from right to left. To find out whether I was either awake or I wasn't, I turned on my flashlight and looked at my wristwatch which showed it was about 4 a.m. I then looked at the dog thinking that he too would awaken, growl and, perhaps, bark at our noisy intruder but he slept blissfully on. To make sure I was awake, I put my hand on his body long enough to feel his warmth. His body heat convinced me that I was really awake.

Although I had camped alone in isolated backwoods locations on several occasions, I always feel somewhat uneasy and a speck of hollow loneliness when I do so. This makes me more alert to night sounds and to the whims of my overstimulated imagination. Fortunately, at that time I had not yet visited the Ohio Historical Center in Columbus and seen the skeltons of the extinct giant sloths and mastedons that once frequented this region, for my fertile imagination might have conjured up one more remaining but so far undiscovered non-extinct breathing specimen of the species who was about to devour me. But my imagination did well enough on its own for out there in the darkness, yet unseen, was something the size of a lumbering Stegosaurus passing uncomfortably close to my thseshold. but its form was more like a giant praying mantis whose forward motion was not propelled by hind legs, but by two metal tractor wheels twelve feet high that clanked by the front of my small tent.

As the sound moved further away reason finally conquered fear and I unzipped my tent door waving my flashlight in all directions. The beam picked up nothing of an unusual nature. The snowing had stopped but the cold night air that hit my face again convinced me I was not dreaming. I sealed myself in my tent, crawled back into my sleeping bag, and surprised myself by soon falling asleep. The morning was bright by the time I awakened and, as I expected, I could find no lug tracks or monster foot prints in or near the general locations of the sounds. I shared my breakfast with the dog who, I discovered had a dislike of oatmeal that exceeded mine. My brown four-legged friend seemed to be a permanent part of my retinue and I wondered if he would try to get into the car with me when I reached the parking lot at Point A later in the day. The mid-morning was bright and the sun soon obiliterated all signs of the snow. As we walked the dog began to disappear and appear as he had done the day before, and I rehashed the night incident in my mind. A result of too many nips on some 100 proof stuff or puffing grass in camp, you suggest. But the last alcoholic beverage I consumed was a single can of beer three days before and my only brief encounter with marijuana was 20 years in the past. I know how real dreams sometimes can be but I'm convinced that I was wide awake and the noise was not my imagination. I later checked the topo map and found the only road was a small gravel one more than a half mile away. What I heard could not have been more than 30 feet from my tent.

I had been walking less than two hours when the problem of the dog attaching himself to me resolved itself for after making several reappearances that morning and early afternoon, the disappearing periods began to lengthen again until finally the dog did not return at all. Our friendship was ephemeral, almost the same as sometimes meeting a fellow hiker in or near a camp who was a total stranger. Two solitary walkers becoming fond friends in the evening and morning before breaking camp then each going his separate way, never to meet again.

Since that time I have camped alone on several occasions with a sharper atuned ear for night sounds. Nothing since has ever happened out of the ordinary, but if I ever spend the night at Camp #8 again, I am going to have at least one other human with me. If you're camping alone there, pleasant dreams. But back to our immediate concerns with treking the switchbacks.

Continuing on the main trail walking toward Point R, the climb out of the saddle is not difficult and if you did not go to Camp #8, this will be the first time you will encounter the results of the disasterous April fire in 1981. You may be surprised, as I was, to find the results quite different than the total scorched-earth type so familiar in the West for although the damage was extensive, you will see that many large sized trees survived. The openess and high weeds attest to the loss of the smaller trees and the stretch of trail is far different than the forest closeness that existed here before the fire. Many trees have charred scars as high as ten feet on their trunks. This must have been a bleak walk during the summer of 1981 leaving a blighted black terrain. Today you will find that the natural regrowth of plants have covered the worst scars and it is interesting to see how nature regenerates itself. Yet it sets one to wondering about the imbalance of the human mind when faced with the appalling statistic that roughly 85% of the forest fires in Shawnee State Forest are classified as arson. Many of us hike these trails so we can escape the constant reminders of terrorist bombings, hijackings and idiotic wars, only to find such irrational acts follow us beyond the borders of

*Large Fungi growth on South Loop Trail*

urban civilization with trail signs that are hacked apart, vandalized automobiles and forest fires that are deliberately set.

Except for the scarring of the trees, one might assume this part of the trail suffered no serious damage, but when one walks out of the burned area and returns to the thick forest the contrast is quite noticeable.

Continuing along the ridgetop through and beyond the burned area, you will find that the trail then drops off the right side of the ridge and goes down a moderately steep grade which is about a five minute walk away from Point R. When you come to a small auto lane with a back up area for turning around you are practically there. This is so close to the road that it is often used for off-road parking for certain romantic encounters that are spiced with beer, booze and fast food, the containers of which are scattered around the ground. In a few litter ridden feet this little road hits the maintenance gravel road at Point R. This is State Forest Road 16 and the beginning of the R.A. segment is directly across the road.

**Segment R.A.** From Forest Service Road 16 to the parking lot at the trailhead and State Route 125.

DISTANCE:  4.8 miles
HIKE:  Moderate
WALKING TIME:   2 hours 10 minutes to 2 hours 45 minutes

GENERAL REMARKS:   It's nice to know that this last leg of the South Loop is one of the easiest for it begins near the ridgetop and stays on or near the crest, never really descending into a hollow until it drops down to Turkey Creek Lake. Downhill sections are generally gradual even though the trail drops over 400 feet in altitude. Unless you are overtired or have developed some physical problem during the hike, it should prove to be a pleasant walk with only one short rocky downhill section to slow the pace.

TRAIL DESCRIPTION: The sign for this segment is not on the road but back about thirty feet. Beyond it there is an easy climb up to the ridge top. For most of the rest of this segment the trail is sometimes on the top, sometimes just to the left or right of the crest. It has several easy up and down sections as it traverses saddles and U turns around the edge of knobs. To write of them all in detail would be a study in boring redundancy going on for several paragraphs. Since this segment is not only well marked, but also is walked frequently enough to keep the foilage back from the trail without suffering from the hang dog ear marks of overwalking it is almost impossible to make a wrong turn. You will come about 2½ miles of this terrain which should take you about 1½ hours before you come to the descent to Turkey Creek Lake.

When the trail drops off the crest of the ridge as it has done many times on this segment, (but this time hitting an old wagon road), you know the drop down to trail's end has begun. The trail turns right on the road which soon became fairly indistinct. About this time the trail drops off to the left of the old road bed and begins to angle down the ridge side. After two switchbacks that are rather close together you encounter the only brief section of this segment where you have to walk fairly cautiously for the trail follows a water runoff whose course is full of rounded rocks and makes for unsure footing. Just beyond this small boulder bottom, the trail has a rounding switchback to the right. After making this switchback you can look down to your left and see the wide hollow formed by Lampblack Run below you. The trail levels off hanging on the side of the ridge with two quick switchbacks raising you up a little bit. From here, the trail descends easily. You will be able to see the maintenance building for the park and Lodge on the opposite side of the hollow. The trail seems to abruptly end when it hits a narrow-paved road close to the beach area. From there, you can look slightly left and see a wooden footbridge which you take across the headwaters of Turkey Creek Lake. Once across you will see another shorter bridge just beyond it. Cross this shorter bridge and climb the 18 cement steps up to the paved Lodge Road. Turn right and follow the road and bridge across Turkey Creek to the parking lot at Point A on the other side.

## WILDERNESS SIDE TRAIL N.S.T.P.

GENERAL REMARKS: About 1/3 of this trail's 10½ mile length goes through the Shawnee Wilderness area, an 8000 acre tract set aside to reduce the influence of man and allow the land to return to a natural state. All timber cutting has ceased and the roads are closed. Aside from hunting and hiking the only other human activities in the area are for fire and insect control when needed. At this writing, this is the only such designated wilderness area in the state and it offers a unique hike which you should seriously consider if you have the time for the walk. Its most unusual and desirable feature is a beautiful walk of about 2 miles along an abandoned road that follows along or near a ridgetop. Originally of gravel, this road was rather new when the wilderness designation was given to the area and although closed since 1972, it is clearly marked on the 1969 edition Buena Vista topographic map. This walk along the deserted road is unique for, although the gravel base of the road is still there grass and other plants have grown up enough to cover the surface. Except for very level walking along a wide path you might not be aware that you are on a road at all. Most hikers bypass this loop, but if splendid isolation is your thing this road hike seems to move one to another time and place where the only modern intrusions will be from an occasional airplane. For most hikers this side loop will add another day to their hike and Camp #7 is nicely situated at the end of the loop for an overnight stay. The trail sections up to the ridge top road walk and back to the main south loop are not unusual. They are quite similiar to several areas you will have already covered, but it's the deserted road walk that makes the difference. With three major stream crossings on this trail, you will find that the two over Upper Twin Creek are easily crossed by nearby bridges if the water is up, but the crossings of East Fork right at the trailhead at Point N is sometimes impossible. At normal levels, the crossing is easy but if the water is up, above the level of the knees, it is best to be avoided for the current is fast and you could easily be swept off your feet. The map is on page 184.

**SEGMENT N to S** from East Fork at Camp #6 to Upper Twin Creek Road

DISTANCE:  2 3/10 miles
HIKE:  First part strenuous, second part moderate.
WALKING TIME:  1 hour 15 minutes to 1 hour 45 minutes.

GENERAL REMARKS:   This segment begins and ends at two of the largest creek crossings on any loop but only the first, at East Fork, need concern you if the water is high. There is a 400 foot climb on this segment but it is well-engineered, making for steady moderate climbing most of which is behind you after the first half hour.

TRAIL DESCRIPTION:   After crossing East Fork the trail moves diagonally away from the stream and in about 20 feet comes to the Camp #6 fork. Turn left here and start uphill. If you are coming from Camp #6, walk past the privies and turn right at this fork.

The trail angles up the ridge then levels off paralleling a pretty stretch of East Fork some 50 feet or more below on the left. Gradually the trail swings right into Mudlick Hollow and follows the wash at its bottom over some very rocky, uneven terrain. Leaving the wash, the trail goes up rather steeply in front of a narrow protruding rock face on the right where a switchback to the right now takes the trail over the top of that rock face. There are two more switchbacks, then the trail angles up the ridge at a moderate grade. After a steady climb, the trail swings left, passes over the crest of a declining ridge finger, and almost goes down into a side ravine. Just before it drops, the trail turns right and continues to angle up to the ridge top.

After turning left on the narrow ridge crest, there are many short up and down sections to follow, as the trail goes over some knobs, skirts others and drops in and out of saddles. Most of this ridge walk is easy but there are a few short puffy uphill stretches. It will probably take you about a half hour to cover this ridge walk, but when the trail begins skirting a knob to the left followed by a switchback to the right the downhill drop has begun. The trail angles down moderately with a curving switchback to the left where you will soon see a ravine developing on the right. As you continue to go down you will see another ravine developing on your left and you continue to drop down between the two ravines almost to the point where they join. The trail turns left, crosses that wash, then follows it downstream. Soon it passes the stream junction until you see a large flat gray rock about a yard wide that parallels the left side of the trail and leads you toward the stream. You make a diagonal stream crossing then angle away from the creek with an easy stroll out to Twin Creek Road. Just as the trail comes out of the trees it cuts left, angling down to the gravel road. As you look across the road and Upper Twin Creek, you will see that the opposite shore is made up of a long flat natural stone surface.

To find the beginning of the S.T. segment cross the road and the creek to this stone shoreline. Turn left and walk to the end of the stone surface where you can look right and see where the trail is cut through some very heavy bushes. If the water in the creek is too high turn right on the road and use the road bridge over the stream.

**Segment S.T.** from Twin Creek Road to Camp #7 and Upper Twin Creek Road.

DISTANCE:  4.5 miles
HIKE:  Moderate
WALKING TIME:  2 to 2½ hours

GENERAL REMARKS: All the difficult parts of this segment, both in following the trail and the climbing, occur in the first half hour, when you will have a moderate elevation gain of about 300 feet. Once on the ridge top you have the marvelous path that follows the abandoned road through the wilderness area. The width of the road and its gravel foundation, now covered by plant growth, will give you a delightful stroll in any season if the weather is the least bit cooperative. The descent to Camp #7 is an easy one making the last 2/3rds of the segment quite pleasant. Although the white blazes are sometimes rather scarce, once on the ridge the trail is easy to follow.

TRAIL DESCRIPTION: As you walk directly away from Upper Twin Creek through the heavy bushes the trail soon returns to the forest and continues straight ahead for about 20 feet before turning left. You continue in that direction on a trail that is not too distinct until you come upon two washes that parallel one another. You cross the smaller one, then turn right, proceeding upstream between the two washes. The trail continues to parallel the larger branch until it crosses a side wash whose quick drop down to the larger stream has left its bed with many large exposed rocks. Just after crossing this wash the trail drops down and crosses the main branch, follows it briefly upstream, and crosses it again. Not long after this recrossing, you will come to where two tributaries join to make the larger branch. Upstream from that point, the trail crosses the right branch and begins to follow its ravine upstream, then turns left, angling up over the small ridge between the two ravines and begins going up the side of the second ravine. It continues in this direction until the crest of the ridge is reached. Turn right on the abandoned road. If you're winded a bit after your climb you have about an hour of unstrenuous and joyful walking ahead of you. There is a prestine other worldliness about this walk, which is enhanced by small groups of long needle pines that occasionally line each side of the trail road, making it feel as if it were an deserted part of the Appian Way after the fall of the Roman Empire. One might imagine hearing some faint metalic clanking, only to round the bend and encounter a well-armed phantom detachment of a Second Century Roman Legion marching to Brindisium. I've never seen the ghost of a Roman foot soldier here and if I do I promise you I'll turn myself in. But I do remember two unusual, if not mysterious, happenings on my first walk over this delightful bit of trail. I noticed the trail was often lined with blackberry bushes, heavily laden with fruit. Since it was only June 14, the berries were still quite green and I thought of the succulent treat that hikers would enjoy during July and August. But one group of bushes apparently had their monthly clocks out of whack for despite the fact that there had been an unseasonably cool spring and early summer, I found this group offered me two handfalls of berries matured to their best ripeness.

If I am hiking strictly for pleasure I pay only fleeting attention to the time it takes to cover a trail. But for purposes of determining approximate hiking times I often use a stop watch. My original time estimate for the ridge top walk was approximately one hour. My actual walking time shown on my stop watch was 59 minutes and 44 seconds. Since so many unforseen things usually set my times all haywire, it was nice to know that I am right once in awhile.

If you are worried about missing the road turnoff, you will find that the evergreen trees that frequently line the edges of the trail gives you an easy clue to its where abouts. You will come to one such grove that is decidedly longer than the preceeding ones, being over 100 yards in length with taller trees, some as high as 10 feet, lining both sides of the road with a slow sweeping curve to the right. Keep an eye on the right side of the road and you will come to a seven foot long break in these pines close to the end of this green corridor. A sign there facing the road says:

## BACK PACK TRAIL

The trail drops off the ridge to the right here. But if the sign is vandalized, you can easily find the break in the pines and the trail starting down the forested ridge. There is also a maple tree with three prominent while blazes to reassure you that this is the turning point.

The trail easily descends into the bottom of a small hollow which has a magnificent grove of poplars. If you notice how straight the trunks of these magnificent trees grow you can easily see why the early settlers preferred this tree to all others in making their log cabin homes.

You follow along the main wash, which is on your right in the downstream direction, and eventually cross it. Unless you go back to Camp #7 this branch remains on your left all the rest of the way to Upper Twin Creek Road at Point T. There is one place where the trail looks as if it might cross the branch. By looking left across the stream bed you can see a trail on the opposite bank. This is the trail back to Campground #7. A sign there reads: CAMPGROUND. During the two minute walk back to the camp the campground trail crosses a side wash twice.

If you are staying in the campground, the drinking water is not located there but is found by continuing down the main trail.

You are now in Little Gum Hollow where the trail soon joins a rut road and follows it directly ahead. When you join the road you can see that it swings right, eventually making a circle. This is the turnaround for the water truck. For finding the water supply and continuing on the main track, do not follow the road as it turns right. Instead, proceed directly ahead on the road. You will see a short path to the right that leads to the water tap. From this junction, it's just a short easy stroll to the maintained gravel road alongside Upper Twin Creek and Point T. If you are making the short day loop hike, you turn right at the road which will take you back to Point S, 1.3 miles away. To find the trailhead T.P. for the last lap of this side trail, turn left on Twin Creek Road, and immediately cross ove a culvert that allows the wash from Little Gum Hollow to pass under the road and empty into Upper Twin Creek.

Just after the crossing look right where a trail leads away from the road down to Upper Twin Creek. A sign there says:

BACK PACK TRAIL<br>SEG TP<br>↑

**SEGMENT T.P.** from Upper Twin Creek Road to the junction with the South Loop trail.

DISTANCE:3.7 miles
HIKE: Moderate to strenuous
WALKING TIME:1 hour 45 minutes to 2 ½ hours

GENERAL REMARKS: This is the longest segment of the wilderness side trail, but it is no longer in the designated wilderness area. There is a crossing of Upper Twin Creek that can be avoided if the water is high. About a third of the trail is an easy walk up a rather flat hollow. Then, after a quick moderately-steep climb of about 200 feet, you are at the beginning of a long ridge top walk. Although shorter than the lovely ridge top S.T. road walk, it seems far longer, for it meanders much more going down and up saddles and jumping from ridge knoll to ridge knoll requiring much more physical effort. The walking is slower too, for I found that this is the most overgrown section of trail at Shawnee with underbrush and brambles creating a narrow path much of the way. Although never really difficult to follow, the narrow trail in many areas makes the walking annoying and slow for many walkers and downright agonizing for those foolish enough to hike it in shorts. The white blazes, although infrequent at times and, at this writing, a bit faded are still visible as frequently as need be.

TRAIL DESCRIPTION: When leaving the gravel road, the trail quickly returns to the forest and immediately crosses Upper Twin Creek with a short steep climb up the opposite bank. If you should find the waters of the creek too high for comfortable crossing go back to the road and turn right. In a short distance another gravel road T's into this road from the right. Turn right on this road taking the bridge over the creek. Follow the left side of this road beyond the bridge until you see a path to the left with a sign that says: BACK PACK TRAIL. Turn left here and you're back on the trail.

If you successfully crossed the creek, the trail gradually angles left and, in about a five minute walk over flat terrain, you will come to a maintained gravel road. Cross the road heading slightly right and you will see a trail leading off to the left with a sign that says: BACK PACK TRAIL. This trail soon returns you to the forest and to a small creek where it turns right and follows the creek upstream. You now have a long easy walk of about 3/4 miles straight up the hollow which crosses the branch several times and should take you about 20 minutes.

When the trail begins angling right going up a side ravine, the real climb begins. There are switchbacks that swing you up and around to the head of the main hollow where it again switches back twice, taking you to the ridge crest.

Once on top, the trail turns right and begins a long ridge top walk. Although never terribly difficult, it is a slow walk because of the combination of heavy underbrush and the meandering, up and down character of the trail. You will come to many areas where it seems you are about to drop off the ridge only to find you have only gone into a low saddle or connecting side ridge and have to hike up again. There are so many of these false ridge endings, that I felt on my first walk, that I had been cursed by an angry hiking god and I was doomed to walk on a seemingly endless ridge for a 100 miles. After erroneously thinking that the ridge walk ended at least a half dozen times I thought a good name for it would be Endless Ridge. But, of course, it does end; however most hikers will find that it will take more than an hour on the ridge before dropping down to Point P. You may also be aware that the trail is making a long gradual swing to the right.

You will know you are nearing the segment's end when it follows the right edge of a saddle down, then cuts left across the bottom of the saddle with a second left turn dropping the trail off the crest of the saddle and angling down the ridge side in the opposite direction. After a switchback to the right, the trail hangs on to the side of the ridge and swings slowly left around the head of a hollow on your left. Once around the head, the trail starts down with four switchbacks easing the descent. Then you find that the main hollow is on your left and a smaller ravine is on your right. You reach the branch in the main hollow about the time these ravines join together. As the hollow widens, the trail crosses the wash once just before coming to Point P. When this side trail T's back into the main South Loop, you can see the major trail is wider and easier to follow, simply because it is walked more frequently. If you are completing the South Loop, turn left and you should see a sign which says:

## SEG PQ
↑

You have a short easy stretch to Point Q. Turn to page 210 for the trail description of the main trail. For those doing the shorter loop, returning to Point J as explained on page 190. Turn right here where you should see a sign which says:

## SEG OP
↑

When you climb the ridge to Point O, turn left on the gravel road and follow the directions forund on page 190 back to the parking lot at the C.C.C. Camp.

# SILVER ARROW TRAIL
## Introduction - General Remarks

This trail, maintained by the Scioto Council of the Boy Scouts of America, was the first official loop hike suitable for backpacking in the Shawnee forest, for it was completed about 10 years before the Shawnee North Loop. Although well marked, this 14 mile loop trail is not generally known except by Boy Scouts who often hike the trail to qualify for their Shawnee Trail patch. This trail crosses the Shawnee North Loop three times and when I noticed these easily seen crossings on my initial hikes on the North Loop, I assumed that the trail was part of the extensive network of horse trails that exist in the Shawnee forest. My assumption was not entirely wrong, for horses are permitted on this hiking trail, but not on the official Shawnee Backpack Trails. The horse traffic is light, so encounters with the equestrians is rare if at all.

I found out about this loop quite by accident. Since part of both the North and South Loops pass through the grounds of Boy Scout Camp OYO I wanted to know about the possibilities of day hikers using their camp's handy parking lot near the H.I. segment. While making enquiries, I met Ron Miller, OYO's Camp ranger who oversees the camp. When I told him about the purpose of this book, he asked me if I was going to include the Silver Arrow Trail. I admitted that I didn't know it existed and asked him to tell me about it, which he obligingly did. It sounded like the kind of trail that should be included in this book and so it is. This is one of two loop trails described in this book that are maintained by Boy Scouts Councils, primarily for scouts seeking to qualify for special trail patches. Since the trail begins and ends on the Camp OYO grounds I asked Mr. Miller if they preferred to keep it primarily a scout trail or whether it was open to all. He assured me that, like the scout trail at Tar Hollow, the trail was for everyone's use and other hikers were welcome. I found that he and another scout leader Russell Otteny, now deceased, had laid out the trail in the early 1960's and on its dedication day over 3000 people successfully completed the circuit.

Since the completion of the state's backpack loops, most hikers have ignored this trail and boy scouts are its most frequent users. Yet it is hiked in enough numbers that the trail is easily followed but does not have that over-walked feeling. After hiking the trail, I was delighted to find that this trail offers several features that are not found on the backpack loops.

First, this trail is a ridgetop trail for almost its entire length and, although there are up and down sections, the only serious uphill and downhill stretches of any length occur at the beginning and the end of the trail.

Second, the 14 mile distance gives the hiker the option of doing a tough single day walk or a more leisurely overnight backpack trip. Covering the 14 miles in a single day should be considered only by the most physically fit hiker who is accustomed to covering long distances. The pamphlet issued by the Scioto council suggests a walking time of 6-1/2 to 7 hours for the entire loop. This might be a reasonable time for a healthy 15 year old but in most cases it is far too fast for older and much younger hikers doing it all in one day. To me 8 to 10 hours seems a more reasonable time.

Third, this length makes it well suited for an easy overnighter backpack trip. Not quite half way, there is a camp with a water supply next to Bear Lake. But there is a fly in the ointment. The camp is especially designed and designated for the exclusive use of horsemen and camping is forbidden here to others. Don't rise in righteous indignation saying this is unfair for this is the only campground in the area where people with horses may stay. The camp also parallels a road, so any feeling of a wilderness campground is destroyed and the proximity to the road makes for possible difficulties with hoodlums. If you camp there, state forest personnel may insist that you move. But there is a quite legal way for backpackers to spend the night near this loop, although it requires a rather testy climb on the second day and increase the distance of the first day's walk. At a handy junction point, you leave the Silver Arrow Trail and follow the North Loop Backpack Trail down to Camp #1. You must decide on this option before you start on your hike, for it is necessary to register at Point A for your overnight stay in the backpack camp. No registration is necessary to walk the Silver Arrow Trail. The directions to Camp #1 are included in that section's trail description.

Fourth, for those who like a moderate day hike and have a driver who can drop you off or pick you up at the Bear Lake dam, that point almost divides the trail in half with the western walk from Camp OYO to Bear Lake about 6½ miles and the eastern half a longer 7½ miles. Directions to Bear Lake are included in finding the trailhead for the Silver Arrow Trail.

Fifth, this trail has several unique features that hikers may enjoy. In almost 60 miles of Shawnees' North and South Backpack Loops, there is not a single overlook point where a panoramic view of the quasi-mountains terrain of these Appalachian foothills can be seen. Yet the far shorter Silver Arrow trail has two such overlooks, one of them being the Copperhead Lookout tower.

Although the trail has more road walking than either of the larger loops, these two brief road stretches cover a combined distance of only 1-4/5 miles on a narrow gravel backwoods road which passes no houses and only an occasional automobile intrudes into the hiker world. The trail is blazed by silver arrows with aluminum colored paint.

If you are a scout or a leader of scouts and are interested in obtaining the Shawnee Trail patch after hiking the trail, the present cost of the patch is $2.50. Inquires for the patch may be made by writing:

SHAWNEE TRAIL<br>
P.O. BOX 1305<br>
PORTSMOUTH OHIO 456662

or phone

(614) 354-2811

## FINDING THE SILVER ARROW TRAILHEADS AT CAMP OYO AND BEAR CREEK LAKE.

From Point A at the intersection of State Route 125 and the Shawnee Lodge Road follow 125 east for about 2.2 miles to Hobey Hollow Road. There is a Camp OYO sign on the left. Turn left on Hobey Hollow Road, where almost immediately you will see the entrance to Camp OYO on the right. Directly across the road from the entrance is the parking lot for Camp OYO enclosed behind a chain link fence. This parking lot may be used for hikers except for a weekend or two in the spring and fall when Camperalls are held at OYO. Usually you will find the parking lot nearly empty, but if you should hit it on a busy weekend, then you will have to use the backpack parking lot at Point A.

To find the trailhead from OYO parking lot turn right on Hobey Hollow Road and almost immediately you will see a smaller paved drive on the right that drops down and crosses Harber Fork, using a combination ford and culvert bridge. Follow this drive across the creek until it dead ends a short distance away in front of Turkey Creek. Take the one-lane gravel road to the right, which is the water truck road for the water supply near Point H. Follow this road a little ways uphill, and as the road swings to the left, you will see a trail that proceeds straight ahead uphill. This is the Silver Arrow Trail.

To locate the trail at Bear Lake, go a short distance west beyond Point A on State Route 125 and turn right onto Straight Fork Road (#3). Go almost 4 miles to a junction with Bear Creek Road (#4) where you turn right. You go almost 1-2/10 miles to the Bear Lake Horseman's Camp. Drive through the camp until you come to the dam of

*Overlook in Shawnee State Forest on the Silver Arrow Trail*

Bear Lake. Walk across the earthen dam and cross over the wooden fence at its far end. The Silver Arrow Trail is on the other side of the fence. See page 223 for trail description from Bear Lake to Camp OYO.

## SILVER ARROW TRAIL
See map on page 176 & 178

DISTANCE: Entire Loop: 14 miles. To Bear Lake 6½ miles. To Camp #1 8.7 miles.
HIKE: Entire loop in the same day, strenous. As two single day hikes, moderate.
WALKING TIME: Entire loop 8 to 10 hours, To Bear Lake 3 to 4 hours, To Camp #1 -4 hours.

GENERAL REMARKS: Most points about the trail have appeared in the proceeding introduction of the trail. Remember that the blaze marks are made with aluminum paint in the shape of an arrow. The trail is almost always wide and easy to follow.
TRAIL DESCRIPTION: Once the trail leaves the water tank road it continues to climb a wide finger of an inclining ridge at a moderate grade and soon crosses another well defined trail with orange blazes. This is the G.H. segment of the North Loop. The moderate climb continues until you have gained about 320 feet up to the ridge top. The trail stays on or near ridge tops until an easy descent takes you to Bear Lake. There are several climbs and descents on the ridge top itself, with most grades being easy to moderate and a few short ones that will make you aware of every pound you are carrying.

After walking about an hour, you find that the trail drops off to the left of the ridge top going through a lovely flat forested area where you will eventually see a ravine on your left as you walk above it uphill, moving toward its head. The trail T's into the narrow ridge crest and turns left passing above the head of the ravine. Then it climbs rather steeply to a new higher point on the ridge where the trail continues to follow the quite narrow ridge crest. There are two rather long downhill sections which still stay on the ridge with the second one taking you to a maintained gravel road. It will take most walkers more than two hours walking time to reach State Forest Road #6. Although the official trail turns right and follows the road, before doing so, turn left on the road and in less than 1/10 mile you have an excellent roadside panoramic view to the south, showing you several of the forested ridges giving you a good idea of the type of country these trails traverse and why the name, "Little Smokies of Ohio", seems not inappropriate.

Back on the official trail, you will follow the road east for 1.3 miles. In about a half hours' walk, you may see where a trail crosses the road, which is Point C on the North Backpack Loop. Alongside this trail as it leaves the road on the right a sign next to it says:

### SBP TRAIL
### SEG C B
↑

Directly across the road another sign says:

### BACKPACK TRAIL
### SEG C D
↑

Although you do not turn here, this junction lets you know you are close to the point where the Silver Arrow Trail leaves the road. In about another two or three minutes of walking, the road starts down off to the right of the ridge crest while the trail stays on the top and proceeds straight ahead.

After parting from the road, the trail does not stay on the ridgetop very long. It curves left and descends down to Bear Lake. Before you reach the lake, the trail branches into three different sections. Take either the middle or right fork, for they soon join again. When you are almost to the Lake's dam, there is another trail to the left. Instead of taking it, follow the one that angles to the right which shortly takes you down to a wooden fence at one end of the dam. The official trail does not cross the fence, but parallels it, finally turning right along a backwater of the lake. If you want a better view of the lake and the horseman's camp or if you wish to replenish your water supply, walk out on the dam. The dam was built by the C.C.C.'s in the 1930's and the present horseman camp was at one time the site of a large C.C.C. Camp. To locate the drinking water, follow the spillway down the side of the dam into the horseman's camp and in about 50 yards, you will reach the hand water pump which is enclosed in a wooden fence.

The fence on top of the dam is the northern-most point of this trail and the beginning of the eastern return section. Once across the fence you turn left, paralleling the fence on your left, and walk down toward a small inlet made by a small stream. As you walk back along this inlet on your left, you will soon be in a hollow. Briefly follow the trail up the hollow made by the wash until it turns left, crosses the wash and swings left crosses the wash and swings left again towards the lake. As the trail comes to the ridge end just in front of the lake if forks, the right one going rather steeply up, the other swinging round the end of the ridge where it turns right and begins a moderate climb up the crest of the ridge. The latter is slightly easier than the other fork, which soon joins it. This moderate climb ends at a maintained gravel road. Turn left on the road where you will see a parking lot above you on the right from which you get a view of the rolling countryside to the north west. The Copperhead fire tower is immediately on the left and it will take you about 15 or 20 minutes to reach it from the lake. If you climb the 72 steps up to the eighth platform and the weather is cooperating, you have a grand view of many tree-enclosed ridges on this large forest area. If you suffer from acrophobia, the view from the road is almost as good.

Continuing east on the State Forest Gravel Road 6 just exactly a half mile from the fire tower, there is a dirt road going off to the right with a sign that says:

SERVICE
VEHICLES
ONLY

This is the water truck road for the water tap at Point D and the turn off if you want to spend the night at Camp #1. If you wish to use that option, follow this one-lane road for a very short distance to a small clearing. Looking left there you will see a trail starting downhill with a locked culvert pipe standing upright alongside the trail. That is the intake for the water supply. Go by it and, a little to the right of the trail, is the water spigot. The trail to Camp #1 is between these two and goes on downhill. For the trail description to the camp see page 189.

If you are continuing on the Silver Arrow Trail, you remain on the main gravel road just briefly beyond this junction. The Forest Service gravel road goes downhill and as it starts uphill again you will see a trail going off diagonally on the right with a large stone beside it, displaying a painted silver arrow assuring you this is the correct turnoff.

Just after leaving the road, there is a fork in the trail. Take the right fork which begins another long ridge top walk with several up and downs over high knobs and saddles. In a few minutes, you will junction with the D.E. segment of the Backpack Trail where those who spent the night at Camp #1 return to the Silver Arrow loop. Proceed straight ahead at the junction, avoiding the trail that veers slightly to the left, for if you get on that trail you'll soon notice the orange blaze marks which tells you that you have made a wrong turn. As you continue along the ridge top the trail comes to a small clearing on the left where it turns right going easily downhill then crosses the paved road, which is the last road crossing on this trail. The trail continues on the ridgetop almost to its end with a few short stiff climbs over knobs. After about a half hour's walk from the last road crossing, you will find a small clearing to the left. At this point the F.G. segment of the North Loop Backpack Trail crosses the Silver Arrow Trail. The Silver Arrow Trail proceeds straight ahead, and if you begin to notice orange blazes, you'll know you've turned when you shouldn't have.

After reaching the top of one of the higher knobs, the trail makes a right turn and begins a steep, treacherous descent over badly eroded ground down to a lower ridge. This is the first of two difficult downhill stretches that come almost at the end of the trail. It's a bit tricky to negotiate if you are carrying a heavy pack and it becomes even more testy if the weather is wet. The trail follows this lower ridge right to its end, where you come to the second difficult downhill section, which is longer than the first one and takes you into Camp OYO. After passing a large cabin on the right, turn right on the camp road which soon takes you to the Camp entrance just across the road from the Camp parking lot.

# EAST FORK
## INTRODUCTION AND AREA DEVELOPMENT

Up until the beginning of the 1980's backpackers and hikers from the Cincinnati area seeking the longer loops were forced to travel two to three hours by car before arriving at the trailhead of any overnight loop walk. But because of two dams built quite close to Hamilton County, the hiker from the greater Cincinnati area now can often be on the trail in less than a hour from his home. The better than forty miles of trail available to the hiker backpacker at East Fork as well as the additional loop hike of approximately 40 miles at Caesar Creek State Park place interesting and worthwhile backpack loops and long day hikes almost within the backyard of Hamilton County residents. The development of the East Fork area happened at a most opportune moment, for Clermont County has seen a wave of industrial development in the vicinity near the present lake, which in no way intrudes its presence into the area of the state park and reservoir but has caused land values in the area to rise to such a point that a later recreational development of the area might have became cost prohibitive.

As with many of the loop hikes and the lakes they surround described in this book, East Fork and Caesar Creek dams owe their existence to the Flood Control Act of the federal congress passed in 1938. The lake at East Fork known officially as the William H. Harsha Lake in honor of a retired local U.S. Congressman is generally known and called by its earlier name, "East Fork Lake," by the long time users of its waters. Dam construction began in 1970. By 1978 the dam was operational resulting in a lake of over 2000 acres at normal pool and over 5 miles in length with 35.8 miles of shore line. East Fork derives its name from the major tributary of the Little Miami appropriately lying to the east of that stream. The lake and surrounding land was purchased by the federal government. Construction of the dam was carried out by the U.S. Corps of Engineers who still control it, the spillway and surrounding areas. Although still owned by the federal government, the rest of the 10,222 acres surrounding the lake are now leased to the state and have been developed by the O.D.N.R. into a state park which includes a Class A campground, with over 400 sites, seven major boat ramps, a large public beach, numerous picnic grounds and well over 50 miles of bridle and backpack trails, making it an outdoor recreational area of high quality, almost in the backyard of a large metropolitan area.

The bedrock formations of the area go back to almost 400 million years ago and proceed through at least three major geologic ages. The subsequent erosion through the area by the East Fork and its tributaries has cut a myriad of stream beds, many of which are surfaced with several layers of attractive stone terraces covering the complete width of the stream bed. Several sites of both the Adena and Hopewell Indian cultures have been found in the area suggesting ancient Indians inhabited the area as early as 3000 years ago. Of the modern Indians the area was controlled by the Erie tribes until they were wiped out by the Iroquois in 1665. Despite the favorable hunting and farming grounds, the area was little used by the Indians after that date. By the time of the Greenville treaty in 1795 this area was inhabited by farmers, who coveted the fertile land. Soon thereafter the nearby towns of Bethel, Bantam and Williamsburg were established. Because of the gradient of the East Fork and its fairly reliable water flow, there were many excellent sites for both water operated saw and grist mills. The most unusual enterprise in the area however was the establishment of two operating gold mines in 1869 within the confines of the modern park. One was located close to the north shore of the present lake. All vestiges of both of them however, have entirely disappeared.

226

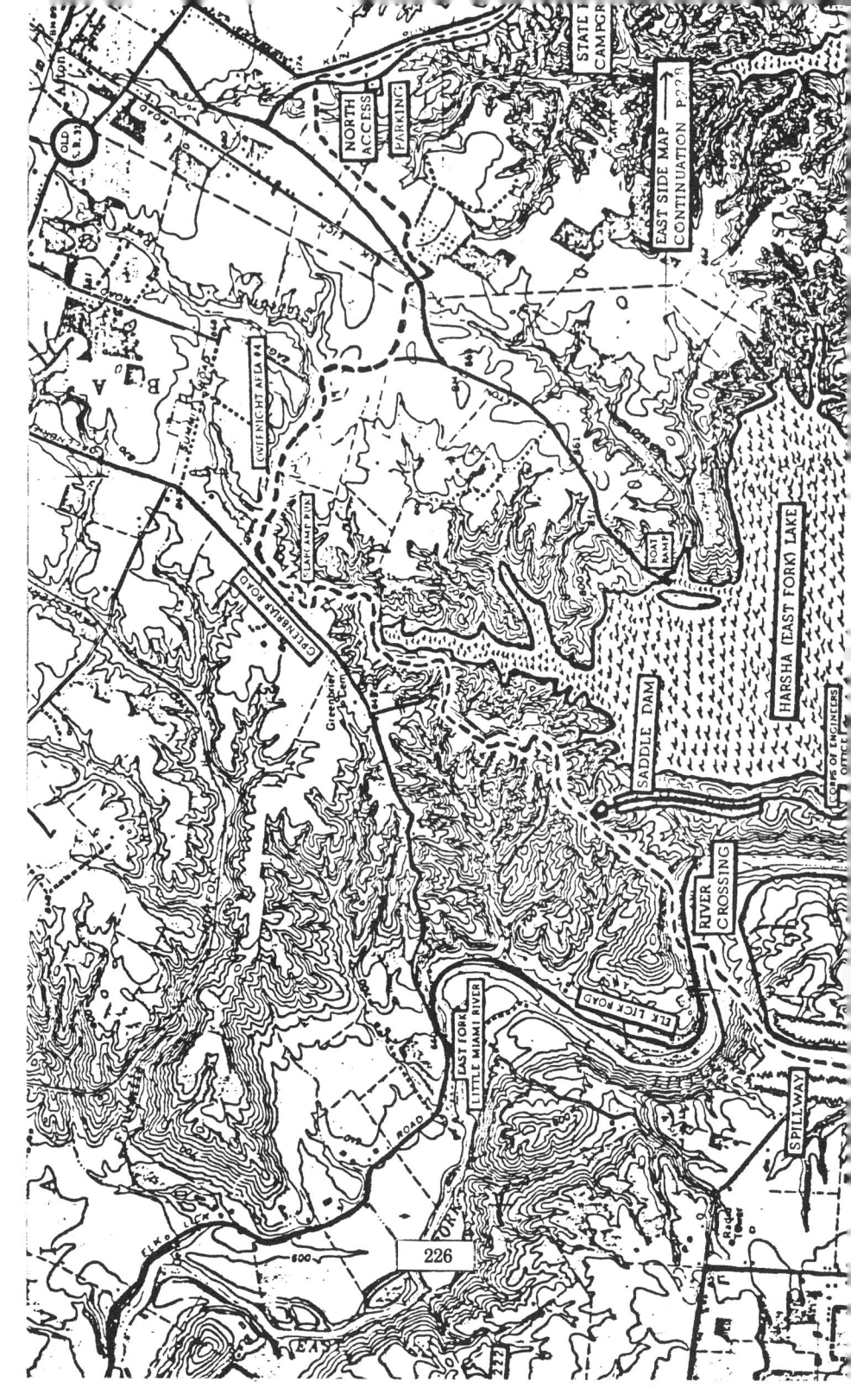

EAST FORK TRAILS
WEST SIDE
EAST FORD LEGEND
BACKPACK TRAIL
BACKCOUNTRY TRAIL
SLADE ROAD
DAM
BOAT RAMP
BEACH
FRONT WHEEL DRIVE
BOAT RAMP
S. R. 222
SOUTH ACCESS
PARKING
OVERNIGHT AREA 01
WILLIAMSBURG BANTAM ROAD
WILLIAMSBURG
STATE PARK OFFICE
S. R. 125
Bantam
Substa
South Bantam Ch
Trailer Park
Tabernacle
Bantam Ch
Hulington
CAMPBELL
SUGARTREE
OVERNIGHT AREA 02
SUGARTREE CREEK
TO A T
A
B
C
D
E
F

228

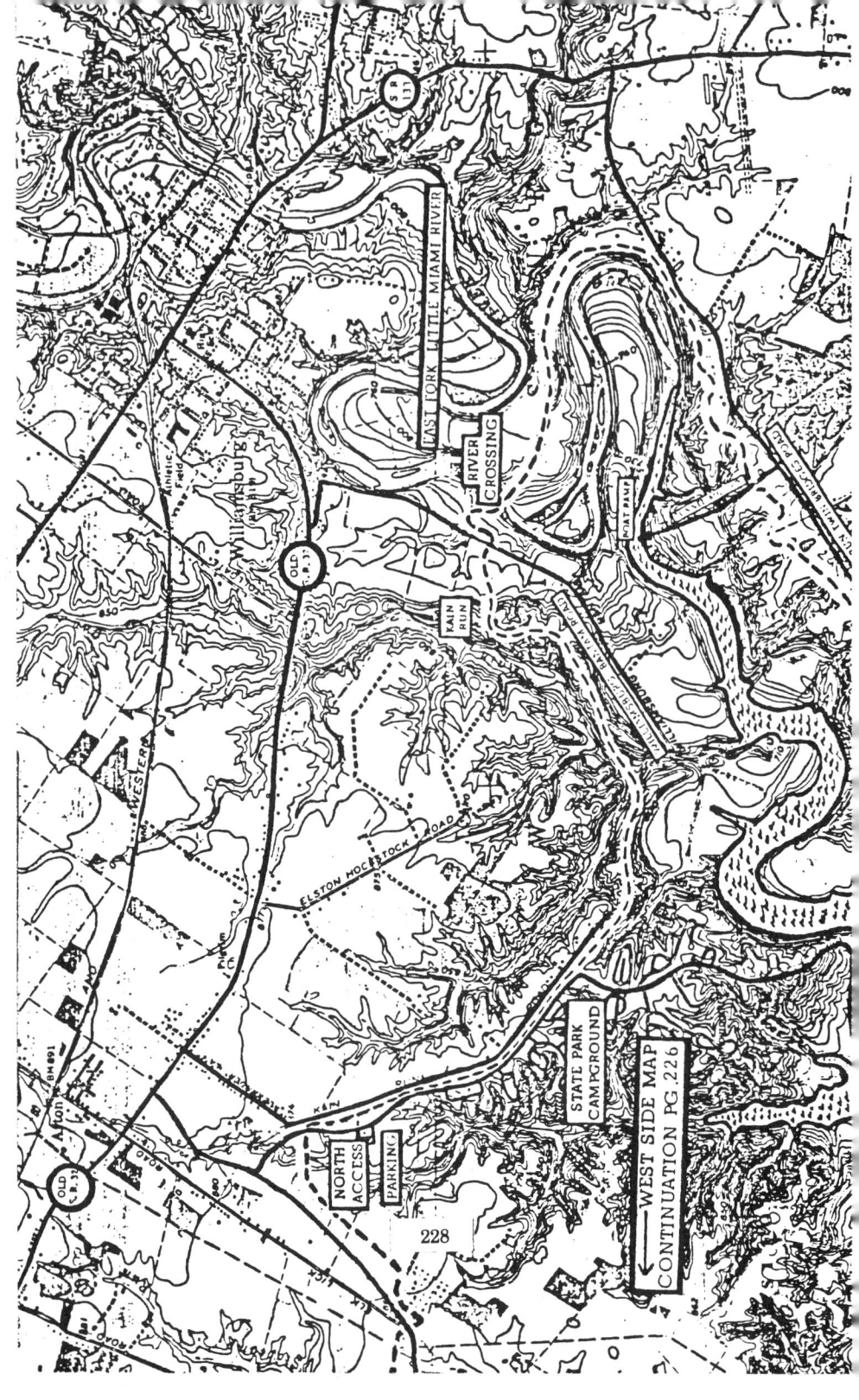

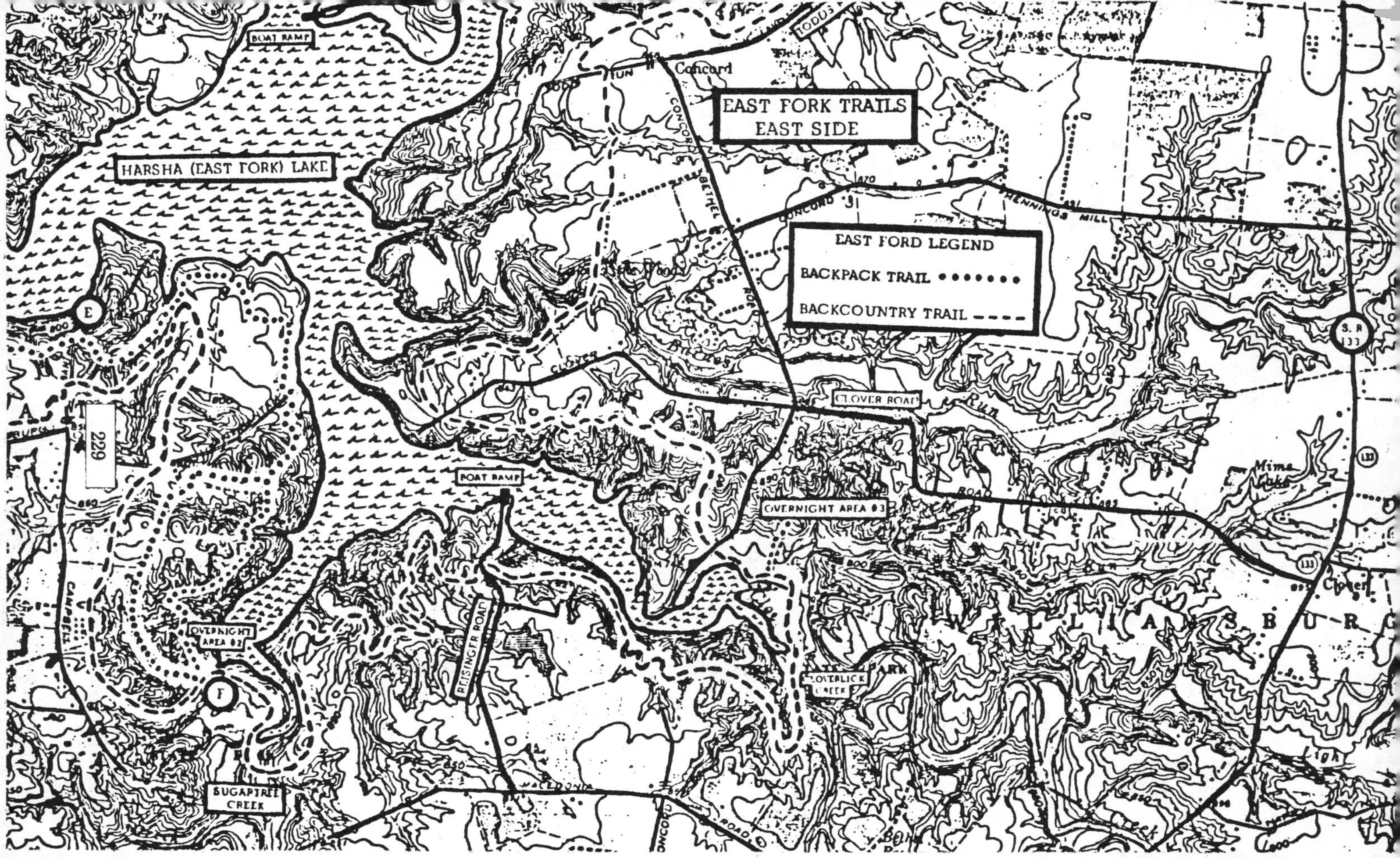

EAST FORK TRAILS
EAST SIDE
EAST FORD LEGEND
BACKPACK TRAIL
BACKCOUNTRY TRAIL
HARSHA (EAST FORK) LAKE
BOAT RAMP
BOAT RAMP
CLOVER ROAD
OVERNIGHT AREA #3
OVERNIGHT AREA #2
REISINGER ROAD
LOSTALICK CREEK
SUGARTREE CREEK
HENNINGS MILL
CONCORD
BETHEL
ROAD
Concord
Clover
Run
Mima Lake
WILLIAMSBURG
S. R. 133
133
E
F

## HOW TO GET THERE AND FINDING THE TRAILHEADS

Most hikers will find the east side of I-275 around Cincinnati the easiest access to the East Fork area. If you want to hike the Backcountry Trail starting at the North Access parking lot, follow State Route 32 east from 275 for a little over 9 miles passing Batavia, then take the Batavia Road - Front Wheel Drive exit. You immediately hit a stop light. Turn right at the stop light and almost immediately you will hit a second stop light. Turn left and in less than a half mile the road dead ends into Old State Route 32. Turn left and you will soon enter the small hamlet of Afton, and in less than 2 miles from the turn on Old State Route 32, you will see the entrance for the state park on the right. After this right turn, you will come to a road coming in from the left that goes to the campground. Follow that road to the campground office and the parking lot on the right side. Use this lot for the North access. Once in the lot, you can look across the road in front of the campground office and see a sign on the other side facing the road which says:

### BACK COUNTRY TRAIL
### NORTH ACCESS

Although it is not here at this writing, there will be a self registration booth built there. After filling out your permit, walk past the sign, and in a very few feet you will hit the loop trail.

If you want to start the Backcountry Trail at the South Access of the Backpack Trail, follow State Route 125 east through the town of Amelia. When State Route 222 comes in from the left, you have about 1½ miles to go before you turn off Route 125. When 222 turns off to the right, you make a left turn off 125 on Bantam Road. After you go only a short distance you will see a large sign indicating the park entrance on the left. Turn left here and go about ½ mile where you will see a sign facing you on the right side of the road which says:

### ◄——— BACK COUNTRY TRAIL
### SOUTH ACCESS PARKING

Turn left on this one lane gravel road, which takes you between two ponds. Once past the ponds, you arrive at the South Access parking lot with the self registration booth on the right. To follow the Backpack Trail, with the parking lot at your back, walk past the registration booth and you're on the trail. For the Backcountry Trail, with the registration booth on your right and the parking lot on your left, follow the dirt road that continues on beyond them and you are on the trail.

### PLACES TO STAY

While East Fork has neither lodge nor cabins there is a Class A campground with over 400 sites complete with electricity and hot showers. There are no primitive campgrounds that one can drive to.

### HIKING THE BACKCOUNTRY AND BACKPACK TRAILS
### AND THEIR VARIATIONS

**TOPOGRAPHIC MAPS:** Batavia, Williamsburg and Bethel quadrangles.

**TRAIL BLAZES:** Backcountry - green,
　　　　　　　　　 Backpack - orange.

Hiking the East Fork loops ..................................................... 231
The Backcountry Trail ........................................................ 231

Dayhiking possibilities ..................................................... 234
Backcountry Trail from the South Access to the North Access ................ 234
Backcountry Trail from the North Access to Overnight Area #3 ............... 241
Backcountry Trail from Overnight Area #3 to Overnight Area #2 .............. 246
Backcountry Trail from Overnight Area #2 to the South Access Backpack Trail
................................................................................ 249
Backpack Trail from South Access to Overnight Area #2...................... 252
Backpack Trail from Overnight Area #2 to end of the loop ................... 257
Maps:
West Segment ............................................................. 226
East Segment ............................................................. 228

    There are two loop trails suitable for backpacking in East Fork State Park. The oldest and longest of these two trails is the Backcountry trail. Completed in 1976 it is 33 miles long, encircling and occasionally in sight of William H. Harsha Lake. Open for use by backpackers, day hikers and horseriders, the trail is blazed green and also has green signs showing a backpacker framed by a horse shoe. The newer and shorter Backpack Trail is 10 miles long which is entirely on the south side of the lake and frequently in sight of it. This newer trail opened in 1982 is restricted for use by hikers only and is not a true loop for it has only a small loop at its end which circles around heading you back over much country you have already covered to the South Access. This makes the complete hike about 20 miles in length. Self registration is necessary before you start out on either trail. For those hiking the Backpack Trail or wishing to begin the Backcountry Trail on the south side of the lake, there is a self registration booth at the trail heads. For those hiking the Backcountry Trail starting at the North Access there was no registration booth there in the Spring of 1983 but there eventually will be.

    East Fork State Park has one interesting addition to its security staff that no other state park has at this time, for two of the park's rangers are often on horseback. You may find them anywhere, on the park roads, the Backcountry Trail and both in and around the campgrounds. The only place you won't find them on their horses is the Backpack Trail. So East Fork has its own version of the Canadian Mounties except their uniforms are green instead of red. Both of these mounted officers are very nice and so are their horses. Another addition that you will find at East Fork but is not found at any other of the state's backpacking campgrounds is all four of the overnight primitive campgrounds have bunkhouses. Overnight Areas 2, 3 and 4 have two with four bunks each, but don't expect Holiday Inn comfort, for the bunks are made of plywood. Overnight Area 1 also has 2 bunkhouses each but they are lower accommodating only two campers each on the ground. If you don't like carrying tents or do not have one, the bunk houses are handy. If, like me, you prefer to use your own backpacker's tent there is an area for tents at each campground. Only one of the Overnight Areas has a safe water supply within a reasonable distance from the site so carrying enough water or effective water purficiation supplies is a must for overnight stays unless you cache water at various road crossings before you hike. This is easily done for there are nine open roads that the trail crosses that are mostly spaced nicely apart. Key places for doing this closest to the overnight areas would be at the end of the saddle dam for Overnight Area #4, Concord Bethel Road on the north side of the lake for Area #3 and Reisinger Ramp Road for Area #2.

# THE BACKCOUNTRY TRAIL

    Shortly after this 33 mile loop trail was opened, I talked to aquaintances who had hiked parts of it and at least two of them described it somewhat negatively as a trail that kept going in, out and around people's backyards. Since the area is so close to a

*View of Harsha Lake from the East Fork saddle dam*

major metropolitan area this disappointing opinion did not surprise me, but after hiking it myself I found that such an opinion was, in general, happily misleading. Even though buildings are occasionally in sight, only twice does the trail come close to dwellings for any appreciable length of time and my overall impression after covering the entire trail twice was that most of the trail travels through a pleasant combination of woods and field which mostly seems far removed from the usual urban enviroment we wish to elude. Despite the fact that this loop is a hair's breath from a population center of over a million people the crowds of people that flock to East Fork congregate at the beach, picnic area and Class A campground while the trail walker is left in happy isolation hardly aware that there may be large crowds not far away. Many a pleasant day I've walked large segments of this trail and never encountered another human being.

If you hike this trail you will soon find that it rarely follows the shortest distance between two points, for the general purpose of the trail was to create a walk or ride in the most available pleasant locales with enough distance to make it a long and interesting loop. The mostly pleasant surroundings of the trail show how well the planners succeeded because the trail architects efficiently isolated the trail rider and walker in a cocoon of semi-wild forest and field in an amazingly small area. The climbs and descents along the trail are almost never severe, and the hikers will generally tire more from the distances covered than a series of lung busting climbs. But after becoming reasonably familiar with this trail, I came up with some rather ambivalent feelings toward it. Despite some of its obvious good points it has some real drawbacks. A few of the more rugged hikers may look at these drawbacks as an advantage. It all depends on your point of view. Generally this trail is not well suited for beginners because the distances are long and following a trail also used for horses is much tougher to walk. There are enough difficult places on the path as well as many unofficial and confusing side trails, and several crossings of large streams which might make this an unappealing trip to all but the experienced backpacker. But East Fork's newer "Backpack Trail" is a beginners delight, so if you are looking for a shorter and less taxing hike check out East Fork's Backpack Trail on page 252.

All trails can be adversely affected by heavy rains but, like the Burr Oak loop, great amounts of precipitation can make a hike on East Fork's Backcountry loop an impossibility. Both of these long loops come so close to their respective lakes at low enough altitudes that when the lakes are used to hold the runoff of excessive rains to prevent or lessen the danger of severe flooding downstream, there are many areas of trail that are totally submerged and loop hikes become impossible. There are some other drawbacks caused by high waters at East Fork that are generally not found on the other hikes described in this book. After the water has receded, some of the areas previously inundated remain terribly mucky for days. Not only does plodding through ankle deep mud tend to irritate the hikers, but often the new deposits left by the receeding water make the trail exceedingly difficult to find. There is hardly a trail in this book that does not have its swamp-like segments even after many dry days, but East Fork's Backcountry Trail has more of them than any other trail. Add to this inconvenience the irritation of having horses churning these spots into gluey quagmires, this trail becomes a test of human tempers which is best not attempted by the faint of heart. This is one of two loops in this book whose entire length is open as a bridle path. Trails open for equestrian use are generally far more difficult to traverse for the hiker than those where horses are not allowed. But if you wish to hike this loop don't cuss the horses and their riders but bless their existence, for the horse riders actively campaigned for this trail and without them the trail may not have existed at all. Maintenance of 33 miles of trail is a big job and many trail rider groups have aided the park personnel in a large capacity in keeping the trail open and usuable. Of all the long loops described in this book, this is the only one I hiked where the trail was almost entirely clear of downed trees.

There are other drawbacks. The Backcountry Trail is also the only trail described in this book that crosses a river and crosses it twice. Fortunately the East Fork of the Little Miami River is a very small river so crossing it safely is often possible, but there are many times that the river crossing is too dangerous to attempt. If the water is high, the lower crossing can easily be avoided, which is explained in the trail description, but the upper crossing has no easy alternative because the walk to the the nearest upstream bridge is far enough away to make it impractical. This crossing is usually possible after a day or two of dry weather providing there haven't been days of persistent rain saturating the ground preceeding the dry spell. Don't try either crossing when the water is up to the trees because even at high normal levels these crossings can be tricky. The crossings are never low enough to stone hop dry across the stream and even at low levels the water will often be up to your knees so carry an old pair of tennis or jogging shoes along for the crossing because you never know what kind of foot cutting debris may drift in and getting a good pair of hiking boots soaked can be both expensive and very uncomfortable. You can find if the lake level is low enough or if the release of water from the dam is small enough to make the river crossing by phoning the Corps of Engineers between 7:30 and 3:30 weekdays year round and on weekends during the summer months at Area Code (513) 797-4766. Ask what the lake level is and what the C.F.S. release from the dam is. It's a local call for people living in the Cincinnati area. The summer pool of the lake is 733 feet. If it is two or three feet above pool stage the trail is still above water and anything below is fine. C.F.S. means cubic feet per second of water passing a given point. I was told that any release up to 100 C.F.S. was crossable by hikers. I crossed it at 42 C.F.S. and it was fairly easy. Fifteen C.F.S. is the minimum release. At that level the crossing would be very easy. The only way to check the upper river crossing would be to follow Route 133 to Williamsburg where the route crosses the river just a little ways upstream and make a visual check.

I suppose you could sum it up and say this trail's most trouble-free conditions occur when it has been dry, dry, dry for an extended period of time. Its 33 mile length makes the Backcountry Trail the second longest in this book. Except for the exceptional young hikers in excellent physical condition, the length of the trail puts it beyond the point of completing the loop on a double overnight weekend. However, it does fit nicely in a three day weekend for a conditioned backpacker. The distance, river crossings and the mucky places make it a good training ground for those in shape to test the durability of equipment and the general temper, personalities and fitness level of companions before making more extended and physically demanding trips along the Appalachian Trail or any of the longer high trails in the West. For people living in the Cincinnati area, it means they can be on the trail in about an hour where the rougher and longer loops of Shawnee are close to three driving hours away. By getting a morning start loop hikers beginning from the South Access should be able to make Overnight Area #4 or starting on the North Access to Overnight Area #3 before dark.

If you are going to do the entire loop starting from the South Access, you have a rough second day of 14 miles between Overnight Area #4 and #3. By starting at the North Access the hike to Overnight Area #3 is shortened by about 1½ miles and on a triple overnighter you will have no hike longer than 12 miles by using Overnight Areas #3, #2 and #4. This leaves an easy 1½ mile walk on the last day back to the parking lot.

Some may wonder why my trail description follows the clockwise route rather than the other way around since the campsites are numbered in the anti-clockwise direction. There were two reasons for this decision. The one that influenced me the most was an option to follow the new Backpack Trail from Overnight Area #2 toward the end of your trip by cutting out a very dull section of the Backcountry Trail. Also by getting a morning start in the clockwise direction from the South Access you would cross some very boggy spots while you are still fresh followed by the more interesting spillway area and river crossing at midday leaving a rather easy segment for late in the afternoon.

## DAY HIKING POSSIBILITIES

There are many day hiking possibilities if you have two vehicles or someone that can pick you up at the end of your hike but there are no short loop possibilities on this trail. You can figure your own day hikes by using the map and seeing where the trail crosses usable roads. East Fork, like Burr Oak, also has the possibilities of day hiking using a boat and depositing or picking up day hikers because the trail comes very close to the Tunnel Mill and Reisinger Road boat ramps. Also, at this writing Concord Bethel Road on both the north and south shore of the lake is open and goes right to the water's edge although they do not have boat ramps. The dam area ramp is also handy if the hiker leaves the trail at the spillway and follows the road across the dam.

**Backcountry Trail.** from the South Access parking lot to the lower crossing of the East Fork, Overnight Area #4 and the North Access parking lot.

DISTANCE: To River Crossing 4½ miles, to Overnight Area #4 9½ miles to North Access parking lot 11½ miles.
HIKE: To spillway - strenuous, from Spillway to overnight area #4 - moderate, from overnight area #4 to North Access parking lot - easy.
WALKING TIME: To river crossing 2½ to 3 hours, from river crossing to overnight area #4 1½ to 2 hours, from Overnight Area #4 to North Access parking lot 1 hour.

GENERAL REMARKS: This segment has the unusual feature of passing through

*Hikers on East Fork's Backcountry Trail walking through the spillway area*

the spillway, the river crossing if the water is low or going across the dam if the river level is up. Although rarely in view of the lake, a very short walk off the trail will offer the best lake view possible. If you are starting a loop hike from the South Access, the 9½ miles to the first overnight area is a good distance if started early in the day but a very poor one if you are getting an afternoon start. The biggest drawbacks to the hiker are a few places on the trail that almost never seem to dry up especially one the horsemen call "the swamp". The going in a number of places is gooey enough to bring the thought of uttering a few blue words. Almost all the climbs and descents between the two parking areas are moderate to easy, so the biggest deterrent to progress on this section is mushing through the bogs. There is another camp that can be used and if you arrive at Overnight Area #4 early and you are still not overly tired, you could hike on to the North Access and camp in the Class A Campground. The advantages of doing so would include shortening of your second day's walk from about 14 to 12 miles and access to the camp's water supply and hot showers. But disadvantages include paying a camping fee ($7.00 a night per campsite at this writing), and any feeling of wilderness seclusion is destroyed.

TRAIL DESCRIPTION: To find the trailhead see page 230. Follow the dirt road past the registration booth. This road soon bears to the left and ends at the edge of the forest. Once in the trees the trail begins descending to Ulrey Run at a mostly moderate grade with one steep section. I remember going down this section on my first walk here which unhappily coincided with a torrential downpour and the going was slippery indeed. On subsequent drier days I found it easy enough. Just before the trail reaches the creek it T's into another that parallels the stream. Turn left here and you will find the trail follows Ulrey Run upstream for a couple of minutes walking before turning right and crossing it. Once across the wide trail turns left and again follows the creek upstream. In less than five minutes of walking the trail forks. Both paths are wide but turn right here and you will find the trail takes you into open country and after a gentle climb you will pass an old rusty remmant of farm machinery on the left.

This area was once the farm of a retired sea captain named Pinkham who settled here in the late nineteenth century. George Rooks, the assistant manager of the park, told me that the magnificent brick house that stood nearby was unusual enough to be considered for restoration, turning this house, other building and the surrounding area into a working farm using tools and techniques of the nineteenth century and thus creating a working museum of the past. But because of prohibitive costs (the cost of restoring the house alone was estimated at over a half million dollars) the project was abandoned and the house torn down.

Just past the old piece of farm machinery you are confronted with the trail splitting in three directions. Take the middle one straight ahead, and it soon leads you to an abandoned narrow road. When the road curves to the left, the trail proceeds straight ahead. If the weather has been wet, a little easier way is to follow the road just around the curve, and about twenty feet beyond it you will see another trail going off to the right. Take it for it parallels the main trail on a little higher ground with an old fence in between and soon rejoins the main path.

Shortly beyond this point the trail passes along the right side of a pond and goes over a cement culvert that drains the pond.

As the trail returns to the woods you are entering a quagmire the horsemen call "the swamp." It doesn't resemble the usual swamp with high weeds and cat tails but the mucky footing is usually a nightmare even after long spells of dry weather. Both hikers and horsemen looking for firmer footing have created a number of paths here which turn out to be all equally grim and gooey. Probably the best route is to hang close to the right side and plod through until it T's into another trail as you come out of the trees. Turn left here and as the trail briefly returns to the trees you have another gooey section that has an easy grade downhill. As the trail comes out of the woods you will find a little rise in front of you with a trail going straight ahead up the rise and another that goes to the right following the edge of the trees. Take the path to the right and you will find that it soon swings left into the field where you will be able to see a white house off to the left and a good ways in front of you. Although the trail never gets closer to the house on the left side, just before the trail is abreast of it the path swings right and soon hits another fork. Take the left fork which almost immediately crosses a closed paved road. As you cross it you can look left and see the road barrier which is at the end of a residential street called Yellow Lane. Shortly after crossing the road the path veers into and turns left on a well used gravel path, but stays on it for only about thirty feet before turning off of it on the right side, and almost immediately it passes a small pond on the right.

As the path returns to the forest, it begins a moderate descent to Back Run. You will soon see this large creek below as you head in the general upstream direction. It will not be long before you will arrive at a junction. You will see a trail coming in from the right. Turn right here and the trail goes directly down to the creek and crosses it. Once across Back Run, the trail turns right and briefly follows the creek in the downstream direction. When it turns away from the stream you have the only steep uphill climb of any length in this entire segment, which is eased a bit by a double switchback. Once you are up on the wooded ridgetop all the other up and down sections are moderate to easy for several miles. You will soon cross a trio of small washes quite close together with high ground between each one making the trail go up and down like a miniature roller coaster.

When the trail hits another open but somewhat narrow field, it swings left, and soon a house and barn are in view on the left. But before coming up alongside the structures, the trail turns right and returns to the forest.

Dropping easily down and crossing a small wash with a solid stone bottom and adjoining rock ledges, the trail swings right and goes gently downhill and will soon bring you in sight of a small arm of the lake below you on the right. Then the trail brings you out of the woods and into the spillway area where you immediately cross a wash that drains in the spillway into the lake. Look down to the right here and over a cement chute built to prevent bank erosion. If the lake is in pool and you are walking in the summer months the lake is 62 feet below you; in the winter, 65 feet. The highest the lake has been so far is 765 feet above sea level which it reached in 1979. Thats 28 feet higher than the normal summer pool and 35 feet below the level of the spillway (795 feet). The chances of the water reaching the spillway are quite remote but if it ever happens I won't have any time for hiking for I'll be too busy building my Ark. Once across the wash the trail turns left into the spillway area. You will see two parallel hills forming the sides of the spillway that run almost ¾ of a mile. Since little grows in the spillway the whole area has a sort of forlorn and lonely look almost like a small patch of flat desert among the green and rolling hills. Following along the spillway area, the trail soon crosses the paved road that cuts directly across the spillway. This road goes across the dam and saddle dam.

You have a nice view of the lake from the saddle dam but it is about a mile away from this point and if you are planning to spend the night in Overnight Area #4, this side trip will use up a lot of hiking time. It is also easily reached on a short walk of less than 50 yards about 2 miles ahead on the Backcountry Trail after the lower crossing of the East Fork. If they are releasing too much water to make a safe and easy crossing across the East Fork of the Little Miami River you can avoid that crossing by turning right on this road up and across the dam.

If you decide to follow the road up and across the dam, you will pass the Corps office on the right and then cross the saddle dam. At the far side of this dam the road ends with a loop turnaround. When you reach this loop you will notice a well worn path about ¾ around going uphill into the woods. In less than 50 feet this trail T's into the Backcountry Trail. This is an option open only to hikers and may not be used by horses. For continuing trail description see page 239.

If you are going to stay on the main trail and make the lower river crossing, you will find the trail becomes very indistinct in the spillway. Walk diagonally through the spillway making for the far right corner. When you reach that point you will see a paved road that follows along the right wall of the spillway but curves right almost at the end of the spillway and goes through a breach in the embankment and then downhill to the foot of the dam. Right at that curve you will see a trail going up the embankment to the left of the road. This is the continuation of the trail but you also have another option here. By adding just a short distance to your total mileage you can follow the road down to a picnic area and lavatory at the bottom of the dam.

It's really exciting to see the water come roaring out of that tunnel when the water's up, but if it is running fast enough to give you a good show, it means a safe river crossing by foot is impossible. The maximum amount that can be released is 5000 C.F.S. (Cubic feet per second). I once saw the flow when they were releasing 3900 C.S.F. and it was a real giant wave making torrent and the river crossing below was safe only for seals.

The restroom is of the flush type and is open during the warmer seasons. It may look like just a normal john but due to environmental regulations the sewage treatment system necessary to operate this lavatory ran the cost up over $100,000 so if you like relieving yourself in expensive surroundings, be the federal government's guest.

On your return to the main trail it is not necessary to walk back up to the spillway for you will notice as you follow the road down to the dam that about 1/3rd mile from the spillway there is a small gravel parking lot on the left with a barrier gate across a small dirt road on the spillway side of the lot. On your return take that little dirt side

*Hikers making the East Fork river crossing below the dam at lowest water level*

*The same crossing location as above after heavy rains when a safe crossing would be impossible*

road for it leads directly to the trail crossing of the East Fork in about 50 yards.

If you decide against this side trip and wish to follow the official trail, when you reach the point where the road curves and goes through the break in the spillway wall climb up the embankment. Once up, you will begin the descent to the river, at first steep but soon moderates to an easy grade.

On my first walk through this area, there were strong uplift air currents rising from the river which four turkey vultures used to hover almost motionless in the air above me. As beautiful as it was to watch, knowing I would be shortly crossing the river I wondered if they were anticipating a diet of drowned backpacker somewhat downstream.

The trail drops down to a small flat treeless area, crosses it, curves to the right merges into an old rut road and follows it briefly with the river visible to the left. The old road soon T's into another once paved small road, turns left, and in a few feet brings you to the banks of the river.

When the river level is low enough, the easiest way to cross is to look upstream where two branches of the river rejoin after going around an island. By crossing right at the top of the island, you cross the two branches and the water level is below the knees when running about 40 C.F.S. You can go directly across but there is a pool where the water gets well above this level. When you reach the river, you have covered about 4½ miles from the South Access parking lot which leaves 4 miles to cover to Overnight Area #4 or 5½ miles to the North Access parking lot.

Once across the river you will find yourself on an old road angling upstream from the crossing point, which at one time served as a ford for wagons. This little road soon takes you between two stone gate posts where this smaller lane hits a larger paved but now closed section of Elk Lick Road. It is at this point that the Buckeye Trail joins the Backcountry Trail for about three miles, so you will see blue blazes until the trails part company at the point where Slabcamp Run enters the lake.

You turn right on the road but follow it only about 100 feet where the trail turns left into the trees and begins an angling climb up the ridge until it turns left and continues a moderate climb up an inclining ridge finger. You will soon see the loop turnaround at the end of the saddle dam on the right side. Just after this sighting the trail comes to a small clearing where another trail comes in from the right. Unless you are terribly pressed for time or have previously been on the dam road, follow this little trail down to the loop and a little ways out on the saddle dam for an excellent view of the lake and, by looking right into the valley of East Fork, you can see how much you have climbed since leaving the river.

In about a five minute walk from this junction the trail hits the end of an unused narrow road that was once paved. Turn left on it and follow it a short distance until it junctions into another road that curves in front of you. You proceed straight ahead at this junction for only about 100 feet before the trail takes a not easily seen abrupt right turn off the road going up very steeply for a few feet back into the woods. The next stretch alternates a good deal between small patches of forest and open wild fields. In less than five minutes of walking the trail crosses a one-lane gravel road that is not open to public vehicles. It is not long before the trail again hits the road but this time turns left on the road briefly to avoid a steep gully on the left. As the road begins a curve to the left, the trail leaves the road on the left hand side returning to the woods where you can see a deep hollow on your left. After doing a swinging U turn around the head of that hollow there is a fork in the trail. Take the right fork which soon leads you another road crossing. If you look left at the crossing you can see the locked white gate which keeps public vehicles from entering. Just after this crossing you will pass an old farm pond on the left. Once beyond the pond the trail begins a steep descent down a ridge finger where the lake is soon visible on the right. After crossing a small wash almost down to the lake level, the trail turns left, climbs slightly and T's into a wide gravel path that once may have been a very narrow road.

Turn right on it, and the lake will soon be visible again on the right as the gravel path peters out.

You will soon come to a division in the trail with one path going slightly left away from the lake. The trail to the right crosses a good-sized hollow ending in a finger of the lake.

You can follow the trail to the left or go down a few feet on the right trail until you come to a trail post. You are now in Slabcamp Hollow and the trail crossing the hollow is the continuation of the Buckeye Trail, while the trail to the left going up the hollow is the continuation of the Backcountry Trail. Since the two trails join again just beyond the North Access parking lot, I orginally felt that following the Buckeye Trail from this junction would be a nice alternative because the Backcountry trail covers mostly open field areas whereas the Buckeye Trail remains close to the lake and in heavy forest most of the way. But after walking the Buckeye stretch I changed my mind. The Buckeye alternative has several nasty climbs which would be real lung busters for anyone carrying any kind of a load and would prove difficult even for light traveling day hikers. This segment would be rated as very strenuous. Both trails are also used by horses, but the Buckeye creates the greater handicap because the long steep climbs and descents are made more difficult by the quagmire created by poor water runoff sloshed to muck by the horses hooves on the slopes in all but the driest of seasons. Although the distance covered is about the same, the Buckeye alternative will take you about twice as long and does not come near Overnight Area #4 leaving a distance of over 15 miles from this junction to the next legal camping area at Overnight Area #3. So my recommendation is to stay on the Backcountry Trail.

As you climb easily along Slabcamp Hollow, you can often see the stream below you before reaching the ridgetop on what was once probably an old trace road. When reaching the top of the ridge, the trail breaks into an open field where you can see some barns directly ahead. At this point there are two different horse trails running together and it is not long before the Backcountry Trail turns right, away from the white blazed horse trail. It then goes into the woods, crosses a wash, climbs out again into the the field and rejoins the white blazed horse trail. Both trails enter a small parking lot alongside Greenbriar Road which is used by horseman. At the far side of the parking lot the trail divides again, but this time the white blazed trail turns right away from the road while the Backcountry Trail proceeds straight ahead. In a little over 100 yards the trail turns right, away from the road at a point adjacent to a gravel driveway on the other side of Greenbriar Road. The trail then returns to the woods, crosses a wash with a solid stone bed and then T's into another trail that parallels the stream. You turn left and briefly follow the wash upstream before curving to the right and returning to and staying in open fields with some clumps of small trees for quite a distance covering several minutes of walking time. The trail briefly returns to the woods, crosses a small wash with a cement bottom, climbs slightly and returns to the fields. As the trail enters a lightly wooded area you will soon see a sign on the left side of the trail facing it which says:

## OVERNIGHT AREA NO. 4

Follow the trail down a little further and the camp is in plain view on the left. The tent area is behind the farthest bunk house.

Just beyond the Overnight Area as the trail goes up over a little rise, the trail forks. Take the left fork for it is slightly easier. You soon run into and turn right on a paved but no longer maintained and closed section of Half Acre Road. As you come into a large open area you follow the road as it swings left and ends just short of a maintained public highway, which is the North Shore Ramp Road. Cross the ramp road and turn left paralleling the road for about 75 yards and you will see a bark covered path that turns right away from the road. After going over a ditch this trail takes you up to another stretch of abandoned paved road. It follows the old road around a left curve, and just before the road again abruptly ends the trail turns right, moving away from it heading toward a fence. This is another area where ground water seems almost never to dry up, and the walk to the fence can be through a real quagmire. At the fence line you can see an old gravel road that goes more or less straight ahead but the Backcountry Trail turns left and proceeds into the open field following the fence line. This field has very poor drainage and more than its share of exasperating wet, boggy places that you can't go around.

After leaving the field, you pass through an area that is partly wooded interspersed with small open areas. You will know when you are getting close to the campground road when you cross the small gully of a wash. When you hit the paved road, the trail crosses it. If you are in a hurry to get to the North Access parking lot, turn right and follow the road. It is only a short distance to the campground office and parking lot. If you follow the trail, it soon turns right and moves in a narrow strip of open land between the campground road on the right and Kain Run Road on the left. When you come adjacent to the campground office there is a small trail to the right which leads over to the campground road and the North Access parking lot.

**BACKCOUNTRY TRAIL,** from the North Access Parking lot to Overnight Area #3

DISTANCE: To river crossing 4 miles, to Tunnel Mill Ramp Road 6 miles, to Overnight Area #3 12½ miles.
HIKE: To river crossing - easy. From river to Tunnel Mill Road - moderate. From Tunnel Mill Road to Clover Road - easy. From Clover Road to Overnight Area #3 - moderate.
WALKING TIME: 6½ to 7 hours.

GENERAL REMARKS: This segment of the trail should only be attempted after several days of dry weather for there is no easy or reasonable way to avoid the upper crossing of the East Fork. The rest of this segment is on fairly high ground and day hiking from Tunnel Mill Road to the crossing of Concord Bethel Road is unaffected by the back up of high water from the lake. Part of the approach to Overnight Area #3 is underwater after long periods of heavy rain. The hike starts out on one of the least interesting segments with public roads paralleling both sides of the trail. But this boring stretch does not last long, for when the trail begins the drop to Kain's Run and the East Fork river crossing scenic interest is greatly improved with only one public road crossing and no close proximity to housing. Once across the river there is another brief stretch quite close to human habitation, but the scenery down to the river makes it worth it. Beyond Tunnel Mill Ramp Road there is a pleasant mixture of field and forest walking with an occasional building in sight but not really close to the trail. In general this whole section offers pleasant if not spectacular scenery with no really strenuous climbs of any appreciable length. But the 12 mile distance between the North Access and Overnight Area #3 makes for a long day which is best not attempted for beginners or hikers badly out of shape.

TRAIL DESCRIPTION: To find the trailhead see page 230. If you are starting from the parking lot look across the campground road in front of the office and a sign facing the road says:

## BACK-COUNTRY TRAIL
## NORTH ACCESS

You follow a trail from the sign just a few feet until it T's into the Backcountry Trail where you turn right. The trail is now between two roads with houses visible on the left and several loops of the Class A campground on the right. The Buckeye Trail soon joins this trail but stays on it only briefly before it crosses over to and follows Kain Run road on the left. This is only one of two places on the entire trail where this loop stays close to homes for any length of time. Not long after you see the campground road curving to the right away from you, the trail crosses a small gulley and hits a closed section of Kain Run Road. The general feeling is to turn right and follow the road downhill, but the trail turns left following the road for only about 20 feet before turning right going into the forest. It is at this point the Buckeye Trail rejoins the Backcountry loop. As the trail follows the descending ridge down to Kain's Run, the scenery is much improved. When the trail reaches this large creek you will see there are several rock ledges across the stream bed both in the upstream and downstream direction. You can look across the creek and see a well defined old road leading away from the stream. The great temptation is to cross Kain Run and follow the road as I did on my first hike in the area. But the trail does not cross the creek at this point but turns left, immediately crosses a wash, and proceeds upstream with Kain Run on your right. It is not long before you do cross the stream at a point where the creek bed is made up of long sections of flat stone. Be careful of areas where the water covers the stone bottom for it can be treacherously slippery. After this first crossing the trail very shortly recrosses the creek diagonally upstream and heads up the middle of a small branch on the opposite shore before turning right and leaving the smaller stream bed. When the trail makes a big U turn to the right you will soon be making your third and last crossing of Kain Run. Once across, the trail turns left and begins a moderately steep climb up the ridge and soon moderates for an easy walk to the ridge top. The Buckeye Trail again cuts off to the left but soon joins the trail again. You can follow it if you want to, but the loop trail is shorter, easier and faster. The Buckeye Trail again rejoins the loop when the trail takes a sharp turn to the right and starts downhill on a rocky surfaced, tree-lined old farm road. As you move down this lane you will be able to see that beyond the trees that line both sides of the road there are cultivated fields on each side. As the trail comes out of the tree rows it proceeds straight ahead along the edge of the cultivated field on the right soon arriving at the paved Williamsburg Bantam Road. Although this road is still open to vehicular traffic the lake interferes with it continuing on to Bantam. If you do the entire loop, you will cross a closed section of this same road on the other side of the lake. The Buckeye Trail turns left on this road and parts company from the loop trail for the last time. At this point the Backcountry Trail goes directly across the paved road and then turns left skirting along the edge of another cultivated field. At the end of the field the trail turns right and follows along the end of the field until it ends. The trail then turns right following the edge of the field only briefly before angling left down to the river bank of East Fork. You can see the continuation of the hike on an old road that angles away from the opposite shore. The horses usually proceed straight across but it is best for hikers to look left a little upstream where the suggestion of an old wagon road curves around to the stream at which point there once was a wagon crossing. By following this old crossing the hiker finds that the stream is more spread out, making the water shallower and the current less swift than it is going directly across the river.

On my first crossing of this stream, there had been no rain for six days although there had been a long previous spell of heavy precipitation. By following the old ford the water was still up to my knees. A direct crossing would have been deeper. The current funnels towards this bank making it quite swift and somewhat hazardous. Except for extended periods of drought the water seldom is below this level and often higher. Even before flood stage is reached, at the normal high levels this crossing should be attempted only by hikers with a great deal of experience in these crossings. Making a crossing at this high level is far harder than it looks. If the stream is out of its banks and into the trees no one should attempt to make this crossing. Remember, that if the water is at a passable level, to unfasten, your pack hip belt before crossing and cross either in bare feet or, better yet, wearing old tennis shoes brought along for this purpose. Getting your hiking boots soaked may make the rest of your hike quite uncomfortable and possibly miserable.

Once across the East Fork you may find the first parts of this trail less defined than the trail leading to the crossing. This is probably due to the fact that the river crossing is frequently not safe and wise hikers and riders have turned back. From the river bank the trail climbs about 100 feet in altitude in less than a half a mile but the rise is so gentle one is hardly aware of it. The trail begins to follow an old dirt road which is very indistinct and in some places not visible at all. Swinging to the left the road moves directly away from the river and follows along the left side of a cultivated field. About halfway across the field the trail swings left away from it and goes up a slight rise. Once up the rise, the trail seems to stop at the edge of another field with no path along its edge. On my original walk I looked left hoping I would see a path skirting around the left side of the field or at least a suggestion of one that went directly across it. But neither existed. Soil erosion sometimes obliterates this trail. If you look directly across the field you will see a bare spot on another small rise which is part of the old road the trail follows. Cross the field directly to that spot. Once up that rise the trail has a little jog to the right and again crosses through cultivated fields but this time there is a definite space left between the two fields at the beginning. This division gets less distinct as you move further across the field. For guidance you can see two distinct clumps of trees with the trees on the right being taller. The trail passes between the two clumps. Once you are there the road becomes far more distinct and you will have no trouble following it.

As the trail and road rise a white house becomes visible on the left. You are approaching the only other area on this loop where the trail is quite close to a group of houses for any length of time and for a very good reason. As you pass the house you go by a locked state gate across the road. Beyond this point the gravel road is public. If you wondered why the trail was routed on this road so close to the civilized world you will see the reason when you begin to pass the second house. Look to the right for a marvelous overlook with the river quite close but far below you. The embankment is so steep that the trail had to be located on the ridgetop. This is the only time the trail is located on an open public road for any distance, but even here the road is narrow, the distance is short and, being on a dead end, there is no through traffic.

As you approach a red brick house which does not face this little road but the paved Todd Run - Twin Bridge road, again look right for another impressive overlook. Just beyond this overlook and just before the little road curves left toward the paved highway, the trail turns right off the road. Once off the little road the hiker finds that the area is still narrow between Todd Run - Twin Bridge road and the dropoff to the river. The trail wanders through both open fields and patches of woods sometimes close enough to the road that you can see the traffic and sometimes on the brink of the drop where you can see the river below. There are several easy crossings over washes, but when you come to one that takes you steeply down about 30 feet with a less demanding climb out after the crossing you are almost to the paved Tunnel Mill Road and boat ramp. When you come out of the forest into a cleared area you reach this road which leads to a public access and boat ramp to the lake. Painted green arrows on the road indicate a left turn on the road for a little over 50 feet before turning right and away from the road. You are about half way between the North Access and Overnight Area #3. If you want to use the toilet facilities you can turn right on the road and walk the short distance to the latrines at the boat ramp. There is no drinking water at this ramp.

The name "Tunnel Mill" is related to an interesting bit of history. If you look at a topographic map in the vicinity of the Tunnel Mill Ramp you can see that the river makes a long U curve to the east, and when the river bends back again, the

*Lunch in front of a bunkhouse at Overnight Area #4*

downstream area is very close to the upper area at the beginning of the U. Two local men realized that the water level of the river at the upper part of the U was better than 20 feet higher than the lower water level and by connecting the two by tunnel the drop would create a fast water flow capable of being used effectively for a water powered mill. By simple dead reckoning, the two brothers began to dig a five foot wide tunnel, one started digging at the upper end the other began at the lower. When the met, they were only two feet off from having their respective sections of tunnel directly lining up. A successful mill was operated nearby the ramp for many years.

This section is often close to Todd Fork - Twin Bridges Road, but the eventual crossing of the road does not occur until the road is closed for public use and the next crossing of a maintained public road does not occur for almost 6 miles.

After crossing a wash, the trail turns right and skirts around the west end of a field. Once at the end, the trail enters the woods only briefly before following the other side of the field and moves toward the public road. But before reaching it, the trail turns right and goes through a small overgrown section and you soon are between two fields following a fence on your left that parallels the road. After passing through another clump of small trees and underbrush where you will cross a small wash you climb slightly to another field where the trail turns right following its edge. Soon you will be able to see the Concord M.E. Church on Twin Bridge Road that was founded in 1839. The trail skirts along the rear of the church cemetery. You do not go far past the cemetery before you can see an old farm pond on the right as the trail turns left on a rut dirt road. In about 50 feet, this rut road T's into a more prominent gravel road and you can look left and see the locked white gate across it. You turn right on this road but follow it only a little over 100 feet where the trail takes an abrupt left turn and goes rather steeply uphill for about 20 feet. The trail soon leads you to the largest field encountered since crossing the river. This field is growing back to its natural habitat.

The trail follows along the edge of the field and slowly curves around the forest perimeter. After partially completing a shallow U turn, it looks as if the trail again starts to the right to follow yet another U around the edge of the woods for another extension of the field, but the trail does not turn right. Instead, it proceeds across the field toward a large tree which stands isolated in the field. Once you arrive at the tree, continue in the same direction, and in a few feet you will hit a paved closed section of Todds Run, Twin Bridges Road. When you reach the road a green arrow painted on the pavement indicates a left turn. In less than 40 feet another green arrow indicates a right turn off the road.

After crossing the closed section of Twin Bridge Road, the trail passes through patches of scrubby forest before coming into and following the edge of a field. Just after passing a fence on the right side, the trail hits an old dirt road and turns right on it. The road soon swings left and crosses the open field. As the trail heads straight toward a large isolated tree, it turns left about 50 feet short of the tree and skirts the field briefly before turning into the woods. After reaching a small wash in the woods, the trail turns right and follows it downstream briefly before crossing it and climbs slightly moving directly away from the stream bed. After crossing another very small wash, there is a moderate climb of about 50 yards. At the top of the climb, the trail comes out of the forest into a field where you can see a house and garage to your left on the other side of the field and soon passes through a corridor of trees before entering another field. The trail then passes a small pond on the left then drops down into the trees first crossing the wash that drains the pond following it briefly downstream where it passes an old dump on the left. You can see a deep ravine off to the right formed by Barnes Run, and the lake is sometimes visible there. Coming into the fields there is private pasture land to the left where barns are visible before hitting Clover Road. This paved road is still open to the public at this point, and just before reaching the road you will see a sign to the right facing the road which says: AREA CLOSED FROM 10 P.M. TO 6 A.M. OPEN ONLY TO HUNTING AND FISHING BETWEEN THESE HOURS. AREA PATROLLED.

Upon reaching the road the trail turns left and goes about 10 feet before turning right into another field. Again you find private cultivated fields on the left which the trail skirts. After passing through a row of trees the trail follows a cultivated field almost to its end where it angles right, and returns briefly through a patch of woods. It then enters and crosses another field before turning left following along the edge of the trees. The trail then cuts right into a heavy forest dropping about 50 feet down into a ravine with a moderately steep grade where it crosses a wash and climbs out again. After crossing some smaller washes, it again drops into another hollow, crosses the wash at its bottom, turns left and climbs to the ridgetop at a moderately steep grade. It follows the ridgetop in the downstream direction crossing an old road whose ruts are now filled with grass and which is often mowed. The trail drops into two hollows in much the same fashion. It goes down to the hollow's stream and turns left, following the washes in the upstream direction and as the trail hits the trees, crosses the washes and climbs diagonally up away from the hollow. As you climb out of the second one, you will hit a mowed path about four feet wide between the trees. Turn left on this mowed path but keep an eye open for an abrupt turn to the right where the trail turns off the mowed section into a narrow path. It's easy to miss, and I did miss it the first time and ended up in somebody's backyard. There is an easy way to tell if you do go by it without going that far afield, for just a few feet beyond the turn off this mowed path there is another path which is also wide that goes off to the right with a sign facing you saying: PRIVATE PROPERTY. When you hit that mowed path you have gone about 10 feet beyond the Backcountry's Trail turnoff and by going back you should easily find it. After the turn, the trail drops down to another wash. You can see there is a very steep six foot drop down to the wash, but the trail avoids this by angling easily down to the wash turns right, returns along the wash to the steep section and easily climbs out of the little ravine into an open field where the power lines are quite visible in front of you. Just before reaching them the trail turns right and briefly parallels them before coming to a fork in the trail. Follow the left fork which takes you under the power-lines. When you are directly under the wires, there is another fork in the trail. This time take the right one which leads you easily down to the paved Concord Bethel Road which is open to the public right to the edge of the lake.

The trail immediately crosses the road but since Overnight Area #3 is quite close you might want to replenish your water supply. If so, turn right on the road and follow it 2/10 miles almost to the water's edge, keeping your eye to the right where a pipe sticking straight up out of the ground gushes water from a natural spring.

When you return to the trail, you follow it down to the lake where the trail turns left on an old road near the lake shore. Not long after the turn, you will see a sign on the left which says:

## OVERNIGHT AREA NO. 3

Facing you on the right side of the trail there is another sign that says: BACK-COUNTRY TRAIL. You can see there is a split in the road, the Backcountry Trail proceeds on the one straight ahead and the road to the left leads to the camping area. It's about a five minute walk back to the area and you will know when you are almost there for the dirt road briefly becomes a very narrow cement road just before reaching the campground. As you approach the Overnight Area you will first see the privies on the right. After you walk past them the bunkhouses come into view on the left. If you are looking for the tent site, look to the left of the bunkhouses where you will see a little cleared rise. That is the tent area. Although it has a sign, it is often hidden in high grass. As you approach the bunkhouses, you will come to an old farm pond in a very attractive setting with a picnic bench along its banks. On my first visit there I met a fisherman who told me the man who owned this land had built the pond by himself and didn't want to sell it to the government. After viewing this lovely setting, I can understand his reluctance to sell, for this is the most beautiful location of the four overnight areas.

**Backcountry Trail,** from Overnight Area #3 to Overnight Area #2.

DISTANCE: To Reisinger Road 2.2 miles, From Reisinger Road to Overnight Area #2 2.3 miles.
HIKE: To Reisinger Road - Strenuous
From Reisinger Road to Overnight Area #2 - moderate
WALKING TIME: To Reisinger Road 1 hour 20 minutes to 1 hour 45 minutes.
From Reisinger Road to Overnight Area #2 1 to 1½ hours

GENERAL REMARKS: This is another segment to avoid if the lake level is a few feet above normal pool for it backs up and covers much of the trail in the area around Cloverlick Creek and Sugartree Creek. Even if the lake level has returned to the normal pool both creeks are big enough to be very difficult or impossible to ford during or soon after any extended period of heavy rain. This segment goes around the two southwest arms of the lake created by the drainage of the two aformentioned creeks. The area proceeding the crossing of Cloverlick Creek can often look quite desolate for the trail crosses a flood plain of the lake where silt and debris are often left by the retreating waters. Once across Cloverlick Creek, the trail then traverses one of the loveliest wooded sections at East Fork. Much of the forest is mature, and if the walking up and down the various ravines is a bit testy, the surroundings make it all worthwhile. From Reisinger Road the trail is in more open but pleasant country.

Overnight Area #2 sits on a bluff high above the lake making it another pleasant setting for an overnight stay.

TRAIL DESCRIPTION:  From the junction of the Backcountry Trail and the side trail to Overnight Area #3 the Backcountry Trail follows the old road and soon crosses Trimble Run where you can see the stone abutment on the left for a bridge that once crossed the stream. If the waters of the lake have covered this crossing in the recent past, you may have to retreat upstream before making your crossing, for the surrounding area is a sea of muck. If you make this crossing upstream when returning to the old road you'll encounter another wash running alongside it covered with heavy underbrush. Don't force your way through but turn left and in a few yards you will come to an old culvert that easily takes you to the road. This road gives out as it enters a grove of small trees and the trail curves to the right, swinging around the headwaters of this arm of the lake. The ground in this area is fairly level, and much of it is underwater when the lake basin is used to hold excessive runoff water. As the trail swings to the left, you can look down and see Cloverlick Creek, which is one of the largest that flows into the lake. The trail follows it in the upstream direction until it gradually swings to the right reaching and crossing the creek. This crossing is not difficult if the lake is in normal pool and the area has not recently been covered by high water. You cross to a little stony path on the opposite shore which is the bed of a very small wash. Follow the stony bottom which moves directly away from Cloverlick Creek for a few yards where the trail returns to the woods and swings left on the suggestion of an old road.

If the lake pool has beeen up and covered this area in the recent past this crossing can be very hard to follow, for flooding often covers the visual landmarks. If this is the case you may find it easier to go upstream a few feet to where a usually dry wash V's into the larger creek. Cross at that point and once on the opposite bank walk in the downstream direction diagonally away from the creek. In about 30 feet you will hit another distinct but usually dry wash with a very stony bottom. Turn left on the wash and in a few feet you will see that a trail crosses this wash. There you turn left and you're back on the trail in a deep woods.

As you walk in the upstream direction of Cloverlick Creek it is not long before the trail forks. Take the right fork which angles uphill with a moderate climb up to the ridge top. You will notice a deep ravine below you on the right. The trail follows above that ravine in the upstream direction easily climbing the inclining ridge. Eventually the trail turns right, drops down to the wash, crosses it, and turns right following alongside the stream bed about 30 feet before it steeply climbs out of the ravine. Still moving in the downstream direction, the trail gradually swings left away from the ravine, and soon you will see another ravine developing on the left in an area of quite large trees.

After following the ridge above this ravine, the trail then turns left and drops steeply down to the bottom of the ravine and crosses the branch just below the point where two smaller streams join together on the left. After this crossing you have the first fairly long steep climb up to the ridgetop in many a mile followed by a mostly level walk in perhaps the most beautiful mature forest at East Fork. The trail drops about 30 feet, crossing another wash, and as it climbs back out begins to follow an old fence on the left. As the trail crosses another wash, it goes through that fence line and climbs to the ridge top. It soon drops into a small flat hollow with a pleasant semi-open area where some old fire rings can be seen. The trail T's into another trail which runs lengthwise in the hollow and turns left on it. You will soon come to a point where two small hollows join together in front of you from the larger hollow you are in. There the trail turns right and goes up a moderate grade out of the hollow with one steep stretch of about 20 feet before arriving at an unused section of the paved Concord Bethel Road. You crossed another part of this road on the other side of the lake just before Overnight Area #3. Turn right on the road for about 1/10 mile.

Just after the lake comes into view, there is a green arrow on the pavement indicating a turn to the left leaving the road. This is followed by a moderately steep climb to the ridgetop. Once up, the trail turns right following a finger of the ridge towards the lake until it drops off the left side, crosses a wash, turns right and follows alongside it until the lake comes into view. There the trail swings left and stays near the top of the ridge, paralleling the lake below. Gradually the trail swings right and drops close to the lake shore near the flood level of the lake where you may see much flotsam deposited near this shore line. After crossing a small wash the trail then follows close to the lake shore in an area that is often quite unattractive because of the debris that floats in during high water. Soon after the trail passes under the powerlines it turns left and follows them, leaving the lake shore area, and climbs up to the corner of one of the steel towers. There the trail turns right and covers the short distance to Reisinger Road. But before turning, look left at the tower for a nice view of the upper lake. Reisinger Road is a paved maintained road leading to a boat ramp and parking. There are toilet facilities there but no drinking water.

An arrow painted into the road surface indicates a left turn on the road. The trail goes a few yards in that direction until another painted green arrow indicates a right turn off the road. You have about 2.3 miles to go to reach Overnight Area #2.

You have an easy climb paralleling the powerlines until you hit an old, very narrow, closed paved lane which you follow to the right. As you follow it downhill almost to the lake, you can see it curve left into the lake. When this comes into view the trail turns left and has a moderately steep climb in open country back up to the ridgetop and goes under the power lines with one of the towers just to the right. After you have gone about 100 feet beyond the power line, the trail reaches an open field where a barn can be seen off to the left. From that point there are mowed areas angling to the left and right. There is a cultivated field between the two mowed areas and a group of small signs stand along the border on both sides of the field indicating the boundary line between public and private land. The trail follows the mowed path to the right almost to the forest line where a wooden post indicates a right turn away from the field following another mowed corridor.

As the trail easily curves right then left before entering the forest it joins an old rut road that follows a pretty stream to the right in the upstream direction. The trail and road go diagionally across the stream but about 20 feet beyond the crossing the trail turns right leaving the road and then does a horseshoe curve to the right and soon comes out of the trees into the edge of another large cultivated trail. Following along the right side of the field, the trail proceeds to the corner of the field where it turns left and continues to follow the edge of the field. On past walks I found parts of this segment of trail very indistinct. Keep following the edge of the cultivated field until you get to its end where you turn left again and skirt it on its third side. After the trail passes through a small break of trees it then turns diagonally to the right, reenters the trees, crosses a small wash, swings left again and is once more running alongside the plowed field. But this time it follows the field only briefly before it cuts diagonally to the right crossing a wild field with a path cut through a bramble patch. After passing through another wall of trees, it enters a scrubby field with many small trees and finally returns to the forest where it soon approaches a large creek. The stream is Sugartree Creek and the trail turns right and follows near but not close to the creek in the downstream direction. Soon you will pass an interesting ruin to the right of the trail, which looks like the remains of a small brick house. About a third of one brick wall remains in place, and upon close examination you will find that the original wall is three bricks thick. This indicates that the structure possibly served as what is known as an 'upground cellar' for preserving various types of fruits and vegetables. due to its close proximity to Sugartree Creek, it might have been an ice house with the triple brick walls giving grater insulation in the prerefrigerator days. A large patch of ivy growing on and around it enhances its charm. Just beyond it on the left side of the trail you can also see an old well.

The trail then heads diagonally left towards the creek at a point that is almost at the head of the lake and crosses it. If high water has recently covered this low lying area, it manages to obiliterate the trail. If the trail is hidden under a new layer of silt, cross Sugartree Creek diagonally going just a bit downstream. Once on the opposite shore, continue walking diagonally across the rocky bank until you hit a primitive deserted dirt road which also heads towards the lake. Follow it only about 20 feet where, if you look left, you will see the trail rises up an embankment which is high enough to miss all but the highest of floods and the trail once again is fairly distinct. The trail momentarily links up with the old road on higher ground but soon angles left away from it and the lake and comes into a large open area which it skirts on the right.

Almost immediately after returning to the woods, you will see a sign on the right side of the trail which faces the opposite direction. As you pass it, you will see it reads: BACKCOUNTRY TRAIL and just to the left you can see Overnight Area #2 nicely situated on a bluff above the lake. As you move toward the Overnight Area, you will see a narrow trail off to the right with a sign alongside it facing you which says: HORSES PROHIBITED ON THIS TRAIL. Underneath the words ON and TRAIL are two triangles, the left one painted orange and the right one white. This is the beginning of the side trail that links up the Backpack loop with the Overnight Area. About 10 feet beyond this sign further down this side trail is a sign facing you which says: BACKPACK TRAIL. Another reminder that this trail is not to be used as a bridle path. If you are returning to the South Access parking lot you can walk (but not ride a horse) back to that point via the Backpack Trail. It is longer but scenically far superiour to the remaining portions of the Backcountry loop. The total distance from the junction back to the South Access is 10 miles on the Backpack loop versus 5½ miles on the Backcountry Trail. You can also use another variation with approximately the same distance as the Backcountry from this point. Walk the Backpack Loop to the side trail that takes you to Overnight Area #1 then follow the Backcountry Trail from the Overnight Area to the South Access. For this trail description see page 257.

As you approach the Overnight Area a large sign says: OVERNIGHT AREA NO. 2

**BACKCOUNTRY TRAIL** from Overnight Area #2 to the South Access Parking Lot.

DISTANCE: 5½ miles
HIKE: easy to moderate
WALKING TIME: 2 hours 15 minutes to 2 hours 45 minutes.

GENERAL REMARKS: The first part of this segment is pleasant with a nice mixture of forest and wild field walking. But once you make the crossing at Campbell Road, the walk is monotonous if not downright boring for most of it is close to public highways in not particularly attractive open country, often in sight of houses. If you have the time a far pleasanter walk is to return at least partway by following the south loop of the Backcountry Trail as previously suggested.

TRAIL DESCRIPTION: To continue on this trail from the Overnight Area follow the F.W.D. road that lies between the camp and the bluff overlooking the lake downhill. When you reach the bottom, you will see that another dirt road goes off to the right down to the lake. Don't turn here but proceed straight ahead on the road you followed downhill only about 30 feet beyond this junction where the trail turns right off the road. The trail follows within sight of the road for awhile before turning right going up through a little break in the hillside and easily climbs an inclining ridge. The trail

*Dam at East Fork releasing water at a rate of 3900 C.F.S. (cubic feet per second)*

wanders through the woods, crossing a couple of small washes, but then you may notice that it begins skirting an open field on the left where it soon reaches a fork in the trail. The right fork is correct, but the left fork quickly leads to the field and a small pond. It is not long before the right fork also turns into the field, a quasi open area with the power line in front of you. Soon the trail angles under the power lines and briefly returns to the forest. When the trail enters another wild field, it immediately turns right and cuts across one end of it and again returns briefly to the woods. It soon enters and crosses another large field where the trail is easy to follow. Once back into the woods the trail descends easily down to and crosses a flat stoned bottom of a usually dry wash before it easily climbs out. The trail then swings right until it is following a fence on the left where it skirts along another field. The trail then turns left and crosses the field. In that field the trail crosses a narrow once paved road, swings left and passes into and through a lovely stand of four rows of man-planted pines. Just after the pine grove, the trail drops easily down to but does not cross a wash where it turns left and follows the wash a brief distance to a closed section of the paved Williamsburg Bantam Road. A green arrow painted on the road indicates a right turn. You follow the road less than 200 feet where another painted green arrow indicates a left turn back into the woods.

After crossing a small wash and easily climbing up to and passing an old shed on the right, the trail descends easily into another wild field. While crossing the field the trail passes through an old fence, then turns left, and follows the fence which is on the left. Eventually the fence line moves several feet to the right possibly at the location of an old gate. You continue to follow this fence line, but now it is on your right. This is a particularly lovely field walk, and I have found on pleasant days that walking these fields that are now growing wild to be well worth the time and is fondly remembered. You follow the fence line until it makes a 90° turn right. The trail then begins a slight curve to the left heading towards the woods. As it approaches a large solitary tree the lake comes into view for the first time since leaving the last Overnight Area. The trail then returns to a wooded area and follows alongside a wash on the left until it joins a larger wash not far from the lakeshore. If you look straight ahead, you can see a small wooden bridge that crosses the larger wash downstream. If you examine it, you will soon be aware that it is not for horses and is part of the Backpack Trail. This is the only point where the main Backpack Trail and the Backcountry Trail (not side trails) are in sight of one another until the trail's end at the South Access. Again you have an alternative route. By crossing the bridge and following the orange blazes, hikers can follow the Backpack Trail to the side trail to Overnight Area #1 and eliminate a long and not very interesting field walk on the Backcountry Trail.

If you are continuing on the Backcountry Trail, it turns left and crosses the wash it had been following just before that wash joins the larger stream. It follows this other wash only briefly before turning right and crossing it. Then you have a moderate climb through a largely open area that is pleasantly dotted here and there with small bushy evergreens. Then, after passing through another fence line, the trail hits and turns left on a closed section of Campbell-Bantam Road and follows it for about 1/10 mile. A green arrow in the pavement indicates a right turn off the road. The trail moves away from the road only about 30 feet before turning left and parallels the road until it T's into a large path. It then turns right again, moving away from Campbell Bantam Road. But it only stays on this path about 50 feet before turning left into a scrubby field.

When the trail hits an old fence line with only the posts left, it turns right following alongside the posts. Soon the trail comes close to an open section of Williamsburg-Bantam Road and parallels it. Although the traffic is usually light along this road and the houses along it are few this is possibly the most boring stretch on the entire loop. The trail soon hits an old deteriorating paved side road, turns left on it for about 15 feet then leaves it on the right. The trail passes through a tree line and then approaches a few old trees that are alongside a dirt rut road. The trail turns right on the road and remains on it a short distance to its end then angles left still heading away from the Williamsburg-Bantam Road. The trail turns right, briefly returning to the forest. Returning again to an open field, the trail turns right and begins to follow along the bottom of a man-made dirt fill embankment on the left with the edge of the forest on the right. When the embankment declines, you will be able to see the Park's red brick service building to the left. The trail takes you to the corner of this open area, then turns left towards the service building following the tree line on the right. You will soon see a sign on the left side of the trail that faces the opposite direction. When you pass it, you can see that it says: BACKCOUNTRY TRAIL. Just beyond it facing you on the right sitting in between a fork in the trail there is another sign which says: OVERNIGHT AREA NO. 1. If you want to use the Overnight Area, take the right fork back into the woods following the white blaze markers. It's about a five minute walk back to the camp. If you choose to follow the Backpack Trail instead of the Backcountry loop to the South Access, walk past the privies where you will see a HORSES PROHIBITED sign that faces you alongside the trail. Follow the white blazes to the Backpack Trail. It's a prettier way to return to the South Access, but it is also 4 miles longer.

The last segment of the Backcountry Trail is very brief and is almost exclusively in open country back to the South Access. After crossing a small wash, the trail turns right skirting along the edge of the trees and soon passes a small pond to the left of the trail. The trail does a U turn left around the end of the pond before coming up to the paved Elk Lick Road that leads to picnic areas, bathing beach and boat launch. You take the little gravel road on this other side of Elk Lick Road which passes between two small ponds arriving at the registration booth and parking lot at the South Access. For those continuing on to the North Access see page 235.

# BACKPACK TRAIL

As my personal interest and participation in backpacking increased, I had often wished that a trail of moderate length existed close to my home where it would be easy to take off at a moments notice and quickly dissolve out of the urban scene with my house shrinking from several rooms to the pack on my back, where I was dependant on only the trees for company. One of the pleasant surprises I found when I began my first exploration of the East Fork area was that just such a trail had recently come into existence. Jerry Boone, who is the present manager of East Fork State Park and a backpacker himself, told me that he felt that a special trail for those desiring an overnight hike separated from the horse trails was needed. So in 1982, this trail became a reality.

Here is a trail whose length and difficulty make it perfect as a first trip for novice backpackers. It is just long enough and has adequate hill climbing to let the beginners carrying a reasonable overnight load feel their way into this activity without catastrophic physical demands being made on one hand, but demanding enough to give the hiker the sense and experience of trail walking with enough bite to raise it above the level of a pancake flat stroll. What a nice trail to see if you and your new equipment are getting along with each other. If you find your boots are providing blisters, your tent leaks, your stove doesn't work, or your load is far too heavy, you can easily abandon the trip by using handy road crossings or suffer through the short trip making adequate adjustments later.

I have friends who are eager for their first crack at backpacking. This trail is where I will take them for their introduction. Better a short overnighter practically in the backyard of Cincinnatians than a disaster at 9000 ft. a couple thousand miles away from home. It is also a handy trail to know about for the experienced backpacker as well as for the person who has had a long inactive spell and wants to limber up a bit but time available excludes a longer trek. Voila! Here it is. For you who live in the Cincinnati area and suddenly get an uncontrollable urge to go packing at 3 O'clock on a Friday afternoon, if you can throw your gear together in half an hour you can be at the trailhead by 4:30 and setting up camp in Overnight Area #1 before 6 P.M.

This trail can be used as a nice single overnight two day trip or an easy two night short mileage trip. Mr. Boone and his staff cleverly laid out this 12 mile trail near the lake's south shore, offering many lake views. Except for the skirting of one picnic area and three early road crossings, the trail is beautifully isolated from the madding crowd. Overnight Area #1 and #2, already in existence for the Backcountry Trail, are utilized for the camping areas. They are linked to the Backpack Trail by side trails. The restricted space makes a complete loop hike impractical so it was designed with a loop at the far end of the trail near Overnight Area #2, leaving much of the outgoing leg to be repeated on the return. But with this trail laid out in such pleasant wooded areas, the return segment is anything but unpleasant. You can do a complete loop walk if you want to by following the Backcountry Trail on your return to the South Access from Overnight Area #2. This is not recommended because most of that stretch is dull and close to roads. If you are pressed for time on your return you could follow the return Backpack loop to the side trail junction that takes you to Overnight Area #1. From there, you can follow the Backcountry Trail which quickly returns you to the South Access.

Although the orange blaze marks are frequent and you often are assisted across washes by little wooden bridges, there is one section of the trail that, at this writing, is difficult to follow simply because it isn't walked enough. With the appearance of this book more hikers will know of its existence so the one short indistinct segment should soon be easy to trace.

**Backpack Trail** from the South Access parking lot to Overnight Area #2.

**DISTANCE:** To Point B (Junction with side Trail to Overnight Area #1) 3.9 miles, to Overnight Area #1 4.1 miles, To Point E (Crossing of a closed segment of Campbell Bantam Road) 5.6 miles, To Point F (Far End of Backpack loop) 9.8 miles, To Point G (Overnight Area #2) 10 miles.

**HIKE:** To Point B moderate, From Point B to Point E, easy. From Point E to Point G, moderate.

**WALKING TIME:** To Overnight Area #1 - 2 to 2½ hours. To Overnight Area #2 - 5 to 6 hours.

**GENERAL REMARKS:** Although this trail begins near a fairly congested park area you will find that it conceals itself nicely from the beach and the boat ramps and, except for the noise of the motor boats, it leaves you mostly isolated from civilization. The trail is also quite easy to follow up to the crossing of a closed section of Campbell Road at Point E and most of it is in the woods to that crossing. Remember there is no water at either Overnight Area #1 or 2 so you will have to carry your water supply for the entire trip. The orange blaze marks are far more frequent on this trail than the green ones are on the Backcountry Trail.

**TRAIL DESCRIPTION:** To find the trailhead see page 230. With the South Access parking lot at your back, walk past the registration booth and you will see a sign facing you which says:

**EAST FORK**
**BACKPACK TRAIL**
↑

Only a few feet beyond this sign there is another which says: HORSES PROHIBITED ON THIS TRAIL. Then you will soon pass another sign on the right side of the trail which says: OVERNIGHT AREA #1   4M. OVERNIGHT AREA #2  9.5 M. This beginning section is not too definite at this point but once in the woods the trail is easy to follow until you are well past the side trail to Overnight Area #1.

The trail comes to a wash, turns left and follows it downstream, then log steps take you down its steep sides with stepping stones to use across the small stream. After the crossing the trail turns right, climbs moderately steep up to the ridge top, turns left and heads toward the lake. You soon cross a couple of small washes both having small wooden bridges and you will see a larger stream far below you on the left. As that stream enters the lake the trail U turns around the edge of the ridge where there is a wooden bench for contemplative viewing. You will then cross a series of small washes, some with bridges and log steps to aid you going down and up until you hit a fork in the trail. At that junction you can see by going straight ahead the trail would take you into an open area, but you take the left turn skirting along the perimeter of the woods. The trail then comes out of the woods where it is high enough to give you a beautiful view of the lake. From here the trail goes directly across a paved road leading to a picnic area, then has a steep descent which is not difficult because the trail has a series of log steps to aid you. It looks like the wide trail then takes you right down to the water's edge, but the Backpack Trail only follows this path about 60 feet beyond the log steps, then turns right reentering the woods. This turn is hard to see during the growing season, but once you know where to look, it should give you no trouble. After crossing a small bridged wash, the trail climbs into another open field using another wooden bridge to cross a drainage area. The trail turns right skirting the woods on the left on the field drainage area on the right. When the trail returns to the woods it has a long gradual descent down a deep ravine. Just before reaching the stream at the bottom of the ravine, the trail turns right, crosses a branch of that stream and follows the larger water course upstream before crossing it without the aid of a bridge. Following along a smaller tributary of that stream in the upstream direction, the trail then turns left, crossing the wash and continues uphill. As you approach the ridge top there is another fork in the trail. Take the right fork, which soon leads you out to an open field with brambles to the left and the fringe of the forest on the right. In the growing season the path here can be hard to see. Follow the perimeter of the forest to your right, for in about 100 feet the trail turns right and returns to the forest. Immediately after coming out of the forest the trail crosses the paved road to the beach area. As you cross the road, you can see a picnic area to the right where water is available during the warmer seasons alongside the parking lot. There are also toilets nearby. The trail skirts right going around the picnic area and is very close to it. There are many trails made by picnickers that go in many directions. The Backpack Trail does not go downhill but stays pretty much on the same level and, once around the corner of the picnic area, continues in the same direction until it T's into a U turn of another trail. Follow the curve to the left. After you go down some log steps another prominent trail goes to the left downhill, but the Backpack Trail stays to the right and then T's into another trail where you can see a wooden bridge crossing a wash to the left. Turn left and cross the bridge. Once across don't follow the trail straight ahead downhill but turn right.

On my first walk here a group of teenage boys were coming uphill and met me at the junction. Just previous to our meeting, I was talking into my small tape recorder taking the original notes for this book. They had seen me do this and eyed me suspiciously. When they were abreast of me one of them frowned and asked me "Are you with the F.B.I. or something?"

After making this right turn the trail crosses a small wash which is followed by a moderately steep descent down to another wooden bridge which has the unusual feature of a handrail. After an easy climb, the trail follows the rim of the ridge with the lake quite a bit below you on the left. The trail then turns away from the lake and crosses a bridge over another small wash where you climb up rather steeply out of the wash for about 12 feet. You will soon come to a sign to the right of the trail which says: OVERNIGHT AREA #1  .2 M. This is point B where you can see a trail to the right blazed white which leads to the Overnight Area. If you are planning to spend the night there it will take you less than ten minutes to reach the Overnight Area. This side trail immediately crosses the paved Tate Boat Ramp Road where you will see a sign that says: HORSES PROHIBITED ON THIS TRAIL. The trail skirts an open field following a tree line on the right. When the trail gets to the end of the field it curves to the left and passes through another tree line entering another field briefly before going into the woods where the camp is located.

When proceeding from the side trail junction on the Backpack Trail at Point B, you will see another sign on the right side of the trail facing you which says: OVERNIGHT AREA #2  4 M. This is to warn hikers who are starting their hike late in the day that there is at least a couple of hours of hiking to go before reaching this second camping area. Consequently, if the hours of darkness are soon approaching you might opt to stay at the first camp. Shortly the trail crosses the paved Tate Boat Ramp road, which is the last road open to public traffic that this trail crosses. Then the trail crosses a no longer used very narrow paved road. Not long after this crossing, the trail follows a wash that is to the right of the trail. You do not follow this wash any great distance before the trail turns right and crosses it. About 60 feet beyond this crossing, the Backpack Trail takes an abrupt right off of the more prominent trail. If you miss this turn, you will soon find the trail ends at a small stream. Retreat and look for the turn. Shortly after this turn the trail passes an old dump on the left and T's into another trail, turns left on it and soon enters a partially open area. The trail is sometimes indistinct here, but it swings left returning to the woods, has two switchbacks down a ravine and then across a small wooden bridge over the wash. Shortly you will pass a rustic wooden bench to the right of the trail where it is pleasant to rest a spell and, perhaps, consume a handful of gorp and wet your whistle. You then drop down and cross a wash where there are log steps on both sides to help you negotiate the steep banks. Following this you will cross three more small wooden bridges across washes before coming into a quasi-open area where you cross the dike of an old farm pond on the right. The trail soon crosses an unused narrow paved road which is closed in by heavy growth making it impossible to use for vehicles. Turning left, the trail parallels the road briefly before turning right coming out of the woods and down some log steps into an open area, immediately crossing a closed section of the paved Campbell-Bantam Road which is point E on the map. You have a little less than 4 miles to cover from here to Overnight Area #2.

Just after crossing Campbell Road, the trail is in a large field and soon has a fork. On my first hike I assumed that this might be where the outward and return parts of the loop join together, but this is not the case. A look at the map will show you that this division does not occur until you have crossed a closed section of Williamsburg-Bantam Road, which is still about 2 miles away. Follow the trail's left fork which soon takes you into the woods and in sight of the lake. You will soon approach a footbridge which is higher and longer than most of the ones you have crossed. Turn left at this point and see where the stream enters the lake. Once across the bridge there is the suggestion of an old road running alongside the creek and the temptation is to turn right after the crossing which actually brings you to the Backcountry loop. Aside from Point A, this is the only place that the Backpack and Backcountry trails are in sight of one another. After you are across the bridge, turn left towards the lake. When you are almost to the lake shore, look right and you can see the trail going up a small hill in open country. Follow it and after an easy climb you have a good view of the lake while the trail easily crosses a large field. The trail returns to the forest only briefly before crossing a smaller open field where you can see a peninsula to the left jutting out into the lake. The trail then passes through another narrow wooded area and crosses a small wash. When the trail returns to a large field, the path turns right and follows along the perimeter of the forest briefly before cutting left diagonally alongside a briar patch then turns more to the left and goes directly across the field and returns to the woods. After crossing a small wash with its little wooden bridge the trail makes a sharp left turn and follows close to but high above the lake and soon parallels a barbed wire fence to the right of the trail. When the fence stops the trail turns right, goes over a wash, and climbs into another large field. If the growing season has made the trail somewhat indistinct, follow close to the forest edge on the left and cross the field. Just after you pass through an old fence line you can look down and see a closed paved road which is on the Old Williamsburg-Bantam Road.

It is not long after you cross this road before you come to the loop portion of this trail. The outward bound section of the loop (i.e. the one closest to the lake) is not hiked hiked often enough at this writing and it can be devilishly difficult to follow. Keep an eye out for the orange blazes. I hope this book will encourage more people to hike this segment, for it wouldn't need a great deal more usage to make it more distinct.

The trail goes directly across the road, climbs slightly and passes by another old fence line. Once past it, keep looking left, for you will see where it drops rather steeply down to the left and crosses another wooden bridge. Once over the bridge you climb slightly in a partially open area in the general direction of the lake. When the trail retuns to the trees you are quite close to the beginning of the loop section of this trail. Shortly you will see that one segment of the trail goes straight ahead while another makes a right turn. The outward bound section of this loop (i.e. the one closest to the lake) is not hiked often enough to make it easy to follow so keep your eye out for the orange blazes. On my first walk here, which occurred during the month of June, plant growth made it extremely hard to follow in the field and woods. The return loop does not suffer from this trail vagueness and is far more distinct, so if you have too much trouble following the outward bound segment you can always return to this junction and follow the eastern part of the loop in both directions.

From this junction proceed straight ahead for the loop closest to the lake shore, and you will return here coming from the trail on the right when you complete the loop. The distance from this point to Point E at Overnight Area #2 is about 2½ miles. You briefly follow an old fence line before the trail turns right and again heads away from the lake going into and directly across a field. As it returns to the woods, the trail becomes less distinct since much of the forest floor is covered with an ivy-like plant. The trail turns right and briefly continues in that direction before turning left and passing between two trees that are quite close toegether. After passing two small washes, the first with a stone aided crossing, the second with a small wooden bridge, the trail seems to disappear. Look for blaze marks which indicate the trail goes almost straight up the hill at a moderately steep grade. Then the trail swings right, and with a ravine on your left, the trail again goes into an open field. The trail crosses this field bearing slightly to the left and goes over an old narrow paved lane of which little is left before reentering the forest. Once back in the trees, the trail goes downhill at a moderate grade and follows the bottom of a usually dry wash before it T's into a very distinct gravel trail. You turn left on this trail but you only stay on it for about 20 feet where the Backpack Trail turns right and starts angling down in the upstream direction of a deep and large ravine until it reaches a large creek. Once you hit the creek, the trail turns right and goes upstream about 100 feet where the departure point from the stream bed is hidden by a tree until you walk past its trunk. From there you have an easy angling climb in the downstream direction. Once on top, the trail follows the ravine you just crossed far above it in the downstream direction.

As the trail enters a grove of man-planted pines, it disappears among the fallen pine needles. Walk about half way through the grove, then turn right going uphill directly away from the lake. This leads to an open area which is almost on top of the hill. The trail turns left leading you to the edge of a mostly treeless deep ravine that shows steep bare banks that are eroding rapidly. Turn right following the edge of this somewhat barren ravine until you reach its head where you turn left and pass it. Almost immediately you reach a second ravine with bare slopes but this time you are at its head and you pass it on your left. Soon you come to a wide open swath kept clear for the power lines. I will always remember my first walk across this area although it was such a nightmare I'd just as soon forget it. The trail totally disappeared in the tall grass that obliterated any trace of its direction. It was quite hot, and as I forced my way through these grasses the pollen from them covered me with what looked like a fine dust and partially clogged my nasal passages. Fortunately I do not have serious allergies or I would have had to retreat back to the forest. Once you know the way it is not a hard crossing, but only having a general idea of where the trail went, I treked back and forth through this grass for well over a half hour and was about to give up when I accidently stumbled on the correct solution of this open crossing.

When you come out of the woods, turn right going easily downhill until you reach and cross one of the small wooden bridges that are frequently found on this trail. The bridge takes you over a very tiny wash. From there look partially left uphill away from the lake at the power line tower which is closet to you. Walk diagonally uphill to the tower passing it on the left side where you will see an orange blaze mark painted on one of its steel legs. At this point you are fairly close to the woods that border the other side of the power line open area. When you are close to the forest's edge turn right and follow it. Keep looking left until you see a tree with a large arrow carved pointing upwards on the trunk of a tree. The size of the arrow suggests that it was possibly made by a confused, frustrated and concerned hiker who had preceded me and apparently encountered as much difficulty as I had in locating the trail on the other side of this power line area so he/she carved this arrow large enough that few would miss the turn into the woods. It is also nice to know that the camping area is not far away. If you look at the map, remember that the power lines are quite a bit south of where the present U.S.G.S. topo sheet shows them.

Once back in the woods, the trail briefly follows the edge of the ridge but soon turns to the right away from the lake and begins the only long steep descent on this entire trail. As you drop down you can look and see a ravine on both sides of you. It looks as if they are two separate ravines that will join when actually it is the same ravine with its course curving in front of you. Once down to the creek level, you can see the curve and the bridge to take you across the creek. This bridge occasionally gets wiped out by high waters, so if it is not there cross the creek and look left and you will see a sign which reads on the reverse side: RETURN LOOP. Once you have crossed the creek, the trail to the right is the beginning of the return loop and if you are day hiking and do not wish to go to the Overnight Area, follow the orange blazes. If you are going to Overnight Area #2 turn left past the sign and follow the white blazes for you are now following the side trail to the Overnight Area. The trail quickly takes you to another wash also with a bridge which occasionally is uprooted by high waters. Once across this wash, you are on an old dirt road that soon ends at the lake. Turn right on the old road following the white blaze marks. There are two ways to go from here. If you want to take the official trail, you follow the road only about 100 feet before you turn left and begin a moderately steep climb uphill. You will soon pass a sign facing the other direction which says: BACK PACK TRAIL. Almost immediately beyond it you will come in sight of the camping area. A slightly easier way is to stay on the road and follow it a short distance until it hits another. Turn left here on the other road and climb the hill until you see the campground on the right.

**BACKPACK TRAIL.** From Overnight Area #2 to the end of the return of the eastern loop

DISTANCE: 2.3 Miles
HIKE: Moderate
WALKING TIME: 1 hour to 1½ hours

GENERAL REMARKS: This pleasant segment, functioning as a return on the Backpack Trail from the camping area, is far easier to follow than the western part of this loop. If also offers the people hiking the Backcountry Trail the option of finishing their hike by following a trail designed only for hikers which offers pleasanter scenery from this point than the Backcountry Trail. It does make the hike longer, but if you want to shorten it until it is close to the same length as the Backcountry Trail, you can use the side trail to Overnight Area #1 and use the Backcountry Trail to the South Access.

TRAIL DESCRIPTION: For you who did not use the outbound section of this trail you can follow the side trail with white blazes to the loop. Across the closed dirt road that runs alongside the camp you will see a sign that says:

**HORSES PROHIBITED
ON THIS TRAIL**

About 10 feet beyond this sign there is another sign facing you which says: BACK PACK TRAIL. The trail takes you downhill somewhat steeply to a dirt road. Turn right on the dirt road and follow it about 100 feet where it turns left going over a wooden footbridge. If the bridge is missing or down, turn left and cross the wash and follow the trail. In a short distance you will see a sign facing you which says: RETURN LOOP. Take the trail to the left with the orange blaze marks that does not cross the creek and follow it upstream for about 50 feet before turning left. There you will see the trail begins the only moderately steep climb on this return loop going diagonally up the ridge. Once up the ridge you will cross two small washes each with small wooden bridges that empty into a ravine on the right. You cross that ravine on another wooden bridge and soon enter the cleared area for the power line. On my first walk, I was dreading this crossing because of the terrible time I had finding the trail on the outbound section. But I happily found that this one was quite easy going directly across the open power line area.

Back in the forest the trail crosses a fence line and soon hits a field. The trail crosses the field going just slightly right. Look for a small beech tree which is growing in the field just about 15 feet from the forest perimeter on the opposite side. Turn right at this tree which has orange blaze marks painted on it and follow the line of the forest about 50 feet before returning into the trees. After you walk into the woods for about 30 feet, the trail turns right and skirts the field and gradually angles to the left. The trail then descends moderately steeply for a short distance down to a wash where it turns right and follows the wash downstream until it joins a larger branch. You cross over this usually dry stream, and climb easily up the ridge going through an old fence line on the way, and pass into another field. The trail crosses the field again bearing just slightly right and crosses an unused paved narrow road before returning to the woods. This forest is in a glen where the trees are not close together and thus has a more open feeling as more light hits the forest floor. After crossing a small wash in this delightful glen, the trail turns left and passes the only unsightly part of these surroundings for to the left of the trail there is an old dumping ground for worn out auto and tractor tires.

It is not long before this trail T's into another and if you came out on the Backpack loop you will recognize this as the point where the loop begins. Turn left here, and in about a five minute walk you will cross a closed section of the paved Williamsburg-Bantam Road. From here follow the orange blaze marks back the way you came. Or if you want to shorten the return leg take the Overnight Area #1 side trail to the Backcountry Trail junction and follow it back to the South Access trailhead. For those who previously followed the Backcountry Trail to the last Overnight Area, but switched over to the Backpack Trail continue to follow the orange blazes back to the side trail that take you to Overnight Area #1 and proceed on the Backcountry Trail to the South Access or, if you have the time, follow the orange blaze marks all the way back to the South Access which adds about 4 miles to your hike.

*Ranger John Gillespie on patrol on East Fork's Backcountry Trail*

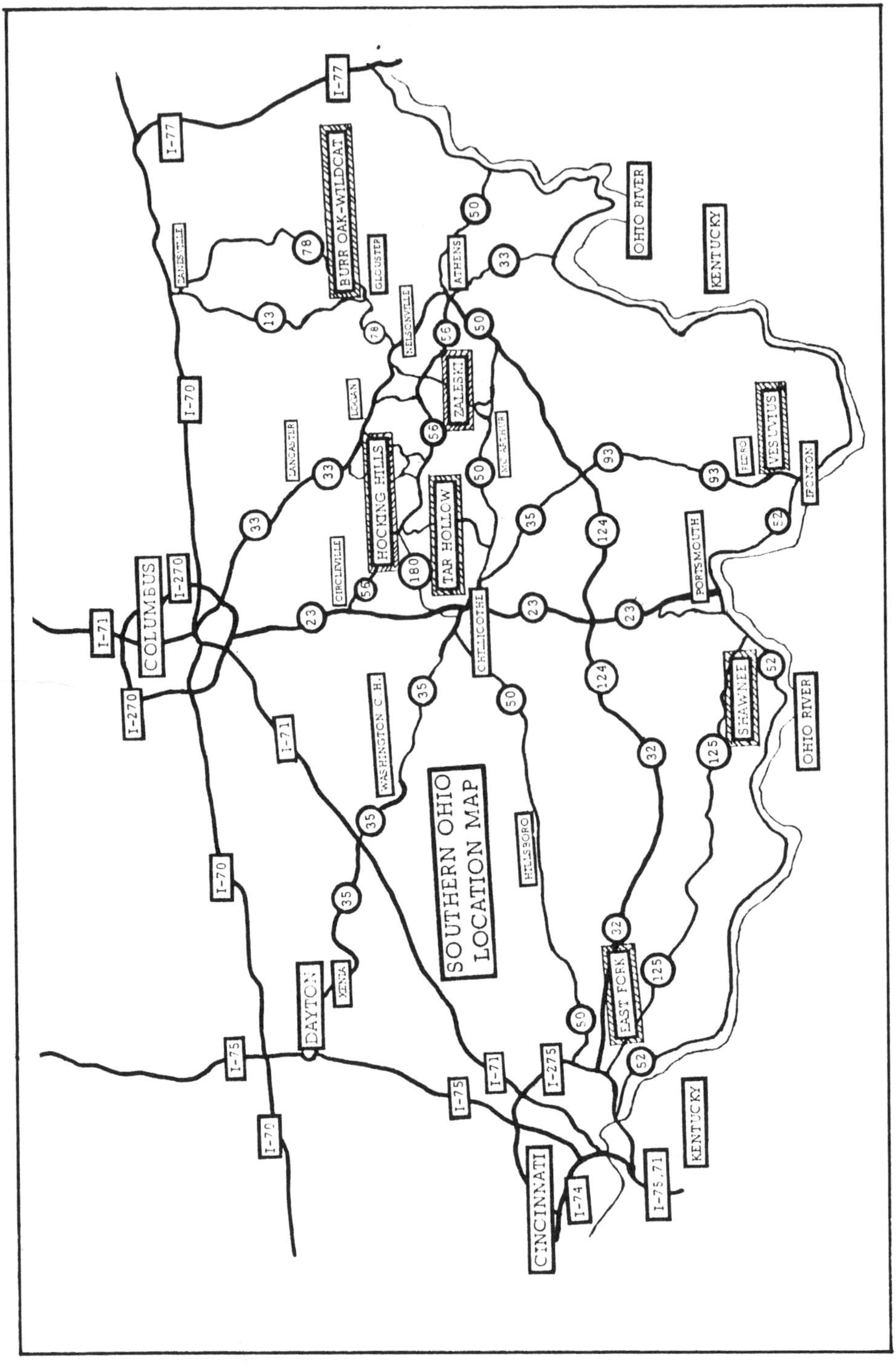
SOUTHERN OHIO LOCATION MAP
COLUMBUS
CINCINNATI
DAYTON
KENTUCKY
KENTUCKY
OHIO RIVER
OHIO RIVER
BURR OAK-WILDCAT
HOCKING HILLS
TAR HOLLOW
ZALESKI
VESUVIUS
SHAWNEE
EAST FORK
ZANESVILLE
GLOUSTER
NELSONVILLE
ATHENS
LOGAN
LANCASTER
MC ARTHUR
CIRCLEVILLE
CHILLICOTHE
PORTSMOUTH
PEDRO
IRONTON
WASHINGTON C. H.
HILLSBORO
XENIA
I-77
I-70
I-71
I-270
I-75
I-275
I-74
I-75,71
13
78
33
50
56
93
35
124
180
23
52
32
125